RALEGH
AND HIS WORLD

RALEGH
AND HIS WORLD

BY
IRVIN ANTHONY

CHARLES SCRIBNER'S SONS
NEW YORK · LONDON
1934

COPYRIGHT, 1934, BY
CHARLES SCRIBNER'S SONS

Printed in the United States of America

All rights reserved. No part of this book may be reproduced in any form without the permission of Charles Scribner's Sons

A

TO
CORNELIUS WEYGANDT

FOREWORD

Consciously or unconsciously, every man is guided by standards of his own discovery, often far too blurred to be called concepts, sometimes but little more than half-perceived visions. To relate a man's reactions to his philosophy makes the events of his life unfold themselves in a tale which denies the existence of mystery. The facts of Sir Walter Ralegh's life are generous, but not perfect in continuity. At tantalizing moments the light grows dim, and these spots of shadow have become controversial. In themselves they are but a failure of knowledge. We simply do not know, since the records fail us. They have tormented scholars into creating a miasma of doubt and wonder which has become tradition. There is no sesame for those doors behind which the truth is forever locked away. In despair, biographers have sought clues for the solving of the riddle of their own making without examining the philosophy of the knight, the well from which his behavior sprang.

Sir Walter was no Hobbes, no Bacon. He was too much caught up into the woof of active life for that. He was drawn to the one political philosophy of his day, the doctrine of Machiavelli. Of all the moderns of his time, Sir Walter, in his own writing, quoted only from the practical Niccolo. Every court in Europe was a mirror to those maxims and remained so more or less until the French Terror. Sonnets, blank verse, Palladian palaces, foreign rapier play—it was all new, for England was discovering Italy. Sir Walter was of his time and studied the Florentine. In another age it might have been religion, or democracy, or oratory, or the practice of the doctrines of Lenine. In Elizabethan days all success had to be sought through politics. All that Sir Walter desired had to come through the Court, and for that the eminently practical Machiavelli pointed the way.

The system of Niccolo required a prince to be served. It implied a contact with that prince, for the ruler was the centre of the network of intent which led on to fortune. So long as Sir Walter had a prince upon whom he could focus the process of success he prospered, single handed and in spite of his enemies. It was not until he lost every intimacy with his prince, so that no medium remained through which to exert power, that he failed, and even then the system of the Florentine might have given him a foothold had not time added its afflictions to the animus of James to produce tragedy.

This, then, is my tale; this, if anything, is new; the attempt to reveal Ralegh in the dizzy whirl of his day while he followed a credo which was open anathema in every land, and in every land practiced assiduously. It is a sufficiently elastic setting for the true history of a soldier, sailor, courtier, scholar, explorer, colonizer, governor, poet, historian, philosopher, metaphysician, scientist, and patron.

IRVIN ANTHONY.

On Board the *Pirate*
   July, 1933.

CONTENTS

		PAGE
FOREWORD	. . . .	vii

CHAPTER		
I.	THE QUEEN IS DEAD	1
II.	FLANDERS FIELDS	13
III.	THE ROAD TO GLORY	27
IV.	UNTO THE CELTS	42
V.	RISE SUN	55
VI.	FATUOUS FIRES	69
VII.	INTENTIONS AND VISIONS	83
VIII.	VIRGINIA	97
IX.	THE ARMADA	112
X.	A SHEPHERD PIPING IN THESSALY . . .	126
XI.	ARMS AND LOVE	140
XII.	GUIANA	153
XIII.	OVER SPANISH SEAS	166
XIV.	ESSEX	185
XV.	THE HALTING OF THE TIDE	203
XVI.	LONG LIVE THE KING	220
XVII.	TREASON	237
XVIII.	ROYAL MERCY	255

CONTENTS

CHAPTER		PAGE
XIX.	THE LONG YEARS	268
XX.	ELDORADO!	286
XXI.	DEATH	302
	NOTES	319
	BIBLIOGRAPHY	321
	INDEX	323

RALEGH
AND HIS WORLD

CHAPTER I

THE QUEEN IS DEAD

THE long vigil of the wan woman was over. At midnight, on the 16th of November, 1558, for the last time the host had been elevated before her. Queen Mary, daughter of Henry VIII by Catherine of Aragon, could not move nor speak. Her eyes were fixed upon the body of her Lord. In a last ecstacy, fervidly her mind drank in the significance of the moment. Its spell tapped the hidden springs of her life and they ebbed away. Her head dropped back. Her eyes flickered and closed. She lay so until an hour before the tardy dawn. Death stole in as the pale torches flared and guttered low.

It was really ended. Thursday, November 17, would never know her reign. The moonlight would come and go over the terrace at Hatfield, but the ghostlike royal form would glide no more from shadow to shadow. Her fierce unrest was still. She had been a riddling ruler. England had been hers at the outset. The nation was ashamed of Henry's treatment of her mother. Catherine of Aragon had bulked saintly over the years of Mary's childhood. England was ready to serve handsomely, eager to make amends for old harms, but Mary proved difficult. She was fire and ice, now all faith, now suspicion, in a breath both discreet and reckless. She burned Latimer and Ridley at Oxford in the town ditch before Balliol College with the fervor of a Latin. Cranmer she crassly had executed while England cried shame upon her deed. At that moment the Queen turned coldly from her people, whom she had never understood. She married Philip of Spain, as she declared at the altar, not out of any concupiscence, yet from the consummation of her marriage she prayerfully hoped herself pregnant. When imagination failed of foundation in fact she rebuked heaven which had so slighted her faith. Faith's testament, cruelty, had brought no merit in the sight of God. She had punished heresy savagely. Where was the infinite justice, the reward for the support of dogma?

Elizabeth, her half sister, rode through Smithfield and Old Bailey, along Fleet Street unto Somerset Place. The company of her Grace's gentlemen, gay, in velvet coats and bearing gaudy chains upon their breasts, her Grace's men at their heels in gleaming red, broadly guarded in black and bravely slashed, passed before the Queen's eyes. In a cheery roar the popular good will rose to the Queen's ears, sickening her with jealousy. Had Mary Tudor passed that way the lip praise would have been faint, lifting out of fear, not kindliness.

Spain, grotesquely bearing the olive branch, England possessed beyond doubt: these she had in title sound enough, but in substance she was not of them. Her Catholics feared the reaction certain to follow her ardent assault upon her heretics. Her people kept her poor, so poor, even the funds for the most necessary expenditures could be secured only by forced loans. She could not maintain her pride, let alone finance a war. Yet, when she permitted poor Wentworth to surrender Calais to the French, she was abused roundly by the nation. For two hundred eleven years Calais had been English. She had betrayed her trust by cowardice. None looked to see why she had not prosecuted a defence. The nation was no more just to her than heaven had been. Utterly estranged, bowed under the shame of hurt pride, she withdrew from the world and shut herself up at Hatfield. A thousand torturing doubts, flashing suspicions tormented her. Since she had lost the love of her people she yearned after it as she had longed to bear Philip's child. She drove her ministers willy nilly. Wild, accusing notes were despatched to the cold, politic Philip. Faith had gone out of her. Through the days she brooded in darkness. Nights she passed stalking about the galleries at Hatfield. By such paths she was brought to sitting upon the ground with her knees drawn up to her face, all her energy spent in a vain questioning within her mind. Its regrets, its interests, its pitiful mistakes; through them she examined her failure. Sometimes she shed maudlin tears over her letters to Philip, or flashed into a fury at a trifle, but for most part her lonely suffering was locked within a wooden silence that led toward a dark frenzy, until death swallowed her sorrow, and the lonely vigil came to an end.

Philip II took the news of Mary's death quietly enough. He was a man of iron, with a narrow, hard, set path before him. From the moment of his father's abdication he had been all severity. He had a critical and able audience in Don John of Austria and Margaret of Parma, his natural brother and sister. The marriage with England had been a failure. He wasted few tears upon the loss of Mary. He paused in his acts of faith, the rites of slaying Moors and Protestants, to weigh the matter. At the time, marrying England had not seemed impossible. He had not mounted the throne as yet, and calmly enough he had taken his time about consummating the union. His bride was twelve years older than he and reported to have bad health. Although he was only twenty-seven, he chose Mary in cold blood and sheerly for politic reasons. The English people were unfriendly to him, that he knew, but he was not a peasant marrying out of the heat of the flesh. It was his second nuptial. Two years after the marriage, in 1556, he was Prince no longer but King, and was called back to his realm to fight France. He did not go to England again, although

Mary waited hopefully. It was a land of heretics. When next he approached it he would carry the might of righteous wrath. Mary's death took as little from him as Mary's marriage had brought, but it touched him in one matter—a Protestant would probably take the throne. Philip turned to his task feeling the pressure of time. From the first he had worked like the monk he was. To the chanting of his priests he meditated upon temporal power. An ever growing corps of spies served him. From every corner of the earth the winds of the world sped news to his hand. He commenced to groom his armies.

He was only thirty-one when Mary died, but he knew England was lost to him. In the little body of attendants about the Princess Elizabeth, on the London streets, upon the fringes of Parliament and the court, even in the theatres his enmity was taken for granted. Hatred implied fear. The same spies who brought him hate from England could carry into England dread and suspicion. He could become a tradition against the day when he would invade that realm of heretics. From the west poured in the wealth he would use. Portugal might be "Lord of the navigation, conquest and trade of Ethiopia, Arabia, Persia and India," but the Treaty of Trodesillas improved upon the papal bull of Alexander VI and gave to Spain all the lands west of a meridian passing through a point in the Atlantic three hundred seventy leagues from Cape Verde. Plate ships idling across tropic seas from Callao and Guayaquil. Pearl fisheries of Panama. Fabulous mines of Cusco. All the gorgeous pride of the Spanish throne could be maintained by these riches. True, the English knew of the lands oversea and heeded neither bull nor treaty. Curiosity could well be curbed. Tonson had gone back to the heretics with his tale of a hidden treasure house, but the English could not hope to threaten Spain. The wealth would flow in undisturbed and be spent upon the faith. He had the grand manner, had Philip.

For a year he had meditated upon his vow. God had given him the victory at St. Quentin's; the French had been routed upon August 10, the day of St. Lawrence. He had pledged himself to build the Escorial in memory of the blessed martyr. It should have seven towers and fifteen gates and take the shape of a gridiron to honor the courageous end of Lawrence. He would make it a fitting palace from which to rule. A mausoleum, a great library, a church, a college, a monastery; there would be room for it all; it should be matchless. In utmost simplicity he would remain true to the iron spirit of the Saint, and when the years had let him keep his vow in stone, he would look down the long aisle of his church past the stern granite pillars, from his brick-paved cell, and seeing God made and eaten all day long he would weigh his men, ships and money before he lost that instant in eternity, his life. For the glory of the faith, England must bow before Spanish arms as France had done at St. Quentin.

Torn as she was by a domestic struggle, France was not then a threat to either Spain or England. Mary might die, Philip might scheme, but Henry II flung the realm of France into the lap of his mistress, Diana de Poiters, and watched the priceless filagree toy tossed and twisted in her scented fingers. Catherine, the Queen, turned away her round face from the spectacle. Royal folly did not seem to her so dangerous as the rise of the Guises. The pieces of her play were a sad lot, weak hostages to an evil fortune, but after all, her four wind-shaken limbs were blood of her blood, de Medici children born to a King of France. She watched the Guises within the realm, ready to match them move for move. Let others look beyond her dream of the succession. When the Spanish and English defeated the royal armies of France at St. Quentin and Gravelines she frowned at mention of Lamoral, the conqueror, but she did not really care. When

Francis, Duke of Guise, took Calais and Guines, she forced a diplomatic smile, for her craft recognized him as a deadly menace to her sons whose father heeded only Diana.

And in England the crown was sure to be Elizabeth's. No madness at Hatfield for her. No trusting to ministers. She would be a Queen, wisely or foolishly none could tell, but positively beyond question. Red-haired, firm mouth, long hands, facile, skilled, eager to control the affairs of the realm. Since she had been fourteen she had known affairs of state. Mary had tried to kill her then, and only her cunning had kept her head upon its shoulders. Had not Mary aimed to make her confess an intention to marry Thomas Seymour without the consent of the Council? She wrote so well in her defence that no minister could find a flaw in it, and she lived. She was a creature out of a pageant. Ruddy against the forest green she appeared. The youthful Virgin of the North bent upon the chase. Diana, gay and radiant, face alight in the flush of the pursuit. Yeomen in gilded caps with golden bows and arrows flanked her. Feet quickened amid the rustling undergrowth. The cavalcade swept past, following the deer. Sylvan the chase, but certain the end. The quarry was brought to bay and doomed. The royal hand unsheathed the jewelled knife and gave the stroke of grace like a player upon the boards. Not so the sincerity with which she watched the light die out of the brown eyes, dreaming of Mary at Hatfield. Then she laughed. She praised skill, speaking roundly to the huntsmen. She made them hers as well as the deer. A huntress she! For her no mewed existence behind gray walls. She was twenty-five, rough and sudden, cautious and proud, her anger not always just, but powerful, her wisdom and learning of her own digging. Now that Mary was out of the way she would be a queen in royal pattern. For her the darkened halls of Hatfield were filled with the light of a new day and that her own. She had no stake of four sons as Catherine had in her struggle with the Guises and the Bourbons. She had no need for virtue to cover the stain of illegitimacy as had Margaret of Parma, whom Philip was sending north to rule the Netherlands at the coming of the new year. All things to all men she might seem, but always one thing to herself she would be to the last hour of her life—the Queen.

2

The news travelled fast. Queen Mary was dead. The couriers shouted it through the market towns. Ships broached it along the coast at every port both south and west. It reached Exeter and was carried out past East Budleigh church to the Ralegh home at Hayes. Queen Mary was dead. To none in all the West Country were the words more comfortable. The news settled like a benediction upon the house and its folk. The smoke lifted cheerily above the thatch of three gables. Nestling into a comb upon the edge of an upland, low and solid, the house seemed gnarled with age. At its threshold to the north, the moor bore its bracken, and gorse, and some heather. At the south stood Hayes Wood of complaining oaks, and beyond, where the land fell away to the channel, the little port of Budleigh Salterton hid below the cliffs. Heavily mullioned windows, a new Tudor porch, low walls of stone under a short roof, the house had been a rugged bit of monastic property in the days of Richard I. Something of its ancient spirit remained. Something of the old Plantagenet blood pulsed in the hearts of the Raleghs living in it. Were not the arms of the Clares and the Raleghs quartered upon the pew entrance in East Budleigh church? There might be a trace of royalty in them, yet Queen Mary's death brought them no sorrow.

Walter Ralegh had little reason to love sovereigns. Henry VII had fined his father heavily, impoverishing the estate of the son, driving him to sea as the owner of a bark with which to recoup his means in trade. He inherited the Ralegh pride and from his mother the dogged Grenville courage, both of which were drawn upon to the full. As for Queen Mary, her hatred of heretics and her persecution made Ralegh of Hayes always fearful for himself, for his wife Katherine (the widow of Otho Gilbert and the daughter of Sir Philip Champernoun), and their children: three Gilberts and three Raleghs. They had been hard years for the lesser gentry. The Gilbert children were older than Walter Ralegh's own, and able to exercise in their own right what they had by way of inheritance, but Carew, Walter and Margaret Ralegh would have found themselves beggared if Mary's reign had lasted until their coming of age.

The West Country families had earned the dislike of Queen Mary. To begin with, they were Protestants, and a lawless lot, who understood each other over a long term of years better than the Queen understood any of them. The Champernouns, the Carews, the Grenvilles, the Raleghs: they were all gentlefolk of long standing in Cornwall and Devon. When the Spanish marriage loomed and Sir Thoms Wyatt plotted to revolt against Mary he depended upon Courtenay to lead the West Country forces to London. Courtenay turned treacherous. The Council was too quick. The revolt died. Suffolk, Wyatt, Lady Jane Grey and her young husband, Guilford Dudley, were condemned to the block. The Queen sent down into the West Country to punish all offenders. Sir Arthur Champernoun was forced to tender his fealty anew, kneeling to Mary at Hatfield. The Carews were a more stubborn sort. Perhaps they were more deeply in and feared the royal presence deservedly, for they would not plead for mercy and pardon. They were cried through the land as traitors. The Queen sent Sir Thomas Dennys after them. She must have known Sir Thomas was of their blood;

perhaps she never really wished to take them. Sir Peter Carew went aboard the Ralegh bark and Walter Ralegh carried him to France. Once there, Sir Peter blamed all his plight upon the Spanish. He went to sea, captured and pillaged Spanish ships and made himself so obnoxious the French throne had to deny him the use of its ports. He was a dangerous man. Walter Ralegh returned in his bark to England and, unmolested, resumed his trade and piracy. Sir Arthur Champernoun, at peace with the Queen, turned loose his fleet upon the luckless French and Spanish. The Carews sent their small freebooters everywhere, but Walter Ralegh did not feel safe: the punishment for treason was hideous and he had aided fleeing traitors. He returned feeling insecure and unsure in his mind how the Queen might strike at him.

When Mary married Philip most of England disliked the idea of the country becoming a dependent province. Distrust began at once to foment fear. In Devon, the Spanish had long been hated. Many of the country families had been plundering them at sea whenever possible and hatred is a defence of violence. The dons, in turn, avenged themselves in the name of God and self protection. All of this was of course quite unofficial, but often sufficiently brutal in method to be thoroughly convincing. Englishmen out of the fishing fleet, shipwrecked in far away Newfoundland, were rescued by Spanish ships and carried into Vigo or Cadiz to have their souls saved by the burning of their bodies. Almost every ship coming in out of Biscay brought its tale of added outrage. Miles Phillips had come back with his story of Englishmen in Mexico condemned to one hundred, two hundred stripes and then sent to the galleys for six, eight or ten years by the Holy Office. All classes in Devon went to sea and all knew the power of Spain. Englishmen at home lost their noses, their ears, their good right hands, at the brutal word of law, yet they cried "God save the Queen," as bravely as might be. There was no mawkish sentimentality over unfortunate countrymen. Much less consideration was afforded the foreigner who married Mary. Devon heaped its wrongs upon the head of Philip and disloyalty stirred.

Once married, Mary submitted England to the Pope's legate, Cardinal Pole. With Philip and both Houses of Parliament, she knelt before him, confessing the sin of breaking from the Roman see. She rose fired with zeal, free of her sin. With a will she turned to rooting out the heretics in her realm. It was a foolish thing to stand in her path after that.

Her officers went down into Devon. It was a time to be cautious. The jails were stuffed with suspects. Walter Ralegh and his wife would not shrink. With young Walter, Mistress Ralegh visited Agnes Prest, a confessed heretic, as she lay in Exeter prison. The prisoner spoke with so much courage and good sense that young Walter's mother came away unable to win her back to safer ground. For weeks the Raleghs regarded every passing Queen's officer with dread. To have conversed with an heretic, to have carried her bodily comfort, was dangerous. England was becoming something strange and frightful. West Country folk were not given to cowering and their patience with royal folly was wearing thin. From Orkney, Ireland, Iceland and Newfoundland, the crews came home to strut and gossip. They talked of pirates, kings of far ports, the new world, baits, depths, North Atlantic winds, but more and more the talk was of Spain and the empire overseas. Devon and Cornwall were one with the Norman and Breton seafarers to the south and east, below the sea rim. The French and English coast families were intermarried, one clan despite queens and courts. On both sides of the Channel there was rage at the Spanish influence which engulfed the West Country, patrolled the seas and threatened Normandy and Brittany. Mutterings grew loud.

Then, rather swiftly at the end, came Mary's death. Elizabeth was suddenly upon the throne. Henry Carey, Lord Hunsdon, Sir Arthur Champernoun: all the great men of Devon would be going up to court and finding office. Walter Ralegh no longer was afraid of royal zeal. Walter Ralegh's children had opportunity at last. Their uncle, Sir Arthur Champernoun, would be vice-admiral of the West Country. Young Walter was a mere child of six, not fit even to be a page, but he would grow and that under a young Queen, without fear, free from the menace of heresy, safe from the doubt and suspicion in which Queen Mary had lapped the land. England now would never be Spanish. Persecution would fail and die. God's servant from Madrid had best stay at home, or Elizabeth would send him packing in short order. The Spanish ambassador might tell her that Philip had favored her succession; she was not deceived for a moment.

There was much virtue in the magic of her name—Queen Elizabeth. The fortunes of young Walter Ralegh were bound up in it. In addition to his general connections with the great of her court he had two intimate contacts. His step-brother, Humphrey Gilbert, had served her the last two years she was a Princess, one of the loyal retinue which Mary had so envied. A dreamer, but of a practical sort, a man all gentleness, conscious of how the fate of England rested upon the deeds of his Queen, Gilbert was very close to her counsels. He was a fine figure of a man although a trifle too modest, and much too serious to succeed with the hearty, rugged daughter of Henry VIII and Anne Boleyn. She would use his loyalty and reward him only as she chose. She was shrewd and quick to catch the worth of a man. Even so early her trust was in him, and he never failed her to his death. No more stalwart advocate for young Walter Ralegh could be found.

Closer still to Elizabeth, and with a greater claim upon royal favor, was a kinswoman of the Raleghs—Kate Ashley. Kate was a talkative soul, not very wise but somewhat learned. Under the guidance of Roger Ascham, she taught Elizabeth. Despite the stern old tutor's commands, she spoiled the Princess at every opportunity and in turn Elizabeth loved her as none other. Kate knew every intimate, human turn of the Princess's mind, her hopes, her fears. In the trying days when Queen Mary was seeking the death of her half sister, Kate did what she could to defend Elizabeth, and Elizabeth boldly exonerated Kate from every blame. After the coronation, Dame Ashley was a garrulous soul. Young Walter's name was bound to be mentioned in the royal presence. True, she might not live long enough to let the lad grow up and use her favor, for she was much older than the Queen, but Elizabeth had a long memory, even of the chatter of an old soul who once really loved her.

Let young Walter grow to be the man his Devon kith and kin were, let the Queen but need men, as her vigor promised, and the path to favor led fair out of the gloom of Mary into the sunlight of Elizabeth.

CHAPTER II

FLANDERS FIELDS

FROM the moment of Mary's death, Elizabeth grasped the sceptre. At the news she fell upon her knees. The eyes of all England were upon her. The ears of her people were open. When she spoke it was with the dignity of a queen.

"*A Domino factum est illud, et est mirabile in oculis nostris.*" Out of dark memories the words of the psalm rose to her tongue. It was indeed the doing of the Lord, she was reverent enough to believe. Besides, whatever brought it about, it was well to let the nation see her faith and worship. "Marvellous in our eyes." So, at a word she became regal. She was newly moulded to the pattern of an astute ruler. At fifteen she had written sagely to Somerset, "They are most deceived that trust the most in themselves." At twenty-five her self-esteem was perfected; she was ready to govern her kingdom.

When the shock of the new reality had been met she became more casual. She passed the Little Conduit in Cheapside at her coronation with "Time, and time has brought me here." She smiled happily when a voice in the crowd cried, "I remember old King Harry the Eighth." In privacy, after being anointed, she told her tiring woman, "The oil was grease and smelled ill." From the first day of her reign she was shrewdly practical yet assuming at ease a mystical attitude. "By God's son! I am no Queen," she would cry out and then write gracefully in her little prayer book of sixty-five pages, vellum bound in shagreen, clasped with gold and set with rubies, "O most Glorious King and Creator . . . Hear the most humble voice of thy hand maiden." Even in her oath she was never less than the hand maiden of God.

With Sir William Cecil as Secretary of State to "take pains for me and my realm" and Thomas Parry, knighted and given the controllership, she set out upon her path of glory. Robert Dudley had helped her when Mary sought her execution; him she raised to be Master of Horse and shortly after the Earl of Leicester. It was her policy to reward a few of the faithful so that hope might be bred in others.

As a mission she undertook to undo all that Mary had sought to establish. She saw with clear vision the ridiculous gestures of other nations. England was its own friend. There was no deceiving her. Elizabeth could not have her people at each other's throats; they were too necessary to the security of the realm. Her Catholics were first English. Her Protestants should be restrained, but not antagonized. One of her first acts was to order the Church service read in English. Diplomatically, she remained non-committal upon the point of her personal faith. Candles burned upon her altar before the chapel crucifix, yet it was forbidden to bind the pictures of the Saints into the prayer books. Statecraft could save the country from its enemies, but there was no need to cavil too fiercely at divergent beliefs.

At a bound, she became an apparent leader of the nation, mingling among her people with little or no protection. Leicester tendered her lavish pageants. All the court vied with him. She shone in splendor, living dangerously. Popularity with the masses grew. For the intelligent she presented the mind of a scholar and became a patron of learning. The instruction of Roger Ascham and her own hard work stood her in good stead. When she began her "progresses," royal visits of great honor to the recipients, but ruinous in expense, she did not forget to put the universities in their place as offering the most acceptable path to preferment at court. She frankly looked to the seats of learning to provide her with young men of schooled ability. She made "inland breeding" synonymous for the culture of Cambridge and Oxford, the highest in the land. Since Oxford had been the scene of so many of Mary's zealous acts of faith, she bestowed the Earl of Leicester upon that university, as Chancellor with the task of inspiring toleration. She gave him two years to work and in 1566 she visited Oxford to see what had been done. In no uncertain terms she declared herself for moderation. The puritanical Doctor Humphreys was greeted with, "Mr. Doctor, that loose gown becomes you so well I wonder your notions should be so narrow." She laughed with Doctor Westphaling in St. Mary's Church. He had memorized his address and dared not break off until he had finished, despite the royal command to stop when the Queen had wearied of him. Her coming added no fuel to the fires of religious difference. "Her sweet, affable and noble carriage counselled all to moderation." She charmed her hosts, displayed her learning cleverly, and left the university proud it was English, and rather forgetful of religious controversy.

It was all part of a plan. Her church must win the Protestants and leave the Catholics untouched. Matthew Parker, her newly created Archbishop of Canterbury, would be the man for the new times. In her six days at Oxford, she swung academic opinion into line. Her progress passed into tradition. The effect was immediate. Protestant exiles returned from Strasburg, from Zurich, from Geneva. Reassured, fewer Catholic scholars followed their gifted leaders into the seclusion of the new seminary of their faith at Douay. Brilliant students thronged into the colleges. Francis Bacon entered to polish the facets of his deadly mind and sound the depths of all learning. Richard Hooker began his studies that he might later take the nephew of the martyred Cranmer under his tutorial care. Philip Sidney, whom the Queen was soon to hold "the choicest jewel of my court," took up residence. Oxford called to Thomas Hariot who discovered the sun spots before Galileo and the moons of Jupiter simultaneously with him. Camden, on his way to be the greatest scholar of England, paused for his degree. Gentlemen were quick to see the royal patronage of learning and caught the way of it: Greville on his path toward favor; C. Champernoun, the cousin of Walter Ralegh, and Humphrey Gilbert destined for the wars in France; poor foreign scholars, such as Stephanus Parmenius of Buda. An enlightened England, united in spite of the clash of faiths, was a goal toward which to work.

Finally, in 1568, Walter Ralegh, listed as a commoner of Oriel College just below the name of C. Champernoun, joined the elite of Oxford. He was only sixteen, but his age was one of early maturity, so his precocity was not so startling as it might have been in another era. Before Ralegh went to college he knew two things at least: he hated the sea and could never be a sailor, for he was always sea sick on board ship; he hated Spaniards with all the rude candor of a true West Country man. He was grown tall and supple. His glance was too straight and challenging to be friendly. His air of boldness promised the dignity of his manhood to come. To carry off such personality among the collegians required him to have a heavy hand and a facile wit, both to take the place of a more modest man's compromise. New as he was in the community, Camden caught his character in a flash. Bacon noted a single incident of him in his *Apothegms*. A cowardly fellow at the university happened to be a very good archer. Another student abused him to the point of insult. The coward asked Ralegh what to do. "Why, challenge him to a match of shooting," answered Ralegh. Slight, to be sure, and easily matched in undergraduate prespicacity the world over, but the only Oxford legend of Ralegh. It seems Ralegh once borrowed a gown of an unknown T. Child and wholeheartedly forgot to return it. In all else the life at Oxford is without evidence of interest, except for the friendships which may have begun there. The wonder is that he earned any notice whatever, for after a residence of little more than a year, at the age of seventeen, he was snatched away into the maelstrom of military life long before he could earn his degree.

2

The way of it was this. Seven years earlier Elizabeth had watched the Huguenot revolt in France with some misgivings. By nature, she hated and feared the despising of authority, but she recognized all Europe was taking its religion very seriously. When the movement promised success she was offered Havre in return for her support against the Guises. She preferred a Protestant neighbor to a Catholic, especially a Protestant who would be beholden to her. Then too, she hoped to exchange Havre for Calais that Mary had lost. She ran some risks, for victory was by no means certain, but in 1562 she decided to aid the Huguenots.

At the outset, Count Montgomerie was cooped up at Rouen and Vidame de Chartes was beleaguered at New Haven (Havre) by the all too powerful Guises. Montgomerie had many friends in the West Country. The daughter of Gawen Champernoun became his wife. The Queen was anxious to help the besieged, but unwilling to entertain the costs. The Devon men offered their services. Eager to assist Montgomerie, they only waited for royal sanction to rush pell-mell into action. She nodded her head and they were off. It was a golden time for young Humphrey Gilbert to get his first taste of war and escape the silken dalliance of the court. He was twenty-three, old enough to have sense, young enough to be fearless. Behind him, at home, he left his half brother, Walter Ralegh, then only ten years old and unfit for feats of arms.

Scarcely were the British into the fracas than the French factions came suddenly to terms without treating with Elizabeth, leaving the English in possession of Havre which she refused to give up. The plague attacked her people, driving those who did not die back to England. Left thus in the air betwixt heaven and earth, Elizabeth dallied with what face she might until 1564, and the acceptance of the terms of the Peace of Troyes. Havre was gone, and she signed away all claim to Calais for 220,000 crowns. Despite the money in hand, it was a poor gesture for her, but the Guises and the Huguenots were but at a pause. The fire of faith would yet flare fiercely. Presently, the truces of Amboise and Longjumeau languished and died. Elizabeth refused to be drawn in as the unwelcome foreigner, in whose menace the French might again find an excuse for peace and union. She was taking her first steps in the long march of diplomacy. Duplicity had acquired a recognized value for her. Publicly, she denied the existence of the situation. She affirmed to the French Court none of her subjects had her consent to take part. Meanwhile from her ports sailed away ship after ship carrying armed volunteers. The West Country paid its score of affection. Henry Champernoun raised a troop of one hundred gentlemen, sending his call even to Oxford. Walter Ralegh heard and left the classics to join his cousin's force. His residence at the university had been short, so short it is surprising Camden made a scholarly note of his departure. The troop was quickly overseas, and reached the Huguenot lines on October 5, 1569, two days after Lewis of Nassau began his retreat from Montcontour. Walter Ralegh wrote years later in his *History of the World* "of which myself was an eye witness, and was one of them that had cause to thank him for it."

At seventeen he plunged into action. From the first his initiation was dispassionate. He was of an auxiliary force, willing to fight for the Huguenots, but in zeal and belief holding itself aloof. The campaign was vigorous. The fighting was open and gave abundant chance for stratagem and device. The country was strange. Moving in such chaos Ralegh kept his head. He saw clearly enough that the heart must not be squandered in war. Hero worship of an impersonal sort was a delusion. Admiral Coligny "advised the Prince of Condé to side with the Huguenots, not only out of love to their persuasion, but to gain a party." Ralegh wrote those words out of clear vision, a youthful memory of disillusionment.

The war was an opportunity to learn of attack and ambuscade. Long days in the saddle, the feel of armor and the use of weapons, the need for caution, the responsibilities and restraint of command: for Ralegh it was a school which hurried him toward manhood. The enemy broke. The Huguenots were victorious and vengeful. They hunted the Catholics into the hilly and faulted country of Languedoc, smoking them out of caves when they hid, slaying such as made a desperate stand. Young Ralegh learned the violence, treachery and cruelty of irregular warfare. Elizabeth had disavowed the existence of the troop to the French even as she hastened to license it secretly. Something of the brigand, of the reckless schoolboy, of the callous mercenary is bound to touch troops so much upon their own. Out of independence grows a frightful insolence. Ralegh began his practice of arms in a ruthless, wanton school. As a mere trooper he performed duties he despised, but he perceived to what an extent war was only a political device to advance leaders and factions, nothing to get excited about. With that vision clear to his mind, he passed from the boy to the man, courageous, far seeing and not to be easily deceived.

3

A year or two more and the Netherlands gave the Queen much to consider. She loved the sovereign power of princes. The Netherlands were seething in revolt against Philip. Naturally, she was somewhat sympathetic with Philip as a king whose subjects were disloyal. She detested all extremes but her own. Subjects should not rebel, for insurrection was sinful in the eyes of heaven, but neither should monarchs threaten other monarchs by innuendo and exhibitions of force. Philip massed troops in Flanders, well knowing that England watched, only the narrow sea away from his theatre of war. Elizabeth, as a neutral, was to Spain a menace; diplomatic pressure grew heavy, Spanish counsel gave her no peace. Protestant as she was, she secretly favored the Dutch side. At last the somewhat irregular admiral of William of Orange, De la Marck, sought harborage in English waters. At a Spanish whisper Elizabeth regretfully ordered him to leave the coast, but she was touched in her spleen by the necessity. De la Marck obeyed her order, put out of Dover, and in desperation sailed to take Brill at the mouth of the Meuse. The city fell on April 1, 1572. Elizabeth remembered the Spanish insistence, and at once the scales tipped in favor of the Dutch cause. The Spaniards had not been discreet enough to flatter her growing sense of power.

What was in his Queen's mind Burghley phrased neatly. He was always the man for that work. Thinking of the threat of invasion which lay in the Spanish force then gathered in the Low Countries, he said, "As they are there we must help the Dutch keep them employed." The fetish of united Protestantism came into being. Funds were subscribed. Volunteers were enrolled, and the new recruits began to cross. Having met with such success among the English, the Dutch appealed to the French. Charles IX listened to Admiral Coligny, the Huguenot leader, and was eager to war with Spain. Before anything could come of it Catherine de Medici convinced him the Huguenots intended to murder him, and believing his mother, the King encouraged the swift and terrible massacre of St. Bartholomew. Three thousand Huguenots died in Paris alone; in all of France more than thirty thousand perished. So opened the Fourth Civil War in France, and by the autumn of 1572, the Huguenots looked like winners. The Spanish in the Netherlands had an enemy on either flank. In view of the conditions Elizabeth went into the open, and hastened to lend William of Orange forty thousand pounds, the use of ships and the services of all who would flock to him.

Walter Ralegh was back from the wars, a veteran, looking toward the future for action. Humphrey Gilbert, Sir Humphrey Gilbert by then, had served as Governor of Munster with great severity. He had treated with Irish rebels only after they were marched to his tent between fixed rows of severed heads and had looked into the dead faces of their former comrades. From this active life of the field he went to Parliament from Plymouth, but in this Dutch affair he saw a better means to fortune. He wanted royal favor. Upon it he depended for support of his project—a northwestward passage to China by way of the top of the new world. Parliamentarians who did their duty were often unpopular with Elizabeth. Gilbert had been fortunate amid the violence in Munster, hey ho for the Low Countries. He promptly organized a company of auxiliaries and Walter Ralegh found the action he was seeking in his half-brother's command.

For the youngster, it was out of the fire into the smother.

From a war of two languages he leaped to a combat of three. For the first time since the Queen's coronation the half-brothers were engaged upon the self-same adventure. As befitted his age and experience, Sir Humphrey was in command. Ralegh was to learn something of discipline, of war carried on according to rules. The stability of the siege, the advance of ordered forces, were very different things from the galloping skirmishes with the Huguenots. He had the example of Sir Humphrey before him, and he caught many of the tricks of the trade he was to use later when his career really opened. Physically, he had developed a close-knit frame and glowed with the first vigor of manhood. He was ripe for flowering, eager, keen, but as yet virgin in his mind. Then came George Gascoigne.

Born of gentle blood, Gascoigne caught the culture of Cambridge and then took up residence in Gray's Inn. He was a roisterer, a friend of cut purses and thugs. Proud of his notoriety, he was yet unashamed of his better parts. At the Inn he translated the tragedy of *Jocasta*—Euripides in blank verse—and Ariosto's comedy, *Supposes*, into English prose. Latin, Dutch, French, Italian and Spanish were easy for him. He read omnivorously. Only of his way with women and his successes with them did he do himself the injustice of recording his exploits in verse filled with allusions in very poor taste. In all else he kept his good and gross natures apart. One thinks of the small, shrewd figure of Niccolo Machiavelli with his neat mind separating life of the intellect from bodily behavior. For all his learning, in 1572, Gascoigne found his living precarious, and offered his services as burgess for Niedhurst, Sussex. He had not counted upon the spleen of outraged citizens. The Lords of the Privy Council had addressed to them a petition of objections couched in no uncertain terms.

"Firste he is indebted to a great number of personnes. . . .

"Item he is a defamed person and noted as well for manslaughter as for other great crymes.

"Item he is a common Rymer and a deviser of slanderous Pasquelles against divers personnes of great callings.

"Item he is a notorious Ruffianne and especialle noted to be both a Spie, an Athiest and Godles personne."[1]

The damning plea was heard and Gascoigne did not become burgess. With a grimace and a swagger he hastened overseas to Flushing and joined Morgan's volunteers with a commission as captain. He reached Brill shortly after the Sea Beggars of De la Marck had taken it. Under Sir Humphrey Gilbert, who commanded the English forces, he took part in the siege of Tergoes. If he practised with the army any villainies of the sort laid to him by the petition of Niedhurst, they were undetected. With discreet ardor he flung himself into the campaign and in the intervals between engagements wrote a narrative poem of his adventures. *Dulce Bellum* he called it.

Ralegh was twenty, an age quick to accept leadership, eager for example. Gascoigne's swashing manner, his man of the world air, invited the youngster's imitation. Gliding from notable to notable, making a friend of William of Orange, seeing all through the cynical tints of full experience, Gascoigne was working to get on at court once he was home again. He knew he was a man of parts, but he had never touched the hem of fortune's robe. Young Ralegh interested him. Their friendship ripened. A man in his forties does not in those shrewd years let such a valuable contact slip away. Together they talked of those things which all the young bring to maturity; metaphysics, history, politics, theology and philosophy. Gascoigne could open the reasoning of Machiavelli of whose doctrines all Europe was talking. Ralegh could bring to bear the favor of Gilbert, and Gascoigne gained thus another acquaintance at court. Had these three no other bond than their interest in the strange lands overseas, it would have been enough to ground a lasting friendship.

Gascoigne courted Gilbert. Once all three were safely home in England with Dutch affairs out of mind, he called often upon Sir Humphrey. It was a time of dejection for the knight, living quietly in his home in Limehouse, waiting for the Queen's permission to undertake the Northwest Passage. The Queen seemed never likely to yield. Gascoigne could assist with the published journals of contemporary voyagers. Languages were no bar to him. Dutch voyages, French discoveries, Spanish histories: these he could unlock at will for the knight and his half-brother. Among *Cosmographicall Mappes and Charts* and the *Tables of Ortelius* in Sir Humphrey's study, Gascoigne unearthed *A Discourse of a Discoverie for a new Passage to Cataia written by Sir Homfrey Gilbert Knight*. He urged the knight to publish that the Queen might read. He wrote a foreword for it, "From my lodging where I march amongst the Muses for lack of exercise in Martiall exploytes, this 12 of April, 1576."[2] Unfortunately, not even the energy of a Gascoigne could make a self-seeking courtier of Gilbert. He ever asked but poorly for anything of his own.

On the other hand, Gascoigne's exploits of evil savour were swiftly forgotten when the Earl of Leicester began to take note of him. These attentions were synchronized with the period in which Gilbert and young Gilbert and young Ralegh had easy access to the Earl. In July, 1575, Elizabeth, upon her royal progress, spent seventeen days at the Earl's castle. Gascoigne was entrusted with the creation of fitting entertainment. He did himself proud, not neglecting afterward to write as an eulogy of his own cleverness, *The Princelye Pleasures at the Court at Kenelwoorth*. Giving himself again to "literary diligence" Gascoigne eclipsed his previous service when the Queen reached Woodstock in September. Whatever qualm Sir Humphrey may have felt at endorsing so unstable a man as Gascoigne, he had succeeded in pleasing the Queen. With a manner that stood the test of any company, boldness beyond the smirch of cowardice, a swagger the envy of every youngster at court, he had a finesse that kept him from blundering.

Ralegh had watched him understandingly. He did what he could for his friend. When Gascoigne published *The Steele Glass* it was prefaced by verses of "Walter Rawley of the Middle Temple" and that there need be no doubt as to who Rawley was, a Bencher's list of all residents of the Middle Temple reads under February 27, 1574-5, "Walter Rawley, late of Lyons Inn, Gent. Son of Walter R. of Budleigh, Co. Devon, Esq."

So Gascoigne had climbed to favor. So he was when his last sickness took him. He, who had exulted in the casuistry of Machiavellian attitudes, found himself seeking after comfort. It was a long bout and before he succumbed he had lost every vestige of his courage. His ego shrank at every assault, as if his mind were attacked and not his body. In the end, his repentance was abject, his humility a disgraceful denial of his former wild freedom and his growing fear of death pitiful. He died in October, 1577.

Ralegh had seen the change. He had plumbed the man's fear and he learned of death at first hand, realizing that strutting before the dread gates was very difficult and that irreverence brought its own reward. Faith in the sixteenth century sometimes cried aloud and Gascoigne died stripped of his worldliness and its clear-eyed denial of religious faith. Ralegh clung to much of his philosophy, in one gesture completely acknowledging the influence of the man. Sick or well, he would never fail as Gascoigne had failed, but then he would never be so foolish.

Tam marte quam Mercurio had been the lifelong motto of George Gascoigne. As much for Mars as for Mercury. As much for war as for affairs. Mercury—sometime the messenger escorting souls toward the shadowy Hades. It was a fit phrase for a rover in the days of the unlocking of the world. Nothing silly nor ribald touched it, but instead something of steel, high resolve and discerning pride. Perhaps something of prophecy was visited upon Walter Ralegh. Gascoigne had taught him to soar on the wings of thought; the fire of accomplishment Gilbert had breathed into him. To do and to understand, yet be one's own always! Like a mantle the motto rested upon him. He made it his own in a flash and he never surrendered it. The years of surmise were ended; he moved into the years of affairs ready to fight or think.

CHAPTER III

ROAD TO GLORY

THE road to glory in the reign of Elizabeth, whether travelled with Mars or with Mercury, was difficult. The years had led far from the simplicity of the Middle Ages. A new political philosophy was being debated in the courts of Europe. It had begun in mediæval query: Which power should be sovereign, the church or the state? Here was a daring flight of the mind, a rattling of fetters about to be broken. Born among the most active minds of Italy, poets, philosophers, soldiers, the dispute was echoed everywhere. Upon the wings of ubiquitous Latin the matter filled the ear of all Europe.

At first it was but the tilting of two political factions, the random shivering of lances between the popular and the aristocratic, the Guelph and the Ghibelline. The Guelphic thinkers held the city of mankind must be subject and sacrificed to the city of God. Morality was the highest good and religion the triumph of God in man. The Pope was the sun. The state could only reflect papal light—a veritable moon. The reasoning lacked method and any vestige of scientific bent. The thinkers had contempt for lay society and scorn for the history of Pagan antiquity. The two most prominent among them were Egidio Colonna and St. Thomas Aquinas with his *De Regimine Principum*.

The Ghibellines endeavored to escape from dogma to abstraction. They denied the Pope was the sun and the Emperor the moon, because both were but accidental circumstances of the race of man. In support of this side of the question Marsilia da Padova wrote his *Defensor Pacis* in 1327 and Dante Alighieri offered his *De Monarchia*. Man was created on the sixth day while the sun and moon were made on the fourth; therefore God was illogical and inverse in the order of creation, providing for the accidental before the substantial. So Alighieri's sophistry ran, without his seeing that these arguments, being equally serviceable to both sides, were worthless.

It was a question that was unsolved in its day and which has reappeared in different ages; the struggle between Christian and practical philosophy. Witness Professor Carl Prantl writing in twentieth century German[3]:

"Thomas Aquinas was guided and inspired by Albertus Magnus and it would be a great error to regard him as an independent thinker. He is simultaneously restricted by two authorities, by the Christian-dogmatic and by the Aristotelian (transmitted by Albert's erudition), and whoever preserves or attains his religious freedom will glimpse nothing in the whole so-called philosophy of Thomas Aquinas, but an incomprehensible union of two essentially disparate standpoints. It is merely a matter of a cloudy understanding if one believes it possible to retain the Aristotelian idea of substance together with the Christian trinity or if one debased the Aristotelian ethics into Christian moral theology."

The city of mankind at war against the city of God gave life to heavenly doubts. A mood of inquiry led on toward the greatness of Niccolo Machiavelli and his *Duca Valentina*. An outgrowth of the Ghibellines, apparently aristocratic in sympathy, he denied the church the right of dominance, he challenged morality as not being the highest conceivable good for the state, and in the impassioned eulogy of his own Prince, Cesare Borgia, he firmly closed the door upon the mediæval in statecraft. He finished *The Prince* in 1514, but neither it nor the *Discourse* was printed in his lifetime.

Both had an extensive circulation while he lived, probably quite beyond the restricted audience for which he had designed them. Two manuscript copies of *The Prince*, made by Buonaccorsi, are still to be seen in Florence. When the little man died in 1527 it was five years before Blado, at Rome, published *The Prince* and opened the modern era of political thought.

In place of platitude Machiavelli poured out practical maxims. He used as a starting point the lower register of human emotions and he never forgot that a ruler without a state to rule would be nothing. A prince should appear: "pitiful, faithful, humane, religious, thorough" but "it is well to have your mind so trained that when it is expedient not to have these qualities you may know how to become entirely different." By way of comfort the prince is reminded, "Every one sees that which you seem to be, few feel that which you are." Above all, "Let the prince then determine to conquer and maintain his state; the means employed by him will always be deemed honorable and universally praised."

The prince was admonished never to deprive the citizens of property nor insult their women. He must preserve a reputation for gravity and courage. He should never exasperate the nobility, but should always favor the people to avoid ruin. A statesman's belief or unbelief is a question of private conscience. The method of ruling should be canny rather than violent. "Conquest, in fact, gives offense to many; and those who are benefitted by it expect more than can be conferred by the change." Power must always rest with the prince to support his intentions. "Love is maintained by a bond of obligation, which, owing to the wickedness of human nature, is always broken whenever it clashes with private interest; but fear is maintained by a dread of punishment that never abandons you." To be feared without being hated is ideal for the prince. Finally, a general law of action dictates, "a prudent lord neither could nor should observe faith, when such observance might be to his injury, and when the motives that caused him to promise it are at an end."

Such concrete commentary upon the ways of life was a long way from the abstractions of either Guelph or Ghibelline. It was the way things happened. It was reality and common sense opposed to theories so shadowy that only a cleric could differentiate the terms of their tenets. Every thought crashed like a stone through the windows of convention. Freedom is always alarming, none more so than freedom from prevailing cant and dogma. At once Machiavelli was attacked, but at once *The Prince* became a hand book for politicians. Italian was not so well known as French. Translations were speedily made. Charles V had pronounced the ban of the empire against Luther, whose followers had accused the newly formed Society of Jesus of unchristian methods. Now the Jesuits turned upon the son of Charles V, reproving him as anti-christ and Machiavellian, thus completing a triangle of abuse and misunderstanding. There is no doubt Philip II did study Machiavelli, but so did Catherine de Medici who took *The Prince* into France with her. Jesuit and Huguenot alike revolted at so unchristian a book taken to the hearts of their rulers, but they daunted neither the dead Machiavelli, nor the living princes. The mode grew. Richelieu studied the Florentine. William of Orange slept with a copy under his pillow. When Henry III was murdered at St. Cloud by the monk, Jacques Clement, and Ravaillac assassinated Henry IV, each monarch had upon his person, at the moment of his death, a copy of *The Prince*. It remained a book in fashion for a long time; witness the copy of Christina, ex-Queen of Sweden, whose French translation *Il Principe*, annotated in 1683, rests in Amsterdam, still bearing her marginal notes—"que cela est bien dit!"—or again—"Verité incontestable!"

Seven years after Machiavelli's death, Cardinal Reginald Pole was thundering, in England, against *Il Principe*. He devoted himself particularly to assailing the dictum that it was better to govern by fear than by love. Boldly the cardinal cried that Machiavelli's works were by the hand of the evil one, that the Florentine had aimed at destroying those he advised and that such a writer's life must be as detestable as his writings.

Stodgily enough, yet in sound Latin, he attacked Machiavelli's good faith, failing to see that the author's intent has nothing to do with the sheer truth or falsity of his maxims. He claimed Machiavelli said of *The Prince*, "That in that book he had been following not only his own judgment, but also that of one to whom he was writing, whom he knew to be of a tyrannical nature; if, however, these things do rankle ... his rule would be short; a thing especially hoped for, since deep down he (Machiavelli) burned for hatred for that monarch to whom he was writing."[4] Pole, fortunately for him, lived only two days after Queen Mary and so probably escaped both the stake and the sight of the triumph of Machiavelli.

The new doctrine had come to England in the days of chaos, a doctrine of a clear head and a cold heart, and Elizabeth early showed signs of heeding its devious practice. She had candles always burning before the shrine of her private chapel, but her religious training at the hands of Bernadino Ochino had been broad and her patronage of Giacomo Acantio had taught her that dogma was very like "stratagema satanae." Any trend of a queen's actions is sure to stir opposition and very soon came into being the doggerel

> An Englishman Italianate
> Is a devil incarnate.

At court some stood staunchly against the invasion of such realism. "The reconciliation of enemies may prove safe, and honorable, where the ciment on either side is worth. So as this Florentine precept concerning reconciled enemies, deserves worthily to be buried with unworthiness the author of it," wrote Sir Fulke Greville as he told the life story of Sir Philip Sidney.

While the Queen, meshed in a maze of duplicity, toyed with the Lowlands and Spain through the year 1572, her own Archbishop Parker wrote to Lord Burghley, "This Machiavell government is strange to me for it bringeth forth strange fruit." Sir Robert Naunton, writing of Leicester, high in Elizabeth's favor, disparaged him by pointing out, "He was too well seen in the aphorisms and principles of Nicholas, the Florentine, and in the reaches of Cæsar Borgia."

The court was, much of it, of Elizabeth's opinion, both in public and private. The Italian idea stimulated thought. The keen mind of Bacon, weighing all the skein of life within his philosophy, declared of Machiavelli, "Gratitude was owed to him and to all who, like him, had studied that which men do, instead of that which they ought to do."

Queen Elizabeth certainly found comfort in the practical expediency of the new thought. She found it convenient to say to one of her most trusty servants, Sir Henry Sidney, the Governor of Ireland, "Si violandum jus regnandi causa" —if the right must be violated it must be for the sake of rule. In the presence of her court she saw fit to boldly announce "The friendship of princes does not go beyond their convenience," which might have been a speech of the Florentine himself, dead then already half a century.

What more natural than that Walter Ralegh should set store by the example of Leicester and the teaching of Gascoigne? Machiavellian thought was in the air, the banter of gallants, the utterance of sages. To compete he studied *The*

Prince. The proof is easy. Most of his writing was concerned with demonstrating something; proving the general by the particular, ransacking life for instances. He was destined to possess a world of learning before he died. He quoted in his writings from Tacitus, Livy, Aristotle, Cicero, Tibullus, Suetonius, Pliny, Euripides, Homer, Plato and many others. Almost all of his allusions are to the ancients. Once or twice he quotes Thomas Aquinas, showing he had a knowledge of the Guelphic school. No modern, close to his own time, is more than mentioned except Machiavelli. When he writes of tyrants they must be Machiavellian in subtlety. When he seeks an illustration, it is a Florentine proverb made original. In argument he follows sometimes the mediæval precedent of proving his point from holy writ and the classics, only, in the same breath, he will quote the words of Christ and reconcile them with a Machiavellian precept. The bluff boldness of Drake and Frobisher he could meet naturally, but at twenty-five, home from the wars, he had to weigh Leicester and Burghley, he had to estimate the favor of a Queen changeable as the hours, but given to devious practice, and the subtle delights of statecraft. Ralegh needed all his natural gifts plus the learning of Camden and Ben Jonson. The road to glory was hard to hit in such an age and Walter Ralegh had trouble to set his foot upon it in the midst of chaos and marvellous indirection.

2

William Cecil had survived the service of Queen Mary to become Lord Burghley. From the day of Elizabeth's accession, when his note of twelve points told her exactly what to do, Cecil never slackened rein, yet he drove moderately and prudently to the end. Had he been able to advise Walter Ralegh how to get on, his words might have been much the same as those he really wrote to the Earl of Bedford, appointed Governor of Berwick in 1564. "Think of some great nobleman whom you can take as your pattern . . . weigh well what comes before you. Let your household be an example of order. . . . Be hospitable, but avoid excess. Be impartial and easy of access." Ralegh, fresh from the wars, would have felt the advice cold to his young blood. Not for him, then, the judicious, cautious method. Yet he needed to make a friend of Cecil, for his was an ability, an understanding that held England as its first interest, and close behind, the fortunes of Lord Burghley. French, Spanish, Dutch, Portuguese, Catholic, Church of England, Puritan, every faction was a tool to the craft of the great Lord Treasurer.

On the other hand Ralegh might find favor with the Dudleys. Robert Dudley had passed through the early dream of marrying Elizabeth, when he was willing to side with the Catholics, to a belated enthusiasm in which, although in the pay of Philip of Spain, he was vociferously for the cause of the Netherlanders. The dizzy maze of affairs, the sudden shiftings of Dudley, whose manly charms had made him Earl of Leicester at an early age, what way did these things pull upon Ralegh? As a soldier he had been broken to accept change from day to day. Direct action, youthful zest would attract him to Leicester. Any cynical pose of mawkish twenty-five would put him studying the velvet device of Burghley. The lordly gestures of each he could only espy at a prodigious distance, Machiavelli had laid down no maxims for coming to terms with greatness in such straits.

The court of Elizabeth was a theatre for the struggles of many others beside Burghley and Leicester. Some fifteen hundred, from statesmen down to stable boys, danced regular attendance upon the Queen. Most of them were men eager to present suits, able to connive at all manner of stratagem. Of one hundred fifty-eight persons at one time connected with the privy chamber only eleven were women. Even at the end of her reign, Elizabeth had only twenty-eight ladies attached to court. Every courtier sought position and power that his suits might not be in vain. The most humble, the most servile of graces were exacted and recompensed at court.

To make all more difficult for a bold, aloof nature, seeking success, Ralegh had to struggle in a court which was very much one great family. Lord Hunsdon of the privy council and Sir Francis Knollys were first cousins of the Queen, one by blood, the other by marriage. Sir John Perrot, if likeness and rumor can lead on to truth, was her illegitimate half-brother. Lord Buckhurst, Lord Howard of Effingham, Lord Derby, were kinsmen to the Queen. The courtiers were intermarried in many ways. Leicester, Pembroke and Sir Henry Sidney each married three times, complicating relationships no end. Perhaps the most extremely involved lady of marriage was Penelope Devereux. By a third marriage of her mother, while Penelope was in her second, the two became sisters-in-law. The ramifications thus set up took years to learn and were constantly increasing. Naturally the court had a tendency to become a family affair. Robert Cecil followed at his father's heels. Burghley's nephews, Anthony and Francis Bacon, were being groomed for preferment. The Cecils, the Howards, the Norrises, the Knollyses, all played for favor and none too gently. Against all this Walter Ralegh had to bear up, engage and thrust home. It was the hand of destiny that opened the way for him, that and the fact that he belonged to no faction by blood and so escaped entangling alliances.

3

The first step toward Fame that Walter Ralegh made was to take up residence in the Middle Temple. To be admitted to any of the four societies in the Inns of Court required the endorsement of two barristers, and in the Middle Temple, the testimony of a bencher to show he is "aptus, habilis, et idoneus moribus et scientia." Once admitted, the candidate became entitled to use the Temple library, claimed a seat in the church or chapel of the inn and could enter his name for chambers. When Ralegh took up quarters, the Middle Temple Hall had just been built. The fountain, which "sprang to a vast and almost incredible altitude," was much more active than now. The Temple was in its heyday. At Christmas, Hallowe'en, Candlemas and Ascension Day there were splendid feasts governed by an elected Master of Revels. The Lord Chancellor, Judges, and Benchers danced a triple round in solemn abandon about the sea-coal fire.

To be admitted to the Temple did not guarantee that one studied law. Lord Burghley was an inmate, but in later years regretted that he had not used the occasion to become familiar with common practice. Ralegh, at his trial, denied that he knew the way of the courts, which presupposes that Ralegh's time at the Temple was a matter of residence only. It was a proper gesture of a young man hoping to climb. No doubt the regulations of the benchers were onerous to him, but it was not an age when laws were fully enforced, even among the lawyers. Only knights and benchers might wear hose and doublets of bright colors, except crimson or scarlet. Velvet capes, scarlet wings to the gowns, white jerkins, buskins, velvet shoes, double shirt cuffs and feathers or ribbons in the cap were all proscribed in the interest of the prerogatives of the court. It was unthinkable that young men of the Temple should rival the gaiety of the courtiers. Ralegh was acquainted at court and the Devonshire lad returned from the war had learned already to get what he wanted. In 1576, he was surely in residence at the Temple, but as surely in 1577, he was resident at Islington.

It seems William and Richard Paunsford resisted the watch and upon arrest acknowledged themselves servants of Walter Ralegh. Bail was necessary and the master signed the recognizances one as "Walter Rawley, Esq. of Islington" and the other as "Walter Rawley, Esq. de Curia." So in December, 1577, Ralegh dwelt in Islington. Islington or Isheldun, the lower fortress, was then a place of pleasant, open fields, touched by silence and repose. Landed estates, shooting butts for the practice of archery, and the country places for the rising nobility—that was Islington. It had a reputation for polite wickedness. Lord Burghley owned a fine house there which later became the very comfortable Queen's Head, a famous tavern that was pulled down in 1829.

Just what may have been Ralegh's residence in Islington is a matter of surmise. How did this youngster of the provinces find the funds to keep two servants, to enter the Temple and to live in the suburb of Islington? Perhaps the explanation of this lies in that second recognizance and the signature, "Walter Rawley de Curia." His gentle blood, his acquaintance with George Gascoigne, his being half-brother to Sir Humphrey Gilbert, the indeterminate date of his attachment to Leicester, with whom he was a person of some importance by 1580: these may have furnished channels of revenue. To be of the court was the mark of a young gentleman seeking the privileges of his birth. It was of use in case a man struck a thorn while sowing his wild oats. The army had left its roughness upon Ralegh, Machiavelli had made his mind free of prejudice, and no doubt a little heedless, and the gay blades of London for company led him into a licentious enjoyment of his leisure. Perhaps it was as well he had no great fortune to lavish. His father was alive until April, 1578, after which nothing is known of him.

This was the same year Humphrey Gilbert came into his

own. Patiently he had waited at his house beside the highway, "with fine elm trees on both sides; that the same hath now taken hold of Lime Hurst or Lime Host, corruptly called Lime House." He had attempted to organize an abortive effort against Spanish ships, but the government would not sanction it. Then came a Royal Charter to Gilbert giving him authority over six years to explore and occupy territory not actually possessed by other Christian thrones than the English. It was a dream that had come out of the days with his friend Hakluyt. What more natural than he should employ the idle Walter Ralegh? There might be fighting. In fact the expedition may really have been directed against the Spanish rather than the finding of "Norimbega" or the North West passage to Cathay.

Before the end of 1578, Gilbert had cleared with his fleet. There was the flagship *An Ager*, two hundred fifty tons, bearing Sir Humphrey's own motto *Quid non*. The *Hope of Greenway* measured one hundred sixty tons and the *Red Lion* with the motto *Now or Never* and commanded by Nyles Morgan of Tredgar with John Anthony as his master, came to one hundred tons. The *Falcon* of one hundred tons completed the expedition, save for the *Gallion*, forty tons. It is difficult to tell from the rolls of the expedition whether this last name should be spelled as a proper or a common noun. For sharp, light work she no doubt would have proven very handy.

The *Falcon* was given to Walter Ralegh to command, but with him as master sailed "Fardinando, the Portugale," a mysterious man supposed to know much of the wonders beyond the seas, but, whether loyal to English or Spanish, still an excellent seaman. Ralegh was listed as "a capitayne of An Ancient by Lande," perhaps by way of excuse of his commanding at twenty-six, without any experience, the "Quenes ship of 100 Tunnes havinge in her Caste peces 15, fowlers 4, doble bases 12." With him sailed Charles Champernoun, John Robtes, Thomas Flerre, Thomas Holborne, John Antoll and William Higford, all gentlemen. The whole number of gentlemen, soldiers and marines in the ship were seventy, a small enough crew to assail the new world. Aloof, elegant was her motto, *Nec mortem pet nec finem fugio.* "I neither seek death nor flee the end."

As was the case with many expeditions of the time the departure was delayed. The Privy Council heard the complaint of a Seville merchant concerning a cargo of lemons and oranges. The county officials were ordered to detain the fleet at Dartmouth. Some one had to be seen. Meanwhile the fleet "victualed with beef for three months." On September 26, the expedition finally left Dartmouth. Wind and weather beat them about so there was no getting to westward. By October 15 they were forced back to Plymouth much battered. The edge had gone from the adventure, but the men re-embarked on October 29 and at last the ships got to sea after tedious waiting. With their sailing the attempt passes into mystery. John Hooker later wrote to Walter Ralegh, "Infinite commodities in sundry respects would have ensued from that voyage, if the fleet then accompanying you had according to appointment followed you; or yourself had escaped the dangerous sea fight, wherein many of your company was slain and your ships therewith also sore battered and disabled." This sole reference to a naval battle tantalizes, but unfolds nothing. Bernardino de Mendoza wrote on February 26, 1579, that Gilbert and Knollys had returned and the sole result was the capture of a French ship with cargo. Hollinshed drops a hint that Ralegh held on his way for America bent upon independent action, but running short of food was forced to give up and return. Walter Ralegh had had his first fling at sea duty. He was never entirely free from mal de mer and yet he performed his duties well enough to please Sir Humphrey Gilbert and leave him with no unwillingness to help his half-brother further.

In February, 1579, he crossed swords with Sir Thomas Perrot who afterward married Lady Dorothy Devereux, sister to the Earl of Essex. The duel had no fatal consequences; both men were arrested and flung into Fleet prison for six days. However, Ralegh was quarrelling with men of note and no doubt creating, by his boldness, much of that antagonism which was to block up his path later. Peer of simple gentlemen, he feared none at twenty-seven.

Burghley had many troubles at the time. He nursed his gout, taking Nicholas Gybberd's tincture of gold and the Earl of Shrewsbury's "oyle of staggs blood," as well as paying heed to the nostrums in Latin from Doctor Nuñez, the Queen's Portuguese physician, and he worried about the young Earl of Oxford. Married to Elizabeth, his eldest daughter, this nobleman was proving himself an unwise son-in-law. His temper was uncertain. His whims lacked discretion and his bent was in no way politic. In 1579, he stormed on to a tennis court where he sought to displace Sir Philip Sidney and several others then playing. Sidney, the perfect knight, would have loved nothing better than to put the matter to a test of arms. Ralegh, naturally on the side of the gentry against the great nobles, and a friend to Sidney, took sides at once. Sir Philip carried the affair to the Queen who fell back upon his undoubted loyalty to her and dismissed the matter with the Florentine counsel, "There is a great difference in degree between earls and private gentlemen, and princes are bound to support the nobility and to insist upon their being treated with proper respect."

As for Ralegh, all the affair brought him was a fine from the Privy Council. Burghley may have had an overbearing fool for a son-in-law, but the Queen had taken sides and if "the perfect knight" had proved unavailing before her, there was no need for a gouty councillor to hazard any of his prestige in an issue already decided in favor of his kin.

So the year closed. Ralegh had established contact with Leicester and Walsingham and possibly with Burghley, to judge by the sequence of events. He had made enemies who probably despised him for his lack of position, and friends who admired his courage, but he was far from the road to glory. Every attempt to set foot upon it had resulted in failure and yet his spirit had struggled on recklessly, more gallantly at every rebuff. His play had grown more high-handed. His wisdom had yet to round into maturity. At twenty-seven his experience had been one to stir all the rough and violent in his nature. To strike, to swagger, to play the man at arms, to feel the beat of the blood surging through a vigorous body, these were the heritage of his youth. Ahead lay the world still undiscovered.

CHAPTER IV

UNTO THE CELTS

THE year 1580 opened ominously for Elizabeth. Philip was fitting out the Spanish fleet with great clamor. He had joined the Pope in forwarding Desmond's rebellion in Ireland. Parma had succeeded. Orange was desperately struggling to reunite Flanders with Holland under Alençon. Every circumstance threatened Elizabeth. If she failed to marry Alençon Flemish affairs might be settled without her and afterwards she would have to face Spain alone. She had toyed with Alençon's emissary Simier with the condescension of some gorgeous courtesan. Her vacillation distracted her ministers and pressed England into a host of involvements.

For the first time since she had come to the throne, Elizabeth's popularity wavered. Her light conduct with Simier and its prophecy of a French marriage had renewed the old rivalry with France and excited the Puritans against the Catholics. There was some ground for this resentment. Allen's English seminary, which had been taken to Douay in 1568, had sought refuge under the Guises at Rheims, and young priests, trained for the missionary work, were being constantly sent to England. The first members of the Jesuit mission, Persons and Campion, arrived in 1580. No wonder was it that Leicester, Hatton and Walsingham were resolved to break off the French marriage. As they succeeded the Queen's position became completely isolated.

All his life Burghley had striven to prevent the isolation of England and to keep the peace. By one device or another he had kept either France or Spain a nominal ally. When Elizabeth turned from the marriage to Alençon, he found need to delve into new diplomacy. Alençon should be encouraged to accept the sovereignty of Flanders, soon to be offered him. This would divert him from a Spanish alliance. All Papists should be made safe at home by removing them from positions of power. The army and navy must be prepared. Desmond and his Irish should be conciliated, justice rendered and "certain private disorders in Ireland winked at." Mary Stuart should be made safe that she should not be a rallying point for disaffected Papists. The Queen should continue to dally with Alençon and pretend to a more friendly feeling for Spain.

Elizabeth heeded his advice. She opened negotiations for Condé, with his Huguenots swelled by a mercenary force of German Protestants, to enter Flanders. English money would support the effort and if the enterprise turned into a threat against England, Alençon would not have a free hand. Ninety thousand men were mustered and the navy, seventeen ships in all, was mobilized. Fourteen had been in commission since the threat of Alba in 1578. Mary Stuart was eventually brought to Buxton instead of to Ashby-de-la-Zouch as originally intended. As soon as Burghley urged a drawing close to France, Leicester, out of rivalry, told Mendoza he desired "to serve the King of Spain." Scotland was strongly Catholic. The Guises had recognized James as the successor to his mother. These complicated relations made the heads of the Councillors spin and sent Elizabeth into a furious flurry. In private with Burghley and Archbishop Sandys, "Here am I," she cried, "between Scylla and Charybdis. Alençon has agreed to all my conditions and wants to know when he is to come and marry me. If I fail he will probably quarrel with me and if I marry him I shall not be able to govern the country. What shall I do?" At the same time she had the resolution not to heed Burghley's advice in Irish matters where the Spanish and Italians were aiding a fully fledged revolt of Munster. She had no great force to hazard. In fact, much of her niggardly closeness may have been a necessity to be careful rather than an unholy proclivity to be mean. Beset as she was, she would not countenance the success of the rebels helped by foreigners. Ireland should be punished.

2

Sir Humphrey Gilbert had been appointed President of Munster in 1569. He had been an absolutist. The Irish were unruly and were poorly armed. "In those days the Irish had darts," wrote Walter Ralegh. Gilbert was even more vigorous than his age. He administered the province with austere severity, dealing out to insurgents what he desired, ruling without consideration. Objections at court became too loud. It is doubtful that Elizabeth was moved by compassion for the people of Munster. Often she let her officials do that to Ireland which she would have liked to do to Spain, France and Italy. It was not a noble attitude but it was a practical relief. Still, she heard the objections. Gilbert was never an adroit courtier. He chose to worship the Queen as the moon, Diana at a distance, and he allowed nothing to shake him from that attitude, with the result that he only won in years what men of less reserve and natures more attuned to intimacy made a suit of a few months. Sir Humphrey Gilbert was relieved of office and Sir John Perrot, the father of the Perrot who fought with Walter Ralegh, was sent out in his place.

Apparently the moderation of Perrot's administration did not bring the people of Munster to terms. The positions were reversed now. Gilbert, busy about his colonization schemes, was at court to look out for his own interests. Perrot was in command in exile, with many miles between him and the Queen. Gilbert was able to urge severity and an iron hand upon a man fitted only for temporizing and when the matter passed to a discussion of methods and instruments, Gilbert had but to proffer the services of a dozen good fellows, including Walter Ralegh, to give the Queen the possibility of action she longed after.

The expedition of 1578 to Norimbega had not been a success. There had been much bickering and some false play. Whoever was to blame, apparently Gilbert was satisfied with the actions of Ralegh. One did not recommend doubtful instruments to the Queen and hope to keep her esteem. Gilbert was dependent upon her good will for the realizing of his American dream. He could afford to make no mistakes when he recommended his half-brother for the Irish service.

From July 13, 1580, Ralegh drew his four shillings a day as a commissioned captain. His company was not so strong as is modern practice; one hundred foot soldiers devoted to suppressing rebellion. Gilbert believed in violent means; Ralegh from the outset of his Irish days was all energy and force. He saved neither his men nor himself and he crushed the poorly armed Irish in no uncertain manner. Lord Grey, the Deputy, through most of the trouble, was an officer who favored severity. Under Grey, as assistant secretary, was Edmund Spenser, who believed, too, that the best way with the Irish was to treat them brutally for the sake of the example made.

The English felt the Irish were savages. They were disloyal to the crown. They consorted with Spaniards and Italians. The Papist cause was, to such rebels, a thing to be championed, particularly since it was anti-English. Through all this maze of feeling, rather than thinking, ran an immense scorn of a subject people. This never left the British mind until recent years, if indeed it is now quite dead. On the other side, the Irish were presumptive that tribal unity was essential to them. Poorly armed, and often indifferently led, they made a brave showing from time to time. Alack, they had every incentive to do so, for English treatment of rebels has always been sharp; in Ireland it was usually outrageous. It was this sense of the overwhelming array against them that drove the Irish to seek Spanish and Italian aid, as the Cubans cried unto the United States, and the Poles unto every nation that has gone to war. The Papist leanings were real, but primarily their hope was to avert the famine which the English operations were bound to bring, since the war-racked land bore next to nothing and ruin stalked everywhere.

Elizabeth seems to have been unmoved by the extremes her men entertained in Munster. She was busy with the rest of Europe, pacifying Mendoza, making extravagant promises, always with reservations, to Castelnau. Ireland was only an added annoyance. Since she had rejected Burghley's suggestion that the rebels should be mollified and irregularities winked at, she was anxious to see her soldiers speedily prove that her policy of rigor was correct. The more strenuous, the more crushing the efforts of her forces, the quicker the Irish would come to their senses and realize their inferiority, their remote and humble place in the scheme of her imperial splendor. She was forty-seven and pride grows with the years, especially in a Queen.

3

Ralegh was plunged into the nastiness of the trouble from the first. James Fitz-Maurice, of the Geraldine family, had landed and on his heels, San Josepho, bearing the banner of the Pope and bringing Spanish and Italian forces in three ships, which landed at Smerwick, in County Kerry. They built Fort del Ore, had it blessed by Allen, the Irish Jesuit, and Sanders, an English Jesuit, and received into it the Irish forces of James and John, brothers of the Earl of Desmond. Thomas Courtenay, of Devon, promptly captured the three ships. Fitz-Maurice was killed and James Desmond wounded and captured by the sheriff of Cork. He was delivered up to Sir Warham St. Leger and Captain Ralegh. He was examined, indicted, arraigned. With remarkably little fuss he was sentenced to be drawn, hanged and quartered, which was done, "and his head and limbs impaled upon the city gates of Cork." It was a grim introduction to responsibility but Ralegh was already a tried soldier. This opening service he performed under Pelham, and almost immediately, on August 12, 1580, to be exact, Arthur, Lord Grey, Baron of Wilton, came into Ireland as Deputy. It was an important change for Ralegh. Lord Grey was an extremist of his own school. It promised to be an easy shift to make, although the Earl of Ormond, then Lieutenant of Munster, was known to be a moderate. There was much opportunity for unrestricted action and only an occasional need of diplomacy.

By November, 1580, Ralegh was before Smerwick. The British fleet, under Admiral Winter, brought culverins and heavy ordnance ashore so the fort could be bombarded both by sea and land. It was a chance for the tireless energy of the young captain, already a veteran of irregular warfare. Captains Ralegh and Denny covered the landing and emplacement of the artillery, with their companies. Ralegh's men took over a battery of the new guns and served them well, hammering the fort so heavily that the rebels made several sorties, but were forced to return to their walls. Gradually the guns were advanced until the fort became a ruin and on November 9, the place surrendered. From a dream of taking Ireland, England and Scotland in a holy war, the besieged surrendered, their only terms a plea for mercy.

Captains Ralegh and Mackworth had the ward that day

and immediately entered and, under orders, fell to slaughter. Four to five hundred died. San Josepho, the Spanish commander, his camp master and a few other Spanish officers were spared and sent to England to be ransomed. Save for a reprieved noble, all the Irish died. An Irish priest and a renegade Englishman had their arms and legs broken before execution. Lord Grey's orders were carried out in both spirit and letter. The excuse was a belief that a relieving force of fifteen hundred was close enough to attack and the English detachments were unequal to dealing humanely with so many prisoners. Europe professed horror at the massacre; perhaps it was but an expression of disappointment at British success. Elizabeth wrote Grey as much pleased with his conduct. Grey did not name Ralegh in his despatch to the Council.

There were other feats awaiting the captain, so what matter his superior's favor? The years of action were upon him, the years when night riding and lone combat, desperate deeds and above all military device, were precious. The winter he spent in Cork, except for a journey to Dublin, where he exposed the sedition of Lord Barry to Grey. The Lord Deputy gave him full permission to reduce Lord Barry to peace and subjection, but somewhere there was a slip. Barry himself burned his castle to the ground and scoured the country round, perhaps to prove his British loyalty. Meanwhile, an ambush was set for Ralegh. Riding homeward with six men, he was attacked at a ford between Youghal and Cork. One of his men, Moyle, was mired in the confusion and likely to drown in the mud. Ralegh rescued him, but lost his horse, which ran off at the fighting. Alone, with his pike in one hand and a pistol in the other, he stood off Fitz-Edmonds, the seneschal of Imokelly, and twenty more. There were a few rough words instead of murder. Fitz-Edmonds did not dare attack. Ralegh out-faced him.

Parley was held from time to time, for the rebellion was really like a family quarrel. Fitz-Edmonds boasted of his valor at one of these. Ralegh charged him with cowardice. Ormond, the moderate Lieutenant of Munster, at that offered to fight it out with the Irish: two to two, four to four, six to six, but the rebels flatly refused. It was a heavy winter touched by bickerings and scheming dalliance. It brought Ralegh the notice of the Earl of Ormond, who was weary of this wilderness with its boastings and treacheries. In the spring he returned to England, leaving the government of Munster in the hands of a commission: Sir William Morgan, Captain Piers and Captain Ralegh.

From the vantage of his share in such authority, Ralegh's energy drove him forward. There was a Lord Roche of Bally seated in a castle twenty miles from Cork, well retained by a strong force. He was a nobleman of parts, friendly with the people of the countryside, but known to be hand in glove with the chief rebels. Ralegh undertook to bring him in for examination. As usual, in Ireland of the time, the news of his efforts got abroad ahead of him. Eight hundred men under Barry and Fitz-Edmonds gathered to intercept the English. Ralegh set out at eleven o'clock of a dark night with his company at his heels. They pushed straight on so rapidly toward Bally in Harsh, Lord Roche's own village, that the ambuscade failed, but, arriving at the place at break of day, they were met by five hundred townsmen. Ralegh at once took measures to police the streets, attempted no violence, and with six men marched on to the castle. He was met by several gentlemen who agreed to take him in to Lord Roche if he dismissed four of his followers. This he did, but managed to have these men of his kept within the walls, so as to receive the others of his company, who, a few at a time, left the town, concentrated upon the castle and were let into the courtyard by their friends within the gates.

Lord Roche was confident in his security. He feasted the well-known Captain Ralegh most amiably. He was amused when the Captain was so facetious as to explain the purpose of the call. Many excuses came to mind. Ralegh grew more bold in his explanations: Lord and Lady Roche must come with him. The commission for the capture was produced. Lord Roche grew more bland. He was in his own castle surrounded by his faithful retainers. This Englishman was ridiculous. Ralegh ordered him to obey. Lord Roche absolutely refused. Ralegh displayed his complement gathered in the courtyard, some watching the gates, some guarding the halls, every man having his piece double charged. Lord Roche bowed to fate and kept his good humor. Ralegh pointed out to him that since the townsfolk of Bally were so ready to protect Lord Roche, they should escort him on his way to the Deputy. Roche assented good-naturedly. It was no light thing to go plunging along in the dark, up hill and down dale, with a chance of his own friends mistakenly firing into his party from ambuscade, but there was no resisting the impetuous Ralegh. Soldiers were bruised by falls. One lost his life, but thanks to Ralegh's tireless vigilance and strength of command, the prisoners were delivered in the morning unharmed. The rebels had lain in wait at a dozen points but had seen nothing of the party. It seemed the work of a devil rather than a man, a deed touched by black art, done by an Englishman who knew nothing of the country he dealt with, but who knew much of determination.

Yet Walter Ralegh played a rash game in Ireland. His soldiers were a poor lot, and he did not hesitate to say so. While the Deputy was writing home to announce success was at hand, Ralegh denied that the trouble could have any immediate end, and placed the blame upon Lord Grey. "Would God the service of Sir Humfry Gilbert might be rightly looked into; who, with the third part of the garrison now in

Ireland, ended a rebellion not much inferior to this in two months." Ormond thought well of Ralegh and his work, but this did not silence Ralegh's criticism of his actions. He shunned no labor, avoided no danger, even that beyond his duty, took all risks, but he saw with clear eyes the true power of his superiors. Their praise could not make him, he would see that their dislike left him untouched. Years were too precious to be wasted in Irish exile, under men who were strangers to success. So he turned his wits to other channels. How would Gascoigne have played it? What episode would he have plucked from such a career and moulded to a climax, bringing advancement? In August, 1581, Lord Grey dissolved the commission administering Munster and made Captain John Zouch governor. Ralegh was left only the command of Cork, but he seems to have shown no spleen against Zouch, and he was not a man to take a rival's success easily, even at thirty.

The fact was Ralegh was already headed for the court career he had long dreamed upon. He was never a man who liked rough work for itself, nor the blood beat of wild deeds, nor the competitive zest of rigorous campaigning. He saw a larger canvas and he saw hard-headedly with an eye to perspective, and foreshortening, and all the play of light and shadow. Even as he spoke full solemnly his opinions of Lord Grey and the Earl of Ormond, he was in correspondence with Lord Treasurer Burghley. His very first letter to Sir Francis Walsingham begins: "I received of late a letter from your Honor wherein I find your Honor's disposition and opinion more favorable than I can any way deserve." Whereupon he poured out to the Secretary intimate knowledge of Irish affairs. Only a day later the young soldier wrote about a personal wrong done him in the affairs of Barry Court. Warming to his subject, he compared the administrations of Ormond and Gilbert, who had governed Munster in 1569.

In short, Ralegh wanted Barry Court, even though Ormond had allowed Barry so long to evacuate that the castle had been dismantled before Ralegh had gained possession.

Walsingham wrote to the Lord Deputy and Grey turned over the Barry land from Rostellan Castle to Fota to Ralegh. This meant the whole northern side of the harbor of Cork and Great Island, on which Queenstown was later built, became the reward of the Devon Captain. Ralegh, in temporary possession, offered to rebuild Barry Court and garrison it at his own cost, if the Queen would confirm his rights in the matter. Apparently his contacts with Burghley were not so sound as those with Walsingham, for the Queen rejected the matter at Burghley's suggestion. Where Ralegh had the money to rebuild the court is uncertain. His father is not heard of after April 11, 1578. His estate may have brought his son funds of a sort, but Barry Court was a ruin and to rebuild it would have been an expensive matter. The episode is the first glimpse of the involved mental processes of Ralegh. There was no man who could plead with a heavier balance of service upon his side. All his life Walsingham gave to the Queen to win an obscure burial at night that none might know how pitifully poor she had kept him. No doubt Ralegh saw ways to finance the matter, if only Walsingham had succeeded in winning the permanent grant for him. Since he did not, Ralegh forgot Barry Court at once and turned to play another card. It was only the dream of a moment, that estate in Ireland, the spoils of war, but the Queen had said no. Ralegh wrote to Leicester.

"I may not forget continually to put your Honor in mind of my affection unto your Lordship, having to the world both professed and protested the same. Your Honor, having no use of such poor followers hath utterly forgotten mee. Notwithstanding, if your Lordship shall please-to think me your's, as I am, I will be found as ready, and dare do as much in your service, as any man may command; and do, neither, so much despair of myself but that I may be some way able to perform as much.

"I have spent some time here under the Deputy, in such poor place and charge, as, were it not for that I knew him to be one of yours, I would disdain it as much as to keep sheep. I will not trouble your Honor with the business of this lost land; for that Sir Warham Sentleger can best of any man deliver unto your Lordship the good, the bad, the mischiefs, the means to amend and all in all of this commonwealth, or rather common woe. He hopeth to find your Honor his assured good Lord and your Honor may most assuredly command him. He is lovingly inclined toward your Honor. And your Lordship shall win by your favor toward him a wise, faithful and valiant gentleman, whose word and deed your Honor shall ever find to be one.

"Thus, having no other matter, but only to desire the continuance of your Honor's favor, I humbly take my leave. From the Camp of Lismore, in Ireland, August 25, 1581.

Your Honor's faithful and obedient,

W. RAWLEY."

This has no sound of a first letter. Ralegh knew whom he wrote and he did not address Dudley only as an earl "of Her Majesty's most honorable Privy Council," he addressed Leicester. He knew the Queen's favorite well enough for his recommendation to have had some value to Sir Warham St. Leger, and in a postscript he ventured to call the Earl's attention to the "pitiful estate" of Fitz-Edmonds of Cloyne, a loyal Geraldine.

It was a bold voice reminding a patron his follower had suffered enough in exile. It was the direct tendering of services and an announcement that Ireland under Grey held nothing for Ralegh. The Queen had had every excuse to give him Barry Court and did not. Nothing more likely would be available. He had served his apprenticeship. If Leicester saw fit to redeem him the time was ripe. Leicester heard. Grey sent Ralegh home in December and four days after Christmas, Ralegh settled his expenses at twenty pounds in London.

CHAPTER V

RISE SUN

IT was the portion of destiny that Ralegh bore despatches from the Lord Deputy into England. Ralegh, the hero of fearful night riding, the man who had stood off the Irish twenty to one, who captured castles without expense to the crown, and before whom the massed rebels broke and ran! His legend ran before him at a court where information concerning Ireland was important. Who so apt to comment intelligently upon conditions as the carrier of despatches?

Ralegh had his occasion made for him. It was not necessary that "Her Majesty, meeting with a plashy place, made some scruple to go on; when Ralegh (dressed in the gay and genteel habit of those times) presently cast off and spread his new plush coat on the ground, whereon the Queen trod gently over, rewarding him afterwards with many suits for his so free and seasonable tender of so fair a footcloth." Oh, Ralegh might have had a new cloak. He was in funds. In February of 1582, he was paid two hundred pounds for his services, a sum equal to about one thousand pounds in our day. Fuller, writing that story forty-four years after Ralegh's death, may have been speaking truth, not amiable fiction. Ralegh was to pursue far-fetched and hectic chivalry to the end of the Queen's reign. He may even have written with a diamond on the glass,

"Fain would I climb, but that I fear to fall," and Elizabeth may have escaped the line with her brusque, Delphic,

"If thy heart fail thee, then climb not at all." Fuller related that too, but it needs none of such magic to favor the young Devon gentleman.

He, himself, made the way for a magician. Doctor John Dee, communicant with spirits, astrologer extraordinary, was brought to the Queen's attention by the new courtier. He interceded as Elizabeth left Richmond for Greenwich and the seer of visions noted in his diary, "At her going on horseback, being new up, she called for me, by Mr. Rawly his putting in her mind."[5] The good doctor had summoned the spirits to help Adrian Gilbert in his plans for the Northwest Passage. Gilbert's half-brother brought to the savant the wonder of a queen's hand to kiss.

Ralegh came into England an experienced soldier known as more than a shadow to Leicester and Walsingham, and as an officer to Burghley, William Cecil. The wretched state of affairs in Ireland had burned at his heart as a young and eager campaigner. He had a text his cool and contemplative mind told him was sound. His superiors, left behind in Ireland, would not like what he would say, but in the nepotic court of Elizabeth his candid opinion would earn him more appreciation than many vain extravagances. It was important to policies of state that the Irish equation be accurately stated.

Behind that tall (too tall, some thought), white forehead was formed a project to make Ireland serve Ralegh now that Ralegh had served Ireland. He had seen that to keep a garrison in the island powerful enough to subdue the rebel bands was impractical. The cost mounted swiftly. The proper administration was to win over the more likely of the chieftains, selecting carefully those of value after winning. Due regard should be taken of tribal alignments. Thrift, as well as efficiency, entered into his plans, and Elizabeth was always eager to save a penny. Ralegh pointed out how "divers lords" might be won to the English cause. This was an about face from his attitude in the field. Perhaps he had caught so much of wisdom from Lord Burghley, or perhaps he turned moderate to catch the sympathy of the powerful Cecil. The Lord Treasurer seems to have seen farther than others of Ralegh's supporters. He had known Elizabeth longer and served closer to her whims. He was quick to catch at Ralegh.

Grey was not uninformed as to what was going on at court. He knew whom to thank for it; Leicester was his bitter enemy. He had had trouble with Ralegh's presumption in Ireland. Leicester, too, felt rivalry from the Earl of Ormond, for even so early he could see that Ormond would be the man to receive credit from the Privy Council for the suppression of the Munster rebellion, as well as the Queen's thanks. Grey insisted Ralegh's plans were impossible. Ralegh was passing on the expense of the garrison in Ireland for the province to pay. Grey pointed out clearly that this was offering impossibilities for others to execute, but his defence was powerless. Leicester had so far overcome the disadvantage of his marriage, revealed by Simier three years earlier, that he was again in favor with the Queen. Ralegh was invited to lay before the Council his plans and was given audience by the Queen.

It is doubtful whether Ralegh cared much for Ireland, save as an instrument to solicit royal favor. He never after was entirely free from contact with Irish affairs, and he was always regarded as an expert concerning them, but he was after larger matters. The dreams of Hakluyt, the example of Sir Humphrey Gilbert, so powerful in his boyhood days, when the interval of their ages was so conducive to hero worship, were not forgotten. The quiet return of Drake in the *Pelican* in 1580 had proved that the Queen loved money more than she feared war. Even when urged by Burghley, Essex and Crofts to restore to Spain the freebooter's gains, she had listened to Leicester, Walsingham and Hatton, and told the Spanish she was the abused party—witness the Papal and Spanish troops sent into Ireland. Drake aided the solution by bribing the Councillors, but in the end, it was the Queen who made something of him as a hero and refused to return any of the captured loot to Spain. Ralegh dreamed of the new world. In the light of precedent he played upon economy in Ireland, that he might win both funds and royal support for his greater ventures.

Why the wonderment, the mystery that is woven about that first audience? Ralegh had risen perfectly normally and not with any undue precocity. He was thirty in 1582 and his Queen was forty-nine. Three years earlier he and his affairs were discussed by the Lords of Council. In the midst of fitting out their expedition Ralegh and Gilbert were ordered "in her Majesty's name to remain on land and to surcease proceeding in their enterprise." That was on May 29, 1579. If the episode of the bridging cloak occurred it would only serve as a contributory circumstance to the career of the young courtier. Many have remembered that Kate Ashley was governess to Queen Elizabeth in her days of trial, while Mary was still on the throne, and claimed that her blood relationship with the Raleghs led to the presentation of Walter. This would be probable except for the chronology. Mrs. Katherine Ashley died in 1565, when Walter Ralegh was but thirteen. Clearly the thing is impossible. Seventeen years after the death of her governess, Elizabeth harkened to speech of Dame Ashley's relative and found him sage and filled with interest. He was able but not entangled with other courtiers. He was already no one's man. For a close friend he had Sir Philip Sidney, nephew of Leicester, but with his knowledge of Irish affairs he was sometimes closeted with the Earl of Sussex, Leicester's enemy. Something of his preference he may have owed to Walsingham, to Sir Philip Sidney, to all the host of men that moved across the royal stage. Certainly, he knew enough of them to have been presented to the Queen at will and he chose the time of his return from Ireland.

The most probable man to intercede for him was his own half-brother who was just then pursuing his dream of colonizing America. Ralegh did not think much of Sir Humphrey Gilbert as a courtier, but then what man of thirty comprehends the actions of a man of forty-three? He had written Walsingham from Ireland wishing Gilbert were in command. "Would God his own behavior were suche in peace as it did not make his good service forgotten and hold him from preferment he is worthy of." Gilbert had been attached to Elizabeth's household when she was but a princess. What chance had Ralegh to estimate his half-brother's influence? When he had been granted audience and Elizabeth knew of herself what manner of man had come out of Ireland with criticism of Lord Grey, she wrote on April 1, 1582:

"For that our pleasure is to have our servant, Walter Rawley, trained some time longer in that our realm [Ireland] for his better experience in martial affairs and for the especial care which We have to do him good in respect of his kindred that have served Us, some of them (as you know) near about Our person, these are to require you that the leading of said band may be committed to the said Rawley; and for that he is, for some considerations, by us excused to stay here. Our pleasure is that the said band be, in the meantime, till he repair into that Our realm, delivered to same such as he shall depute to be his lieutenant there."

Walsingham wrote the Lord Deputy at once, seconding Her Majesty's letter by way of routine, doubtless, and Grey, hating Ralegh with all his heart, replied, "As for Captain Rawley's assignment to the charge of Apsleie's band . . . I must be plain: I neither like his carriage nor his company;

and therefore, other than by direction and commandment, and what his right can require, he is not to expect at my hands." Whether Gilbert was Ralegh's sponsor or not, Grey recognized the young man to be dangerous and apparently not entirely congenial. Had the Lord Deputy known the full extent of Ralegh's court conquest, the future cast of events, he might have dealt more diplomatically with the return of his young captain.

Even so, it was many a day before he had to meet the gentleman he so hated. Ralegh was to stay in England until after the rebellion in Munster had ended. Meanwhile, he served the Queen. Leicester had no objections, at least for a time. Already he saw Elizabeth as "a lady whom time hath surprised," but he left it to Ralegh to say so much later. The service of the Queen was fatiguing. Keyed to a febrile uncertainty, unaware what turn the cruel wit or the more deadly shrewdness of perception might take, a courtier needed all his power of mind. It was a hurly-burly age with a thousand issues upon a thousand tongues. To make a mistake was fatal and the Queen was a person of infinite and changing taboo. When John Stubbs and William Page wrote and printed a thin octavo, *The Discovery of a gaping Gulf*, against the French marriage with the Duke of Alençon, they lost their right hands although the Queen had already decided against the marriage. The line between pleasing and offending was nicely but deviously drawn. Elizabeth expected her courtiers to play the game of love discerningly, stopping where she would have them and she often insisted they go far. Whether courtesan or virgin, scandal was sure to attack Elizabeth because of her extremes in attitude. Stories touched all of her faithful intimates: Leicester, Essex, Hatton, Ralegh, but none reached her ears, for her wrath would have turned destructive in an instant. What intimacies were granted, only Ralegh knew and it was easy to be the gentleman with a Queen. Ralegh never told, but he shortly began to be given responsible tasks, such as Elizabeth could entrust only to men wholly hers. There was, for instance, the entertainment of Francis, Duke of Alençon and Anjou, when he passed some four months in England, sailing to take upon him the government of the Netherlands in February, 1582. It was a piece of work calling for the utmost tact and the purest loyalty, this ministering to a prince rejected as a suitor after being held so long at bay, yet Ralegh shared in it with older and titled heads.

All the extravagant pageantry the Queen loved so well was invoked to pass away the time. There was a tournament at Whitehall. Philip Sidney fought as one of "Four Foster Children of Desire," who laid siege to "The Fortress of Perfect Beauty," erected before the Queen's window. In full armor, all blue and gold, he shot through the lists, the very soul of chivalry. Chivalry and noble deeds were the keynote of the adventure. All the extravagant panoply of the British Court was spread before the eyes of the Frenchman, until the day of his departure for Flushing brought the climax.

The Queen, herself, rode with him as far as Canterbury attended by old Lord Hunsdon, the Earl of Leicester, Fulke Greville, Philip Sidney, Dyer and Walter Ralegh. When the Queen turned back, the gentlemen went on, crossed the channel and carried the Duke on to Antwerp, where they attended him at his investiture as Duke of Brabant. There Ralegh met the Prince of Orange and there too he was detained after the others and sent home with letters for the Queen and a verbal message, "Sub umbra alarum tuarum protegimur," we are protected under the shadow of thy wings, for the Prince was deeply grateful to Elizabeth for her assistance from the beginning of his state.

To crown his value and to assure us that Ralegh was not

only a graceful symbol of regal power, there is among the papers of the Irish Correspondence a joint writing of Lord Burghley and Walter Ralegh named *The Opinion of Mr. Rawley, upon motions made to him for the means of subduing the Rebellion in Munster*. This title, written in Burghley's hand, is self-explanatory, yet must be read with wonder, for it means nothing less than that by October 25, 1582, the sage Lord Treasurer was treating with Ralegh in conference. The cautious diplomat, who for so long matched and outwitted the best brains both Philip and Henry could muster, was accepting the counsel of the young campaigner just out of Ireland. It was a compliment to the Queen's choice of men.

2

It was curious how this Devonshire soldier carried the Queen back to earlier days, raising a ghost of her turbulent youth, a wraith that touched an old memory of fear.

Strong limbed, tall, with a thick mass of curled hair; a beard and a mustache; lips sensuously red; blue-gray eyes that looked a little too straight and piercingly upon the riddle of life, a face with bold, proud features: an arched eyebrow, a strong nose, the nostrils sensitive, the set of the mouth that of a man just within control; and all this promise of violence denied by a tall, pale forehead and eyelids pouched and sceptical.

This contradiction of parts interested Elizabeth. Ralegh would play a high hand with the mature boldness of thirty. Leicester had seemed like that, but the years had made him more cautious. After all, Robert Dudley was the son of the treasonable Northumberland, whose villainy had been stupid. Dudley was naturally no match for this younger mind. This newer, braver figure recalled Thomas Seymour, Somerset's brother, brother too of Jane Seymour, the mother of Edward VI, the third wife of Elizabeth's own father.

For a shadow, Thomas Seymour was very real. He had been bold. He had been handsome and swagger. It had all been a long time before—when she was thirteen or fourteen. Her father had just died and she was living with Katherine, her father's last Queen. Thomas Seymour had courted Katherine when Lord Latimer, her first husband, had died, but Henry had his way of her, and died too, so, without hindrance, came Seymour, newly made Baron, Knight of the Garter, and Lord High Admiral. Under Katherine's roof he found a child of fairer face than Anne of Cleves and of nimbler wit than Princess Mary.

He must have been nearly forty, but he was handsome, free of manner, hearty; not like those side-glancing creatures who tasted of one's words before they were spoken and ran away to mis-report them at court. Katherine, now only Dowager Queen, loved him too, and so he came to live with them. The Admiral he was, but not much in his ships in those days. He had found a fresh bud, untried in worldly ways, but a princess. While he struggled with his brother to control Edward; he could tell a man when he saw one and he knew Edward's kingship would soon end in death, he lay siege to Elizabeth under Katherine's roof. She remembered him and his rollicking. Of a morning he would come bounding into her chamber. Half out of high spirits, half out of delicious dread, she hid under the coverlet. He would tumble her about and fall to striking her over the buttocks and sometimes Katherine with him, both laughing. This was at Hanworth and later at Seymour Place, but later still he grew more gentle. Then Kate Ashley came with a warning of that mood and from the moment seemed to hate the man. Good soul, she knew where the wind blew and the quartering of it. He came oftener. He was like resisting a storm. One day

Katherine came upon them when he had her in his arms, Katherine newly married to him in secret and pregnant, carrying his child. He had been a lusty man, fit for an eastern tale. He had tasted of war in the Netherlands, France and among the far-off Turks, but the Council would not have him and his ambition. He was tried for his effrontery and Kate Ashley was made to confess his conduct before her eyes, while she and seventeen others were mewed up in the tower. When he went to the scaffold, the last thought he had was to send a letter to Elizabeth. She was to conspire against his brother, Edward the Protector. Thomas was sure of the source of his misfortunes and he held a great hate to the end. His boldness never deserted him, even under the axe.

This Walter Ralegh was bold and younger. She knew so much about both of them. There was no withstanding the energy of either: the one she had known so long ago and this new comet, more active than all the seething hordes that hung about her ante-chamber; faces that appeared for a day, a month, a year and vanished into nothingness. Both had travelled and fought in France and the Lowlands. Seymour had bought guns in Germany and Ralegh had subdued the Irish. Both had a way with their tongues. Only her father could outswear the Admiral, while Ralegh spoke as he pleased in the frank dialect of the West Country. It was a brogue that suited her ear and his tongue well. Doubtless the rogue knew of it, for there was none of its roughness transmitted to his writing. He passed Seymour there.

Both men knew the world well. Seymour sailed once against Thomessin the pirate and his fellowship in the Scilly Islands. He had sworn great oaths he would put the fellow down, wipe out his adder nest and bring all to justice, but he sailed away and back again without doing anything. Faith, Thomessin was such a fine fellow he had left him untouched in his stronghold, where the best of entertainment had been provided the Lord High Admiral. No doubt the two had come to private terms. Ralegh might have done that if it suited him. He knew intimately all sorts of people: sailors, poets, alchemists, philosophers, scholars, soldiers, and they thought well of him. There was little difference between privateering and piracy, poetry and libel, alchemy and counterfeiting, philosophy and atheism.

Seymour had dreamed of founding a new country, possibly with the idea of being King of it. Ralegh was set for that like the rest of his clan: the Gilberts, the Carews, the Drakes and the whole Devon lot. Most of these discoverers really aimed at piracy or settling private grudges with the Spanish. They did not care what troubles they made for her and her faithful few. 'Slid, they had best beware of her if the Spanish brought them in to plead. Drake had done many things but they were not all Drakes. Even one was giving trouble enough. She would be ruthless and turn away her face. Cold majesty for her, boisterous laughter for Seymour, words that fitted not his steady, all seeing eyes for Ralegh: each had a method unto an end. Ralegh could be aloof or noisily intimate as well as filled by forethought. He was a cunning fellow.

Seymour was much like him and Seymour had brought close shame and the threat of death. Even Kate Ashley had been unable to stave off the examination. All the damaging details of the love-making had been admitted. Ah, it had been a time of hazard when wits alone brought redemption; royal wits, not Seymour's. Ralegh had a clearer brain than the Admiral.

It was remarkable what the West Country man knew. He was awake to new as well as old learning. He read Spanish as well as the classical tongues. One would think he saw life as a play repeating itself and his knowledge continually supplying him with examples for present needs. To Burghley and his treasury he could quote exact sums and offer economies. For Dudley "Sweet Robin," there served the jealousy of Lord Grey as a rival; for Walsingham the plea of loyalty so pat upon the ear of a principal secretary, ever at the elbow of royalty. Wise, too wise, yet not so wise as to step aside from the heavy path of Walsingham and Sir Henry Sidney, toiling under burdens that gall the backs, duty to the state though they be called. Even there—Ralegh was too well versed in Machiavelli to follow so blindly the simple virtues. Had he but been born of kingly blood, it had been a pleasure to hear him say of the de Medici brood in France, "Tacitus says, we ought to submit to what is present, and should wish for good princes, but whatsoever they are, endure them, and Machiavel terms this a golden sentence, adding, that whosoever does otherwise, ruins both himself and country." Yet for all his thousandfold protest of loyalty, the man read Spanish and drew the glance of every lady in waiting like a lodestone working upon bits of iron. Had he not lived in Islington, noted for its immoral trysts, hidden bowers and dissolute couplings? Like enough he had his history but the heart went out to him. His brain was good, yet that brain might be guilty of treason to Queen and woman, and she had nothing else to hold him by than those two fetishes. Seymour had dreamed of marrying her; Ralegh bowed very low but his eyes looked quite through one without a vestige of modesty. She would curb that insolence. Before Seymour she had been a child; before her, Ralegh was a subject; yet to simulate a dread in delight; there was a new facet of pleasure.

Yet was the dread pretended? Seymour had taken her by storm. No warning had availed. She had been in the first flush of lustihood, tormented by a myriad blind and angry impulses. He had brought her within fear of death. He had shown her shame; the staring eyes, the faces turned aside to gossip, the pause of scandalous enjoyment, for she was a princess then with embittered Mary upon the throne. She had lost to Seymour, lost at one fell swoop. She had not known nor hated. Perhaps—she couldn't be sure—perhaps she had known but hadn't cared. In her heart of hearts had the old love rankled all the years between? She had shared that mad joyousness so long ago. It had been a different Elizabeth, for now she stood afar off from those dead things, dispassionate, with even their memory blurred.

How like they were—not in fact—in memory. She had lost to Seymour. She loved Ralegh but this time it would be different. She would make him pay for old indiscretion. It would be a passage taking her back to her first love: strong arms, firm flesh of youth, fresh passion firing all the body. She would devour him as a symbol for the long lost Admiral and he should pay, he so wise and worldly. Other men had filled her eyes for the moment, some longer. Hatton had been one of fifty gentlemen pensioners and she had made him Captain of the Yeomen of the Guard. It kept him close to her, for the Guard watched over her day and night, securing her person from weapons and poison. Hatton she had knighted five years after and then made him Vice-Chancellor and Privy Councillor. Since then Sir Henry Goodier and Sir Anthony Paulett had served her as Captains.

If she made Ralegh Captain of the Guard he would hear all things and be unable to decide any. She would see the light of ambition flash through his careful guard only to die neglected. New love for old and the old mortified in the sufferings of the new. Ralegh was not tame; no mild Hatton. He must never be Privy Councillor, for he had the violence of a Seymour; even now she might fail in checking him if he were let out of hand. These subtleties clashed with her father's rude blood in her. 'Od's lifelings, that would pay Ralegh handsomely. Men were so different, but the digression was enjoyable. There was the son of the old Keeper with the wisdom of the serpent, young Francis Bacon; he had but a stony gaze while in Ralegh's eyes shone a pride that was noble. She would make that pride bear her trust for all its cunning and the wraith of Seymour and her folly would fade forever. It was a new way, Elizabeth's way, to pay old debts.

CHAPTER VI

FATUOUS FIRES

RALEGH found a court that was opulent rather than brilliant. More than two thousand ounces of pure silver was worn by its servants. The grooms and pages bore embroidered upon their coats an E. R. in Venice gold that dazzled the eyes and taxed the exchequer. Roses and crowns imperial gleamed upon the backs of the yeomen of the Guard. The Queen lavished upon herself, in her love of jewels, a sum that would have gone far toward paying in full the nation's debt of gratitude to the toiling servants of the state. In terms of value of our times, more than a million dollars were expended annually to support the formal round of pomp and pride. Yet there was little of glittering speech and farseeing vision among the courtiers.

From the first, Ralegh was superior to the stodgy, cautious mood of the life. Dark angles of intrigue each have the spring, which, touched, lets them flash into the light. He must have felt scorn for most whom he met there at work. Elizabeth loved and exacted servility: the bent knee, the portentous flattery, were dear to her vanity. When the courtiers passed the Queen's empty seat in the chapel at Whitehall, they made three obeisances. She liked the gesture of love extended into worship. Ministers talked with her kneeling through two hours of conference. In private, these things were replaced with a saccharine intimacy so stilted and unnatural that life became infinitely involved and the important and unimportant jostled each other in every mind. It was thus she preserved her vacillation, her evasion of fixed ideas.

The tempo of the court was ridiculously slow. Burghley, cautious and deliberate, strove to save the country from both France and Spain. Walsingham, determined not to lose the Queen's ear, and conscious of every turn of foreign affairs, measured delay to the last instant. Leicester, knowing that he could not match either of them before the Queen, save by gorgeous display and personal appeal, strutted rather inanely about the stage. Sussex, old and rough in manner, was out of the mode, a good soldier but a poor diplomat. Hatton worshipped the sun that had brought his day. Elizabeth changed her mind as often as a new thought came to her, giving and countermanding orders dizzily. No wonder it took so long to find one's way toward the royal esteem.

It was most necessary for Ralegh to be of the court in a very active sense. The court had legal exemptions, privileged pleasures and exclusive opportunities. Monopolies, appointments, grants of land, profitable licenses, receiverships of fines, lucrative offices, were the rewards given to the fortunate, to those who pleased. It was difficult for a bold, clear-seeing mind to accept the bonds which alone could bring a share in such a government. After all it was domestic, like a great family, in which the relatives earned preferment by pleasing the fabulously wealthy head of the clan. Yet Ralegh, burning with ideas, fired by his youth so soon to be left behind, weighed the situation and moving forward, clear of the factions within factions, set his eyes upon the centre of his solar system and found his days growing fairer and richer for his trouble.

Elizabeth was nothing less than his sovereign hope. It was her method to take from one and give to another. When the estates of Stolney and Newland became hers from All Souls' College, Oxford, she promptly gave them over to Ralegh on April 10, 1583. On May 4, she granted him letters patent for the "Farm of Wines." Each vintner in the realm paid Ralegh twenty shillings annually for a license before he dared to display the green ivy bush above his door and dispense his wares. This gave Ralegh from one thousand pounds to two thousand pounds annually. An onerous burden for the vintners it would seem, yet Ralegh's deputies seem to have been lenient in their collection, for in 1628, when the license fees went directly to the King, the yield was £4,320 10s. 8d.

This seems like generosity upon the part of Elizabeth, hedged about as she was by a host of suppliants, but she ruled by a bureaucracy, and there were never more than fifty men in whose hands rested the power of the realm and whom she had to reward as a guarantee of their service. Within this circle she distributed a plurality of favors. Lord Burghley was not only Lord Treasurer, but a member of Privy Council, the Court of Star Chamber, Head of the Exchequer and Master of the Court of Wards and Liveries. Lord Hunsdon captained the Gentlemen Pensioners and held the keepership of the game in Hyde Park. "Here is much jostling and suing for places in the privie chamber, by reason that most of them being growne old and wearie of waiting would faine bring in a successor," runs a letter of the time.[6] It was thus that Sir Robert Cecil, in his day, succeeded his father in Privy Council and Star Chamber and became besides Secretary, Master of the Wards and Chancellor of the Duchy of Lancaster. Elizabeth had rewarded Ralegh for her good opinion of him, but carefully. It was necessary that he have some means if he were to reside at court; these she provided.

2

For six years Sir Humphrey Gilbert had a monopoly of discovery and settlement in America. His letters patent were due to expire on June 11, 1584. After the failure of his expedition in 1578, he had been compelled to live quietly, paying the debts the effort had left him. Meanwhile, the years slipped away. New faces came to court. New voices secured the Queen's ear. As Ralegh himself knew, Gilbert was no longer an adroit courtier, and his enemies knew it too. Simon Fernando crossed the Atlantic for Walsingham and returned with his report. The cleric, John Walker, went out and roughly mapped a part of the coast. Walsingham interested Gilbert in sending out Catholics and those unable to support themselves in England as colonists. Sir George Peckham and Sir Thomas Gerard lent their efforts, but in vain. The assignees of the plan failed to organize a single expedition. Apparently the undesirables chose to stay where they were. Walsingham had a son-in-law, Christopher Carlile, who was interested in opening up trade to America. Walsingham began to prepare for the end of Gilbert's monopoly. He encouraged merchants in Bristol to appeal for additional shipping. Hakluyt was his go-between to the Bristol men. The merchants subscribed two ships and money of account, to the sum of one thousand marks, as an evidence of good will.

In 1582 Christopher Carlile sailed in the fleet of the Muscovy Company to get first-hand experience of ships, and the next year he laid before that company a proposition of shares to be sold at a ranging value. Carlile pledged his own fortune and would plead with the Queen for special privileges for the adventurers. A company of one hundred men backed by four thousand pounds was talked of, and finally, by September, 1583, preparations were completed. Obviously, Walsingham had been successful in securing approval of the idea at court. On every side, men interested in the lapse of Gilbert's grant began to plan for the termination of his rights, but he was beforehand with them all. Carlile was just a summer late; Gilbert left Plymouth with five ships on June 11, 1583.

The five ships varied much in size. The *Delight* was of one hundred twenty tons and carried Sir Humphrey Gilbert. Walter Ralegh sent out the bark *Ralegh* which was of two hundred tons. Two vessels of forty tons, *The Golden Hinde*, and the *Swallow*, were not so pretentious, but were doubtless as serviceable, while the *Squirrel*, so well named for a saucy craft of ten tons engaged in crossing the ocean sea, might prove too small on the passage, but would be invaluable for work in shoal water, once she survived the hazards of the North Atlantic. Two hundred sixty men made the venture.

Stephen Parmenius of Buda, "late bedfellow" of Hakluyt at Oxford, "adventured in this action, minding to record in the Latin tongue, the gests and things worthy of remembrance, happening in this discovery, to the honor of our nation, the same being adorned with the eloquent stile of this Orator and rare Poet of our time." He sailed in the flagship, the *Delight*, and began his record of the attempt by an embarkation ode of three hundred elegant Latin hexameters. Therein Elizabeth gained a new title. Henceforth she was "Queen of the Seas."

Gilbert and Ralegh were very close in those days. Elizabeth regarded Gilbert as an unfortunate man at sea, and one whom she liked to have at court. Perhaps the very inability to plead a suit readily lent him interest. Yet most that he did cost her nothing, so she let him make ready. Ralegh she would not allow to go. He had eclipsed Leicester in her interest: there should be no risking of his life with a man who had no luck afloat. He was at hand. Gilbert was about to sail. She could not leave Richmond and make the journey to Plymouth, nor did she trust headstrong Ralegh to go in person. He might embark. Her parting wishes she gave to him so that he might send them to Gilbert, and so he wrote.

"Brother,

"I have sent you a token from Her Majesty, an anchor guided by a lady, as you see; and farther, Her Highness willed me to sende you worde that she wished you as great good-hap and safety to your ships, as if hersealf were ther in parson; desiring you to have care of your sealf, as of that which she tendereth; and therefore, for her sake, you must provide for hit accordingly.

"Farther, she commandeth that you leve your picture with me. For the rest, I leve till our meeting, or to the report of this bearer, who would needs be the messengre of this good newse. So I committ you to the will and protection of God, who send us such life or death as he shall please, or hath appointed.

"Richmonde, this Friday morning [March 17, 1582-3]
"Your treu brother,
"W. RALEGH."

There was not the haste that Ralegh then thought likely. Three months later Gilbert sailed. By night of that first, fair day they met a "great storme of thunder and wind," On the third day out, the *Barke Ralegh*, vice admiral, turned back, giving as an excuse contagious sickness among the crew. There was no accounting for such a thing. Perhaps it were best to do as Edward Hayes, the narrator of the voyage, thought well. "I leave it unto God." The *Golden Hinde* moved her flag from the mizzen into the fore top and became vice admiral of the weakened fleet. They dropped down into forty-eight degrees of latitude and for thirteen days met rain, fog and head winds, forcing them to the south until they were in forty-one degrees, below even the summer track of trans-oceanic traffic today, and then north to fifty-one degrees, bringing the ships face to face with the hazard of drift ice. "Our traverse was great," wrote Hayes. Yes, and the fog drove them apart, so they passed spectral mountains of ice "which were carried Southward to the weather." This drifting of the bergs against the wind was natural. They had discovered the Greenland current by the same patient observation which gave them data of the Newfoundland Banks. The landfall was in fog, but they managed to make the harbor of St. John's and found the *Swallow* had turned pirate on her way, but was quite willing to resume her former civil status. Gilbert signalized his purpose of colonization rather than discovery by calling together the mixed populace he found there, and, amidst the fragrance of wild roses and raspberries, taking possession of the land in the name of the Queen of England. He further Anglicized the new possession by declaring the religion of the people should be according to the church of England; any who opposed the English were guilty of high treason; all who spoke anything to the dishonor of the Queen should lose their ears, their ships and goods. The arms of England, engraved in lead, were set upon a wooden post. It only remained for Gilbert to arrange his land rents, draw his "cards and plats" of the coast and hurry on to the south with the silver ore his geologist had found. His company had shrunken so that he left the *Swallow* behind, taking the men into the other ships. He had no desire to winter on the American coast and it had been the 30th of July when he came upon the Newfoundland shore, which he computed to be in latitude fifty-one degrees.

Since they were to go a coasting, Gilbert transferred into the *Squirrel* that he might be in the van of the exploring. He left St. Johns on the 20th of August and made for the elusive Cape Race, determined to chart what he could of the shoals and currents. Thick and dirty, the northern weather buffeted the fleet, until the *Delight*, striking in white water, had her stern torn away and went to pieces. With her were lost the specimens of ore, the new chartings and the life of

Stephen Parmenius, the bard of the expedition. A little longer the surviving ships struggled to southward, but the currents baffled them and the wind did not favor. Gilbert had longed to see the south but he was so fully satisfied with what he had discovered in Newfoundland, and his men were so poorly found, that he was ready to start for home. He "was now become a Northern man altogether." Despite an injured foot, had from treading upon a nail, he would not forsake his little company going homeward, but remained in the *Squirrel*.

Then came Monday, the 9th of September. They had crossed until the Azores were south of them, but they were in the latitude of England. The weather turned foul. The seas were short with no foot to them, breaking pyramids of water that ran willy nilly. "Men which all their lifetime had occupied the Sea, never saw more outragious Seas." The wind blew a gale. By afternoon the little *Squirrel* was sorely battered and nearly cast away. She was overburdened "with fights, nettings and small artilleries, too cumbersome for so small a boate," which had been taken on when she had set out to explore the coast to southward. There had been no later opportunity to rid her of them. Perhaps to reassure his crew, Gilbert sat upon the poop with a book in his hand. When his ship dodged close to the *Golden Hinde* he called down wind, "we are as near to heaven by sea as by land."

The dusk swallowed the two, the *Squirrel* leading the way through the windy welter. At dark, lights were set and the watches passed until midnight, when the *Squirrel's* light suddenly went out and the *Golden Hinde* was left alone to battle her way to Falmouth through thirteen more dirty autumn days. Sir Humphrey Gilbert would never need to borrow ten thousand pounds from the Queen for the spring return. Those who longed after his patent would not have to wait for its expiration. Gilbert's estate had been devoured in the venture. It would seem that the state owed some one something after such a gallant effort. Camden, remarking upon the tragedy, wrote that it was a more difficult matter to carry over colonies to remote countries upon private men's purses, than he and others had persuaded themselves, to their own loss and detriment. Ralegh was, however, of the brood. He had lost much in the dying of his half-brother. They had been very close. He would take up the quest. It was a challenge to him and a legacy. The Queen was mindful of Gilbert's death, just then. The time was fit.

Elizabeth, at the moment, was refusing Ralegh nothing. She granted him a patent that, although all he could ask, was still substantially like that of Sir Humphrey Gilbert. Dated March 25, 1584, the document gave, "to our trusty and well-beloved servant, Walter Ralegh," liberty to discover "such remote heathen and barbarous lands not actually possessed by any Christian prince, nor inhabited by Christian people" as seemed good to him. He was permitted to carry English people into these lands as settlers. Force to defend his intentions was yielded to him, both over the settlers who might go out and the natives of the newly discovered parts. The limits of his authority were generous. He should govern all who "shall abide within two hundred leagues of any such places he or his heirs shall inhabit within six years, next ensuing." Royal sanction was withheld in no particular save that he could not go in person. Elizabeth's happiness came first.

Walter Ralegh had been long a dreaming. He knew there was a stretch of coast to the northward of Florida devoid of white men. Men seeking his patronage brought him news of expeditions. If the latitudes computed, and used, in their navigation by explorers of Newfoundland and Florida were correct, there were several hundred miles of coast in the new world utterly unsettled. Ralegh had read the first-hand accounts of these adventurers: English, Spanish, French and Dutch—he knew them all. An empire, nothing less, waited for him. The possibility made one dizzy. In a month and three days from the receiving of his patent, two barks, commanded by Philip Amadas and Arthur Barlow, sailed from London town. Dropping down to the Canaries they easily reached across to Porto Rico, Hispaniola, then northwest, making sure to pass north of the Spanish settlements before making a landfall. Six score miles they sailed up the coast before they found Ocracoke Inlet, Wokoken Island (Roanoke) and Pamlico Sound. Among the many islands they selected Roanoke on which to take possession of the new land. Five months from the time they had left England, they were back with skins, pearls and two Indians brought as guests, as well as a colorful report to Walter Ralegh of all the wonders he possessed.

It was time to preen the plumage. Ralegh had his arms made into a seal with the legend, "Walteri Ralegh, militis, et virtue." The Queen herself furnished him with the name *Virginia*, although tradition claims he suggested it. In December an act of confirmation of Ralegh's grant was passed by parliament. It was modelled upon the charter given the Muscovy Company twenty years earlier. Men began to flock to him as a patron. In the summer he leased Durham House, a fourteenth century house of the Bishops of Durham, which covered the site of the modern Adelphi Terrace. Elizabeth had lived there after her brother, Edward VI, had taken it from the church. It was well enough to follow the court to Greenwich, Whitehall, Somerset House, St. James and Richmond, but it was better to have Durham House as one's own London home. The Queen reserved certain rooms for herself, and then allowed Sir Edward Darcy to live in them. All sorts found their way there to Walter Ralegh, climbing to his study in a turret that looked out over the Thames. This view was "as pleasant perhaps as anything in the world." Durham House remained his until 1603.

Thomas Hariot, who so often signed himself "servant of Walter Ralegh," and who was to follow him so bravely through the five acts of his life, conferred with him there. Old Doctor Dee, astrologer, expert in demonology, mathematician, diplomat extraordinary, waited upon him as a guest at dinner. Ralph Lane, who was to be governor of the American colony, came for instructions. Sir Richard Grenville, his intractable, stiff-necked cousin, swaggered in with all the self-esteem of a bullying sailor. His brother, Carew Ralegh, called to inform Walter that the merchants of Exeter believed the voyage to Virginia was pretended, and would undertake no trade there despite the reputed markets. Strangers, such as John White, whose water-color maps and sketches show us Indian life and customs as first found by the Europeans, sought audience of the Queen's favorite. By the end of the fiscal year a license to export woollen broad cloth, which the Queen had granted him in March, netted three thousand five hundred pounds, equal to eighteen thousand pounds in our times. Durham House needed some such bountiful revenue. It was indeed a palace.

The Ralegh energy extended into other matters. Ever since America had loomed into the sight of man there had been a hope that some way either through or around it might be found. China and India were the goal. With his brother, Adrian Gilbert, Ralegh became one of "the colleagues of the fellowship for the discovery of the northwest passage." He gave generously of his means and of his spirit. The fellowship was in no way laggard. There came a day when John Davis, at their direction, made a landfall in sixty-six degrees forty minutes of latitude. There he anchored under a brave mountain and "the cliffs thereof being as orient as gold, they named it Mount Ralegh"[7] in honor of their proprietor. It would seem there was gratitude for the favorite's generosity, or perhaps a larger understanding of the patron who would rather have been engaged in natural simplicity than courtly subtleties, had it not been for his boundless energy which caught him up into the very heart of things. For an Englishman of his time, that meant being close to Elizabeth, but it also meant wearing a hat band of pearls worth thirty pounds, thinking in terms of damask silk, strutting among men he regarded as popinjays, dressed in exquisite armor, or bedecked with lace and fur, set off by diamonds, shoes jewelled to the value of sixty-six hundred gold pieces, every gesture a sumptuous, flashing plea for the favor of the Virgin of the North. Out of such expenditure he coined wealth. Amidst Machiavellian finesse he paraded an apparent boldness that to his enemies was a damnable pride and a cursed forwardness. He was no hand at conciliation.

He was surely seated in favor, and so had many friends as the reward of success. He was elected to parliament for Devonshire, one of the shire's two members, the other Sir William Courtenay. To win his way to parliament showed he was popular with the county families in the west, a friendliness he never lost. These electors had to be forty-shilling freeholders, men who had the tenure of land which brought that much rent annually. On July 26, he tried to buy the farm of Hayes Barton Manor because, "being borne in that house, I had rather seat myself there than any where else." Mr. Duke of Otterton did not listen to his fair words with any favor and so refused to sell Hayes Barton. Perhaps it was a natural gesture against a court favorite extending his grip to the possessions of more ordinary men.

Before December 14, 1584, Walter Ralegh was knighted. He had stood the test of intimacy. None had quicker access to the Queen. She granted knighthood with an eye to Machiavellian niggardliness and no doubt an exalted appreciation of its value. She had a precise estimate of her favorite's abilities and he could not easily fill the destiny she had in mind for him as plain Walter Ralegh. It added little to his stature; it took nothing from her, but it signalized his progress.

It was as a knight that Burghley sent him into Devon to make a report upon the stannaries. This tin industry, that had centuries before brought the Phœnicians into England, had its own privileges and practices. As a West Countryman going home, Sir Walter understood much of the men he had to deal with and pleased Burghley with his work. It was February when he was asked to investigate. In July, 1583, he succeeded the Earl of Bedford, Lord Warden of the Stannaries. As warden he commanded the Cornish militia. As warden, too, he sat in judgment upon the customs of the miners. This Stannary Parliament was held in the high wilderness of Crockern Tor, the traditional meeting place. He ruled wisely and easily there, his practices accepted as law for years after his pronouncing them. In September he was appointed Lieutenant of Cornwall, and in November he became Vice-Admiral of Cornwall, and his half-brother Sir John Gilbert became Deputy for Devon. As if all these services to the state were not enough, Sir Thomas Heneage and he undertook an inquiry into the case of Englishmen suffering as Barbary slaves and presented to the lords of the Council a memorial of their findings.

The Vice Admiralty was a profitable post, for it gave a golden opportunity to engage in privateering. Ships could be taken and brought into West Country ports with ease; there the official disposition rested upon Ralegh's will. For the rest, the offices were fraught with abundant labor but with slight return. Hatton and Leicester no longer regarded Ralegh as an outsider. All too evident was his progress and his Queen's favor. He was a rival and therefore a menace to their security, but he promised to be more the beast of burden: the Burghley, the Walsingham, than a comet wheeling in a flashing arc across their sky. Busy, he was no match for them. Each felt confidence, yet was conscious of his sweeping into the royal presence all glamour and good looks. Events do not always cast a full shadow before them.

CHAPTER VII

INTENTIONS AND VISIONS

WHEN Alençon sailed to become sovereign of Holland and Flanders, carrying with him fifteen ships, a gift of twenty-five thousand pounds and the Earl of Leicester, it was much against the will of Elizabeth's favorite to go into the Low countries. On the day Alençon was crowned, Leicester made his excuses and hurried home to the English court. He informed Elizabeth that the French, but especially Alençon, were hated by the Dutch. They had only accepted the new monarch out of deference to her. At the same time Henry III sent word that he repudiated his brother's action; Alençon could shift for himself and all who aided him were traitors to the French throne. Thus had begun a series of expedient moves ending in Leicester, himself, being sent into the Netherlands to rule, four years after Alençon's investiture.

On December 8, 1585, Leicester sailed with five thousand men and fifty ships from Harwich. Alençon had died. Orange had been murdered. The Protestants: Leicester, Knollys and Walsingham had been helped by events to push aside Burghley's twenty years of balance and compromise. The nations tramped toward war. Elizabeth shrank, but yielded, even as she blamed Leicester for forcing her hand. Lieutenant-General of the Queen's forces he was by title, but ruler in his own right he hoped to be. He landed safely enough at Flushing and in two short weeks was intriguing for the sovereignty of the Netherlands. The offer was made him, refused, offered again and accepted in January, 1586. He let the anger of Elizabeth grow unchecked by any explanation from him. Burghley saw that the Queen was really furious at the assumption of royal title by her favorite. He merely absented himself from court. Walsingham and Hatton might plead with the presuming Earl. The Queen sent Sir Thomas Heneage off to Holland with specific orders to Leicester to renounce his office, and then when Leicester and Heneage dallied she raged anew.

At length Leicester sent William Davison to explain his act to the Queen. Davison was related to both Burghley and Leicester but that did not deter the sorely beset Earl from insisting that Davison had persuaded him to accept the sovereignty. The Queen banished him from court. Leicester professed to believe him an insincere advocate of his course.

Meanwhile Holland had measured Leicester as incompetent and as lacking the English support for which they had hoped. They longed to get rid of him. Burghley protested his friendship for Leicester while the Earl was ruining himself at court and in Holland, but he let Davison suffer unrelieved. The militant Protestants were losing caste with the Queen. With so much ostentatious friendship there was still something wrong. "Surely," wrote Walsingham, "there is some treachery amongst ourselves, for I cannot think she would do this out of her own head." Some one with imagination was dictating Elizabeth's position with Leicester ruling in Holland. For once, she seemed to see the possibilities of her course of action. Usually irresolute, she was now all resolution, vacillation was become obstinacy. The Court chattered behind hands. Who was playing this part of Ariel, dealing in spells? Who but the man who had held Leicester for patron, but who since his coming out of Ireland had become the partisan of Burghley, who but Sir Walter Ralegh?

When the word reached Sir Walter's ears he wrote to Leicester that he had been "very pestilent reported" and pleaded for frankness between them. "But all that I have desired att your Lordship's hands is, that you will evermore deal directly with mee in all matters of suspect dubleness, and so esteem mee as you shall finde my deserving, good or bad." And at the close of his letter the informal postscript, "The Queen is on very good terms with you, and, thank be to God, well pacified; and you are agayne her 'Sweet Robin.'" The postscript may have been Ralegh's way of quieting suspicion, that he might the easier damage Leicester and improve his own position. He was all too conscious of the Earl's limitations, of his foolish wit and his overweening vanity. It was not good policy to trust one's career to such a man; rather the astute Burghley, able to foresee actions and to make puppets of councillors out of their very nature. Ralegh had outgrown the peacock preening of Leicester.

The more Elizabeth favored, the more strenuously Ralegh struggled toward privilege. His actions grew bolder, his words tinged with authority. When Robert Sidney, the brother of the knightly Sir Philip, sought to marry Barbara Gamage, to whose dead father, the friend and patron of Ben Jonson, Ralegh was cousin-germain, he wrote almost regally, "Her Majesty hath thrice caused letters to be written unto you that you suffer not my kinswoman to be bought and sold without Her Majesty's privilege to the consent and the advice of my Lord Chamberlain and myself . . . considering she have not any nearer kin nor better." Swagger as he might, Robert had married the lady two hours before the letter came into play and it does not appear to have been an evil marriage; Barbara Gamage became the grandmother of Waller's "Sacharissa." Robert Sidney inherited Leicester's wealth and was later used confidently between Essex and Elizabeth.

Sir Christopher Hatton pressed Ralegh closely for the royal favor. Hatton had still the ear of Elizabeth and his own supporters, such as Sir Thomas Heneage, close to her person. On Tuesdays, Thursdays and Saturdays at nine o'clock he met with the Privy Council. He had had every opportunity. Dignified, handsome, he was often a member of Parliament, faithful to the business of his offices and a thorough courtier, but he was not brilliant, and by nature he was too kindly to live easily among the pushing throngs seeking favor. Surrounded by courtiers ready to live dangerously, men who spent fabulous sums in the hope of gaining other riches, to be spent again in turn, he seemed but a poor creature. Against Ralegh's vigor and determination he was but a shadow. In 1585, when every glance of the Queen fell upon his West Country rival, he left the court for the country, hurt at the favors showered upon another. Elizabeth sent him word that Ralegh was no equal for her "bell wether," her "Lyddes," but she did not slacken in her attentions to the career of Ralegh. Making the best of the passing of time, Hatton became Lord Chancellor in 1587 and had the satisfaction of presently seeing Ralegh cast into the shade, for he lived until 1591.

Elizabeth never rewarded Sir Henry Sidney according to his merits, but she lavished every evidence of esteem upon his son Sir Philip. This paragon of knighthood, the gentleman par excellence, might have been a rival for Ralegh despite their friendship, save that he took himself off to the wars in the Lowlands and was killed in the battle of Zutphen, robbing Ralegh of a friend and the Queen of an idol among her gentlemen.

England was slowly but surely drifting toward war. The Netherlands and the high seas were training men to the trade they would soon need. France as a menace was receding, but word came up from Spain of preparation after preparation. Ralegh wrote Leicester in 1586, when apparently suspected of sympathy with the Spanish, "Your Lordshipe doth well understand my affection towards Spayn, and how I have consumed the best part of my fortune, hating the tyrannous prosperity of that estate, and it were now strange and monstrous that I should become an enemy to my country and conscience." Considering him at his blackest, attributing to him every Machiavellian deviousness that he was constantly practising, Ralegh never dreamed of aiding the Spanish. He was no Leicester, willing to make such a gesture for the sake of forcing policy. In June, 1586, he sent out the *Serpent* and *Mary Spark*, which engaged twenty-four Spanish ships at one time and brought home three captured. He was always sending his wealth afloat in private expeditions, under his authority as Vice-Admiral of the South West, or in support of plundering voyages like that of the Earl of Cumberland to the South Seas. Elizabeth kept him at court for her pleasure, although he was listed in 1586 upon the official roll of sea captains. Others he could send, but for him there was the silken way of homage, the tedious playing for life and fortune against the whim of a woman fifty-three years old, a woman not too wise, who combated age with caprice, ruthless with power, and coy with favor. Chafe as he might, conscious as he was of a natural right to rule, there was nothing to do but obey. For Ralegh there was the illusion of power and that could be gained only through patient service at the court.

Since Leicester was dimmed by distance and time, Hatton in temporary eclipse and the promise of Sir Philip Sidney suddenly put out, a serene day promised to be Ralegh's. Elizabeth continued to smile upon him. The Earl of Desmond was at last crushed in Ireland and his vast estates were confiscated and divided into seignories of not less than twelve thousand acres each. One of these, lying in the counties of Cork, Waterford and Tiperrary, the Queen gave to Sir Walter Ralegh and his heirs with certain privileges and immunities. He and other "gentlemen undertakers" agreed to plant and people the land, for the suppression of Desmond had scarcely left a living creature in the domain. The struggle had been prolonged and violent, sparing neither man nor beast. To his credit, Sir Walter did perform what he had agreed. He planted his quota of eighty-six families and did what he could to help them in their life along both banks of Youghal harbor. In his interest in colonization, Ireland served as well as America, but it was a year of feverish activity, and he could not give the matter more than passing attention. Several undertakers did nothing, but disposed of their grants to the highest bidder. Ralegh might have done likewise excusably for he was approaching the crux of preferment.

Elizabeth made him Captain of the Guard. It was the most important post he had held. He stood in constant attendance upon her, more striking in appearance than Hatton, an abler mind than Leicester, easier and more cosmopolitan than the puritanical Sir Philip Sidney. His orange tawny uniform graced the presence chamber. When asked, his forceful, incisive opinion was worldly wise. His wealth, while always on the hazard of a dozen ventures, allowed him to set off his handsome body at its best. From the first, he felt he was upon the threshold of great things; a share in the government more fitted to his power. He served superbly, his pride denying his humility. When the occasion demanded he could be formal with ease. Stepping forth from the frame in which Elizabeth loved to live a picture life, he could abandon pageantry to match her in roughness and direct speech, when she willed. His West Country brogue pleased her then, but his straight gaze warned he had a way of seeing things as they were, and always he reached toward that cherished power which was to lift him to greatness.

In those days he found men turning to him. The Parisian, Martin Bassanière, dedicated his published account of Lau-

INTENTIONS AND VISIONS 89

donnière's travels in Florida to Sir Walter Ralegh. Richard Hakluyt translated it and dedicated his work to the same patron. James Morgues, sent out by Chastillion to paint the wonders Laudonnière found, published his "draughts and descriptions" at "no small charges" all paid by Sir Walter. An octavo volume, *The Praise of Music*, written by a fellow Oxford man, was inscribed to him, and at once the legend of his musical proficiency flourished. John Peirson, who unfortunately realized the Queen could not live forever, and so couched his thoughts upon the succession in *Reasons why the King of Scots is unacceptable to the People of England*, acknowledged when questioned that he had given one of the five printed copies to "Sir Walter Ralegh, my master." Philosophers, theologians, medical scholars, historians, paid him court. Thomas Hariot profited by his bounty as the patron was to receive in turn his follower's fellowship. When John Udal found himself tried for treason because he accused the Bishops of caring for "nothing but the maintenance of their dignities" Ralegh, hating the casuistry of the law courts, and the rancor of clerical minds, fought to save him from his sentence of death. Others joined the effort, among them, King James of Scotland. It was accomplished but while the theologian was waiting in the Marshalsea for his accusers to decide whether or not he might sail as a chaplain to Guinea, he died. For the only time in their lives King James and Ralegh had united in a common cause. Esteem grew by leaps and bounds. Treatises upon medicine were inscribed to Ralegh. Hooker wrote a long dedication of his *Irish History*, praising the descent, the services and the success of Sir Walter. However, for all those who exchanged favors with him or did him honor, there were many more who hated him.

He was a success. He was the Queen's favorite. He dared too much. Where other men stooped he strode upright, insolent and unafraid. It did not augur well for him with Burghley in the seat of power and more and more Elizabeth had come to rest upon Cecil, the one enduring prop within her all too swiftly changing council. Grave face, snowy hair, a gouty, crippled old man with bright eyes that defied torment, the Lord Treasurer held the realm and Ralegh in his hands. Burghley had long hated Leicester as a minister must hate a favorite. The best plan, years a brewing, might be blasted at a whim of the Earl, and so Burghley until his death never deviated from treating Leicester as if he were a friend. From him Ralegh took pattern. Long after he was out of the shade of his early patron, and even after he was struggling to gain the Queen's favor for himself, he made every pretense of friendliness to Leicester, but he never deceived Burghley. Deep in his accounts, laboring over the Roman numerals he always used, struggling with a long minute to Darrel, directing how the navy might be victualled, or writing in a note to Walsingham, "I cannot express my pain, newly increased in my left arm," the Lord Treasurer never forgot to say to his son, "Shun to be Ralegh," for there lay his dream. William Cecil Burghley would soon no longer be, but for Robert there would come a dawn.

A favorite is limited to favor, as Burghley well knew, and to lose favor is to lose all. Ralegh might stand chatting to his Queen in her room when Secretary Davison brought to Greenwich the warrant for the death of Mary Stuart, but he had no office from which to put a hand upon the matter. So he stood that Saturday and heard Elizabeth tell of a dream in which she had been angered by the death of the Queen of Scots and had been ready to visit her wrath upon Davison. That patient servant of her will demanded whether or not she wished the warrant executed. Then she burst out into oaths, swearing at him for thrusting the responsibility upon her; and on Wednesday Mary died at Fotheringhay. When Talbot, the sixth Earl of Shrewsbury, brought the news the next day, she turned upon her servant ruthlessly and ever after to his death, Davison was a blasted man, disgraced before her. All Ralegh's learning, all his pondering of Machiavel, of Aristotle, of Tibullus might be upset by a moment of misguided loyalty. If a secretary of the crown came so quickly to so ill an end what might not the Captain of the Guard fear from the turn of favor.

The death of Mary Stuart taught Ralegh much. The Queen of seven lovers, beautiful though red-headed, as George Sand put it, was a symbol of insecurity to Ralegh. He looked upon fate, questioning his preferment. Could he enter the Privy Council and so become a member of that dread tribunal, the Court of the Star Chamber, his position would be much surer, his dependence upon mere favor ended. There could be none to match his energy; he had measured them all. His wisdom grew with every day. In his private interests, he knew as much of happenings and intents in Spain, France and the Netherlands as any in England. His spies were everywhere. In every particular he was fit for preferment and the sky looked very clear until he began to observe Lord Treasurer Burghley.

Burghley was a man to whom blood ties meant much. Although his son Robert was as yet too gangling to bear great burdens, he kept a careful eye on Walsingham's failing health. Robert should some day be Secretary, yet meanwhile the Lord Treasurer let the avalanche come down upon his kinsman, William Davison. The unfortunate man was tried, given a long imprisonment, fined until he had scarce a shilling and was lost in obscurity. The reason Burghley let him suffer without effort at alleviation was very clear: Davison had thought himself more a relative to Leicester than to Burghley. He had attached himself to the cause of Essex and so became a stumbling block to the Cecils. Burghley cut him down, mercilessly as Ralegh saw, and when Sir Walter glanced at Essex the sky was clear no longer for the favorite.

2

Leicester had grown red-faced and bloated. His armor, still to be seen in the Tower, proves him to have been almost as immense as Henry VIII. His charm of person had vanished. Ralegh had nothing to fear from him before the Queen save his history of long service. Since her affair with Alençon, Elizabeth had dallied only with young men. It saved embarrassment, complications and the need for permanent attachment. In such times Leicester chose to be favorite by proxy. He brought his stepson to court.

His stepson was born of Frances, daughter of Sir Francis Walsingham, a forceful, dangerous woman, and the Earl of Essex, whom rumor says Leicester poisoned in order to come at the widow. It is only certain the Earl died of a sweating sickness and left his son his title. The youngster was never known as anything but Essex. Leicester was intimately known as Lord Robert, but his stepson was from the beginning an Earl. Leicester, at the best, disliked Essex, and Essex hated his stepfather, but power was not weighed by affection, so the youngster came to court to assail the peace of Sir Walter Ralegh and struggle for favor. At seventeen he was presented to Elizabeth. Leicester worked desperately upon the Queen for him and the Countess used every artifice to forward her son's interest, until she was a nuisance to Elizabeth, waylaying her to present suits, offering untimely presents. To Essex she was a goad, that no effort might prove fruitless. The fear of eclipse was strong upon both the Earl and the Countess.

Essex was large but not handsome, no Hatton certainly, scarcely as well-favored as Ralegh. He felt the blood of royalty in his veins. For some reason he felt his strain to be superior to the Queen's. His face was large, his eyes small and his nose thin, his person long and powerful, but lacking in grace because of his stiffness in motion. His pride was loud in its declaration, his bearing arrogant and self-conscious, a dangerous man for the Countess to push toward his destiny. He despised everybody a little, and Ralegh most of all. Between fiery vigor and sulking lassitude he swung swiftly, a curious man for Leicester to pit against the Cecils, but the stepfather was banking upon the Queen, and his judgment was sound: Elizabeth took the youngster to her heart. His fresh, young life cried out to her weariness, and she dallied with him joyously. He matched her in insolence, in belief in the high estate of princes, in swift change of mood, in alternation between the decorative and the lush plainness of speech. As Francis Bacon wrote to Essex, "A man may read your formality in your countenance"; this she liked for she had so much of it in herself. It interested her to toy with his varied moods. She was never so happy as when she refused him his desire, for his anger spiced her day, and the reconciliations were sweet to her taste.

His following was a boisterous set. The wild, young Earl of Southampton, the epigramist, Sir John Harington, Sir Francis Bacon, Henry Cuffe sided with him. Sir Charles Blount, more sober in cut than the others, ventured to cross him now and then, with the result of a duel, an Essex wounded in the thigh, and a public reconciliation before the Queen. Bacon was the only first order mind that followed him; the rest were a lighter sort. Elizabeth put up with them so Ralegh had to endure their closeness to her. Essex insulted Ralegh openly and would doubtless have been called to account, but that was no way to play the game. Sir Philip Sidney had failed at that with the Earl of Oxford. Sidney had been unique in the affections of Elizabeth and Oxford had held small favor, but she had sharply pointed out the difference between the nobles and mere gentlemen. Young Essex was unquestioned nobility. "Every one sees that which you seem to be, few feel that which you are," wrote Machiavelli. Ralegh heeded the counsel; so much doubtless for the advantage of being fourteen years older than his antagonist. Essex in his wrath seemed foolish. Ralegh chilled his exterior, holding his temper admirably. Inwardly he was rather relieved to share with another the ardor of the Queen's affections, but he nursed the sting of every affront. Ralegh could not escape the Queen's presence; he knew the coming and going of Essex. The youngster was often kept all night by Elizabeth, playing at one game or another. He did not escape to his lodging "till birds sing in the morning," yet Ralegh showed no jealousy.

The Queen went upon a progress to North Hall in Hertfordshire with all her panoply of beauty and gallantry. There she slighted the married sister of Essex, Lady Dorothy Perrot, whose husband Ralegh had once crossed in quarrel. Essex thought this was because of Ralegh and petulantly taxed the Queen with it, speaking scornfully. Elizabeth made play upon the word disdain, assuring the young Earl he had no cause to disdain Ralegh. Grief and anger set free the Earl in full flight. "For myself, I told her I had no joy to be in any place, but was loth to be near about her, when I knew my affection so much thrown down, and such a wretch as Ralegh highly esteemed of her." Elizabeth did not deign to speak. When he blackguarded Ralegh she turned to Lady Warwick, ignoring. Essex swallowed his chagrin. Not even he dare push on when the Queen had closed the interview. And Ralegh at his post saw and heard all.

Essex was taking from him what he was glad to let go. He was not averse to another showering blandishments upon the

Queen. It was a tedious business and touched with danger if one misjudged her pleasure. Released, he was able to dine with Burghley, to meet Arabella Stuart, then twelve years old, to exchange good West Country talk with Drake newly come from the Indies. As the year wore away he saw Essex more in favor. Once Ralegh's attacker had been bebuffed. Ralegh could not be so sure any longer of the position of Essex. He was then "the best hated man of the world in Court, city, and country," for he had climbed alone. Essex was a man of a coterie, willing to be the centre of it, popular wherever he went, trained to security and success from birth. Ralegh merely became more individual. His enterprises went on uninterrupted. He looked upon the antics of Essex, and as with second sight after blindness, recognized his own gestures. Favorites were but jacks, toys of the Queen. He was building an empire of his own across the sea. He had a refuge in Ireland, remote in those days as the Congo in Victorian times, but first he would push on toward statesmanship, toward power.

For a time it seemed his second sight was clouded. Elizabeth smiled upon him. He flashed through the court in his silver armor as uncompromising as ever. Elegant in lace, embroidery and great pearls, with jewelled sword, he scorned the almost universal enmity, for the court was beginning to see Essex as his successor in favor. With Burghley alone was he willing to unbend. He was in the habit of addressing the Lord Treasurer as "the right honorable my singular good Lord" and writing to him elaborate letters, detailed and meticulous. Burghley had no need of him just then. He had come out of Ireland, where so many reputations lay buried under the dusky wings of war. There would be war again presently and his day would return, but the Lord Treasurer was not deceived by his labored exactness; he knew the fine carelessness of the genius with whom he was dealing.

Elizabeth was still liberal to him. Anthony Babington had died for his conspiracy against the life of the Queen. She granted to Ralegh most of the dead man's lands. They lay in three shires: Lincoln, Derby, and Notts, the first holdings in England Ralegh had won. Babington had promised Ralegh one thousand pounds for a pardon, but Ralegh took no heed of the offer. It was a legitimate trade of the day, which had peculiar ways. Many members of the Privy Council itself received Spanish gold regularly as a proof of Philip's friendship for them and it was thought no treason. Nor did it seem even to Ralegh's enemies a monstrous thing that he should grow by devouring the possessions of the unfortunate. It was but the rise and fall of empire on a small scale and a practice that was universal with Elizabeth, who really held a man's fortune her own, at his death, to award where she would, if legal ground could be found.

Liberally, in his turn, Ralegh sent out his fourth expedition to Virginia. The year was dark with menace, and his expenses were unusually heavy, but he would make a last effort before the Spanish threat reached England and rendered it impossible. What might come after none could tell, for Philip was rampant since the execution of Mary Stuart and the success of Parma in the Netherlands. Surely the Spanish would come, and then—Essex was only twenty-one—it would be an hour for men not boys.

CHAPTER VIII

VIRGINIA

SHIPS and men might sail honestly enough to plant Ralegh's Virginia, but their patron dared not stir. Feverishly active, he struggled for his own amid a thousand suits before a sovereign who was swayed by caprice. He joined forces with Sir Philip Sidney. Sidney had served under Coligny in Flanders when the Frenchman was dreaming of a great Protestant state in America. It was to Sidney that LeMoine, the artist, who escaped from the Florida massacre, brought his drawings, his story, and his hatred for the Spanish. Together, they sought out Ralegh as a man who understood. At intervals, when his duties as Chaplain to the English legation at Paris would permit, Richard Hakluyt came over the water to them, to be the third in the Virginian conspiracy. Hakluyt had always something interesting: the story of the last mariner he had sought out for his *Principal Voyages*, or the latest geographical surmise of some clever Frenchman, or a letter from Secretary Walsingham, praising Hakluyt's farsightedness in looking toward America, if only in theory.

What a curious America they conceived! Doctor Michael Lok, a geographer of London, drew a map of the western world for Sir Philip Sidney. It was not so very different from that of Sebastian Münster made in 1540. Much had still to be left to whim and surmise in 1582. Lok showed a tenuous continent, much intruded upon by bays and rivers. At forty degrees North, the land tapered to a misplaced Isthmus of Darien. It was so important that the passage to Cathay and India should be easy that cartographers could not but make it so. Rumor, sketched upon parchment, became truth. Indian legends and fishermen's tales were expanded into geographical certainty.

Sir Walter Ralegh was shrewd in his undertaking. The important thing had been to get an expedition at sea quickly. Scarcely had Philip Amadas and Arthur Barlow left behind the Canaries, in their westward passage, than their patron plunged ahead with his plans. Ralegh was rich, at least by comparison with many who served Elizabeth. He had seen his half-brother, Sir Humphrey, pour into the quest all his estate, and had watched the surviving creditors stripping the heirs. He had learned then that colonization could drain any private purse, however ample. Privateering made fortunes; colonizing devoured them. Amadas and Barlow would bring home a little knowledge, reports of animals, plants and minerals, with some specimens to prove their words, but no booty. When they returned, the next step would be to send out settlers, to begin the real planting; a costly proceeding.

Ralegh turned to the Queen. She could finance a colony if she would. Her cupidity, her pride, her genuine desire for the growth of England; to these he laid siege. She was mean and cautious, but she was just then refusing her favorite nothing. No man in England had a better chance of succeeding with her, and none could so clearly estimate the odds against him. Ralegh sent for Hakluyt.

Richard Hakluyt would cross England to get a sailor's story, or see a map, or borrow an old journal of a one-time venture. With the future of American colonization laid at his feet, he went to work with a will. He would write a Queen's book, a book not to be published, addressed to the gaze of Elizabeth alone. His study of the matter was unequalled. Twenty-one short chapters he wrote in a summer, and in September, 1584, Ralegh saw that the book reached the Queen.

VIRGINIA

The author had written from his heart. He saw his vision as a reality. England must colonize North America. Once established, she could drive the Spanish from the Newfoundland fisheries. With bases in America, the Spanish treasure would be open to easy attack in passage from Mexico and Panama. Stations would be hers from which to seek westerly for Cathay. In such operations the British navy would be trained and kept fit to a degree beyond any other in Europe. Hakluyt played the Queen's closeness against her cupidity. Slyly he explained the advantages of founding the colony: a market for English woollens and linens; a source of increased royal revenue through custom dues. And having suggested profit to be, Hakluyt let blaze the fierce hatred of the Spaniards he had caught from sailormen holding forth under the smoky beams of many a harbor tavern, a spleen Elizabeth no longer cried down. Her people would need all their spirit; the probable course of events was all too obvious.

For the profits of the new markets, Hakluyt urged, "Nowe if her Majestie take these western discoveries in hande, and plant there, yt is like that in short time wee shall vente as greate a masse of cloth yn those partes as ever wee did in the Netherlands, and in tyme moche more."[8] And how much was the English fabric trade with the Netherlands?

In 1550 there were fourteen thousand people in Antwerp who were supported by working these commodities and in all seven states of the Netherlands there were more than fifty-one thousand who lived by the trade.[9] Hakluyt knew how to play upon his Queen's greed.

As for the menace of Philip longing after the salvation of all heretics, the Queen was told, "If you touche him in the Indies you touch the apple of his eye; for take away his treasure, which is *nervus belli*, and which he hath almost all of his West Indies, his olde bandes of soldiers will soon be dissolved, his purpose defeated . . . and his tyrannie utterly suppressed" or later and with cold malice, "He shall be left as bare as Æsop's proude crowe." There was nothing she longed for more than the downfall of Philip whom time had proven the one reality among her threatening shadows. He was steadily amassing ships and troops against her. It would be the part of wisdom to provoke him as soon as possible, but she had no hope of defense when the hour came. To try to throttle Philip in the Indies would bring his hosts upon England at once. Why speed doom upon one's head?

So argument but led the Queen to refrain from noisily entering into the colonizing; argument and her own greed. If she helped Ralegh on the return of his two barks it was with the same secrecy she hid any love passages they may have had, and Elizabeth was not one to bestow wealth in private. As if to slay any slander that might have touched her she named the discovered land Virginia. Ralegh received a report upon the goodness of the land, some pelts, a bracelet of pearls, and had presented to him two Indians, Manteo and Wanchese, lusty enough Virginians to please even an Elizabethan eye.

At once, Ralegh turned to colonizing. Sir Richard Grenville was made General of an expedition to carry out the planters. Ralph Lane was excused by the Queen from service in Ireland and given to Sir Walter to serve as Governor when the colonists were come to land. Captain Philip Amadas went as Admiral of the country. Master Thomas Hariot went out to spend a year among new plants and peoples, lending his skill as an observer without stint, smoking his tobacco with a keen appreciation of Virginia's blessing. Kinsmen of Ralegh: a Gilbert, a Stukeley, went out, Gilbert to stay the year, Stukeley to return with Grenville and ridiculously claim some ten thousand pounds of the fifty thousand pounds taken on the voyage, for Sir Richard Grenville was not the man to let a Spanish ship slip from him because of his colonists.

Grenville led his fleet of seven sail from Plymouth harbor on April 9, 1585. The *Tiger* of one hundred forty tons was his flagship. The *Roebuck* was of the same burden. The *Lion* of a hundred tons, the *Elizabeth* of fifty tons, and the *Dorothy*, a small bark, were rounded out to total seven by the addition of two small pinnaces. From the Canaries they laid a course for Dominica and made the Indies on the 12th of May. Master Cavendish, then but twenty-two, had been lost in a gale in the Bay of Portugal, but caught up with the fleet at Cotesa, having crossed solo. He had been given up, but as he brought his ship in, guns opened to greet him "according to the manner of the Seas." It was a first test for a man soon to startle the world by his daring circumnavigation of the globe. Off Hispaniola, Grenville took one frigate, and off Florida, another. One hundred and seven colonists were safely carried to Wokoken or Roanoke and with them landed Manteo and Wanchese, safe home from their visit to the English Court. Here the ubiquitous Simon Ferdinando came to the fore long enough to ground the Admiral's ship on the bar and lose her. As a pilot, he was not singularly fortunate. Some thought as a Spanish spy he was more successful. On August 25, the General weighed anchor and sailed for England.

Grenville was stubborn and arrogant even for a sailor. He knew nothing of compromise and the colonists had been unable to teach him anything. A silver cup was stolen in the village of Aquascogok. The Admiral was sent by Grenville to recover the cup or secure satisfaction. The cup was not forthcoming, so the town and the ripe corn which had been left standing on stalk were burned. It was a point of discipline to Grenville. To the colonists it was the cause of arousing the Indians against them, ending in plot and counterplot, when Grenville had sailed safely out of the trouble he had created.

In a year the colonists explored as much as they could. They reached Secotan, eighty miles south of Roanoke Island. To the north, they penetrated as far as the Chesepians—about one hundred thirty miles. On foot, by canoe and ship's boat, even by pinnace, a vessel that drew far too much water for the shoal Pamlico or Albemarle Sound, the colonists searched out the country. Ralph Lane knew what he was hunting. "For that the discovery of a good Mine, by the goodness of God, or a passage to the South-sea, or some way to it, and nothing els can bring this Countrey in request to be inhabited by our nation." He was looking after the best interests of his master, following the court in far-off England. Yet there was a distinct centre from which the explorers went out and to which they returned. "The next morning wee arrived at our home Roanoak." Even in such work the English felt the pull of home building, the need for permanence in a land of chaos.

The months slipped away. There was some fighting with the Indians. Manteo, who had journeyed to England and back, was loyal and proved of great value to the colonists. Wanchese, who had shared the same privilege, turned against them. In general, all went well until April, 1586, when Ensenore, the best friend of the English, died and his son, Pemisapan, was free to make trouble. Famine developed among Lane's men. Pemisapan denied the English God who would let his worshipers be threatened by starvation, displayed all contempt for the colonists, and went from village to village rousing the tribes against them. The English took hostages to guarantee their own safety, and presently murdered Pemisapan in much the same ambush he had been preparing for them. When matters had reached this pass, word came up from Roanoke that a great fleet of twenty-three sail had come upon the coast, whether friend or foe none knew. Fortunately, the newcomer was Sir Francis Drake laden with loot from St. Domingo and Cartagena. He was affable and generous, supplying the needs of the colonists; food, weapons, tools. They were furnished with a bark the *Francis*, two pinnaces and four boats. Nothing was heard from Sir Richard Grenville and his relief. From June 1, 1586, Drake waited eighteen days for the colonists to decide what they would do. Grenville should have come before Easter. Lane yielded after a recurring West Indian storm had swept away the *Francis* and given them all a taste of Hatteras weather. Drake carried them all home with him.

While they had been gone their patron had not been sitting at ease in London. Sir Philip Sidney had completed plans with Drake for planting a new world colony of his own, but when Sir Francis came home Sir Philip had been sent by the Queen to fight in Flanders, and Drake had tasted the zest of freebooting and cared for no colonies. England was at war with Spain. In September, came the fatal battle at Zutphen and Sir Philip's death. There would be no more meetings with the ideal knight nor the high talk of dreams. Instead, Ralegh finished and lost a fight with the University of Cambridge which had taken exception to his wine patent. It was one thing to win a royal gift; it was quite another to collect one's due from ancient corporations, dyed in the processes of the law, and steeped in determination to resist the favorite. Moreover, the war began to throttle trade. Restrictions checked even coastal sailings, and the release of ships bound for Virginia was involved in endless bickering. None knew how long the Spaniards would be content to confine the war to the Netherlands. Not the least of the obstacles to be overcome was the feeling that Virginia was after all but a mirage, a figment of the Devonshire knight to trick the Queen.

Yet Ralegh managed; finally, a little before Easter, a single ship of one hundred tons slipped out to sea. She made the passage safely, arriving at Hatteras in fair weather, ready to unload her cargo, but there were no settlers to be found. Her captain made honest search. Sir Walter Ralegh had undertaken this supply effort entirely at his own cost. Sir Walter was a hard man. The master of the ship headed for England to return his cargo unbroken.

Only two weeks after he had left the coast, the major relief expedition, under Sir Richard Grenville, arrived in Virginia. The patron had not rested at the going out of his lone vessel. His proud and testy cousin commanded three well-found ships. The General went ashore. He explored. He considered. He pushed inland to discover any news. Master Lane and his men were gone. How then hold the country for England? Fifteen men were landed on Roanoke Island, and supplies for two years were left with them. Then Grenville sailed for England, calling at the Azores, by the way, to spoil a town or two, but bringing home only negative news from Virginia.

It was time Thomas Hariot should publish his report of all he had found in his year's residence. He addressed it "To the Adventurers, Favourers, and Welwillers of the enterprice for the inhabiting and planting in Virginia." This included by no means all of the court. Success had slipped so far off that Ralegh's enemies felt it safe to scoff. They chattered of pretended voyages, cruel abandonment. Those who testified to the colonists' return with Drake were faced with Grenville's report that they had seen no colonists, and even such a logical agreement of facts took on the air of mystery. Rumor fed upon the confusion, and Virginia became a byword.

But Ralegh would not quit. His other expeditions had not been averse to making an honest pound by privateering.

Colonizing offered hard knocks and uncertain rewards. Privateering suggested sudden wealth, as well as sudden death, and a vessel, once taken, was in itself worth something. Ralegh knew his seamen. From boyhood he had heard and had dealt in these things. His heart was for them, but that way lay no planting of Virginia.

For his new expedition he enlisted John White. He incorporated the Governor and Assistants of the Citie of Ralegh in Virginia under a charter. John White saw a great land swayed by his authority. Each of the twelve Assistants imagined himself the ruler of a province at least. One hundred fifty settlers were gathered. Householders they were, not given to the swagger way of the sea, but folk who were much interested in the tools sent with them, to make easier the tilling of the ground. As a final check against their turning marauders on the high sea, their patron sent them out in three utterly dissimilar vessels: the *Lion*, a ship of one hundred twenty tons, a fly boat, and a pinnace. The most gay and hopeful seaman could not hope to do much fighting with such an ill assortment, and so small a squadron would naturally seek safety in a quick passage to Virginia.

Simon Ferdinando, the eternal pilot, forever going out with one voyager or another, was again on hand. He had served with Captains Amadas and Barlow in 1584. It was his clumsiness in trying to bring the *Admiral* into harbor at Roanoke Island that stranded her and filled her down in 1585. He was no forward, pushing braggart. In the company of Captain Amadas he is listed sixth and upon John White's roll of 1587, he was to stand tenth, yet he was active upon that voyage. More than ever gossip insisted he must be in the pay of the Spanish, who even so early were conscious of Ralegh's position at court and his enmity for them. Knave or fool, Simon suffered from misfortune.

The ships sailed from Plymouth on May 8, 1587. On the

16th, Simon Ferdinando, "Master of our Admiral lewdly forsooke our Fly-boate," which was distressed by heavy weather in the Bay of Portugal. By June 19, Ferdinando had carried his ship to Dominica, and three days later landed at Santa Cruz without seeing anything more of the forsaken flyboat. While the colonists were on shore experimenting with a fruit that swelled their tongues and mouths, and capturing five tortoises of such size that sixteen men could just carry one, Ferdinando sent the pinnace off to the island of Beake or Baque, where he said sheep were to be found. The pinnace rejoined the *Lion* at Cottea without spying a single sheep. When Ferdinando took in fresh water at St. Johns, his men worked so heavily that they consumed more beer than the water they loaded. By July 1, the ships bore along the coast of St. Johns. Ferdinando had had the company prepare sacks to fill with salt when they landed near Ross Bay. Suddenly, he said they could not go into the bay, and as the Governor pressed him for reasons, he changed the course of the ship, until, when he caused the lead to be heaved, the ship was found to be in three and one-half fathoms. Ferdinando began to swear "and teare God in pieces," roaring to the steersman, "Bear up hard, bear up hard." So the ships left the island saltless.

When White wanted to land for oranges and pines to transplant to Virginia, Ferdinando said no, he would stop at Hispaniola. When they came up with the island of Caycos, Ferdinando sent his people ashore to gather salt from the dried ponds, "but it proved as true as finding of sheep at Baque." On the 16th of July, they made a landfall and Ferdinando thought it Croatan. He was only something more than one hundred sixty miles out in his reckoning, for that night they were nearly cast away in the surf of Cape Fear, which they missed by two cable lengths. Once arrived at Hatteras, Ferdinando refused to complete the directions by which he was ordered to pass up the coast to the Chesapeake, of which Grenville had heard so much, claiming the season was too far advanced. On July 25, only three days later, the flyboat arrived at Hatteras. Her master, Edward Spicer, had never been in Virginia, but he had made a good passage despite Ferdinando's treachery. Planters and crews turned to at unloading. It was felt some one should go back to England to serve as factor and so insure supplies reaching the colony. John White was chosen, and unwillingly made ready to return. He left behind him eighty-nine men, seventeen women, and eleven children, all set bravely to live in the new world. By August 27, the two ships sailed for England. Both were touched by sickness, the flyboat held up by head winds, the *Lion* so weakened by sickness among her people that her crew were barely able to bring her into the harbor. It was Ferdinando who had prevented the colony from being as well prepared for Virginian life as John White had intended, Ferdinando who knew the location and condition of the planters which may have been worth money to Philip, measuring his enemy to the last soul.

Landed in England, White found himself checked at every turn. Among the colonists in Virginia he had left his daughter, Eleanor Dare, and his grand-daughter, the first child born to a colonist in America and so named Virginia Dare. His word had been given; his blood cried out for speed; he had to return across the Atlantic. But the affairs of state were becoming critical. Spain was ready to fling himself upon England. The King of France was watching. An embargo was placed upon all shipping. Even Ralegh did not know where to turn, desperate as the plight of his colonists might be. He secured a pinnace and the services of Grenville, but his enemies at court pleaded the danger of England. Grenville was personally commanded not to leave Cornwall. White worked independently after that. The

Brave and the *Roe* he prepared for the voyage. Ralegh's influence got them to sea, but once over the bar at Biddeford they went aroving, fell in with two strong men of war, Frenchmen out of Rochelle, and in two months' time crept back to England badly battered and ravaged. Fifty leagues northeast of Madeira was as close as they had ever been to Virginia. White was desperate.

Hakluyt, himself, had ceased to cry after his "magnificent and gracious prince, Elizabeth of England into whose lappe the Lord hath most plentifully throwne his treasure," to open her heart and bounty in the cause of Virginia. He still felt it was an enterprise far more certain than that Elizabeth of Castile and Aragon had emptied her coffers to undertake, but war was at hand. The church was turning to hearten the nation's defenders. It was a little treasonable to balance the safety and comfort of a few colonists against the need of England assailed. After peace came he would have time for dreams. Even Ralegh had to work secretly and when the battered *Brave* and *Roe* stole home, disobedient and shamed, he dared try no more. He had spent over forty thousand pounds and had nothing to show for it but an empty title and a few struggling souls, castaway from their mother country. When the armada had been overthrown and devoured, he was caught up into public affairs more than ever. Even his gigantic energies were limited. In March, 1589, he yielded trade rights in Virginia to the Adventurers: John White, Richard Hakluyt, Thomas Smith, and a few others. He reserved his patent, but this put the burden of development upon his assigns.

John White immediately contracted for three ships. They were to take on and transport passengers, with their furniture, to Virginia, their owners and masters to be bound to Sir Walter Ralegh or his assigns, for a bond of three thousand pounds posted against failure to perform the contract.

This plan failed. Ralegh's orders were not obeyed. The ships took only White. They lost seven of their chief men and three anchors and cables. By March 20, 1590, John White had landed at Roanoke, seeking for his family and friends. First he found a tree lettered C R O A. Then he came upon a palisade, well-defended by curtains and flankers. Five feet from the ground and to the right of the entrance the bark was stripped away and the word Croatan was carved. It was the signal agreed upon. If the colonists left Roanoke while White was in England, they had promised to so inform him of their destination. In addition, if they were fleeing in distress they were to carve a cross close to the name of their new home. They had graved no cross, but the palisade was grown with brush and grass and nothing was found within it but a few bars of iron, two pigs of lead, and useless odds and ends too heavy to be easily removed. White found his own chests dug out from where they had been buried, rifled and rotted. His things were scattered about and spoiled by weather. Not a word did he learn of Eleanor or Virginia Dare. White returned to his ship, wondering what had overtaken the colonists. He determined to go to Croatan where the baptized Manteo was powerful and should be able to help him. He had not counted upon his shipmates.

That very night the weather turned stormy and the wind drew into the northeast. The ships rode heavily. Their captains were eager to get down among the Indies and when the ship in which White was a passenger lost her third anchor, the three bore away for the south, an eager little flotilla, much more interested in finding John Hawkins and sharing his plunder than in gathering news of Ralegh's colony. So ended White's search at its very beginning. He had not strength, means, or hope to follow farther.

Through all the next decade Ralegh never gave over his hope for a new empire in America. He never heard from his lost settlers. He watched his "adventurers" make nothing of their trading concessions, sorry for their failures but unshaken. His enthusiasm saw Virginia as a new Empire, a Queen's certainty, but the funds to undertake it were beyond him, for he was always flinging his means into the affairs of his career and he knew too well the drain of his dream. All the years of his endeavor he was the cynosure of neighboring eyes, but he was also a hated monopolist, farming his patent on wines. Through paradox after paradox he steered his life. Fired by changing enthusiasms he still penetrated attitude after attitude with Machiavellian clarity, yet amid every involvement, he never forgot Virginia.

Hakluyt had urged men of quality to seek out unknown realms for the Queen. The discoverer was to know that ambition and avarice availeth not. His motives were to be "derived from a virtuous and heroical mind, preferring chiefly the honour of God, compassion of the poor infidels captivated by the devil . . . advancement of his honest and well-disposed countrymen . . . willing to accompany him in such honorable actions." He might have used Ralegh as his model knight in drawing such an actuation.

The fire of Sir Humphrey Gilbert flamed in Sir Walter. His was the heroic mind, vaulting in pride from achievement to achievement. It was at his injunction that Manteo and Wanchese were brought into England and then returned to their people in Virginia. Grenville, Lane, Cavendish, Hariot had been advanced by their experience: only poor John White seems to have been undone by his ill luck. The unfortunate colonists were said not to be entirely honest, nor did they remain well disposed to the Indians. Only in one thing did Sir Walter fail Hakluyt as an example: he never led an expedition to North America. He never saw the blink of sandy Hatteras. He never put foot on Virginian land. He never sailed up the Chesapeake. He never smoked tobacco until Hariot brought back the habit with him, together with the weed worth its weight in silver, and a silver pipe in which to smoke it. Queen Elizabeth would never spare him. She had lost Gilbert and Sidney; she needed a shining knight beside her, especially one who could mix courtesy's falsest extravagance with truth's bitterest wisdom.

There was nothing mawkisk or ill-fashioned about Sir Walter. When eight several expeditions had gone out in behalf of his lost colony and trade and when his Queen was so near death that the only thought of the court was the succession, he sent out his last effort under Samuel Mace. Then he wrote to Sir Robert Cecil asking him to confiscate a cargo just landed from Virginia without the Ralegh permission, and while he rather cleverly reached after his own, he voiced his belief in Virginia, "For I shall yet live to see it an English nation." With the Queen dying he saw the drift of affairs. He knew he was a man with his all upon the hazard of the dice, but his faith was fixed. Even in 1607, when a colony was effected and he was a prisoner in the Tower, he kept up the semblance of his governorship, for Ralph Gilbert voyaged to Virginia in his interest. He was not doddering, only hoping that if times should mend and King James die, he might have a foothold to win back the empire overseas.

When he wrote that letter to Sir Robert Cecil on August 21, 1602, England had not a single visible colony anywhere in the world. Out of Ralegh's faith was all to be made.

CHAPTER IX

THE ARMADA

THE Marques of Santa Cruz, the best seaman in Spain, died before Philip's armada could be made ready. There was so much to be done. Philip named Don Alonzo Perez de Guzman, Duke of Medina Sidonia, Lord of Saint Lucar and Knight of the Golden Fleece, to the vacant command. Don Alonzo objected; he knew nothing of the sea; he knew nothing of war. No one heeded. There was so much to be done.

Pope Sixtus prepared a Cruzado as if Philip were to fight the infidel Saracens. He furnished money. He supplied the expedition with Cardinal Allen to carry the papal bull depriving Elizabeth of all her princely titles and dignities. Allen had it translated into English ready for publication when the army would land victoriously. More than a hundred monks: Jesuits, Capuchins, and friars mendicant, were provided to carry the Inquisition unto the heretics.

Philip felt the black wind sweep about his breezy Escorial and dreamed himself possessed of the realm of England, dreamed himself to be the greatest defender of the faith of all time, and kept his officers in a whirl. There was so much to be done. For a long time his foundries had toiled with brass and iron, his mountaineers had hewn timbers, and his drill masters had perfected the discipline of war. He had ships: sixty-four great galleons, bullet proof in their upper works and in the lower of four to five feet in thickness of ribs and planking, galleases rowed each by three hundred slaves, caravels furnished with trumpets, streamers, and banners, pataches brave with war-like engines. Sixteen hundred brazen cannons and ten hundred iron were mounted to

THE ARMADA 113

serve. Biscuit for half a year, six thousand, five hundred quintals of bacon, twelve thousand pipes of fresh water, fish, rice, peas, oil: here was abundance for the stomachs of the eight thousand mariners and twenty thousand soldiers, although little enough of that abundance reached the two thousand eighty-eight slaves, chained to the rowers' benches. In addition, vast quantities of stores had to be gathered: candles, lanterns, lamps, sails, hemp, ox hides, and sheet lead to stop shot holes.

Into his ships Philip sent five terzaes, or regiments, of Spanish troops, besides Castilian and Portuguese bands with their own commanders. Cannons, double cannons, culverins, and field pieces for land service were stowed below hatches. Horses, mules, wagons, wheels, spades, mattocks were carried. Thirty-two thousand men were to attack England. It was a tremendous effort. Philip estimated it to cost him thirty thousand ducats a day and the toil was more than flesh and blood could stand, but at last all was ready.

The year was already well-worn into spring. The Biscay might be more kind at that season. The Cardinals at Cadiz prayed in valedictory, "Let God arise and destroy his enemies." Couriers went off headlong to Parma in the Netherlands that he might be ready to accept the obedience of the English nation. Philip would have no delay. On May 19, 1588, the gathered fleet left Lisbon for the Bay of Corunna. Four galleys were lost on the way, one by heavy weather, which made her put back, and the other three taken by revolt of the rowing slaves. Eight others lost their masts overside. It was not until the 11th of July that the daily commands from Philip for haste stirred the Duke of Medina Sidonia. He knew he need not rush upon destruction. Of the end for him he had no doubt.

Meanwhile, the Duke of Parma, in the Netherlands, had prepared for victory. He had deep channels dug so that he might move ships easily from Antwerp and Ghent to Bruges and thus to the sea by the way of Sluys. He levied upon Hamburg, Bremen, and Emden for sailors to man the twenty-eight ships of war he had gathered. For ballast he used a great store of beams bristling with iron spikes, and upon their sides hooks and clasps to join them together. At Gravelines he gathered twenty thousand casks, fitted to be fastened by nails and rope into a floating bridge. Pilings, timbers, ironwork: all the material to stop up the mouth of harbors, he made ready. Near Neiuport haven he had a huge pile of wooden fagots laid for the rearing of a mount against the day when captive heretics would be brought to terms by processions of fire ending in acts of faith. He left nothing lacking.

Presently, the Spanish fleet sailed, bearing noble and thrall and a large number of brave soldiers of fortune, unlucky in their birth. There was the Prince of Melito, called the Duke of Pastrana, the natural son of Philip himself, John Medices, bastard of the Duke of Florence, the Marques of Burgrave, one of the children of Archduke Ferdinand and Philippa Welsera, and Amadas of Savoy, base son of the Duke of Savoy. Bravely enough the armada spread its sails. Its like had never been seen upon the ocean sea. At its heels followed the harlots. The penalties had been so severe for bringing women on board any of the ships that even the doughtiest lover had yielded. The harlots, therefore, hired ships of their own, sailing in the wake of the conquerors; there would be loot to earn in England.

Since November, 1587, the English had been preparing for the attack. Sir Walter was busy as a member of a council ordered to provide defense for the realm. Plymouth, Portland, the Isle of Wight, Margate were to be protected by works and garrisons. The Spanish would not dare pass up channel unless they had taken a good harbor to serve as a rendezvous. Should a landing be effected, the people prepared to strip the country of all support for the invader. Ralegh, not content with the general provisions, upon his own initiative implored cannon of Burghley to protect Portland and Weymouth. He saw the sheltering bill, the nearness of Portsmouth and Wight, the possibility of cutting the west from the east counties by a swift stroke toward Bristol Channel. There would be no crossing of Biscay in winter for an armada. The foul climate and westerly gales of England, the icy, brittle weather of the Netherlands were tradition to the Spanish. Ralegh went to Ireland, looking after his estate, watching that his own was not lost to him through faulty deputies. He served as Mayor of Youghal. He supported twenty horsemen as a tenant under the Crown, but his charges were repaid. In March, 1588, he received two hundred and forty-four pounds as his semi-annual due. Then, even to Ireland, came news of the Armada again. Philip was having the lists of his vessels and officers translated into English and Dutch, that all might read and flee. Yet he made a bid to the peace party in England by having it noised abroad the expedition was directed against the Netherlands. Only a few believed.

England had long hated Spain and hatred begets fear. By one impulse bickering was left off. Lord Howard of Effingham, sometimes thought a Catholic although he long had a hand in apprehending recusants, was given command of the fleet. Drake, Hawkins, Frobisher, Henry Seymour served with him. Leicester, whom report had rumored in Spanish pay, commanded on land. What could be done was ready by summer, but Medina Sidonia loitered at the Groine close to Corunna. He was thinking of St. Mary Port and his orange trees, kissed by the soft airs of Cadiz Bay, until the threats of Philip outweighed in terror his own dread of the inevitable. He knew nothing of war or the sea. On July

19, Captain Fleming raced to Lord Howard: he had spied an enemy fleet while scouting in his pinnace. From the twentieth onward there was continual contact at some point or other. At first, the English were very cautious. The Armada was gigantic. It stunned by its size.

All down the shores of England men watched to guard against surprise. There were no idlers. Even the court had scattered to the winds. To hearten her fighters the Queen rode down to Tilbury, on her one hand the huge Earl of Leicester and on the other the young, resplendent Earl of Essex. She sat her saddle clad in a steel corselet, face gaunt with anxiety. Past her filed the strength of her land. She was fifty-four, an age that would allow her no time to recover her realm, if Philip should triumph, and yet, if Ralegh could have seen her glance at Essex amid her anxiety he would have known there was something of love in her for the large lad, and that for him the courtly passages of his first days near the Queen belonged to the past.

Ralegh was down in his own West Country. He had urged the Queen to fit out her fleet. The mobility of the Armada was so much greater than that of an army that resistance on land alone was impossible. The Spanish had only to choose a beach where there were no troops. He had in council with Lord Howard urged against boarding the Spanish ships. They were too big. They were too well manned. The English guns were heavy. Let them stand off and batter the Spanish, follow close, firing carefully, engaging continually, but never grappling. When the Armada arrived in the channel Ralegh was neither beside the Queen nor with Lord Howard. His duty was at Portland and there he heard of a fight between the *Defiance* and a Spanish ship close to the Eddystone. If the Spanish flank were so far to the west the major attack would fall on the south coast, close to Portland as he had expected from the beginning. Like Philopoemen,

Prince of the Achaei, he had spent much of his time of peace weighing this problem of his land invaded; cogitations that would have warmed the heart of Machiavelli as in the early Flanders days they had touched that of Gascoigne. All Englishmen had labored for this day of the Spanish coming. Every turn of Spain was known as soon as conceived. For that Sir Francis Walsingham had given his lifelong ease, from the days when he undertook to study law at Padua and came away with espionage learned and practised. Burghley used him and the Queen profited. His duty was perfectly performed, his homage to her sex never begun. It maddened her; but his unflinching eyes, his sallow, thoughtful face, never blanched at her tirades, never yielded compliment nor needless courtesy. He was inexorable as a man of his work had to be, but he would never let her cast aside his hard won facts. To him she was England, neither more nor less, the focus of all his labors. He subtly bent her will and earned her approval, which he never won. To her, he was dark and merciless, but damnably loyal. She spat when she said it, but thanks to him, she, and what was more important, Burghley, knew every thought of France, of Spain, of the college of cardinals, of Pope Sixtus V, and so, when the half moon of galleons and galleases came up channel with the wind astern, the chain of beach fires leading up the Thames and along the coast were lighted one by one deliberately, without noise and without fury.

Two days after the *Defiance* met the Spaniard off the Eddystone, the invading ships appeared off Portland. Ralegh needed no intelligence service to tell him what to do. The enemy lay at his door. With his gentlemen at his heels, he hastily transferred his land duties to others and went to sea. From behind Portland Bill he swept out in chase, for the Spanish worked to the east with the wind aft. Ships came out to join him. Both fleets made for Dover Straits, the English grown to one hundred forty ships of all sizes and sorts, but with heavier guns than the Spanish, and more ability to work to windward smartly. Ralegh followed to Calais and saw the stratagem of the fire ships, to the shoals off Gravelines, to the breaking moment when the Spaniards had gotten sea room and to flee "cut their mainsails," as Emanuel van Meteran put it in his Latin history of the Low Countries, and then took up the chase of the broken squadrons with the rest. There was no air of piracy, no picking up of prizes. A Spanish ship faltered, fell behind. English fire hammered her, crashing quite through and through until she sank. Then with a following wind her attackers pushed on to hang upon the quarters of another foe.

When "the morris dance on the waves" had ended, Sir Walter wrote with his customary clarity of the coming of the invincibles. "This navy, consisting of a hundred and forty sail, was, by thirty of the Queen's ships of war, and a few merchantmen, beaten and shuffled together, even from the Lizard Point in Cornwall to Portland, where they shamefully left Don Pedro de Valdez, with his mighty ship; from Portland to Calais, where they lost Hugo de Moncada, with the galleys of which he was captain: and from Calais, driven with squibs from their anchors, were chased out of the sight of England round about Scotland and Ireland; where, for the sympathy of their barbarous religion, hoping to find succour and assistance, a great part of them were crushed against the rocks; and those others who landed, being very many in number, were, notwithstanding, broken, slain and taken and so sent from village to village, coupled with halters, to be shipped into England; where her Majesty, of her princely and invincible disposition, disdaining to put them to death, and scorning either to retain or entertain them, they were all sent back again to their own country to witness and recount the worthy achievements of their invincible navy."[10]

Bravely touched off in a few words that, proving a clear eye, an orderly mind, and a puritan upbringing.

As for Philip, walled in upon rocky, windswept Guadarrama, he said to his General: "I sent you to fight against men and not with the winds," but Medina Sidonia was forbidden the court and commanded to his private home. The ships of the harlots reached Newhaven in Normandy. Not for them the flight of the galleons. Sea-worn passengers, Spanish women far from home, landed among an alien people.

Only Philip took the failure calmly. At first he would not believe the defeat possible, but when news upon news confirmed the first report he turned to dreams of a new armada.

Elizabeth, for one of her arrogance, was singularly humble. She had made very little of all the strategy, the tactics, the single ships engaged with stunning shocks. She trusted Howard, the Lord Admiral, and her Vice-Admiral Drake, and as her best and bravest went out she was a little remorseful she had not provided a fleet to meet the emergency, a fleet with generous stores and full magazines. She was even to her dearest friends not mean, perhaps, but careful. When the fleet came home Elizabeth felt relief and surprise. She had a medal struck in honor of the victory which she dedicated by her motto to great mystery. "Deus afflavit!" God blew his wind indeed, she thought, wondering. Sir Francis Drake had made "himself whole with the Spaniards," quits that was for the one little ship of his inheritance, lost to the Dons on his first marauding voyage, in company with Hawkins. There was very little loot saved from the Spanish wrecks, but the ransom of rich Spanish prisoners fell in a large share to Sir Francis, and in equal sum was Sir Walter Ralegh remembered. Howard, from there on, felt him a naval authority.

2

Reverence sat upon Elizabeth with a strange solemnity. Heedless, at her own pleasure, of dogma, she merged in religion all the dread matters she could not understand. She would go to St. Paul's in state. She would lay the victory upon the high altar and when God had taken it again, perhaps her wonder might depart somewhat and her vision be more clear. She hated to live in a maze.

She saw her heralds, gentlemen ushers, and harbingers move to the head of the procession at Somerset House as in a dream. Judges, court physicians, nobles, bishops followed, and then, just before her chariot drawn by white horses, the French ambassador, her councillors, her chamberlain, while upon the flanks filed sergeants-at-arms, gentlemen, pensioners, and halberdiers. The chariot passed along the Strand, canopied and crested by the imperial crown. The Marchioness of Winchester bore her train. The Queen smiled upon Essex leading her palfry behind the chariot. After him followed the ladies of honor and at the end the Queen's yeomen of the Guard.

The Strand and Fleet Street were decked in blue. It was Sunday and the populace thronged to see them pass, a November Sunday of triumph and almost high noon. City musicians were playing over the gateway at Temple Bar where waited the Lord Mayor and the Aldermen, all in scarlet. Citizens in the blue liveries of their companies lined Fleet Street, their ensigns and banners fluttering in the crisp air. Up Ludgate Hill to the west porch of St. Paul's the procession led. The Bishop of London, the Dean, and fifty of the clergy, received the Queen. She knelt and prayed in silence. There was nothing so good as a rite to focus the mind. Chanting the litany, the clergy followed her down the aisle and across the transept to a seat facing Paul's cross.

The Bishop of Salisbury preached a sermon full of regal gratitude that restored Elizabeth much to her self-esteem and her ability to concede her sailors something of their due. They had pressed their ships only to the limits of caution, checking their zeal, commanding a deadly calm to master their heated blood. They had shot four shots to the Spaniard's one, giving one of the earliest lessons in the importance of superiority of gunfire. If only Lord Derby, with the astute young Robert Cecil in his train, were able to come to terms in the Netherlands, one armada might prove enough to quiet Philip. If Catherine should die—it was rumored she was not well—so close upon the murder of Henry III, the last hope for stability in France would be gone. Philip might find enough campaigning just over the Pyrenees with the coming of the Bourbons to the throne. Meanwhile, it was a time to be careful in rewarding; no lavish flinging to the winds, no vain gestures.

Her pointed eyes sought the bearded face of young Essex. A little more than a year he had been at court. Knighted, given the Garter, he was already Master of Horse. There was no need to reward him for his resistance of the Armada, for she had kept him by her. With Leicester he would have commanded the imaginary thirty-six thousand, her bodyguard, to keep her from being haled to Rome, her person conveyed "to the purpose that His Holiness the Pope should dispose thereof, in such sort as it should please him." Essex could not have prevented that had the Spanish landed. She shuddered out of the horror only lately put by. She prayed a little. So chastened was she by the comfort of her faith, that she saw him but an impulsive, lovable boy, and then she saw Ralegh watching Essex.

Ralegh had heard of the flanking guardians at Tilbury: Leicester and Essex in full armor. As the procession had gone up Ludgate Hill his guardsmen's halberds, gilded and with handles set in red velvet, had ceased to glint athwart his vision and he had spied Essex at the head of the Queen's palfrey, at the very heels of her chariot. He stood untouched by humility, by prayer of cleric, or the closeness of the Queen. Tall, among her guardsmen, he showed nothing that he thought. There was no getting behind the tall brow, the straight gaze, so long as he cared to remain impassive. Leicester had made way for him, was he now to yield to Essex? The Queen had never let him go into danger in recent years, not with Gilbert, nor his own Virginian expeditions, nor his privateering ventures. At a time like that just passed she could hardly have seen fit to hold him back, but she had Essex. Was it Leicester over again then? Was Ralegh done? As he looked upon the woman who had been Queen for thirty years he thought of Gilbert and Gascoigne; Gilbert who faced death unafraid, Gascoigne who refuted his every tenet to seek spiritual comfort at his passing. Was he to pass from the life of the court? Was he to die that mocking death in life of a superannuated favorite at thirty-six? What said Machiavelli, "The prince is, moreover, obliged to live always with the same people, but he can easily do without the same nobility, being able to make or unmake them at any time." If Elizabeth would ever undo Essex it would be too late, for his stalwart Ralegh pride would not let him stoop; there was still some impetuous fire in his blood. Gascoigne or Gilbert? By God's grace, Gilbert and handsomely done too, without creeping, without humility. The Bishop of Salisbury had ceased. Elizabeth spoke to the multitude gathered beneath the eleven captured Spanish banners and Ralegh's eyes never flickered. His voice kept the roundness of its timbre as he marshalled his guardsmen, but Elizabeth had moved far away. She was fifty-five and looked it. Close behind her strode Essex, her Guard bringing up the rear.

The Spanish menace was more than ever in the minds of

Englishmen. They felt that something surely must happen in revenge, in attempted retaliation. No sooner did Drake and Norris regain port, after chasing the Spanish north of the Firth of Forth, than they set about an expedition to restore Don Antonio to his throne of Portugal, which Philip had abolished. Should the English succeed they would have a base from which to operate against Spain. Philip would have a thorn in his side. There was much deliberation at court. John Norris was a first-class fighting man but no courtier, nor did Drake often succeed in a suit. It was not until February 23, 1589, that commissions and instructions were sent down to Plymouth by the Queen.

All was bustle and clamor, more like the sailing of buccaneers than an efficient naval movement. The grand manner still clung. George Peele wrote a fiery farewell.

> "You fight for Christ and England's peerless Queen,
> Elizabeth, the wonder of the world."

In April, one hundred fifty vessels sailed. Sir Walter Ralegh went in one of his own ships, unimpeded by Elizabeth. He had no part in the command; that was given to Drake and Norris. Essex ran away from court, rode two hundred twenty miles as rapidly as he could to outrace couriers, and flung himself on board the *Swiftsure* and into the arms of Sir Rodger Williams, who had known of his intent. The Queen made every effort to overtake him, and failing, blamed the expedition for every indignity she felt Essex had heaped upon her. The fleet reached Corunna and hammered the city for two weeks, but gave up the siege and sailed for Lisbon. The delay had permitted Essex and Sir Rodger Williams to have a cruise of their own, but they were in time for the landing. Essex gave his youth vent, reckless as a madman. Don Antonio was put ashore, but the populace feared the Spanish rulers more than they loved Don

Antonio. Elizabeth sent a petulant reminder of her displeasure: she would not pay a shilling of the costs in excess of twenty thousand pounds. The leaders should be responsible for all spent over that. Drake and Norris determined to give up the attempt. They burned two hundred ships on the Tagus, set sail, called at Vigo long enough to set fire to the town, and then swept on to England, tumbling their men upon the English wharves with scant ceremony. If the Queen had no more heart for the attempt they would be rid of it too.

Sir Walter received four thousand pounds out of the general booty and his prizes. Besides, he carried a fight over prize money with Sir Rodger Williams to the Privy Council. It almost seemed like Ralegh versus Essex, and Ralegh was sustained, but the friction was growing serious. Earlier in the year Essex had challenged him to a duel. To have let his blood would have ruined Ralegh forever with Elizabeth; to have paid no attention would have been to allow the young bully to swagger even more tauntingly than was usual to him. The council forbade the challenge, forbade the meeting, forbade the spreading of the news for fear it would reach the Queen and involve every one in her wrath. Since Leicester had died, on his way to Kenilworth, there was none could face her when she was angry. Catherine de Medici had been dead six months, Catherine who, like herself, suggested immutability of character, freedom from time and death. Both deaths were troubling reminders to her of mortality. Sir Walter understood something of this. Better still, he knew the petulant bad nature of Essex would make the most of their antagonism. It was an unequal contest and a little ridiculous; Essex rose so fast, he, Ralegh, waned so slowly. Elizabeth had refused Sir Walter something at last. She would not make Lord Pembroke Ranger of the New Forest, although he requested it. True, she had given it to

Blount who had lately fought a duel with Essex, so the young Earl could not boast a victory either, but Ralegh had been refused.

The expedition was ending. Ralegh commanded his own ship and there was nothing to hurry him to London. Even his Virginia efforts were in the hands of his new lessees. He would make straight for Ireland. It would be a pleasant change to see his estate, and if the stewardship had been poor, that should be put straight. The Queen sent him a chain of gold for his services to her at Lisbon and no other word.

CHAPTER X

A SHEPHERD PIPING IN THESSALY

HE sailed into Youghal Bay, where the greenest hills in the world tumble into the sea, with the thought of setting his house in order. Farther inland, at Lismore, where a castle was being built for him, lay the more proper seat from which to administer his estate, but Youghal was very beautiful with its flanking hills and its sea line; the sweep of St. George's Channel opening to the Atlantic. In the Warden's house of the Dominican Friary, he settled to find his peace. Far off things would seem clearer there. The practical and theoretical, how often he blended them. The thirteenth century town wall made of his garden a bit of a close. He was thinking of Virginia with its great hopes, now postponed until they seemed lost to all but his eyes, so he experimented with the potato and tobacco. From the Azores came the yellow wall flowers and the great myrtle trees that still astonish visitors. The four yew trees twined and thatched into a summer house are unchanged from the days when Ralegh smoked his pipe of comfort in their shelter. It was he planted the Affane cherry that ever since has grown along the Blackwater. Near Cork there thrive cedars he had set out. Through the gates of his garden the tubers, which were to save Ireland from destruction in famine time, went out to the villages of all Munster. In the intervals he lounged by the deep fireplace watching the flames flicker upon the carving of the mantle.

Virginia was impossible for the time; he would colonize his Irish estate instead. From Devon and Somerset he brought faithful English. Lismore lies today in the midst of the coal fields. Even so early Ralegh knew there were mineral deposits there and hired Cornish miners to open mines, seeking, of course, metal. Arrangements to improve the stock of the farmers were undertaken. Sir Walter sought to plant almost three English to one Irishman upon his land; how far he had departed from his early savageness toward the natives is hard to tell. Ireland to him meant a possession to be utilized, a profitable province contributing to his grandeur. For the people he cared very little, for the land—he liked the Warden's house at Youghal and the sea line beyond the flanking hills.

It was time that he trusted most to when he landed. Essex would pass when Elizabeth tired; his wisdom was not great, his courage was only the heedlessness of youth. When the Queen tired of children she might remember Ralegh in Ireland and find the broad face of the Devereux plain, lighted only by the glow of passing fancy. If she wanted the youngster alone, he would spare them. Niccolo said, "The first impression that one gets of a ruler and of his brains is from seeing the men that he has about him." It was a dangerous play but a bold one. When Elizabeth should make him a Privy Councillor, then he would have it all. She was not a fool. Leicester was dead. Burghley was past seventy and unwell. The Queen would be needing men about her and he knew his worth. Could he but win clear of her relatives, of those who lived in closest touch, whom she did not love and yet dared not despise. Was it as Niccolo said, "A prince must provide, therefore he is liberal to those from whom he does not take"? Was the converse true? Would she not raise a maker of gifts who would labor to the last blood for her, for England, and so for himself? Good lack—what of Walsingham, whom she kept so poor shame sat in his eyes for the poverty of his life, and Sir Henry Sidney whom she had ruined by giving him honor beyond his means. Was she not making Leicester's estate pay her back every farthing of the

Earl's indebtedness? If she could not have the man, the widow should not have his wealth. To demand little things of her was easy; to demand great was to find deafness and a stubborn will which neither fire nor ice could shatter. Time was a cunning ally, time it should be for Sir Walter.

While he waited, he read with that hunger he carried with him everywhere. From the great chest of books that even went to sea with him, he chose his favorites. Homer, Cicero, Juvenal, Martial were his from youth, but he turned to Suetonius, to Seneca and Plautus, browsing avidly amid history, tragedy, comedy. He thought upon Aristotle and Plato. He went back to the beginnings of historical criticism with Thucydides. Vegetius, Hesiod, Plutarch, Euripides, Pliny, Martial: he roved at will where interest led. He knew the reign of Hiero, the first King of Sicily, how Strozza was torn to pieces at Terceres, by what means Pope Julio attacked the Bentivoli at Bologna, and all the intimate sidelights the authors of the Spanish chronicles had shed upon the Emperor, Charles V. He scorned nothing as foolish and he penetrated all as with second sight. Youghal was a place of silence where his thoughts rose easily and his vision deepened.

Close at hand, at the ruined castle of Kilcolman near the Galtee Hills, lived Edmund Spenser upon three thousand odd acres of the old Desmond land. Heavily wooded, with a tower to catch the eye, the manor was practically a poor place, but it was Spenser's own and he made the most of it. He was not unknown even then, for he had succeeded Lodovick Briskett as clerk to the Council of Munster. He had known the patronage of Leicester and his nephew Sidney, so soon taken from him by death, and he had attracted attention by his *Shepherd's Calendar*, a poetical invention in twelve books dealing with people of his day. Masquerade and hyperbole were the stage and scenery on which the poet's strength and sweetness were lavished. Dedicated to Virgil, approved by Sidney's Areopagus of wits, winning the praise even of Harvey Gabriel, the Cambridge scholar so set upon establishing the English Hexameters and Sapphics, the *Shepherd's Calendar* became the fashion. There was doubtless a visit to court, for Spenser wrote of Harvey's "desire to hear of my late being with her Majesty." Lord Grey of Wilton had become his patron after the deaths of Leicester and Sidney. When Ralegh was once settled at Youghal he remembered his cousin Sir George Carew, Master of Ordnance in Ireland, then at Lismore, and the author of the *Shepherd's Calendar* at Kilcolman.

Busy as he was Ralegh realized the change that had come to England in recent years: the touch of things Italian, French, Spanish, the cry for the elaborate, the ornate. The courtly world was forced to the caprice of Elizabeth and the Queen was become as a graven image no longer pristine, but craving worship more than ever. She wanted all to think she was semi-divine and "Her peerless skill in making well" stood her in good stead, but a strange artificial air crept upon the court and upon the universities which were the mirrors of the court. Harvey sounded this change. "What news at Cambridge?" he propounded to Spenser and hastened to answer, "Tully and Demosthenes nothing so much studied as they were wont: Livy and Sallust perhaps more, rather than less: Lucian never so much: Aristotle much named but little read: . . . Machiavel a great man: Castilio of no small repute: Petrarch and Boccace in every man's mouth: Galateo and Guazzo never so happy: but some acquainted with Unico Aretino: the French and the Italian highly regarded: the Latin and the Greek but lightly: . . . Turkish affairs familiarly known: castles built in the air: much ado and little help: in no age so little so much made of; every one highly in his own favor." So the false vanity of a Queen swept the country into caprice, into flattery that exceeded extravagance; new effects, posturing, perverted gestures, gilded shamming, sincere nonsense.

Out of such a maze had Ralegh come to Ireland, to find a poet paying no heed to the pedants but writing in the romantic, full-blown style of the older English. A bit florid, his style, ornate now and then, but with a steady pulse. Spenser showed Ralegh the first three books of the *Faerie Queene*, and Ralegh knew at once what he had found. To Spenser he was the "Shepherd of the Ocean," the discoverer of new beauty, the reader of all excellence. Ralegh was doing a deal of dark thinking those days; pondering Italian political aphorisms, weighing historical instances, sharpening all toward one end; his own greatness at court. Here was poetry for the ear of the Queen. Spenser toyed with her pride. At his touch she became Gloriana, Belphœbe, Britomart, Mercilla and with less certainty Amoret. In ten thousand glittering ways the young poet turned her about in all tenderness. Ralegh knew the worth of the lines and sighed for his dead youth reflected there. He would take Spenser to court. Elizabeth could not be so stupid as not to see that Spenser's lines carried Ralegh's heart. One did not laugh at a device so fashionable. To be restored to Elizabeth's good graces was all that mattered.

Three years later Spenser wrote of it all in *Colin Clout's Come Home Again*. Colin Clout was his name for himself. The Shepherd of the Sea had suffered, "great unkindness and usage hard," at the hands of Cynthia, Lady of the Sea, before Spenser and Ralegh read the *Faerie Queene* together.

> "When thus our pipes we both had wearied well,
>   (Quoth he) and each an end of singing made
> He gan to cast great lyking to my lore,
> And great dislyking to my luckless lot.
> That banished had my selfe, like wight forlore,
> Into that waste, where I was quite forgot.

> The which to leave, thenceforth he counseled mee,
> Unmeet for man, in whom was aught regardful,
> And wend with him, his Cynthia to see."

When at last he stood before his Queen he saw her as wonderful as his fondest fancy; like to a crown of lilies upon a bride's head, gay with roses, golds and daffodils, nay more; earthly symbols fail before one divine—she was even "The image of the heavens in shape humane."

Elizabeth heard and liked all. From her touched vanity she granted Spenser a pension of fifty pounds. To be sure he had to struggle with Burghley, nearly dead of gout and caring not a whit for poetry, before the sum was paid, until each time the annual battle was staged, he hated Burghley more thoroughly. At length he squared matters with the Lord Treasurer in the *Ape and the Fox.*

> "No reach, no breach, that might him profit bring,
> But he the same did to his purpose wring."

The *Faerie Queene* was entered in the register of the Stationer's Company on December 1, 1589, the date of the entry couched in Latin, the rest in English, a poem in twelve books, of which three were ready.

Ralegh knew how to float such matters. Every approach must be in good form and point device. Patronage of the right sort spelled success. The published form should be introduced by a host of commendatory poems. Hatton, Essex, Oxford, Northumberland, Cumberland, Ormond, Howard of Effingham, Grey of Wilton, Burghley, Norris, Walsingham, and Ralegh himself were each addressed to befriend the work. When all the panoply was arranged the attack upon the courtly world began by publication in 1590.

Ralegh had not given up his dream of Virginia. He had taken Spenser under his wing and his experience betrayed to him a golden opportunity. He saw to it that the dedication to Elizabeth read: "Queene of England, France, and Ireland, and of Virginia." No monetary check would be for him a permanent defeat. He had leased his rights of trade in America, but all other privileges were still his. In days to come he would find means to his end, when it was once certain Philip could not control the seas between. He saw it as one of the four dreams of power left to him, for he was maturing there in Ireland, perhaps conscious for the first time of fleeting youth. Yet he tinged even his dream with stratagem; he saw to it that Elizabeth was reminded of his Virginia and of her Sir Walter Ralegh. He contrived too that Spenser bowed not too humbly, but presented his work to the Queen, "To live with the eternitie of her fame."

Since he was to ride back into favor on the wings of the poet, Ralegh flung himself wholeheartedly into a sonnet in praise of Spenser.

> "Methought I saw the grave where Laura lay,
>   Within that temple where the vestal flame
>   Was wont to burn; and passing by that way,
> To see that buried dust of living fame,
>   Whose tomb fair Love and fairer Virtue kept,
>   All suddenly I saw the Fairy Queen,
>   At whose approach the soul of Petrach wept,
> And from thenceforth those graces were not seen,
> For they this Queen attended; in whose stead
> Oblivion laid him down on Laura's hearse.
> Hereat the hardest stones were seen to bleed,
> And groans of buried ghosts the heavens did pierce:
> Where Homer's spright did tremble all for grief,
> And cursed the access of that celestial thief."

In answer, as to a patron, one of several sonnets Spenser wrote and printed at the end of his masterpiece:

> "To thee that are the Summer's Nightingale,
>   Thy Sovereign Goddess's most dear delight,
>   Why do I send this rustic Madrigal,
> That may thy tuneful ear unseason quite?

> Thou only fit this argument to write
> In whose high thoughts Pleasure hath built her bower,
> And dainty Love learned sweetly to indite.
> My rhymes I know unsavoury and sour,
> To taste the streams that, like a golden shower,
> Flow from the fruitful head of thy Love's praise;
> Fitter perhaps to thunder martial stowre,
> Whenso thee list they lofty Muse to raise;
> Yet, till that thou thy Poem wilt make known,
> Let thy fair Cynthia's praises be thus rudely shown."

Thereby did Spenser let out the secret of Ralegh's months in Ireland. It would take Elizabeth's fancy that while her favorite had been far from court she had never been out of his thoughts. Fifteen thousand lines of a poem of praise Ralegh had written to the glory of his Queen. "I do express her in Belphœbe, fashioning the name according to your own excellent conceit of Cynthia," wrote Spenser. A gorgeous tapestry these two wove amid the open wastes about Kilcoman, seated there in the island graveyard of reputations, fashioning a net of fancy in which to snare Elizabeth even against her will.

Cynthia was never published. Elizabeth may never have seen it. Ralegh's court circle may not have had it passed among them. All that has come down are fragments—five hundred sixty-eight verses of a manuscript entitled, *"The Twenty-first and last book of the Ocean, to Cynthia."* Dates, proportions, sub-themes, incidents, allegory: all are matters of scholarly conflict. The two poems were similar in theme. Cynthia never emerged beyond a prodigious conceit, talked of by Spenser as a reality known to him. The *Faerie Queene*, carried out of Ireland to the court, did all that the two scheming in solitude could hope.

Ralegh had written other poetry. Every one in the court, except Francis Bacon, turned out verse at will. Popular, academic, and courtly poets were finding their voices. Marlowe, the shoemaker's son, who went to Cambridge a dozen years after Ralegh had left Oxford for the war, was in his hey-day of lilting music and bombast. The collegians, such as Gabriel Harvey, were seeking after classical English, learned rather than natural, resulting in an astonishing bastardy of word and figure. At court, John Lyly, heart sick at hope deferred, entered parliament in 1589, a decade after he had presented the court his *Euphues* and set up an extravagant style well suited to Elizabeth's theatrical tastes. Couched in metaphorical conceits, wrapped in exaggerated allegory, Lyly's manner fastened itself upon the court. He was the Earl of Oxford's man; that would have been enough to put the hand of Ralegh against him, and in addition he was slight, elegant, but without loftiness and always exaggerated in manner. Ralegh's poetry was like his glance, a little too straight, damnably pointed, and independent in viewpoint.

Marlowe celebrated youth and the blessing of rural life with genuine gusto.

> "Come, live with me and be my love,
> And we will all the pleasures prove,
> That grove or valley, hill or field,
> Or wood and sleepy mountain yield.
>
> Where we will sit on rising rocks,
> And see the shepherds feed their flocks
> By shallow rivers, to whose falls
> Melodious birds sing madrigals.
>
> Pleas'd will I make thee beds of roses,
> A twine a thousand fragrant posies;
> A cap of flowers, and rural kirtle,
> Embroidered all with leaves of myrtle.
>
> A jaunty gown of finest wool,
> Which from our pretty lambs we pull;
> And shoes lin'd choicely for the cold,
> With buckles of the purest gold.

A belt of straw, and ivy buds,
With coral clasps, and amber studs;
If these, these pleasures, can thee move,
To live with me, and be my love!"

So ran Marlowe's poem, delightfully pastoral, full of Elizabethan freshness. It was first published in 1599 in company with Ralegh's answer but had been written long before and must have been circulated orally for a long time. Marlowe himself referred to this poem in his *Jew of Malta* in a comic speech in the fourth act, and Marlowe too was dead in 1593. Ralegh's reply must have been written close to his days with Spenser, since he was not a man to answer the dead.

"If all the world and love were young,
And truth on every shepherd's tongue,
These pleasures might my passion move
To live with thee, and be thy love.

But fading flowers in every field
To winter floods their treasures yield;
A honey'd tongue, a heart of gall,
Is fancy's spring, but sorrow's fall.

Thy gown, thy shoes, thy beds of roses,
Thy cap, thy kirtle and thy posies,
Are all soon wither'd, broke, forgotten,
In folly ripe, in reason rotten.

Thy belt of straw, and ivy buds,
Thy coral clasps, and amber studs,
Can me with no enticements move
To live with thee, and be thy love.

But could youth last, could love still breed;
Had joys no date, had age no need;
Then those delights my mind might move,
To live with thee, and be thy love."

There was the answer, realist to romanticist, yet both poems possessing beauty and of a simple sort. Sensuous and passionate too was Ralegh in those short poems he wrote to be read by his friends. None of them were published by him. Some that he did not write were named his by the world, but he did not concern himself seriously in that direction either. He was very French in the clarity of his written thought, not pedantic like the collegians, not ridiculously extravagant after Lyly, not heartened to the gushing sentiment of the popular poets. In this last he lost some of the fine, careless rapture that would have given his songs circulation with the best, but it was always as with Marlowe's pastoral verse; he saw the gleam of posies but he never forgot the dew and frost as well. Restrained, not stilted, cynical, but holding bitterness in disdain, his muse winged his words with the pride of his soul, a cavalier flirt of the cape, the proper gesture for the hour, words of force not lacking grace: these things were of him, body and soul. Oh, he could cap a phrase with a polish and reserve that looked forward to the eighteenth century.

Those years before the retreat to Ireland were years of quandary; how to add position to wealth, how to practice upon Elizabeth the maxims of the Florentine in the search for power. A time of shrewd reflection, when the Queen was but a fact.

"And Lust fell-cold, and Beauty white,[11]
Sat babbling with Desire."

To think of Elizabeth other than as a power to assuage was to overestimate the rising of young Essex. He must not warm to that. From the first he knew he must claim very little from the Queen. He had written in disdain of love,

"Hey, down, adown, did Dian sing,
Amongst her virgins sitting:
Than love there is no vainer thing,
For maidens most unfitting:
And so think I, with a down, down, derry."

At the same time he had praised chastity, for Elizabeth would bear no rival and so he earned the Queen's smile while he might. That was an asset, the first needful thing, but she was even more approachable with a new point of policy, or a quirk of government, and either was more congenial to the mind of Ralegh. Yet it was needful to play the suitor before Elizabeth, and especially to affect the despairing lover, as when Sir Walter wrote,

> "Thus those desires that aim too high
>   For any mortal lover,
> When Reason cannot make them die,
>   Discretion doth them cover.
>
> Yet when Discretion doth bereave
>   The plaints that they should utter,
> Then your Discretion may perceive
>   That silence is a suitor.
>
> Silence in love bewrays more woe
>   Than words, though ne'er so witty,
> A beggar that is dumb, you know,
>   Deserveth double pity!"

One hundred fifty years later, his last stanza was quoted in fashionable London as the words of the Earl of Chesterfield, who was then drawing all things elegant unto himself.

To make a mock passion then was to jest at his first burst of affection ten years earlier, to kill the boyish vision of the Queen seen at Hayes-Barton. Pride suffered. Sinister might be Ralegh's search for preferment, for he dared to toy with the Queen for his own esteem, but even as he played he was disgusted with the show and pretense of it. No wonder that when the fit was upon him he wrote:

> "Go, tell the court it glows,
>   And shines like painted wood;
> Go, tell the church it shews
>   What's good, but does no good.
> If court and church reply,
>   Give court and church the lie.

> Tell potentates, they live
>   Acting, but O their actions!
> Not lov'd, unless they give;
>   Not strong, but by their factions.
> If potentates reply,
>   Give potentates the lie.
>
> Tell zeal it lacks devotion;
>   Tell love it is but lust;
> Tell time it is but motion;
>   Tell flesh it is but dust:
> And wish them not reply,
>   For thou must give the lie."

He spoke with the sting of the whip lash there, recalling the high-hearted insolence of a shadow of a century before, the unforgettable François Villon and his nemesis Louis XI. It was in the spirit of both of them, that rising out of disillusion to sing the freedom of the heart. Ralegh, seeing by troubled light, which showed no path save one he scorned, yet knew to be profitable, was embittered at the prospect. The way of things as they seemed stretched miserably before him, but his vigor remained untouched, he at will struck an attitude with the best of Elizabeth's henchmen and dispraised love devotedly.

> "If love be life, I long to die,
>   Live that list for me:
> And he that gains the most thereby,
>   A fool at least shall be.
> But he that feels the sorest fits,
> 'Scapes with no less than loss of wits.
>   Unhappy life do gain,
>   Which love do entertain."

All love but of Elizabeth was treason. It was a fatal convention, which made marriage an unattainable luxury to her gentlemen and an eternal exile to her ladies. Unreasonable as she might be, through no other could the elevation to Privy Council come. Ralegh cared very little for his poetry.

It was like his stay in Ireland and his bringing Spenser to court, a stage in his battle to climb in the state. When he met the Queen, it was to find himself welcomed. Essex, the impetuous darling of the gods, had defiled the sanctuary of Elizabeth's love. There is no doubting that in some strange, grotesque fashion, he was rooted in her heart of hearts. Since the days of Alençon she had turned to the younger men. The homage was less ridiculous, not so tinged with irony, as that of their elders. Essex had played the game most like to a prince, but Lettice Knollys had loved and lost the model of all chivalry, Sir Philip Sidney; she lay siege to and conquered Essex, the personification of youth, as, at his fall, she was to capture that paragon of the mind, Sir Francis Bacon. His wayward fire had swept Essex into marriage. The Queen flared into a towering rage and eclipsed them both, although her heart and Essex's sulking repentance saved them from being blasted, while she lifted the shadow from Ralegh, receiving him again with sweetest grace. It was a respite out of which to coin his vantage and he flung himself at the moment. Forgotten were Spenser and the muses. Affairs of state swallowed him again.

CHAPTER XI

ARMS AND LOVE

THE monk Jacques Clément murdered Henry III before Paris in August, 1589, one week and seven months after the death of Catherine, the Queen mother. Henry of Navarre entered upon his fighting chance to become King, a Huguenot who was not crowned at Chartres in 1594, until he had abjured his reformed faith. As if wearied of the changing scene and confident he left a France friendly to Elizabeth, Sir Francis Walsingham closed his weary eyes, his life-long service ended. She was angry at Essex for marrying Lady Sidney. Scant shrift was given good Sir Francis in the face of the more present pique and righteous wrath. He was buried quietly, at night, that none might see his poverty. The Queen despised the viper she had nursed and she welcomed Ralegh with all her heart, yet sad to state, she showed no more than her accustomed constancy. On June 20, 1591, Essex wrote: "I am commanded into France for the establishment of the brave King in quiet possession of Normandy." He found a young man's idol in Henry IV and his campaign, heading in the siege of Rouen. He had not entirely fallen out of the Queen's grace. Ralegh found himself Vice-Admiral of a fleet, under Lord Thomas Howard, Admiral, intended to fall upon the Spanish plate ships near the Azores. Then came the discrimination: Essex was allowed to proceed, but Ralegh was relieved, and his place given to Sir Richard Grenville, although Sir Walter's own ship, the *Ark Ralegh*, with Captain Thynne on her quarter deck, sailed with the six ships of the Queen.

The Spanish menace was always in the minds of the Councillors. Not a whit had the destruction of the Armada re-

ARMS AND LOVE 141

laxed their vigilance. The English fleet was seen off the Azores. English spies sent home word the Spanish were sending out fifty-three ships to sail as convoy for the treasure and the Council sent orders to Ralegh to send off a pinnace to warn Howard. Before the pinnace could establish contact, the Spanish were upon the fleet, harbored in the Azores. Grenville covered the withdrawal with the *Revenge*, engaging five galleons with his lone ship, while five more Spaniards stood by ready to relieve. The *Revenge* lost her mast, her crew, her guns. Her very decks were cut out of her by the eight hundred shot she received. She burned three of the galleons and one was put ashore. A thousand Spaniards had died before Grenville surrendered with the guarantee that the crew would be sent to England. On board the flagship, Grenville lived three days, denying pain, refusing to quail before the sureness of death. In mad fervor, to show his captors the stuff of England, he drained his wine, then forced the glass between his teeth, crushing it, only to swallow the pieces, while the blood gushed from his mouth. Strange barbaric ecstacy that, as he watched death stalking up to him through all his three days.

Ralegh, waiting in England, soon had the news. On poor terms with the Howards, knowing the swaggering, stubborn nature of Sir Richard, his cousin, he wrote the *Report of the Truth of the Fight about the Isles of Azores*. In November, less than two months after the fight, he published his account anonymously. The Admiral, Sir Thomas Howard, he praised for his wisdom, defending him against the charge of abandoning Grenville. The Spanish he never spared, still less when he was telling the story of his own cousin's death. Their pride he spat upon, a ruthless people, knowing only ambition: "As if the Kings of Castile were the natural heirs of all the world." In full Florentine flight Ralegh painted them as a blot upon the earth. They had not returned their captives as promised. He wept over their wastage of three millions of the natural people of Hispaniola. "The obedience even of the Turk is easy and a liberty, in respect of the slavery and tyranny of Spain." He knew the story of Moorish captives in Barbary. Was he thinking of that? Spain had conspired with every nation against England, which she hated as a rival, but even more because England had revealed the truth, unfolding the Spanish, "weakness we have discovered to the world." If England would be quits let her set her eyes upon the colonial empire to be had for the taking. Grenville's example pointed out what odds the Spanish had to hurl against one little ship if they would win. This defiant gospel, launched with honest fervor, he poured forth in plain English. Short and crisp, his martial periods fell upon the ears of the populace, for it was for the people he was writing, no Euphuistic court circle of far-flying folk.

So he stayed at home and wrote, but Elizabeth had rewarded him for his self-denial. Down in Dorset, a bishopric had stood vacant three years. Whoever became Bishop of Salisbury would have to buy his office by leasing the estate of Sherborne to the Crown. At last, in January, 1592, Doctor Coldwell accepted the conditions, signing over the castle and grounds to the Crown for ninety-nine years. At once Elizabeth assigned the lease to Ralegh, who gave his Queen a jewel worth two hundred fifty pounds. Some felt such dealing sacrilege, but it was ever her way to reward easily. Harington spoke much of the truth when he said, "She considers it of the first importance that she should live peaceably and pleasantly and pass her days in well being." However, Ralegh had a property to set off even his pride, and Howard had not won great success; Sir Walter had rather the better of the luck. The year that had just closed had been a worrisome one for the government. The Privy Council had met almost daily. In a year they convened on forty-seven of the fifty-two Sundays. Foreign affairs were by no means stable, and the aim of the throne easy to foresee.

Out of uncertainty came word at last. Philip had sent to sea a fleet of sixty ships, reputed to aim at Plymouth. Ralegh begged Elizabeth to strike at Panama, with a chance of taking the plate ships as well as sacking the town. He offered his *Roebuck*. His brother Carew Ralegh tendered the galleon *Ralegh*. Merchants of London proffered two ships. Cumberland lent six. The Queen bought the *Ark Ralegh* from Sir Walter for five thousand pounds. He sank every penny he had in the venture. London furnished six thousand pounds and Elizabeth eighteen hundred pounds. What had begun as an empty intention, timely though it was, turned into a reality, a fleet with Ralegh as its General. Elizabeth, as usual, wavered. Should Ralegh go? Should Ralegh stay? From March to May she dallied. The west wind waxed and failed. The time to attack Panama soon passed. Ralegh was worn out by her. On May 6, 1592, Sir Walter dropped down from Gravesend, outward bound. The next day he was brought to by Frobisher, who had overtaken him with orders from the Queen to return. Four days, through heavy weather, he pushed southward, until he could watch the clouds drift across the stark lift of Finisterre. In plain sight of the Spaniards, half his fleet cruised the coast, while the rest sailed for the Azores, hoping to fall in with the plate fleet. With these, his last orders obeyed, he turned back, doubtless knowing what awaited him in London. Frobisher, the hardest case of all the Elizabethan bullies, carried on in his stead, with Sir John Burgh to help.

2

She was tall and slender, the daughter of a faithful knight, and herself a maid of honor. Her eyes were blue, her hair golden. She was fair and fit to be a hand maiden to any monarch. She wore her jewels delightfully, but with caution as was wise so close to the jealous Queen. Later, she was even fairer in a close-bodied gown, satin, white flowered with black, sleeves close drawn to the wrist, a lace wisp lifting above her shoulders, a bosom bared, and upon its whiteness, a jewelled pendant hanging from a pearly chain about her neck, at her ears, ruby clasped pearl drops, while over all she wore a mantle tufted on the arms. In attendance she was wise in the way of her duty, for she was the daughter of Sir Nicholas Throckmorton and knew the foibles of her royal mistress by rote.

Ralegh cared little for the three or four gentlewomen of the bedchamber, or the seven or eight gentlewomen of the privy chamber. As for the half dozen maids of honor, "like witches, they can do hurt, but no good." Elizabeth Throckmorton bent his proud will and he paused for dalliance in his coming and going about the business of his Queen. It was a year of love. Shakespeare was just dedicating his *Venus and Adonis* to his patron Southampton. The Countess of Pembroke was smiling upon an outburst of lyric poetry tendered her patronage, looking back, no doubt at times, upon the vestiges of old passion she had once known for Ralegh, when she was Mary Sidney, the sister of the perfect knight. Sir Walter, flashing through the court in silver armor, jewels, and satin, saw none but Elizabeth, the maid of honor, forgetting for a moment Elizabeth, his Queen. Scandal throve all in a moment, for Elizabeth yielded to his suit. Robert Cecil arraigned Ralegh's offense as "brutish," but Mistress Throckmorton was past twenty-five and had been at court some years. She knew the penalty, but Sir Walter was her man; it was like that, an attachment that lasted life long. For two years, Ralegh had enjoyed the benefits of the marriage and disgrace of Essex, yet he did not let the

Queen's prudery check the force of his passion. Vice-Chancellor, Privy Councillor, the pride of being made a peer: he snapped his fingers at them and took the woman he loved by storm. It was no blending of inexperienced youth and fancy. Sir Walter touched the maturity of forty in 1592, yet he flung his ambition away boldly, like a swaggering bully of a quarter deck, crazed by desire and denying the imminence of destruction.

In the imperial will lay doom. To love any but the Queen was blasphemous sacrilege; she expected her gentlemen to harp and carp with her at her behest, yet pause like monks at her slightest whim; to pretend to extravagant lust, yet chill the heated blood to the strictest decorum. Rough or smooth there must be no harm done in her play with the many. She was the Queen. Despite her selfish dictum, commanding the lover's gesture of all her gentlemen, love, scandal, and marriage quite naturally held their sway in her court. Dorothy Devereux fell in love with Sir Thomas Perrot, but marriage only followed the embarrassment of scandal. Leicester only married his second wife, Lettice Knollys, after discovery of their relations was inevitable, and the same was true of the Earl of Southampton when he married Elizabeth Vernon. At times, love advanced only to the scandal. Lord Pembroke amused himself with Mistress Fitton until they came upon misfortune and were flung into the tower. Their embarrassment entertained Sir Robert Cecil so hugely that, in the best of spirits, Cecil wrote Carew about them. They did not marry. The Queen was stung into great fury at each lapse. She never forgave such offenses, and usually the lady involved was never allowed to return to court. As a pose, the court affected to be shocked and pained at each exposure, especially when mentioning the matter in such letters as might reach the royal gaze. In reality, flesh and blood were too strong for prejudice. The Queen might have her theoretical virginity and welcome. As age came up unto her she clung more strictly to her demands upon the bodies and souls of her courtiers. None knew this better than Ralegh. He, who had known every intimacy of the royal presence, who had not the youth of Essex to plead; what could he hope from her with his love for Elizabeth Throckmorton discovered?

In the rosy flush of their love he seduced her. It was not an union of convenience, nor of fear, for he married her before the Queen knew of it, a thing not likely to lighten the sin in the royal eyes. "Honorariâ Reginae virgine vitiatâ, quam postea in uxorem duxit,"—having seduced a Queen's maid of honor, whom he afterwards took to wife: old Camden, writing in 1615 put the matter precisely in his Latin, all but the spirit of it, which was altogether different.

The tall, dark Captain of the Guard, heart whole, bent above the golden head in the Queen's chambers. Where all was posture and simulation he suddenly found a new taste to compliment, a hidden delight in each polite gesture. His enthusiasm, his carefree joyance, his determination that counted not costs, led him to assail the maiden. Gone was the railing cynicism of Gascoigne. Machiavelli wrote no chapters on love. The Queen focussed all passion upon herself. Sir Walter lay siege to the maid recklessly. At Hampton, at Richmond, at Greenwich; wherever the movement of the court carried them, they met secretly, knowing the rough jesting the courtiers would deal them if they learned, and hoping against hope the Queen might never know. Whatever the fears of Elizabeth Throckmorton, she doubtless felt the zest of conquest: there was but one Sir Walter Ralegh in the land. As for Ralegh; no other time in the brittle pattern of his days promised so much tenderness, warmth of heart, and the mysterious priesthood of the way of man with a maid.

When the time of need came, they wed. He would pay for that secret marriage out of his high heart and the purple and golden glamour of their joyance. Their first child would be untimely in conception. The Maid of Honor would not be maid, nor have further honor at court. The Queen might set her Captain of the Guard about and set him going, yet Sir Walter knew that his heart was proof against all that could befall them. Instead he would carry his wife with him to the far honors he longed after. His pride should not give over before the malice of a faded woman of sixty, be she devil as well as a Queen in her own right. When their secret was discovered he would make the proper reply, trust his wits for some convincing insincerity, and once Belphœbe was appeased, sweep on with the woman of his heart, past all the cruelty of the Queen whom time had surprised.

3

When Frobisher overtook Ralegh on his way to Spain and loot, Sir Walter kept the orders to himself and held on his course toward adventure. He had known his marriage would become known, but he had hoped to return to the Queen laden with spoil. Her wrath might change to greed. If only they could fall in with the Spanish fleet on the high seas, if the plate fleet could not be found. The Queen might balance love and honor if he should thrash Philip's servants. So he sailed upon the back trail from Finisterre with empty hands prepared for the worst. What had befallen his wife? Was his recall only another vexatious caprice of the Queen? He knew the time was ripe for their discovery. The path of true love was like to prove heavy going.

Once in England, the tempest roared about him. Arthur Throckmorton protested, since he could not find record of his sister's marriage; Ralegh had ruined her. Sir Robert Cecil, Sir Walter's trusted foil against Essex, dubbed his actions brutish. The Queen paid no heed to his existence.

All these things Ralegh digested within the Tower, where Elizabeth Ralegh had preceded him. It was an usual device of the Queen, a chastening of sexual urge which might return to her the attention she demanded. She left Ralegh Captain of the Guard. She made no charges to the Court of the Star Chamber. His imprisonment never became a matter of public record. She confined him in the Brick Tower with his cousin, George Carew, who had quarters there as Master of Ordnance, to answer for him. He entered the old fortress in the heyday of a British June and he watched the year grow old as he looked beyond the North Bastion into the gray light of the shortening days. It made his confinement no easier that in order to display a contrite heart he dared to pay no heed to his wife. Any letter he wrote might have been carried to the Queen. In all the correspondence of his months of imprisonment he never mentioned his wife and he administered his offices by deputy even to the estates in Ireland and Sherborne. Instead, he turned loose all the chicanery he could evolve. It was important the Queen should think of him as well nigh distraught by her unkindness. It was her vanity that was wounded. Good! He would salve it so freely that, unable to untangle the false from the true, she might be brought to a more careless frame of mind and slip the bolt of his prison. He knew well enough how Elizabeth, immured so close to him, was faring. Even so early he knew better than to trust to his cousin George Carew any written words. George preserved everything with politic care. His caution did not prevent news reaching Sir Walter all was well. Then have at the Queen for liberty.

He was still responsible for his guardsmen. He ordered coats for a royal progress and forwarded his account to Cecil, with the strangest letter ever a man of forty wrote about a woman of sixty.

"My heart was never broken till this day, that I hear the

ARMS AND LOVE

Queen goes away so far off, whom I have followed so many years with so great love and desire, in so many journeys, and am now left behind in a dark prison all alone. While she was yet nigher at hand, that I might hear of her once in two or three days, my sorrows were the less; but even now my heart is cast into the depths of all misery. I that was wont to behold her riding like Alexander, hunting like Diana, walking like Venus, the gentle wind blowing her fair hair about her pure cheeks, like a nymph; sometimes sitting in the shade like a goddess; sometimes singing like an angel; sometimes playing like Orpheus. Behold the sorrow of this world. Once amiss, hath bereaved me of all. Oh Glory, that only shineth in misfortune, what is become of thy assurance? . . . All those times past—the loves, the sighs, the sorrows, the desires—can they not weigh down one frail misfortune? . . . I am more weary of life than they are desirous I should perish."

Alexander and Orpheus—Diana and Venus! He was balancing the sexes not knowing if her mood of the moment might be mannish or womanly. She was a strange woman, not the less difficult because she could indulge her whims in her own right as Queen. She would scarcely like to think of Sir Walter in distress, if he were fortunate in finding the right words.

It was a courtly despair, but a mood he thought fit to stir again that July. His letter to Cecil was of course meant for the Queen. In the same vein he cast himself an actor. The Queen was rowing on the Thames. The Queen! George Carew would pray take him upon the river in disguise to catch a glimpse of that fairest of all faces. A sight, a poor sight, or else a heartbreak! but George would not risk it abroad with his prisoner. Out daggers, and so to it with "the iron walking" until Sir Arthur Gorges, finding the farce turning tragic, separated them, getting a slash across the knuckles for his pains. It was brave news for George to write Cecil and he made the most of it, keying his words to the spirit, "Sir Walter Ralegh will shortly grow to be 'Orlando Furioso' if the bright Angelica persevere against him a little longer." Ralegh protested he would hate Carew forever, and doubtless Cecil, hating Essex, and willing enough that Ralegh should rise from his prison to check the new favorite, let the Queen know of the fight in the Tower. False as the devil, all that, and bordering upon the mock heroic, but keyed to the fashion and the factious will of Elizabeth regnant. Even the impudent godson, Harington, and the astute Bacon, tongue guarded as he was by habit, gave their fancy free rein to leave the earth and hover amid unrealities. Usually it was most effective, but Ralegh found it did not serve.

The Admiral, Charles Howard, attempted intercession. Sir Robert Cecil brought forward Ralegh's name frequently. Nothing happened. "A prince, therefore ought always to take counsel; but only when he wishes, not when others wish," wrote Machiavell. Elizabeth was in no mood to heed aught but her own will, grown rather murky and dulled by the burden of the years. The patter of polite wordings, the rough jouncing of crude fellowship, were both stale. She was turning to young Essex as safe, because he was a mere boy. All the rest she trusted most were grown old, save Cecil, and Cecil she treated as a gnome, patronizing him for the service he could render, perhaps a trifle afraid he might not perform what he promised. None might touch her concerning Ralegh. It was well, as he put it in his dedication of his *Voyage for the Discovery of Guiana* to Howard and Cecil, he was "able to hold his soul in his teeth."

In the end his own strategy took him out of the Tower. Frobisher had haunted the Spanish cape according to his orders, while Sir John Burgh cruised to the Azores. There, twenty miles west of Flores, the *Madre de Dios*, a great carrack of more than sixteen hundred tons, tried first to run for the beach, but later was brought to bay. Her crew of eight hundred defended her for sixteen hours, a stubborn fight, ending in the darkest hours of the morning by a surrender of the ship. Nothing like the Crown of Portugal vessel had ever before been brought to England.

Madre de Dios, a dream of the Indies, homeward bound from the coast of Malabar. She was lined with rich carpets of a thousand hues, sarcenet quilts, lengths of white silk and cyprus. In her hold mingled the odors of the east: benjamin, cloves, nutmegs, civet, ambergris, frankincense. Five hundred thirty-seven tons of spices she carried. Fifteen tons of ebony were stowed on board. In chests of sandalwood, she bore rubies, pearls, amber, precious porcelain, ivory, and rock crystal. In her between decks were stowed planks of cinnamon, pots of musk, tapestries, and satins. The pepper in her was worth one hundred and two thousand pounds. The Viceroy was sending home to the King two great crosses and jewelled diamond pieces, which landed in Dartmouth on September 8, a very fitting moment; it was Elizabeth's birthday.

Immediately chaos was loosed. The commanders had fought among themselves at sea. Their crews took it up at once in port, all using the enmities as an excuse for plundering. All the dealers of London sent their jackals hustling to the harbor which began to look like a Bagdad bazaar. A strong hand was needed to guide the distribution. Cecil used a letter written by Sir John Hawkins upon Elizabeth, a letter shrewdly pointing that Sir Walter Ralegh was the only man who could save for the Queen her portion. Cecil himself sped westward, seizing any spoil he came upon, no matter in whose hands, here a golden armlet, there a crystal fork and spoon, each set with rubies. Upon his heels, still in custody, travelled Ralegh, with his keeper Blount. Morose, brooding upon the anomaly of his position, Sir Walter was met with shouts of joy at Dartmouth. Sailormen pressed about him. Sir John Gilbert wept as he embraced him. It was a delirious moment, needing a cool head.

A commission of three: Cecil, Ralegh, and William Killigrew, took stock, paid off the crews, and apportioned the shares. Here Ralegh became diplomatic. He determined to deal handsomely with his royal jailer. By her right the Queen's share was not more than twenty thousand pounds of the one hundred and forty-one thousand pounds. "Four score thousand pounds is more than ever a man presented to her Majesty as yet," wrote Sir Walter. "If God have sent it for my ransom, I hope her Majesty of her abundant goodness will accept it. If her Majesty cannot beat me from her affection, I hope her sweet nature will think it no conquest to afflict me." There was a little quirk there, a sad humor of the royal favor now no longer pristine. Ralegh's own share was thirty-six thousand pounds, the same as Hawkins's. He complained to Cecil, but cautiously, more perhaps by way of record than with any serious hope. He was not returned to the Tower. Gladly enough he retreated to Sherborne to the all too short idyll of his early married life. He cultivated his lands, adding to his buildings, became familiar with falconry, exchanging tercels with Cecil, bred horses. He went to Bath to take the waters. To Weymouth and into the wilds of Devon and Cornwall his duties carried him frequently. At times he lived in London though barred from the court.

Save for his actual appearance there his life seems to have been much what it had been for some years; feverish activity, grave responsibilities, moderate rewards in the line of duty.

CHAPTER XII

GUIANA

THE displeasure of Queen Elizabeth proved powerful. After his freedom Sir Walter looked for favor and saw only Essex, heard only of Essex, touched upon every side tokens of the Earl's success. As a member of Parliament Sir Walter thundered against the Spanish. John Best, Champion of England, performed as deputy the duties of Captain of the Guard. Private spies brought word of the Spanish fleet gathering in the ports of northern France and Ralegh offered both the information and his services as a humble volunteer, and—the irony of it—both were accepted. The Spanish did not come. Irish affairs were going from bad to worse. He wrote for the Queen expert opinions upon the matter, but another tendered them. Angered and baffled, he turned to his books, spending much time up in the tower, in his turret study of Durham House, with its prospect opening upon the Thames. There he read those Spanish histories he gathered all his life and nursed his pride.

"I also believe that he is happy whose mode of proceeding accords with the needs of the time," advised Machiavelli. To be impetuous, to be cautious, which way led fortune? Fortune, a jade to be mastered by force and heat and action, yet the Queen paid no heed to his efforts although no man was more busy in her interests. Fortune, the Queen, both women, both friends to the young. The day was so soon over then and he was still to work with a worn body and weary mind. His pride turned cold. In his histories Spanish hearts had ridden high under tropical skies and come to nothing, but that was better than this despised, shadowed existence.

He began to fit a new word to his tongue, "Guiana." This time he had followed the lust of the venturer. Not a new route to the Indies, but an overland passage through Peru: that was the way the new idea shaped itself. Peru had a heart of gold and through the veins of Guiana flowed its wealth. He knew the thrusts that had been made and the uniformly tragic end that came upon them. Long years before he had known of the city of gold, El Dorado to the Spaniards, but to "the naturals Manoa." From Spanish chronicles he knew that Oreliana had tried, had returned for a patent, and, upon his arrival in America for the second time, had sickened amid the islands and died, while his ships were tempest lashed and destroyed. After him, Diego Ordace, with six hundred men and thirty horses, had essayed, but he was killed in a mutiny on the Guiana coast. His Master of Ordnance allowed his gunpowder to blow up and was cast forth from his company. After lone struggle with the rivers and jungle, this Martines reached the city of Manoa and returned to tell its glories. Pedro de Osua, a knight of Navarre, had gone in by way of Peru, where, finding the river Oia, rising east of Quito, he had descended it toward the Amazon until from the ranks of his men rose Sergeant Agiri, seized the power and was finally slain himself. In 1594, Ralegh was ready for action. He sent out Captain Jacob Whiddon to examine the coast and the rivers leading inland, with special attention to the Orinoco, while he applied for a patent to explore and settle such countries as were not then actually peopled by other nations of Europe. By proxy it was presented and the Queen shocked him by its reception.

He hoped doubtless to be called to court to plead the matter. He was offering a tale of riches, much more entrancing than the hollow story of Virginia. Gold was the lure. Elizabeth was sure to respond to that, for wealth was never known to fail as an incentive with her, even in a fable of tropical mines. It was a swift return Ralegh was offering. He was living on a different scale of time then. Once he had thought his life was long, almost endless. He knew now it would be too short to wring profit from colonizing. There remained but the search for gold. The Queen had so often prevented his going upon quests of honor and fortune because of her desire to have him near. His plan could do no harm. It might lead to reconciliation, which even in his anger and impatience he still wanted. Then, in haste, came his patent. "To our servant, Sir Walter Ralegh," read the document. He was named neither "trusted" nor "well beloved" and he was encouraged to go to the mountains of the moon and beyond for all of her care.

Elizabeth Ralegh knew her man by then. She had seen the urge growing upon him. She wrote Sir Robert Cecil as her friend, "I hope for my sake you will rather draw Sir Walter toward the east than help him toward the sunset, if any respect to me or love to him be not forgotten. . . . I know only your persuasions are of effect with him, and held as oracles tied to them by Love; therefore I humbly beseech you rather stay him than further him. By the which you shall bind me forever." Cecil's part in the affair is shaded. If he heard the womanly plea from the writer who already knew much of distress, his efforts were of no avail. The Queen had struck at Sir Walter's pride in a new way. After receiving his patent, so given, Ralegh would have gone to Guiana had he been certain of the deadly fate which had destroyed every Spaniard who had gone before him. He knew no flinching. His health was bad. The toll of his ceaseless energy was heavy and his body was paying, but he plunged at once into the equipping of his expedition.

On February 6, 1595, he sailed by the way of the Burlings

and the Rock to the Canaries, a fast passage of nine days, not bad for a winter sailing. By March 22, he had crossed the Atlantic to Trinidad, where the Spaniards had long been. Once upon the anchorage of Punto de Gallo the wonders of the new world broke upon him. It was a lush land, very different from the sand and pines of Virginia. It was a new America, only ten degrees north of the line, fired by tropical heat, flaming with sunrises lepidoltic in mauve and rose. His little argosy, paid for largely from his own means, seemed puny and futile against the savage fecundity of the life at hand. He remembered gratefully that Charles Howard had lent him the *Lion's Whelp*, but he pondered more that, should he die before the defiance of this brazen land, his wife and son had not three hundred marks a year left them. His company of one hundred included his nephew John Gilbert, his cousin Captain John Grenville, and such hardy men of experience as Keymis and Whiddon, yet it was but a handful. His purpose was threefold under his commission. He might discover and subdue heathen lands, not the possession of a Christian prince, nor inhabited by any Christian people. He was empowered to resist and expel by force of arms all persons who should attempt to settle within two hundred leagues of the place where he and his people should establish themselves within six years of the granting of the commission. All foreign ships trading within the territory of his domain might be taken. The land laughed at his pretensions, but Ralegh looked upon the raw, high colors with sceptical eyes, disregarded the myriad threats, and fell to work in Trinidad.

Don Antonio de Berreo had spent twelve years of his life upon the coast. He had been sitting in Trinidad when Captain Whiddon had called upon his scouting voyage. He still sat in his new city of S. Joseph when Ralegh landed. Berreo knew many things. He understood how to sell in the West Indian Marguerita, for one hundred fifty pesos, Orinoco maidens who cost him four hatchets apiece. Perceiving that Whiddon's arrival announced the possibility of visitors at any time, he sent to Spain for troops five months before Ralegh landed. Conscious that Guiana was threatened, he had dispatched runners to his son in Nuevo Reygno with orders to levy all the forces he could and come down the Orinoco to Emeria in readiness for defense of the port of Guiana, as he deemed the town. All that Berreo did Ralegh learned and judged. When Whiddon had called, Berreo had betrayed eight Englishmen. Should Ralegh leave his ships at Trinidad and venture to the mainland in boats of little draft as was necessary, he would have at S. Joseph an enemy able to cut off his communication at any moment. Before he went that four hundred miles he must destroy S. Joseph.

When the guard was assembled one evening, Ralegh attacked and killed every soldier. By morning the town was taken and burned and Berreo on board, "stricken into a great melancholy and sadness," and using "all the arguments he could to dissuade me," but Ralegh would not give over. Safe from attack in the rear, he set off with his one hundred fighting men in five boats: an old *gallego* cut down to a galley, a barge, two wherries, and a ship's boat. They had food for a month. It was a rough traverse. "All driven to lie in the rain and weather, in the open air, in the burning sun, and upon the hard boards and to dress our meat, and to carry all manner of furniture in them, wherewith they were so pestered and unsavory, that what with victuals, being mostly fish, with the wet clothes of so many men thrust together and the heat of the sun, I will undertake there was never any prison in England that could be found more unsavoury and loathsome." No scented court life this, yet Ralegh went on musing upon the words of Francisco Lopez. "All the vessels of his house, table and kitchen, were of gold and silver. . . . He had also ropes, budgets, chests and troughs of gold and silver, heaps of billets of gold that seemed wood marked out to burn. . . . Yea, and they say the Incas had a garden of pleasure in an island near Puna, where they went to recreate themselves when they would take the air of the sea, which had all kinds of garden herbs, flowers and trees of gold and silver, an invention till then never seen." For a dream Ralegh suffered the reeking galley, carrying sixty men through a choppy sea, checked by current and wind. At last they came up with the coast and entered the labyrinth of rivers. An Indian pilot lost them among broken islands and drowned lands. They called him Ferdinando; was it out of mockery of the Jonah-like Spaniard of the Virginia voyage? When Ferdinando failed they captured another. Soon Ralegh was persuading his company they had to suffer but a day or two more. Strange fruits, flowers, and trees they spied. "Birds of all colors: some carnation, some crimson, orange tawny, purple, green" flew from the barking of their fowling pieces. The river opened out into more open country, plains stretching away twenty miles, groves of trees unchoked by jungle.

The food ran low but two canoes laden with bread were chased and when the crews abandoned them the English examined the banks, trying to discover the natives. They found a refiner's basket containing quicksilver and saltpeter. This threatened that the Spaniards were close, but also promised they were approaching the land of gold. This cheering knowledge with the captured bread and a find of tortoise eggs upon a sand bar heartened them all. So they came out upon the main course of the Orinoco. An east wind helped them and they sailed past islands upon the river they estimated to be thirty miles wide. The tired rowers rested gratefully, gathering their strength. The banks sharpened to bluffs "for the most part stony and high, and the rocks of a blue metallic color, like unto the best steel ore, which I assuredly take it to be." The next day, the banks showed a very perfect red and very soon the mountains began to loom for they had reached the port of Morequito. At every stop they had denounced the Spaniards to the natives. At Morequito they begged the King of Arromaia, whose nephew Berreo had killed, to come to them. He was an old man and weak and "was every day called for by death," in his own phrase, but he walked fourteen miles and brought his household to make a feast. They had venison, pork, hens, chickens, fish, and stores of bread and wine. They gave Sir Walter an armadillo. He had heard of it and its horny armor. "Monardus writeth that a little of the powder of that horn put into the ear cureth deafness." King Topiawari discussed his neighbors very frankly, but left the English the same day and Ralegh pushed on to the west, exploring one and another of the four hundred odd rivers that fed the Orinoco. The season was over. The rivers began to rise. The expedition made a try or two at travelling afoot, but all was too huge for them. They dropped down to Morequito where Ralegh and Topiawari had a solemn conference. It was then the old man confessed the fear of the Spanish. They had murdered his nephew. They would murder him. For seventeen days they had once led him about like a dog at the end of a chain. Even though Ralegh should return the following year, he, Topiawari would be dead, but he would send his son into England. Sir Walter agreed to leave Francis Sparrow to learn of the land, and a boy, Hugh Goodwin, to learn the language. No nearer could Topiawari be brought to joining forces with the English in a thrust at Manoa, the strength of the place was so great in the eyes of the old King, and the vengeance of the Spanish and Incas so certain.

The return trip was hurried. One hundred miles or more a day, the quickening rivers carried them seaward. The weather was foul. Terrible thunder, nights of storm, deafening showers, the discomfort of tossing in small boats upon angry streams: the gamut of Guiana seemed full of terror. At the very end, at the mouth of the Capuri, they spent a ghastly night, but a little after midnight Sir Walter picked his way out to sea over the sands, where for two leagues there was no more than six feet of water. It was wild work but he reached the harbor of Curiapan at nine next morning. "Now that it hath pleased God to send us safe to our ships, it is time to leave Guiana to the sun, whom they worship, and steer away to the north."

So the land of wonders was left behind them with its round mountains of minerals, its jutting white spar, its cranes and herons, its tiny parakeets and unafraid deer. He had lost one man, a negro eaten in the river of Lagartos, by a lagarto, of course, which Ralegh defined as an ugly serpent. He had moved among the river people without stirring any serious enmity. It had taken severe discipline, for he had to preserve the respect of the savages. "Fear and the absence of hatred may well go together, and will always be obtained by one who abstains from interfering with the property of his citizens and subjects or with their women," wrote Machiavelli and Ralegh followed, "for I suffered not any man to take from any of the nations so much as a pina, or potato root, without giving them contentment, nor any man so much as to offer to touch any of their wives and daughters." His men had opportunities offered, for they often had the native women in their power, "and of those very young and excellently favored, which came among us without deceit stark naked." None can doubt the discipline must have been blameless, else how could he have brought his company safely off in spite of heat, wet, filth, exposure, decayed food, and constant fear of surprise from a land of awe?

The marvels lurked at every turn. In Trinidad he found trees upon the banks of one salt river, in the boughs of which oysters were growing. "This tree is described by Andrew Thevet in his *French Antarctic* . . . and Pliny in his twelfth book of his *Natural History*." Nearby he came upon stone pitch, enough to load all the ships in the world, an asphalt-like substance that did not ooze under the sun as Norway pitch would. He heard of Amazons living in the district of Topago, but he saw none.

Cannibals inhabit the region west of the Caroli, and near them lived the headless ones, Ewaipanoma, who "are reported" to have their eyes in their shoulders and their mouths in the middle of their breasts. Sir Walter did not see them. He did not even affirm belief, but he cautioned that the fables of travel written by Mandeville had for the most part proven true. The matter was trifling. More important by far was the riddle of the poisoned arrows. Not only did they kill, but the victim suffered the agony of the damned; going mad with pain, the body broken by the terrible paroxysms. Ordinary venom could be overcome by a *tupera* juice, which quenched the fever. The Guianians taught Sir Walter their secret cures for all poisoned wounds. In a single journey he had gotten closer to them than Berreo in twelve years, for the Spaniard could never learn the antidotes and treatment necessary to save the life of the wounded.

In a few months Ralegh had gained an accurate idea of the nature of the country. He had gone three hundred miles into the interior by unknown water courses. The animals, vegetation, topography: nothing escaped the study of the travellers. With meager equipment they carried home general truths that were indisputable. Once in England, Ralegh wrote them at the end of his account of the journey. Guiana had never been sacked. The graves were inviolate, the images in their temples, the mines untapped. It could easily be invaded. Three or four thousand soldiers as garrison would be able to hold the land, which would yield one hundred pounds per soldier annually. It could be easily captured, but once taken, two forts on the river would be able to protect it forever. The woods were so thick as to be impassable. The one entrance by sea was shoal and the channel would lead directly under the guns of a properly planted fortress. To cap the matter, there was a prophecy in the temples of Peru that out of Inglatierra should come redemption. Ralegh knew who would read his account.

His attitude towards the Queen was by no means cringing. He came from Guiana a "beggar and withered" yet somewhere he had found courage. His pride never rang truer. "Her Majesty should either accept or refuse the enterprise, ere anything should be done that might in any sort hinder the same." A generality that, yet one that does not sound like pleading, but holds instead the shadow of a thrust of independent action. "To speak more at this time, I fear would be but troublesome: I trust in God this, being true, will suffice, and that He which is King of all Kings and Lord of lords will put it into her heart which is lady of ladies to possess it; if not, I will judge those men worthy to be Kings thereof that, by her grace and leave, will undertake it of themselves."

By late summer he was in London. On October 9, Doctor Dee dined with him at Durham House. Ralegh had a way of gathering up the threads of all that had happened in his absence. There was almost no news. In the court it was as if he had died. His enemies said he had never sailed. Cecil was noncommittal. The assay of some of the gold he had brought home proved it good and of a high degree of purity. He published his *Discovery of Guiana*, which was read hungrily. Four German translations, six Dutch, and two Latin were made at odd times. Court and city talked of it. Shakespeare read it. The twin mountains near Morequito, the cannibals, the Ewaipanomas, these things clung to the playwright until, when he wrote Othello, perhaps in 1604 or 1605, he lets the Moor say in his travel's history,

> "Rough quarries, rocks and hills whose heads touch heaven,
> It was my hint to speak—such was the process;
> And of the Cannibals that each other eat,
> The Anthropophagi, and the men whose heads
> Do grow beneath their shoulders."

He may have known about that: Ralegh in his myriad friendships would have known Shakespeare. He could never have read *Othello* in print, for he was four years dead before a copy appeared. The *Discovery* was one of the three books Ralegh published himself. His Queen was blind and deaf. Then his enemies prepared ships. He asked Cecil to check them, beseeching the government to take it up. In the first days of 1596, he sent Captain Keymis with two ships, but Berreo had moved to check him where the Caroni fell into the Orinoco. He had moved into an old Jesuit settlement of St. Thomas and his batteries closed the country against all comers. Keymis was back in England by July, all of Ralegh's funds spent and all news from Guiana bad except the faithfulness of the native chiefs to Sir Walter.

2

The age was swinging toward its later days. The ghost of the murdered Mary Stuart had laid forever the gay and careless frankness of the court. Some of the heart of Elizabeth had withered at that deed. She welcomed the mask of fantastic formal manners. It pleased her to hide in disguise the wounds of her nature, self inflicted out of the need to rule with safety. She could not be a perfect Machiavellian. There was for her, as for the others, a changing world. She joyed in no more days at Ely House with Hatton. Poor Walsingham would receive her no more at Barn Elms, offering her, out of the means she neglected to make ample, his poor best. Death was coming up with them, these men of hers. The gaiety of her reception at Theobalds, with the quiet speech of the far-sighted Burghley, that too was remote, if time ever brought it again. The Lord Treasurer was an ill man, already moving off almost as far as the portly wraith of Leicester, whom all but she had forgotten. She had left to her the welcome of Keeper Puckingham at Kew, which was fusty, and the entertainment of Francis Bacon at Twickenham. She feared young Bacon. His glance was feral and his mind stupendous. These changes made one too clearsighted to be able to weigh motive and action. Mortality against immortality, with death between. She wanted to forget that and Mary Stuart.

Out of her fear she sometimes lightened her mood as when she added a postscript to a letter to Willoughby on the continent. "My good Peregrine, I bless God that your prosperous successe followithe youre valiant acts, and joy not a little that safety accompanythe your luck. Your loving Soverain. E. R."[12] That was about the same time Essex entered Compiègne, mounted, clad in orange-colored velvet trimmed with gold lace, six pages before him. For himself, he was resplendent in a great cape of the same orange velvet, strewn with precious stones, which covered him and his horse. Six trumpeters sounded before him, twelve squires rode with him, while at his heels thronged sixty English gentlemen. Henry IV came to him, cordial, but worn and shabby beside this splendor. Essex was a figure to think upon, a prop for faith, a heart for love, yet always longing for action.

They all were like that to the eye of Elizabeth. Howard of Effingham had said, "I had rather lyve in the company of these noble shyps than any place." Ralegh had turned a moment's service with his seadogs into freedom, and a far fling at Guiana and scarcely seemed to miss the court. That man strode like a god. Cecil said he was living about London until the royal sun should shine. He even dared to censure her when he wrote the account of his journey. She had made no mistake in keeping him in check. This scandal of marriage, God's blood, but the court knew not how that seemed to her. The man foresaw so much, yet heeded nothing. No man brought more news of Spain to court. None had hazarded more than the Guiana shot in the dark. She could not at once give way. She would see Howard and Essex. "Walter" should be tamed, but he might serve.

CHAPTER XIII

OVER SPANISH SEAS

CHRISTMAS came to Mile End and caught Sir Walter loitering in London. What was the good of going up and down to be seen, consorting with poets, astrologers, soldiers, and philosophers, if none of it was to find the Queen's ear. The year was dying, and for all his heavy waiting she had made no sign. Their hearts—their souls—all that was gilded nonsense. He was forty-three and weary, with no flame to tender her. Anything else went wide. She dallied with Essex after the old pattern, for he was topping twenty-nine. Sir Walter wrote Cecil of sixty ships Philip intended to set upon Ireland, wrote the members of the Privy Council that Philip would cross into England from Brittany when Spring came back, wrote Admiral Howard to plead for a resolution from the Queen for a new enterprise of Guiana. He refused to acknowledge the royal displeasure; to confess it would have violated his bond of faith. True, all attempts at return to favor might prove futile but absolute silence in itself denied the Queen's forgetfulness of him.

Elizabeth was remembering so many things. The wraith of the crushed armada of Philip rose to disturb her. She felt the Spanish anger as a hot breath upon her neck. She turned to Denmark, but King Christian refused her demand for eight ships and admonished her he had treaties with Spain. Elizabeth turned to the Lowlands. The Dutch owed her money. She offered to delay the payment if they would lend her ships. They agreed eagerly and preparations to sail against the Spanish began at once. Elizabeth would lay her fears in the dust of new ruin for Philip.

More than ninety ships were fitted out, in addition to the

twenty-four of the Dutch fleet. Fourteen thousand Englishmen, one thousand of them gentlemen volunteers, and twenty-six hundred Netherlanders were enrolled. Elizabeth commissioned Essex and Howard in joint command. Vere and Clifford for the army, Sir Thomas Howard and Sir Walter Ralegh for the navy, and Sir George Carew, Lieutenant of Ordnance were appointed as a council of war. The two commanders were required to accept the advice of a majority of these councillors at any time. Burghley's draft of instructions was very clear. The commanders were to destroy ships and stores in the Spanish harbors, and to plunder the enemy.

Ralegh had succeeded. Guiana was not thrown away. He breathed freely at last and smiled—at the foolish division of command. Conceived by Howard, delivered by Essex, the idea was amply cared for by Ralegh. Sir Thomas Baskerville had sent into England word of the death of Hawkins and Drake, as he brought home their shattered fleet from American waters. He was ordered not to go into Plymouth where the forces of Howard and Essex were gathering, but as soon as the returned West Indian crews got ashore, their story went the rounds discouraging the best efforts of Ralegh who was recruiting forces. Even pressing men was not simple; there were so many slips between seizing them and getting them on board. Ralegh and Sir Thomas Howard were busy daily, plying the river, "dragging in the mud from one alehouse to another," coming up with the hidden sailors only to find them fled into privateersmen where, by the law, they could laugh at the press gang. The defeated men of Drake and Hawkins were only partially paid off. Sailormen wanted nothing in the Queen's ships. It was hard work for Sir Walter. While the Lord Admiral Howard and Essex waited at Plymouth, Burghley composed a proclamation and had them promulgate it. The intent and purpose of the Queen's government was announced to the world. Printed in

French, Italian, Dutch, and Spanish it was circulated in the Spanish ports. All goods that helped the enemy were contraband and those dealing in them were invited to leave Spanish cities. Essex, not to be outdone by Burghley, compiled a number of articles defining the duties of all officers and had a third document, containing a body of rules for the general discipline of the fleet, drawn up by John Young, an old captain, long at sea. The expedition promised to be well regulated. Still Ralegh scurried about London.

The Queen sent down a prayer which Cecil thought "divinely conceived by her Majesty ... conceived in the depths of her sacred heart ... purposely indicted by His spirit in His annointed Queen." This was to be used regularly wherever the fleet should sail. It was read, translated, and dispersed in far-off Venice, teaching many Venetians that the barbaric English knew of Christ. She was not so fortunate in her leavetaking of the beloved Essex. She had vacillated hither and yon as usual, like a reed shaken in the wind. Her petulance had no room for encouragement at the farewell. "Your unkind dealing the very day of my departure doth stick very deeply in my heart and soul," Essex wrote her, a message to breed remorse should his deeds result fatally for himself. Perhaps he liked the injured air of self-immolation. He was only twenty-nine, Master of Horse, but far beneath his colleague in rank. Howard was sixty and Lord Admiral. The five councillors were all of Howard's war-tried stock. They would crucify the Earl's best intent and his Queen had quarrelled with him. He rode hard from London to Plymouth, making it the fourth day, "weary in body and mind," but he still had to wait for Ralegh.

At last, the fleet was manned and divided into four squadrons in command of Lord Admiral Howard, Essex, Lord Thomas Howard, and Sir Walter Ralegh. Van Duvenvoord commanded the Dutch in a ship of four hundred tons. The soldiers were a fine lot of men, volunteers. The sailors were poor, all impressed, and not of the best to begin with.

Ralegh went to sea in splendor. His cabin was sumptuously furnished, hung with pictures, graced with books. His bedstead was generous, covered with green silk, and served by gilded dolphins as posts. With it went on board his famed dolphin chair. He was often seasick on service; that could not be helped, but he would have what comfort might be. Time was difficult at sea, but profitable to a contemplative mind. He was sailing with much to think upon, but meanwhile, below the sea rim, waited Spain where dreams blossomed. Great fortifications were conceived throughout that land and often partially built, only to lie fallow and disused. Huge galleons of more than a thousand tons, the fleet of the "Twelve Apostles," one for each of the Saints of Christ's fellowship, were designed, but battle never saw the splendid dozen leading the line. The Escorial itself escaped the perfection of Philip's vision. Spain, the monster bestriding the world, yet the realm where the end of every effort lay locked within the veil of tomorrow!

2

The *Warspite* spreading Sir Walter Ralegh's flag, all white, at the head of his twenty-two ships. The *Ark Royal*, the Lord Admiral's flagship, scarred from her service against the armada, unfolding Howard's crimson banner. Essex leading his division in the *Due Repulse,* his orange tawny colors waving in the off shore breath beyond the hoe at Plymouth. Lord Thomas Howard displaying his blue emblem above the *Mere Honour*, the fourth of the fleet commanders. With them, keeping company, the new *Neptune* of four hundred tons, Dutch in every line of her and carrying the Netherlander Van Duvenvoord, Admiral of England's allies.

A "navy beautiful to behold" sailing in close order, a cloud of canvas against the sky, keeping station at the wind's will. Scouts flying ahead, to capture any who spied the fleet. Behind, Plymouth wondering, spies questioning, Elizabeth fretting she had let the ships sail, Burghley counting up the Queen's money against the day of reckoning.

Three Dutch flyboats, two weeks out from Cadiz, hanging upon the flanks of the scouts cannot make off from them. News, news they bring. The harbor of Cadiz is full of ships. King Philip is sick, almost dying. Good luck, Van Duvenvoord! Good luck, Englishmen! Nineteen days the ships keep company, at first the weather checking them. Ralegh is sorrowful at the delay, feeling deeper grief than for anything in this world, but the weather settles, the wind comes fair. At evening of the nineteenth day, shadows upon the skyline lift, then scurry away, racing before the fleet. Ralegh tries to overtake them, but they are lost in the night. The invaders draw together, the better to aid each other.

The sea ghosts race into Cadiz, smart sailers telling of the British coming. Cadiz has twelve hours. Philip is sick. The land is in chaos. All the officials want to act. None can find the authority. There is a wild scurrying all over Andalusia. The English are near. Reports conflict. Medina Sidonia, governor of the district, remembers the icy waters, the foul wind that tempers the blood of these foreign sea dogs. He shakes his head and hastens to make defense.

At dawn the fleet rises out of the sea, ghostly in the half light before the sun. Medina Sidonia does not know the *Warspite*; she is new, but he sees the *Ark Royal* and nods at her as an old enemy. The townsfolk are all aflutter. The bells in the monastery of San Sebastian clang dolorously. Troops tramp resolutely into the fort at Puntal. Four of the "Twelve Apostles," newly come from their launching at Genoa, and eighteen galleys make ready for action.

A half league from the shore the English greet the morning. The city glints in the young sun, straggling along the straitened neck of shell limestone. The harbor gleams clear silver and behind lifts the beauty of the Sierra de los Gazules, Spanish mountains in reality, when anxious eyes look at the thirty West Indiamen nosing at the wharves. Cargoes of oil, wine, quicksilver, silk, powder, and shot have poured their wealth into Cadiz. Far off to the left a few ships make sail, northward bound toward Rota. Ralegh sees them and makes after. They lead him for a time, but as he heads them, they come about and run off toward the harbor. Essex, strong with young fire, looks toward the long swells breaking upon the beach of Caleta, the whole city rising right behind. He sees the town in his hand. Two boats lower away and pull to the sharpening swell. The seas crest, barely visible from seaward, but powerful, hollowed to break. The boats drive on under the thrusts of the oars, crash through into the smother, sheer drunkenly, and fill down. Eighty men drown. Essex orders more away from the ship. Slow work, launching boats in the fleet. Ralegh, sailing back from having driven the Spaniards to port, sees the bashed hulls tossing in the surf, begs the earl to desist, and sails on to ask the Lord Admiral that the attack be directed upon the ships first and the city left until later. Lord Howard wonders why he had not thought of that first, but agrees. Ralegh sails smartly to Essex, roaring out the news in passing: "Intrabimus." We shall enter. It means a hot fight within the harbor; galleons, fort, and troops greeting them with a hail of fire, but it is an action after the gallant heart of Essex. He snatches his plumed hat from his head and excitedly flings it into the sea. The day passes before the old orders can be countermanded, the boats taken back on board. The Spaniards look on amazed.

A council is held in the *Due Repulse*, the Earl's flagship.

Howard has the Queen's ships to answer for and she is a woman jealous of her own. Howard has the person of the young favorite to bring off safely, yet with honor. He dares not lead the attack himself for fear Essex should resent his presumption. Vere and Clifford are veterans ashore, but novices afloat. Sir George Carew, a man of suspicion and caution, but without brilliance in action. There will be a merry hell within the harbor, blood flying and life at no price at all. Ralegh and Thomas Howard are the men to lead the van. The night passes in preparation; the fleet a city of lanterns floating before darkened Cadiz.

"At peep of day," Ralegh and Thomas Howard stand into the harbor from the north, leadsmen in the chains. A shoaling of five fathoms deepens off to seven and then to ten good fathoms. Six feet of ebb and flow at Cadiz; no generous British tides to float them should they ground. The eighteen Spanish galleys wait such a mishap. The channel narrows. Full light comes. The four great galleons withdraw before them, anchoring under the guns of the fortress. Puntal. Ralegh cons the *Warspite* in, all cold courage, as every available Spanish gun opens upon him. The Spanish fire in well-ordered salvos. Ralegh answers each round with a snarling blare of trumpets. Ahead lay the *St. Philip* and *St. Andrew*, the galleons that did Sir Richard Grenville to death. Revenge! Ralegh's guns open. Five English ships come up and join him. The fight becomes a cannonade at anchor. The guns fire as rapidly as muskets. For three hours the battering goes on. It is worse for the *Warspite* than if she had boarded, but she is a Queen's ship and not to be risked needlessly. The flyboats, which were to board the Spaniards, did not come up. The *Warspite* can stand no more. Ralegh rows in a small boat to ask permission of Essex to board. His ship will sink if he does not, his ship may be burned if he does. Essex tries to frighten him with the wrath of Elizabeth, but yields. Essex will second him. Back on board the *Warspite* he finds Marshal Vere has put a hawser on board from the *Rainbow* and drawn ahead. Sir Thomas Howard who has left his *Mere Honour* comes up in the *Nonpareil* bringing the Lord Admiral with him, and in Ralegh's absence noses past the *Warspite*. It is a moment of strained relations.

Sir Walter will hold "single in the head of all." He orders the *Rainbow's* hawser cut. He slips his anchor. Holding his own reputation dearest, and remembering his great duty to Her Majesty, he lays out a warp to the side of the *St. Philip* since the wind does not serve to bring the ships together. The *Due Repulse* and the *Nonpareil* imitate the manœuvre. The Spanish go crazy. They slip their anchors. The *St. Philip* and the *St. Thomas* burn themselves. The *St. Andrew* and *St. Matthew* are assaulted from English boats and taken before they can be fired. Soldiers pour oversides, a human stream, fleeing from fire, wounds, capture. The Dutch flyboats butcher them mercilessly in the water. The three-hour big-gun duel is ended, but Ralegh has been grievously hurt, a blow in the leg, interlaced and deformed with splinters, but the city of Cadiz is at hand for the taking.

Five thousand burghers, one hundred fifty professional soldiers, and some eight hundred mounted gentlemen come down to resist the landing, but the English fury daunts them. Sunset finds the fighting desultory, midnight all but the citadel conquered, and dawn will see it surrendered. Ralegh has the honor, he wants to guarantee his share of the sacking. His men carry him ashore, but he cannot sit his horse or stand the jostling of the soldiers looting the town, who, "being then given to spoil and rapine, had no respect." He goes on board for the night, in much distress. In the morning he sends his stepbrother, Sir John Gilbert and Lady Ralegh's brother, to ask permission to attack a fleet reported to be bound for the Indies. Lord Howard cannot be found. Medina burns every Spanish ship in the harbor. He hates Cadiz and he hates the English.

Howard lodges Monday night in the priory, Essex in the fort. The loot is being collected, a motley sort: armor, lead, wine, church bells, carpets, raisins, tapestries, almonds. It all finds its way below hatches. Essex would stay and hold Cadiz, but the Lord Admiral gives thanks he has preserved the Earl so long and the Council of War support him. They will take Essex home to the Queen although first they will call at Faro. Here they take the volumes and manuscripts of Bishop Mascarenhas and carry them home to the newly founded Bodleian Library, together with one of the eighteen volumes in white vellum taken from the Jesuit college in Cadiz. The other seventeen are in the library of Hereford Cathedral. By August 10, the fleet is back in Plymouth, news of their work home before them. The Queen's temper has not improved. The plunder does not equal her expectations. She limits the popular reception of her heroes to London. Months of wrangling over the booty begin. Essex is preached of, at St. Paul's, as the greatest general of all time. Duvenvoord is a knight, both Essex and Howard giving him the accolade. Spanish property worth about one hundred and seventy thousand pounds has become English. The Dutch have proven themselves true enemies of Spain, establishing a breach wide as the sea between the two nations. Philip is so embarrassed by his losses that he defaults his November payment to the Florentine bankers.

Ralegh has a crippled leg and the conditions agreed upon, giving him his share of the loot, are not carried out. He has silver royals valued at thirty pounds, thirty-seven ounces of wrought plate, more than one thousand Indian hides, a half-worn Turkish carpet, nine pieces of gold hangings, some household stuff, and a chest of books. These he has by purchase, the whole worth seventeen hundred and sixty-nine pounds and five shillings. Marshal Vere has three times as much and lesser officers have shares as well, so Ralegh lifts up his voice, making no small to do about the matter. Essex is busy soothing the Queen. Howard is well pleased to bring Essex safe home. The Lord Admiral is feeling his years. Ralegh alone smiles in private and publicly voices his wrongs. To have won so much is a signal to hide his new-found wealth. The cloud has gone from the sun. Belphœbe will presently shine in all her perfect beauty, but others must not know, must not see, a shadow will else remain and wounded Ralegh lets none see his content in the days that followed upon the adventure of Cadiz.

3

From the start Ralegh has been all discretion. He aimed at being a minister, a councillor, and that out of the disgrace of a scandal ending in his marriage. He conceived of a minister in Niccolo's image, "When you see the Minister think more of himself than of you . . . such a man will never be a good minister." None knew better how the Lord Admiral would chafe to find his wisdom used as a drag upon the youthful indiscretions of Essex. Ralegh already had a reputation with the Lord Admiral as a "Captain of old." He entered under the dual command determined to win the goodwill of Essex, for that way lay the heart of Elizabeth. His friends looked on wonderingly, strangers astonished. They saw his carriage toward the Earl to be "with the cunningest respect and deepest humility." In action Ralegh looked after the welfare of the youngster, advising him cannily, leading him out of the faulty landing at Caleta, supporting him in his desires, bearing the brunt of a three-hour fight, which, so soon as Essex was likely to find at a standstill, Ralegh turned into a victory and a Spanish rout.

They marvelled at it after. George Carew, cautious, suspicious, wrote Cecil, "For Sir Walter Ralegh ... I do assure your Honour, his service was ... so much praiseworthy as those which were formerly his enemies do now hold him in great estimation; for that which he did in the sea-service could not be bettered." Sir Anthony Standen, a man of Essex's making, wrote to Burghley of Sir Walter, "I never knew the gentleman till this time: and I am sorry for it, for there are in him excellent things, beside his valor. And the observation he hath in this voyage used with my Lord of Essex hath made me love him."

Through it all Ralegh made it plain he served his Queen. When he checked Essex in his first mad dash it was for "her Majesty's future safety." When he led the attack at the order of the Lord Admiral, he refused to be headed, out of his great duty to her Majesty. Every word would fly to Elizabeth. He trusted Cecil in those days. The father had conferred with the young captain out of Ireland ten years before; the son used him to reach and overreach Essex, for Cecil had his dreams of power, Essex of hot-headed chivalry, and Ralegh of public esteem. Cecil worked upon Elizabeth's cooling anger. Essex had buried his arrogance, his petulance and joined Cecil in Ralegh's interest. Ralegh bowed as far as his pride might permit. Essex left town. Cecil took Ralegh to the Queen on June 1, 1597. Cadiz had brought its reward. She was gracious, if reserved. She was visibly older than when he saw her last, and seemed tired, not so certain of herself, nor the world about her.

In a single leap, Sir Walter was himself again. He was Captain of the Guard and came and went as boldly as ever. He filled the vacancies among his men at once. In the evening he rode with the Queen. She was never happier than when in the saddle, unless it was when dancing, and she graciously talked with him in private while they rode. It was an appeasement rather than a surrender and as full of surprise for the court as any reconciliation in that year of miracles. Cecil had made friends with Cobham after a long estrangement. Francis and Anthony Bacon were well recommended to Elizabeth by Cecil although they had been ignored before. Essex and Ralegh sat often at dinner and Cecil conferred with each of them. Men realized the old heads had gone. Tottering Burghley had upon his knees begged the Earl to deflect the Queen's anger, which he had incurred because he differed with her concerning the division of the Cadiz booty. The way for young men was open. Great stakes waited. The play left no room for minor grudges. Ralegh shook hands with Vere with whom he had quarrelled at Cadiz. Essex led them both into a new stroke against Spain.

It was one of a family of efforts. Spanish ships must sink. Spanish towns must burn. The Queen was attacked by the triumvirate and promised more government aid than usual. The Earl of Essex was in full feather, prinked in the glory of flight. He did not ask for command. Twice Francis wrote to urge him to let the honor be pressed upon him. A rumor in April became a fact in May. On June 4, 1597, the formal commission made him sole commander. Bearing seven titles of nobility and three of office, he was ordered to sea. A council of six: Lord Thomas Howard, Ralegh, Vere, Carew, Lord Mountjoy, and Sir Ferdinando Gorges, were appointed to advise him. Ten Dutch ships under Van Duvenvoord, and three squadrons under Essex, Thomas Howard and Ralegh, comprised the fleet, one hundred twenty vessels in all, which sailed from Plymouth July 10. Fair weather at sailing turned foul over night. No sooner had they gained sea room than a northeast gale ramped down upon them. The Queen's gentlemen volunteers were to learn what sea duty could be. The Earls of Rutland and Southampton, Lords Cromwell, Grey, and Rich found no silken dalliance in the buffets their ships took handily. John Donne turned from metaphysical meditation to look stark fear in the face and wrote *The Storm*. The wind veered to southwest and lashed them again. The fleet broke into a rout of flying ships and singly struggled back to English ports, all but Howard's squadron, which kept contact and pushed on to the Spanish coast. He waited for the fleet within sight of Ferrol, but when none came, he sailed home to Plymouth, fearful of what had overtaken it. Much talk went up about that. There were so many gallant gentlemen cooped up in Plymouth, their spirits chafing to come to grips with the Spanish. Essex could not afford to fail before so many critics. He conferred with Ralegh and together they rode to court.

The Queen loved success, but she listened to new plans for troubling Spain with an eye unto economy. The two favorites asked that the expedition be only naval and the troublesome troops be left ashore. The Queen thought the beginning so bad no good could come of the affair. Essex wanted to strike the Spanish fleet within the harbor of Ferrol. Elizabeth watched his gestures as he described the attack. He was gorgeous, too gorgeous to be lost by her. She forbade his leading the attack. She forbade the use of her vessels in so dangerous an undertaking. Ralegh, seeking to satisfy, offered to go in with the two "old carts" the *St. Matthew* and the *St. Andrew*, captured at Cadiz. With a few merchantmen and fire ships he hoped to ruin the Spanish. Elizabeth saw the cheapness to her and agreed, not too graciously. Essex would stand by outside to lend help and prevent interference. Elizabeth sent them back to their ships and immediately began to vacillate. She wrote them heartily. Then at sunrise on Sunday, she became obsessed of a fear Essex might attack Lisbon, wrote a letter forbidding it, and sent for Cecil. The Secretary tried to dissuade her but ended by couching her meaning in formal words and when he had finished the draft with the great "Elizabeth R" at the head, and the signet at the foot, he sent them both to Essex. So much frankness sometimes saved a man's life and he was still friendly enough to Essex to give the Earl what aid he could.

The Queen's troubled mind was not eased by the sailing on August 17. The fleet dropped down upon the Spanish coast easily enough but the easterly wind kept them at sea, standing off and on outside Ferrol. The weather turned bad. Ralegh was glad all the troops but a thousand Dutchmen had been left at home. The *St. Matthew* lost her foremast and Carew worked her into Rochelle with difficulty. The *St. Andrew* was driven helter skelter and could not be found. Ralegh, with his own main yard broken, led twenty vessels before the gale into the open sea. Ten days he knew no bed, but was constantly upon his quarter deck. He wrote Cecil of his hardships. Essex gave up the attempt against Ferrol and sailed to Flores in the Azores. He sent Sir Robert Knollys home to inform Elizabeth and placate her if possible. He made much of Ralegh's absence as an excuse for giving over the effort, yet when Ralegh joined him he "seemed to be the joyfullest man living for our arrival." The Earl was still hoping for success to make all things well, but he was preparing for failure too.

From Flores, Essex and Ralegh sailed to lay waste Fayal. Ralegh arrived first. The Spanish forts opened. The people began to flee out of their city, Horta. Essex did not come. Two Portuguese swam off to Ralegh. They told him the people would receive him gladly, and help him gain the forts. Ralegh's squadron needed water. Essex did not come. In the articles of the expedition was one forbidding any to land troops without the General's presence, or, in his absence, his order. The Earl did not come. Four days did not bring him. Ralegh's officers were angry. The Spaniards were growing better prepared every day. Ralegh did not regard the attack very seriously, but he waited so that the title of the exploit might be reserved "for a greater person." At last he gave the orders to land.

"The defense of a coast is harder than its invasion," he told his officers. Two hundred sixty seamen and volunteers went with him into pinnaces. They rowed in upon an open beach. Two to one, the Spaniards began firing. The boats slackened, the invaders questioned going in under a musketry there was no answering from the heaving boats. Ralegh watched, a little amused, then ordered his barge to the beach. The boats followed in imitation. Men jumped over, oars came in, the English were climbing over the rocks. Their guns rattled as man by man they came into action. Sir Walter knew by then he had no veterans of the older school to depend upon, men seasoned in Flanders and France. He took a leading staff and sauntered along in front without armor. The garrison in the lower fort withdrew. It was time to push on. The English would not advance. They were doing very well where they were. The Dutch soldiers who had joined them were of the same mind. Sir Arthur Gorges, Captain of Sir Walter's flagship, had come ashore with him. He wore a red scarf, Sir Walter a white. Sir Walter laughed when his men would not go forward. He understood, but the Spanish must not retreat in order. Gorges and he with eight or ten threaded their way over the strange terrain. The scarfs offered beautiful marks, and the balls clipped merrily at the rocks about them, but they found the best way through, and their men followed. With a final rattling burst of fire the Spanish abandoned the upper works and the fort. Gorges and Ralegh had carried their men successfully through a dangerous landing upon a protected beach.

The General brought the main fleet to harbor the next morning, the day of the autumnal equinox. Blount, Shirley, Meyricke, and others, who sought favor by suggesting to a man the action nearest his heart, incited Essex to discipline Ralegh. The one daring chance had been snatched from under the nose of the Earl. Ralegh boarded him at once. The Earl threatened court martial and execution according to the articles of the expedition. Ralegh claimed the article in question applied to the captains but not to him. Did not the General realize he was in line of command in the absence of the General and Sir Thomas Howard? He assumed the whole responsibility. His officers should not be punished. The Earl was noncommittal and cold. Ralegh prepared his squadron to leave Essex, or, if necessary, resist him. The Earl lacked counsel to sway him. The expedition waited, prepared for anything.

No longer being able to confide in Ralegh, Essex turned to Lord Thomas Howard. The Vice-Admiral was not disposed to flatter. Essex was always surrounded by men who made his vices his virtues: petulance became righteous wrath, careless banter the flash of sterling wit, inactive wonder a royal aloofness, headstrong stubbornness a princely will. Lord Howard spoke roundly. It would do Essex no good at court to discipline the one man of the expedition who had performed a feat of arms and earned a victory. It would not strengthen the General in the eyes of the fleet. Nothing could undo the offense, and it was only a military exigency which Ralegh had solved handily, deserving approval rather than censure. Essex wavered. He had something of Elizabeth's vacillation. Lord Howard saw that Ralegh might bridge the gulf and pledged Sir Walter his assistance if violence were offered by Essex after an attempt at a reconciliation.

Ralegh had sounded the mind of the Earl by then and met the occasion by the proper gesture. He apologized formally for his hurried action. Essex accepted it with gusto and the ceremony ended by a dinner on Ralegh's *Warspite*, where all the important officers of the fleet could see for themselves the amity of their leaders. Essex saved his face by omitting the capture of Fayal from his report, but Ralegh had already sent word of his victory to England, where it was remarked that from the main fleet there was no word, but of a coming and going without booty or success. Ralegh subsided into a passive commander, third in rank.

The fleet sailed. They missed twenty-five laden West Indiamen bound to Seville. Six of the galleons were carrying silver bullion. Monson, in the *Rainbow,* did what he could, but they made the protection of Angra before the stately Essex came in sight. Ten million pesos went safely to Spain. Ralegh had been left at St. Michael. He took a ship from Cuba, a vessel of four hundred tons, carrying gold, civet, musk, ambergris, cochineal, and indigo. He was touched by cynicism. "Although we shall be little the better, the prizes will in great measure give content to her Majesty, so that there may be no repining against this poor lord for the expenses of the voyage." He took a ship out of Brazil worth, in England, the wages of all his company of the *Warspite.* The expedition lost an eighteen hundred ton carrack, whose people burned her when the Dutch ships pressed too close. The rest he left to Essex: the chivalry of treating captured women as guests, of fighting a rear guard action at St. Michael on horseback, smoking a pipe of tobacco, while failing to get all his materials on board despite his coolness.

At last the fleet sailed for home. It had failed to destroy the Spanish fleet in the harbor of Ferrol. The merchant fleets had not been met. A foothold in the Azores had not been won. Northeast gales lashed the ships mercilessly, thereby saving them from a probable tragedy. They were worn and sea battered, short of food and ammunition. The same gales that assaulted them also drove back to port Philip's fleet which had sailed for England. All Essex needed to complete his destruction was to fall in with the Spaniards, but the storms saved him. He was home in Plymouth, October 26. Burghley wrote him on October 29, "with a weak hand and sore eyes, besides other infirmytes," but joyful at his return. To all eyes Essex, Ralegh, and Cecil were as friendly as ever. Ralegh had landed at St. Ives and found Cornish hearts still loyal to him. The coast people feared no Spanish fleets with Ralegh by. What blame there was fell upon Essex. The Queen was cold. Essex was vexed. Lord Admiral Howard had been handed his patent as Earl of Nottingham by the Queen as she came from chapel, just three days before Essex had docked. The Queen spoke at his installation. Cecil read the patent. The new Earl would precede Essex in Parliament. He was given credit for being the conqueror of Cadiz. Essex demanded satisfaction of a commission, of the Queen, of the Lord Admiral: anything to keep up his precedence. Burghley urged him not to sulk, but to play the man. The Queen sent for Ralegh. One favorite was to aid her in the interests of another. The Lord Admiral would not have his new dignity abridged in any way. Ralegh wondered why the Queen so often set him thankless tasks and went to confer with Cecil. Sir Walter saw Howard who professed love for Essex, but who was already enamored of being Nottingham. There were always means to meet necessity. Ralegh carried back to the presence a solution. The Queen could make Essex an earl marshal. It was an honorary office last held by the Earl of Shrewsbury, who had died in 1590. A law of Henry VIII listed a marshal as in precedence of an admiral. The Earl of Essex, therefore, took his seat in the House of Lords on January 11, 1598, next below the Lord Chamberlain, the Earl of Oxford, but just above the newly made Earl of Nottingham, Lord Admiral Howard.

Ralegh, deep in his long neglected affairs, smiled a little wanly at the strain Essex had put upon his relations with the Queen for a bauble of title and wondered when some fiery petulance, some unforgiven frankness would be misinterpreted for the last time and Essex be removed from his path. Subtleties were useless against him; folly, the Earl's folly, was a rival's best ally. So full in the eye did the glory of Essex strike him that he had no sight for the embittered Howard. Jealous, outraged that a lifetime of service should be capped by a device of expediency, to satisfy a peer no more than a puling youngster, in deeds of war, the Lord Admiral laid away his white staff, served no more as lord steward, but, retiring to his home in Chelsea, brooded upon his wrongs and hated the sailor Ralegh, so quick to invent the cause of his misery.

CHAPTER XIV

ESSEX

EVENTS crowded the last two years of the century. Philip II closed his eyes upon his last sea-ravaged fleet and gave his soul to God. Burghley lingered until midsummer, moderating, expostulating for peace to the last. Brokenhearted by his sufferings at the hands of the Irish in revolt, Edmund Spenser died and was interred beside Chaucer in the Abbey. Elizabeth failed to find life so endless as it once seemed, and ceased to laugh at the witty banalities of her godson Harington. Cecil, sent for two months to Henry IV, that the Secretary's perfect Florentine statecraft might defer a Spanish-French treaty, failed when France signed the Peace of Vervins and the Triple Alliance perished. The Queen celebrated her fifty-sixth birthday, wondering about the loyalty of the Netherlands, and thinking upon the toll of death taken from among her councillors.

It was a fit time for the new to arise, for the young to lift England to new greatness, but the urge, the boldness that sprang from dreaded dangers, the glamour of the new and strange: all that was of another day. Cecil, devious as a sophist, pledged to any extreme that promised the Machiavell certainty of success, had Elizabeth's ear. She was no longer so active, although as perverse as ever when aroused. Essex pouted, Essex raged, Essex pleaded, Essex smiled. She regarded him from a vast remoteness, now and then dealing him a sore stroke out of seeming spite, and again humoring him in all the little familiarities he had seized for himself. She was really treating with a shadow, however precious that wraith was to her. When he touched her pride she still struck fire, but coldly, as of habit.

It was this change the Earl did not perceive. In July, 1598, the Queen advanced Sir William Knollys as Lord Deputy to go into Ireland. The Earl, disliking Sir George Carew and keen upon having him away from court, urged the cautious knight's appointment. Elizabeth rejected his arguments curtly and the Earl, to show his indifference of her disdain, turned his back upon her. Queen and woman rose at that. She "gave him a box on the ear and bade him get him gone and be hanged." She had kept councillors kneeling for hours. She had never dreamed of such disparagement. He had never stood taunt from man in his life. Cecil, Howard, and Windebank stood watching. The Earl glared angrily at his sovereign and put his hand to his sword. The old Lord Admiral was not so slow but he interposed. The Earl snarled that he would not have stood such an indignity from King Henry VIII himself, and thrusting Howard aside, rushed from the presence and the court. He was one of the five hundred mourners at Burghley's funeral in August and in the fall he had returned to town and Essex House and was again at court by the middle of September, 1598. The steps of reconciliation no one learned. It is certain the Queen did not know of his philandering six short months before with Elizabeth Bridges, one of her maids of honor, although the Countess of Essex, then pregnant, had known. Elizabeth complained to Vere of the Earl's ambition, but also of his humors. From the moment he touched his sword hilt, the royal mood was never the same. She moved farther than ever away from him, and, save for one brief instant on a dusky morning, he was completely a spirit that no longer stirred her blood.

Ralegh, looking on, knew his moment. "The fires of hatred are cinders of affection." The Queen was purging her court. The presumption of Essex had reached its limit. Machiavelli had heralded the Earl. "He is rendered despicable by being

thought changeable, frivolous, effeminate, timid, irresolute."
It was never Niccolo's way to give much countenance to
things of the heart and Essex was nothing with his affection
away. When the Queen came to judge him dispassionately
her distaste might soar like a flame, blasting him utterly.
With Essex gone and the dead lost there would be a need for
a councillor. Sir Walter Ralegh sitting in the Court of the
Star Chamber! It was a dream of a vagrant moment, but it
did not come often, he was too busy and idleness too rare.

He sent spies into Spain to watch the gathering of the
ships in the ports. He wrote on Irish affairs, which had gone
from bad to worse. He was an extremist there, approving of
the murdering of rebels. Jesuits classed him with Cecil and
Lord Admiral Howard as marked men. He paid for the
victualling of West Country ports, paid garrisons, defending his miners against merchants, supporting the ancient
tenures of Cornwall, attacking levies upon the salting and
packing of fish. He was hated in Spain, known in France,
and the Duke of Finland urged him to go again to Guiana
to find more wonders.

In the court he was in a thousand affairs. In the House of
Commons he spoke and served on committees. Projects for
the defense of the realm and conferences with the Privy
Council took up much of his time, but he managed to play
primero in the Presence Chamber, superintend his new house
building at Sherborne, endeavor to get his cousin's son out
of jail, take treatments for his bodily troubles at Bath, and
obtain a governorship of Jersey for himself, besides a host of
activities which never found their way to public record. He
played it all gravely, with a manner. What had been a
roistering swagger had become a gallant air. The years had
brought ease of carriage, adroitness in repartee, and yet his
courage had not died. Youthful zest, wild eagerness, careless fire: these things were all gone, replaced by a clarity of

mind that had ground its facets to a blinding brilliance. At times the old, mad eagerness made him turn to force, trusting his strength. Often, thus, he failed and so came to use his wits and deny his emotions. His was an Elizabethan mind at its finest.

He was forty-six, his life rounding to its sum. Its fullest bloom might not extend to the office of chamberlain, constable, marshal or admiral and steward. He was not so close to royalty in blood, yet he had the illusion of affairs. To sway men's fancies, to quietly inspire them to act as he planned, to feel the nation swerve at his touch, all these lay at the heart of his dream. It was for these things that he strove to be a Privy Councillor, giving a hand to every project, letting nothing that might please a royal whim pass without his touch. At last, he might so grow upon the Queen that he should take his state easily, no other in her mind to question it.

For the rest at court, envy raised him enemies in profusion. Essex, the public's chivalric darling, suffered from the Queen's injustice, but Ralegh, as often a victim of her heckling, only got what was good enough for him. Cecil, ruling with a Queen, might be a model of Italian diplomacy, but Ralegh was the dark Machiavellian like to sell his people to the Spanish and buy a place in the sun for himself from the French. He knew the feeling of the populace, of the nobles, and worked to overcome it. Seagoing men he won easily and soldiers. Popular playwrights he enjoyed for the flash of their genius. Early friendly with Christopher Marlowe, who also had the patronage of the Earl of Oxford, he knew too Thomas Kyd, "who ran through every art and throve by none," to quote the sharp spirited Thomas Nash. Thomas Lodge, whose *Rosalynde* Shakespeare fashioned into *As You Like It*, was of his own college, and George Peele was of his own time at Oxford. He paused to drink with them where the carven mermaid topped the doorway and blue-clad drawers, with white aprons, hustled about under the dark beams of the low ceiling. It was there he missed most the dead Spenser, and Marlowe of the swaggering mien and bold word. He made out well enough with those fellows.

It was the citizenry he could not appease. They thought of him scandalously as a favorite. He was a plundering tyrant, who oppressed the weak, who devoured the land, who exploited the Queen, who befriended the Spanish, dealt treacherously in league with the Irish, and was bolder than Satan with it all. The whole legend of ignorance, born of prejudice and envy, he could never escape.

At court, he chose Cecil as his nearest friend, entertaining his young son William, later the second Earl of Salisbury, at the new mansion at Sherborne. "Poorest and truest friend and servant," he was to Cecil, playing upon the man, himself a master player upon men. With Essex he kept contact, out of policy, urging the Earl toward foreign service, but the followers of Essex saw to it the Earl heard of his thousand rivalries. There was the Queen's birthday, November 17, 1598, when the usual tournament that graced the day was going forward. Ralegh had ordered orange tawny plumes for his retinue. It was a color Essex often affected. When he heard of Ralegh's plan he headed a larger troop and entered the lists with visor down, his men wearing two thousand orange tawny plumes, making Ralegh and his men seem but a company of squires and pages sent as a harbinger to the Earl's arrival. It was the expression of an ambitious brooding. Its advantage soon passed, wiped quite out at the tilt, for Essex "ran very ill," and his party fared no better. There was no avoiding rivalry with Essex; he would not have it. For any vacancy that Sir Walter or any one else advanced a man, the Earl of Essex had his own candidate and spared nothing to see the place fall to his share of the honors.

When he lost, for the Queen could not surround herself by his party alone, and so he often lost, he was maddened, attacking outrageously Ralegh, or Cobham, or whomever stood in his way. Discreetly, Ralegh worked toward his goal of being a councillor of the Queen.

Irish affairs had gone from bad to worse. Ralegh, Sir Robert Sidney, and Sir Christopher Blount were considered for command there. None wanted the post. The Queen felt secure, with Ralegh in command of the defense of the West Counties. His name alone was worth much, if the Spanish came, for they feared him. Ralegh should stay at home. Sir William Russel declined the honor. "A fair way to destruction," the post promised to be, as garrulous Rowland Whyte clearly enough pronounced it. A pestilential island that was always a wound in the side of Elizabeth cried for a master. Ralegh could not have gained it for himself. Essex would not have had that. Ralegh shrewdly turned to support Essex. If the Earl would not let others go, he should be sent himself. Ralegh was quite willing to aid Cecil in presenting Essex with that which no one else could have. Ireland, or rather the timely leaving of it, had brought Ralegh his start at court. Who knew what it might bring Essex? Sir Walter was very near his desire. He was not made Vice Chamberlain nor a Privy Councillor, when the way opened in 1598. It was even rumored, perhaps at the instance of his enemies, that he was going out again to Guiana. He was playing a very close game with an aging Queen. If Essex went to Ireland he was as far away as Lord Grey of Wilton had once been, while Sir Walter Ralegh would be at home at the Queen's ear.

Essex went to Ireland. All London watched the departure of his army on March 27, 1599. The people cheered their champion. He led the largest force that Elizabeth ever sent out of England: sixteen thousand men, beside thirteen hundred horse. John Norden wrote a prayer in which he was offered to God as a peer of Moses, Gideon, and David. Shakespeare compared him with no one less than Henry V fresh come from Agincourt. Elizabeth refused to allow him his stepfather, Sir Christopher Blount, as a councillor, but made him take him as an officer only. Essex, as soon as he signed his commission, made the Earl of Southampton his General of Horse, resulting in royal action and counteraction. In the end Elizabeth had her way and Southampton remained a troop commander. She refused to conciliate. Essex felt no encouragement. He rode through the streets, listening to the popular roar, cold with apprehension, sick with his Queen's slights.

Ralegh had hoped for his reward. Efforts at peace with Spain were forever going forward and failing. No man could have carried more weight in that service than Sir Walter. He knew both tongue and character. Elizabeth set her face against his going to Boulogne as a Commissioner. She had settled all that long, long before. To have made him Commissioner would have confirmed his title to a Privy Councillorship. It was too serious to him for a flurry of temper. He kept his wits. By summer Elizabeth was berating him roundly. He held his anger and retreated to Ireland. Just then he found her compassion his best resource. She repented and invited him home. He left Sir George Carew in Munster and appeared at court.

Essex was given little chance to recover. He too had to put up with what seemed to him the oppression of the Queen. His delusions of grandeur clashed with those of malicious persecution. It was Ralegh who was doing all this, he wrote the Queen, Ralegh who was poisoning her against her favorite, Ralegh who was helping the Irish, who was interfering, standing in the path of Providence, checking both the progress of the Queen's army and the fortunes of the Devereux. It was too early to campaign in Ulster. South and west of Dublin, he went into action even while he waited for the Queen's approval of the plan. Cecil was in power at home and Ralegh was at Cecil's shoulder with local knowledge of Ireland and Irish chieftains. Essex did not succeed and every failure resulted in nagging letters, severe in criticism. By August 13, Elizabeth wrote, forbidding his return, although, like other men of state of the period, Essex had permission to return to England at will, so that his return would not hurt his cause in Ireland. Essex had concluded a truce with Tyrone and nervously broken, worn down by constant bowel trouble, he deputized his power in Ireland, drew his salary ahead, and with Southampton and Danvers, left for London on September 24.

It had not been a quiet summer in England. Strange fears had stirred. London was barricaded for a fortnight in August. Ralegh, as Vice-Admiral, under Lord Thomas Howard as Admiral, bade good-bye to the court and went on board the fleet which lay in the Downs for almost a month. Elizabeth had remembered the Earl of Essex putting his hand upon his sword in her presence. She remembered too that the Devereux had under his command the largest expeditionary force she had ever sent anywhere. She could depend upon Ralegh. He hated the Spanish. She gave him orders to stand by to resist a possible invasion from Spain and meant to use him should Essex come back all wrath and injured pride. Wild talk had reached her from her troops. Sir Christopher Blount, before the headsman's block, later admitted there had been some such intent in the army to march upon London. It was well Essex returned almost unattended.

At ten in the morning, mired and dirty, Essex alighted at Nonesuch. "And made all hast up to the Presence and soe to the Privy Chamber, and staied not till he came to the

Queen's Bed Chamber, where he found the Queen newly up." Her hair was about her face, her glory strangely missing, but he kneeled to her. He kissed her hands. They talked privately, he pouring out his tale of wrongs, but speaking most of the wonder of his Queen. It was nearly noon when they met again, all point device, she combed and perfumed, he cleansed and at ease, with a strange trust upon him, as having found calm at home. She was gracious. He was merry. Somewhere a shadow crossed her. She was old but she was fond of this one. They had talked of her marrying Leicester when she was young, but he had been no king. This one was kingly but she was old; all the crabbed bitterness of her lone command struck her heart. Unconsciously she reflected her latest company, the long hours with Robert Cecil. She saw Essex after dinner, but she was braced to be the Queen. She could check and bridle Ralegh. She would outface Essex. What did he mean by leaving Ireland against orders? He had forsaken his post. Why had he not been more active in Ulster? Was this bringing in the rebel Tyrone? In confusion he retired, stunned, speechless. She never saw him again, a bitter farewell to remember. He talked with the lords for an hour. Twelve hours from his arrival at court, the Queen issued an order confining him to his chamber.

The full Council rose to greet him when he was summoned next morning, but he knew he was on trial before Cecil began to read the complaints against him. The Earl had affirmed Cecil would sell the realm to the Infanta of Spain. He had attempted to remove the Secretary from the Queen. It was only one of the bitter, clouded visions that had followed his "banishment and proscription" into Ireland. In the same mad mood he warned King James to make sure of his succession for conspiracy would place the Infanta upon the English throne. Ralegh, Cobham, Howard, Lord Burghley (Robert Cecil's brother), and George Carew were accused of being in league to betray the country to the Spaniards. That was the reason Ralegh had removed to Sherborne, where he could plan unseen and then had asked for the governorship of the isle of Jersey. Ralegh was the guest of Cecil when the appointment came, August 26, and by October Ralegh was in Jersey sending out ships in Newfoundland trade, but that was a blind. Spain was a better winter passage. Cobham had himself made Warden of the Cinque Ports to yield the southwest coast, Burghley was President of the North and Carew, President of Munster, also out of treachery. Essex never spared of wild words and what was worse, believed all these hallucinations he created.

Cecil read the complaints against the Earl with the satisfaction to be gotten from evening a grudge and doing a clearheaded piece of work. The favorite had returned against orders, had intruded upon the Queen, had not obeyed his orders to proceed against Tyrone immediately, had insisted upon appointing Southampton as General of Horse, had exercised his privilege of making knights too promiscuously, had written presumptuously to the Court, had behaved indiscreetly, treating with Tyrone alone for more than half an hour, the Earl standing at the bank of a ford, Tyrone astride his horse, which stood belly deep in the stream. Essex answered as Essex would. The Queen, a day's contemplation of the matter ended, ordered him into confinement at York House under Lord Keeper Egerton. The Earl of Worcester's coach carried him from Nonesuch to Westminster. Elizabeth confirmed the truce with Tyrone and other of his arrangements in Ireland, but it was half a year before he was allowed to live in his own house, still with a keeper. When a year was almost gone he was released. His friends had angered the Queen by murmuring against his confinement, and she, out of temper, decided he should await her pleasure. Men in London, passing York House, had cheered Essex. Soldiers in Ireland had cried: "Essex or none." Libels were spread against his enemies, pamphlets were written and circulated, railing speeches were made in taverns. Elizabeth had her way. The Earls of Southampton and Rutland, as bosom friends of Essex, took a short sojourn abroad, and upon their return, spent their time "merely in going to Plaies every Day." They thus avoided being useless centres of disaffection. Lady Scrope, cousin to the Queen, wore black for Essex. The Earl had many friends but Elizabeth had power. She tried him by a commission of nineteen, with two hundred invited guests. When Essex entered none acknowledged him. He stood for a while, then was given a cushion to kneel upon, and at last a stool on which to sit through the eleven hours of legal castigation at the hands of Yelverton, Coke, Fleming, and Bacon. On August 26, 1600, he was told he might go where he would, but must not attempt to frequent the court. One honor, his first, the mastership of the horse, was left him.

Red rage ran through his blood in those days. He wrote Elizabeth, "I sometimes think of running; and then remember what it will be to come in armour, triumphing, into that presence, out of which both by your own voice I was commanded, and by your hands thrust out." He could still send defiance to the aging face he would never see again, but among his friends he felt no restraint of being the soul of chivalry returning from the wars to wipe out wrong and error. He spoke freely, what he felt, and Sir John Harington wrote of his sayings: "His speeches of the Queen become no man who hath *mens sana in corpore sano.*" He had neither a sound mind nor a sound body. Often ill, living a quiet, brooding life, broken by attacks of awful rage, he was doing all that was desirable in the eyes of Ralegh and Cecil. In proper Florentine aphorism, years later, Ralegh wrote,

"Undutiful words of a subject do often take deeper root than the memories of ill deeds." The Earl of Essex had said that the conditions of Queen Elizabeth were "as crooked as her carcass." Failing as she was, Cecil needed to do no prodding after that, nor Ralegh any counselling. "Princes are lost by security, and preserved by prevention," Ralegh wrote Cecil, even as he spoke it in the Queen's ear, who, knowing the words of Niccolo, heeded the spirit of Ralegh's.

The century died with Essex approaching desperation. He was forever saying he would "stand upon his own strength," he would "put himself again into the court." It was primarily his inability to reach the Queen that drove him to madness. He asked five of his friends to meet at Drury House, the London place of Southampton. There he had given them a list of one hundred twenty he believed faithful and a series of projects in his proposed "alteration of the state." No injury or violence was to touch the Queen. She was to lose her government, her councillors, her court, and become a prisoner at Whitehall. Beyond that the plot became a very shadow. Essex was to mould all to some sovereign pattern. Five were too many to keep the secret. Five, and their servants, are the whole world, in a scheme touching treason. Sir Ferdinando Gorges, a veteran of the Azores expedition, was asked by Ralegh to meet him at Durham House. Gorges often left his captaincy of the Plymouth defenses without leave. He was advised by Essex to meet Ralegh only in a boat on the river, for else he might be murdered. Essex was convinced Cobham and Ralegh would attempt to murder him in his bed. The more general state of depression had yielded to the delusion of persecution.

Cecil, Ralegh, and Cobham were not the men to let danger go unwatched. The Queen had rebuked the pride of Essex and proven his humility, but she had also broken her man. It was a thing Ralegh would never have told her in any case and the Earl's friends she would not hear. Ralegh had her ear then, never so completely. He knew everything imaginable. He tendered her, perhaps partly from habit, the adulation of the old court. She talked much with him in private. They had known so many who had belonged to an earlier day. Pembroke, young Southampton, Essex, even Cecil himself were youngsters. Forty-eight was so, so much closer to sixty-seven than youthful thirty-three or even her Secretary's thirty-eight. Besides, Ralegh had never been rashly rewarded and so, unlike Essex, was her own beyond all doubts. She "took him for a kind of oracle," even more than in those first, fiery days, when he was fresh come out of Irish campaigning. He kept an eye upon the moves of Essex. He saw the court guards doubled and waited for what Essex would do.

Sunday morning, February 9, 1601, saw men admitted to the buildings and gardens of Essex through a guarded wicket opening on the Strand. Gorges left by the water gate and met Ralegh on the river. Sir Walter warned Sir Ferdinando to leave a sinking ship and flee from madness. Sir Ferdinando threatened Sir Walter with "a bloody day" both speaking symbolically. The gathering at Essex House was known at court. The most favorable ambassadors to be found, shrewdly selected, were sent with a message from the Queen: Sir William Knollys, uncle of Essex, Worcester, Egerton and Popham. Elizabeth was willing to be persuasive. Essex locked them up and dashed off for London crying "For the Queen, for the Queen; there is a plot against my life." From there on the affair grew pitiful and silly. Essex was cheered in the streets, but none armed to join him. Finding Cheapside had failed him, Essex rode to Paul's churchyard, where he walked back and forth alone, uncertain what to do. When he met Sheriff Smyth he seized his bridle and held horse and man for a quarter of an hour, reciting his wrongs and hardships. Official London was about his ears. He fought his way through Bow churchyard, and retreated down Bow Lane to the river at Queenhithe, and by water rowed home to Essex House. There he melodramatically burned papers which he took from a casket, and a little black bag, and offered to lead the residue of his followers to death, fighting the Queen's men. He had no hostages; Sir Ferdinando Gorges, realizing the wisdom of Ralegh's warning too late, had released the imprisoned councillors as a pledge of faith to the Queen. The gray, winter dusk shut in quickly.

Two thousand men, headed by the Lord Admiral, beset Essex House. Ralegh, Cobham, and Grey were in possession of the garden. The banqueting hall was seized. Cumberland, Lincoln, Greville, Sidney, and Compton joined the attackers. Two guns and petards, to blow in the doors, were sent from the Tower. The Lord Admiral was ready at last. In the darkness he stood in the garden. Essex spoke from the roof trying to make terms, but failing that, at ten he surrendered. With Southampton, Essex gave up his sword and went to the Tower.

Ten days passed. Westminster Hall was prepared for the trial of the two Earls. Lord Buckhurst, Lord Steward, sat in a chair under a canopy. Eight judges faced the prisoners. Seven of the Queen's finest were ready to conduct the prosecution. Nine Earls and sixteen Barons comprised the court. A gentleman usher displayed his white wand, and seven sergeants-at-arms bore their maces. The Lord Steward followed them and when the court opened a gentleman usher entered. He carried in his hands the ax, its edge carefully kept to the front, for at his heels tramped the two Earls, as yet innocent of the treason they had committed.

Ten hours sufficed. There was, as usual, no counsel for the defendants nor any witness for the accused. The court considered three charges. The prisoners had plotted to seize the court. They had imprisoned the Queen's councillors at Essex House and had attempted to incite rebellion in London. The testimony on these points was indisputable. Essex found the court knew more of his friends than he did. He attempted counter charges, but when he accused Cecil of sharing a conspiracy to betray the country to Spain, Cecil rose to deny "so foul and false report" and to demand who said he had declared the Infanta's title to the throne of England as good as any. Like a shot came the answer, "Sir William Knollys." Cecil sent for this uncle of the indicted Earl, who was Comptroller of the Royal household. Either Essex or Cecil would be caught in a lie and for either ruin was very close.

Court: "Did Mr. Secretary ever use any such speeches in your hearing or to your knowledge?"

Knollys: "I have never heard him speak any words to that effect."

When, after more questioning, Knollys had retired, Cecil, clinching the lie in the throat of the Earl, "I have said the King of Spain is a competitor of the crown of England and that the King of Scots is a competitor, and my Lord of Essex I have said is a competitor for he would depose the Queen, call a parliament and so be King himself."

With this return to the subject, the Judges were soon asked to expound. What was the law of the case? The facts were self-evident. The Judges averred each charge to be treasonable. The verdict was clear. "Since I have committed that which hath brought me within the compass of the Law, I may be counted the Law's Traitor in offending the Law, for which I am willing to die," pronounced Essex, and then, in curious contrast, "I never had any treacherous or disloyal intentions toward Her Majesty," and then, grovelling, his pride stripped away, looking possibly for that stifling pity he should have despised, he said, "I know my sins unto her Majesty and to my God . . . I am the greatest, the most vile and most unthankful traitor that has ever been in the land." It was wasted, all that self-denunciation. The law was satisfied. Cecil was content. Ralegh and Bacon breathed more freely and Cobham and Grey held the law as sound and the court just, none of the four realizing that in time each would find himself a sacrifice to the law and its half truths.

When the peers had given the verdict the Lord Steward uttered those words of terror, "They shall be returned to the Tower of London, and from thence through the city of London they shall be drawn to Tyburn, and there they shall be hung, and living their entrails shall be removed from their bodies and burnt, and their heads shall be cut off and their bodies divided into four parts and their heads and these parts shall be placed where the Queen shall assign." With that the Lord Steward snapped his staff in two, the sergeants-at-arms abandoned their authority, Sir Walter Ralegh relieved his forty guardsmen of further duty, and the mazed prisoners were led off to the Tower, the gentleman porter walking behind them. The edge of the headsman's ax which he carried was now turned toward the convicted traitors.

Elizabeth quailed before her own justice. Shaken, suddenly old, she used a cane coming downstairs after the court had sentenced Essex. The Earl of Lincoln opened his eyes very wide at the Queen's refusal to let mercy eclipse her law. Twenty times he had seen Essex and the Queen kiss; would she let "one with whom she had been so familiar" go to the block? Confessions and petitions filled the galloping hours within the Tower. The Queen let the warrant go, signed with her own hand. The Earl waited, resigned. On Thursday, February 24, a servant of the Order of the Garter went to the Tower and took away his jewelled George. In the evening came his executioners; two, that one failing, the other could perform the sentence. Next morning, in black velvet and satin, walking with the clergyman, Essex faced the block in the Tower courtyard. Elizabeth had forgiven him the disgrace of Tyburn and the hanging, drawing and quartering. Seven noblemen and a hundred others saw him take off his hat. Pardon he cried. Prayer was his staff. Pity, submission, the men of his age could not understand. Marshal Biron of the French court, moving rapidly toward his own execution, felt Essex to be dying contemptibly, not like a soldier, but a cleric. Humbly the gown, ruff, and doublet were laid aside. He lay upon the scaffold in a scarlet waistcoat, his arms outstretched in long, red sleeves, his hair still fair about his sanguine face. The executioner struck askew. The first blow cut through the shoulder, the second through the head, but the third severed the neck. It is said the first stroke produced unconsciousness.

Sir Walter Ralegh watched from the Armory. Men had murmured when he stood close to the scaffold, so he had removed to the White Tower, where he studied the Earl's humility as something beyond his comprehension. Death had toyed with him less than a week, certain death, and the Earl's passion had gone out of him. How could a man once so filled with rebellion look up at those low, squared walls and towers, breathing the air of resistance, and defense against all comers, and bend his heart to acceptance, even to the welcoming of the end of his world? It was a strange glimpse of the human heart that left Ralegh brooding. He went out from the Tower by the water gate and as his boat pulled up river he weighed the miracle. Death moved everywhere and always. Perhaps there was a time when a man came to know that, and then the struggle for mastery went out of one. Violence, bravery, and even pride vanished. Essex a bowed suppliant, heedless of the triumph of Cecil, disregarding that it was Sir Walter who carried the order of execution, and asking for Ralegh in those last moments! His malice, Ralegh had thought that fixed, his royal presumption eternal. Rather alarming, this last-minute surrender of every soldierly virtue. Death, how could any be sure of meeting that stroke fairly and out of one's own high-heartedness? Cecil had done most toward this. The way was clear of Essex, but Cecil was powerful, and the Queen leaned heavily upon a cane now, and could seldom take her saddle any more. Traitors used the Tower water gate, traitors and sometimes the condemned. The low Surrey fields were fair, but wintry with frost. Ralegh wrapped his cloak about him to keep out the gloom and chill.

He secured pardons for such of the conspirators as could pay for it. Littleton wrote him and others. It was a legitimate trade in his day, and when he could not get a full pardon he could at least get a remission of sentence. The public writhed for a day, but Ben Jonson wrote *Cynthia's Revels*. When it was produced four maids of honor confidently claimed they were the prototypes for Ben's four virtuous ladies, and Cynthia, who was a pattern of justice, had treated Essex with consideration. Oh, it was flattering, championing the cause of Elizabeth at every turn, and when the play reached the final "By God 'tis good; and if you like't you may," the Queen slapped her thigh and clucked in her throat; her people liked it, but she seized it as her first reward for breaking her heart and weighing the welfare of her land with accursed unselfishness.

CHAPTER XV

THE HALTING OF THE TIDE

ESSEX had been unable to await the coming of the Scotch ambassador, but he had left behind him a statement of the imaginary plot, in which Ralegh, Cecil, and Cobham were to betray England in the interest of the Spanish Infanta. The Earl of Mar and Edward Bruce started south in February, but when they arrived in London in March, Essex was dead. James of Scotland had been ready to heed the guidance of Essex. When his envoys reached London new instructions were sent them: they were to pledge confidence to Cecil and his party. Would Cecil secretly foster the idea of succession? James would reward him. Cecil answered as if Elizabeth could live forever. James should form no popular party in England, nor interfere with Elizabethan policy, nor even hint he was impatient to succeed to his right. Given faith, Cecil would do all, secure all, even the throne for James. The envoys did not journey to London for nothing.

The Queen received them graciously. They were beyond the veil that lay between her and the world. She did not need to know that James and a half dozen councillors in each country were parties to a correspondence where many played for a new royal favor and the booty discussed was her throne. She saw the Scotch faces of the envoys and heard their northern tongues and their coming melted into the passing away which was growing upon her so fast. Of course, they were come in the interest of their gangling King, who had just had his thirty-fifth birthday, and what real interest could he have but the succession. It made her sad, angry once, but sad now, with a heaviness she had never thought to feel. They were too deep for her, this new generation, too suave and discreetly venomous. She belonged to a heartier day. She was Queen, so she had a bill passed prohibiting the publishing of any book upon the theme of the succession, but that could not shut out the changing world. Bacon had turned upon Essex at the trial and was clinging to Cecil. Oxford carried his animus for Ralegh into her presence as she played mournfully upon the virginals. Harington was looking toward Edinburgh with that damned cynicism she had once admired. A will to be more alone, to digest this new moodiness, to make peace with herself, grew upon her. She was never more kind to Ralegh. He was close to fifty then, a little stooped, with a slight limp from his leg wound gotten at Cadiz, hair no longer untouched by gray. He was worth them all to her just then. From entertaining a Spanish envoy, come to arrange a truce, he would run down to Sherborne for a few nights under his own roof. From there his health would take him to Bath for the cure in the summer, but returning to London while Elizabeth was on progress to Dover, he received Sully and took him to the Queen. On September 5, the Duc de Biron came to London, to announce the marriage of Mary de Medici and Henry of France, and missed the nobles assigned to be his escort. Ralegh, with the aid of Sir Arthur Savage and Sir Arthur Gorges, took Biron and his retinue to the Abbey to see the monuments, and to the Bear Gardens, at last guiding them into Hampshire where the Queen was at Basing House. Ralegh saw all housed and set off late at night to ride to London to get a plain taffeta suit and a plain black saddle so he might appear more at one with the French guests. Elizabeth, weary as she was, appreciated his efforts and for his pains knighted his brother Carew Ralegh.

Somewhere within the years of 1600 and 1601, he found

THE HALTING OF THE TIDE

time to govern the Isle of Jersey. He had asked the governorship of Elizabeth on April 6, 1600, and in August, while Cecil was his guest at Sherborne, the appointment had been sent him. In October, he undertook the administration, strengthened the fortifications, relieved the inhabitants of an onerous system of military service, projected trade between the island and Newfoundland, and judged such cases as waited upon a court. At the same time he was despatching voyages to Guiana and Virginia, combatting the avarice of John Meere, his bailiff at Sherborne, and following the court as the Queen moved restlessly about.

It must have been in those days he walked through the heart of the city, along Goldsmith Row from Cheap Cross, to turn down Bread Street and pause under the blue mermaid carved above the door. Long and low, half timbered, the inn was a place for meetings, with several exits for sudden flights, and rooms on the upper floor where wits might gather. It was a place of legend and youth to Ralegh. Spenser had frequented it, Marlowe and Kyd were gone, but their friends were still there. Poverty-stricken Dekker, always in debt to that magnate of the theatre, Philip Henlowe, cursed fortune under the smoky beams. There were rooms above where young Selden washed away the dust of the titles of honor he was always seeking. John Donne meditated upon his metaphysical muse and Beaumont and Fletcher conjured with wit against the fashions of their day. Robert Greene moralized upon his sins, Shakespeare sipped the rich Canary wine, Ben Jonson roared out his bludgeon sentences. Even cool Francis Bacon paused to watch the lesser minds, unable to grasp all learning, carve out immortality for themselves. For Ralegh it was a gift after the stuffiness of parliament, or the intricate by play of paying scores at court. He suffered from no condescension. The way that carried him to the hearts of sailors was acceptable to playwrights. He was safe from lampoon upon the stage while he had the wits of the Mermaid at his shoulder.

For the rest, life was never a more hurried scramble for him. His access to the Queen was easy and the envy of the court. Cecil he treated with the frankness of a friend. His duties, manifold as they were, he performed well.

In June, 1601, there was a chance to make him Privy Councillor. He longed for it more than to be raised to the peerage. He liked authority, to move men, to direct events, and he never lost his liking. Cecil opposed him. He swung Sir George Carew to his side by saying he would never consent to Ralegh being a Councillor unless Sir Walter surrendered his Captaincy of the Guard to George Carew. It was typical of his work. His end was to keep Ralegh out, his plea, friendship for Carew. Carew's reward was to be paid by another and cost Cecil nothing. He had said nothing against Ralegh. The device was the very soul of Machiavellian policy, yet Ralegh never lost faith in Cecil. There were some things to which Ralegh never applied his policy of statescraft. Such faith must have amused Cecil busy with Sir Walter's own doctrine.

In accord with Cecil, but proceeding by a very different route to a similar purpose, Elizabeth acted. All things were moving far off, but that made the near and distant alike. Death and life were blending in her mind so that she had her thoughts of the succession. She heard of Arabella Stuart in love and longing to marry William Seymour. She hated Arabella as she hated the Spanish Infanta, as she hated any who might succeed her. She would not think of herself dead and yet death was not far away. This Seymour, who would marry Arabella, was of the blood of that other Seymour whom she had feared. So the old comparison rose: Seymour, Thomas the Admiral, a figure out of her years of puberty, and Ralegh, Sir Walter laying siege to her in the wintry days of her reign. She changed not a whit, only a shade of her wrath at Arabella clouded the hopes of Ralegh.

Lords Shrewsbury and Worcester were sworn in as members of the Council. Ralegh could say nothing to any. Cecil was contented. The Queen had again laid the ghost of Thomas Seymour. Unwittingly Ralegh had moved from the status of an Essex to that of a Walsingham. His era of rewards had passed without his knowing it. Since the fall of Essex, he had known the Admiral, Lord Charles Howard, hated him, even as his bailiff Meere, whose wife was a relative of the Devereux, hated him, but he paid scarcely more heed to the one than to the other. Henry Howard made Ralegh's loss a family triumph, knowing well it was the lifetime ambition of Sir Walter to enter the Privy Council.

Ralegh, carrying the multiple burdens of the state, kept his faith in Cecil. They were very close, their households mingling with every show of affection. Cecil protected Ralegh's minor interests, Ralegh guarded Cecil's. There was always a following at Durham House, for Ralegh had not relaxed his service to the state. Spies came and went. Courtiers paid him the honor of tendering their suits through him as promising them success. All the queer horde of travellers, poets, necromancers, and seamen poured their knowledge into his ears. It was a compliment to his ability, although some thought the traffic at Durham House greater than an honest keeping of his station would warrant. His enemies were always catching at straws, before his impetuous passage would brush them aside and leave them gaping. Even Cecil may have envied him his freedom. He trusted few, but by every sign he loved Cecil with a splendid friendship, which excluded every pettiness, but Cecil was a younger man whose fortunes were not ended. The Secretary cast his eyes upon the failing Queen and faced the succession of a new dynasty as a certainty. Every one in London wrote to Scotland, but James trusted his mounting the throne to Cecil, and then cannily felt the pulse of all Englishmen of note.

In November, 1601, the Duke of Lennox came to London. Ralegh, like the rest, had been in touch with Scotland. He acknowledged that none but James could reach the throne and yet he urged against any discussion of the matter. The Queen still lived and needed not to name a successor. In a very carefully penned memorial he addressed her upon the subject, mentioning his loneness, his danger of eclipse by his enemies, noting as a gracious memory those "celestial beauties" of her Majesty. In spite of, or perhaps because of this attitude, Lennox was sent from James to confer with him. Sir Arthur Savage brought them together. The Scottish Earl could see at a glance that Ralegh was the man of strength he was reputed to be. Lennox proffered his master as a candidate for the throne. Ralegh had a bid made for his services, while Cecil had to seek his. James aimed at purchasing Ralegh's support. His resistance might prove a possible menace to a peaceful coronation and James was the man for peace. Ralegh was rumored to have said that the people might, at the death of Elizabeth, take the staff of government in their hands and establish a commonwealth. What he really had said was that "in every just state some part of the government is or ought to be imparted to the people." Lennox was patient with his arrogance, which grew no less as time lengthened. He bided an answer.

Ralegh knew by his own channels that James despised his friendship and loyalty. He would lack under James the two things he counted upon under Elizabeth. She had barred him as a Privy Councillor, but he held a portion of her favor. Under James he would be regarded as an actual menace to the Crown, no matter how he conformed, for the King of Scotland regarded only his own prejudices and opinions.

Ralegh told Cecil that his gratitude and his services to the Queen had been too deep for him to think of seeking favor elsewhere. Then, with that twisting flash, courtier-like, he urged Cecil to tell the Queen his speech. Cecil convinced him he was boasting of a weakness rather than displaying resolution that was laudable, and kept silence.

All the court was writing to Scotland. Henry Howard, turning from his versifying of the Psalms of David, poured into James' ears attacks upon "those wicked villains, Cobham and Ralegh." With malice, he suggested a conspiracy to place Arabella Stuart on the throne, the instruments: Lady Shrewsbury, Lady Ralegh, and Ralegh. The guilty sting of his conscience might prick James at the mention of Arabella. He had robbed her of her father's earldom, not stopping at her mother's jewels. Adding Northumberland to the faction and apparently considering the Raleghs as one, not two, Howard wrote, "Hell cannot afford such a like triplicity that denies the Trinity." If only James should think them atheists, they would be marked forever in his mind. It was a stroke of the embittered hypocrite informing the dogmatic. A shrewd ambition, that, of Henry Howard; to discredit every one who wrote James but Cecil and himself. Frances Howard, Countess of Kildare, newly married to Lord Cobham, was a fool, although a confidante of Elizabeth. Cobham was trying to discredit James with Elizabeth. The Earl of Northumberland was reputed to have said, "he had rather the King of Scots was buried than crowned." None but Howard would write the truth; King James could disbelieve all others.

Cecil both damned and praised in his letters. Of Cobham and Ralegh, "They would not stick to confess daily how contrary it is to their nature to resolve to be under your soverainty." James was asked to believe nothing Ralegh wrote about Cecil. Again, James was reminded Ralegh is a person "whom most religious men do hold *anathema*." Ralegh and Cobham had little chance to advance "their fonde and giddy offering you themselves." At the same time Cecil praised the wisdom and sincerity of Henry Howard, "faithful 3." All of the correspondents were referred to by number: 10 was Cecil, 20 the Earl of Mar, 30 King James. Cecil had changed his attitude toward Ralegh in one short year. Ralegh knew nothing for a time of the correspondence, but he saw Cecil and Bacon drawing closer together and knew the Howards had hated him at least ever since he had helped Essex to eclipse the Lord Admiral by becoming Earl Marshal. His ties to Cecil were so intimate that he never suspected the Secretary of treachery. Content to let Henry Howard be more obvious in his attack upon Sir Walter and Lord Cobham, Cecil wrote to Sir George Carew, still in Munster, "Our two old friends," Ralegh and Cobham, "do use me unkindly, but I have covenanted with my heart not to know it ... in shew we are great. All my revenge shall be to heap coals on their heads." Then he warned Carew that the two offenders showed all men's letters to every man.

Ralegh refused the offer of the Duke of Lennox. He was reconciled to being a superannuated favorite, a relic of earlier days. By his refusal to involve himself with the struggling factions he might the better keep his own; the honors and wealth he had won under Elizabeth. He was imputing generosity to James. When Ralegh was a dark Machiavellian he could toy with the fiercest of his age, but when he expected a matching of his native frankness by James he failed. James was greedy and without set purpose except becoming King. His mind was narrow, cramped by prejudices of a violent sort, and the riches of England distorted his imagination. He was vain and loved adulation as much as Elizabeth, but with a more fixed sense of his own importance. He was inquisitive, but only within a narrow

THE HALTING OF THE TIDE 211

mould. Ralegh saw he could not hope to please a monarch with whom he had so little in common. It was the penalty of being a favorite, to pass with the Queen, and yet, who knew? His loyalty to Elizabeth might be regarded favorably in the eyes of James. It would be a fair fight when it came, but to forward a succession—Ralegh refused the Duke of Lennox.

After that there were more letters written. Sir Robert Cecil sent missives to King James sealed with three impressions, bearing a lion rampant. His text was the destruction of Ralegh and when he wearied of it he wrote, "I will therefore leave the best and worst of him and other things to Lord Henry Howard's relation." He was checking Ralegh's relations with Lennox and so asked James who dealt between them, whereupon the royal Scotchman, as a proof of his trust in Cecil, named Sir Arthur Savage, but asked that no harm befall the honest, plain gentleman, since a kingly honor was involved. Meanwhile, Henry, Earl of Northumberland, wrote King James the only letter which ever treated Ralegh patronizingly.

"Sixteen years aquaintance hath confirmed to me, I must needs affirme Rawleighs ever allowance of your right, and although I know him insolent, extremely heated, a man that desires to seem to be able to swaye all men's fancies, all men's courses, and a man that out of himself, when your time shall come, will never be able to do you much good nor harm, yet must I needs confess what I know, that there is excellent good parts of nature in him, a man whose love is disadvantageous to me in some sort, which I cherish rather out of constancy than policy, and one whom I wish your majesty not to lose, because I would not that one hair of a man's head should be against you that might be for you."

Ralegh watched the coil of affairs twisting before his eyes without understanding the skein of fate. He knew much of the intrigues, but the whole pattern was of course imperceptible, or it would have fallen apart in a moment. The Queen was not well, although never complaining. Ralegh went to Bath for treatment at the same time Shakespeare was there in 1602. Essex was not yet out of mind. As he watched life change, Sir Walter conveyed Sherborne to himself for life, with successive remainders to his son, Walter, to any sons born later, and to his brother Carew Ralegh. In that same summer of 1602, he refused a challenge from Sir Amias Preston, which experience may have been the direct reminder to settle his estate. He cared nothing for duels, but his dislike did not touch his valor; that was beyond question. It was a world of quicksands and morass in which he was living, and none could be sure to emerge alive.

In the year when so much was being thought of new rulers, Ralegh bade good-bye to another of his splendid dreams. Once he had thought of himself in power over an empire, the opulence of Virginia. Once too he had deemed his Irish holidays a refuge from disfavor, a retreat where something of pastoral peace awaited him, but he had cut much timber, set two hundred men at work in a hogshead factory and been robbed by his lessees, which ultimately had gotten him into a wrangle over the disposal of his product in competition with others. In December, 1602, he sold his Irish holdings, excepting only the ancient castle of Inchiquin Ralegh. He was bidding adieu to his fondest hopes. He had once come out of Ireland triumphantly, but not even there would his spirit find things of pride his own, should fortune strike at him. It was a turning aside of the face, a refusal to look life in the eyes, or else, it was flinging of the gauntlet in the face of fate, demanding the turn of the wheel. Only Ralegh knew what his gestures meant, be they winged as Niccolo's or regarding first causes as Bacon's, or stupid as Cobham's, they were his own and part of his counsel which he shared with no man.

2

It was a queer Christmas, the last of Elizabeth, filled with contradictions, careless talk, and unrest. Sir Walter Ralegh loved the Queen too much to discuss the succession, but he went down to Sherborne for his holiday and carried off Lord Cobham and Lord Compton with him. Sir John Harington wrote to his wife that the Queen was in a "most pitiable state" yet he turned from her "show of human infirmity" and invited Rutland, Pembroke, and Bedford, Sir Henry Carey and Sir Robert Sidney to spend Christmas with him in the pastoral Rutlandshire. The Queen's plight affected her godson so much that he sent off to James a letter, some verses and a curiously wrought lamp, this last accompanied by astonishing words, "Lord, remember me when thou comest in thie Kingdom."[13] Sir John was playing the avarice of James against royal reverence and seemed to forget he was quoting the words of a thief, even though crucified.

At court; plays, bear baiting, dancing, and cards were all quite as gay as usual. Cheer was afoot. Cecil lost eight hundred pounds at play in a single night. Those of the household took no heed of their mistress. Elizabeth could no longer ride for an hour without resting two days. She held a cup in her hands and pretended to sip from it, but neither drank nor ate anything.

Since the Queen was shrouded with melancholy, mystery stirred. Old tales about her were bruited through the city and throve unpunished. She had married her daughter to the Prince of Condé, she had murdered a son delivered at Hampstead at midnight, she had loved her ministers by the dozen, lewdly making a mock of the passions she had indulged. Midwives, barbers, indigent gentlemen, vendors: all the claque who applauded such horrors and outrages struggled for guarded notoriety. With her were libelled her nobles.

Cecil had murdered poor Essex. The Secretary was ready to betray his country to Italy, where he had established credit. The army was half paid. France and the Netherlands stood ready to invade. Cecil was in league with the Pope. Complaint in parliament brought no relief. Some of all this reached the presence chamber. Since Ash Wednesday, throughout the year, Elizabeth had grown steadily worse. On that day, the anniversary of the death of Essex, she had burst into tears. She would not see Doctor Barlow, who had preached against him, and when Harington recalled a word of Essex she fell aweeping, beating her breast and making great moan.

When 1603 began, she had her coronation ring, which had grown too small for her, filed from her finger and then as if to give the lie to superstition, she moved the court to Richmond where she received the Venetian ambassador. She was bejewelled, panoplied in taffeta, brilliant with necklaces and bracelets. He bowed before her, congratulating her upon her good health, and she, from the dais, made all show of majesty the occasion demanded. This was on Sunday, February 6, and a foul, wet winter was drawing to an end. The Venetian awaited a second audience. A month brought only postponement, for which the Queen's health was not made a pretext. No better announcement that she was ailing could have been offered. Then, in March, the Countess of Nottingham, the wife of the old Lord Admiral, died. Another link with the days of struggle was gone. Elizabeth felt her ailments heavily. She had an aching in her bones. Her feet were always chill. Neither day nor night brought sleep. She could scarce swallow for the soreness of her throat.

It was a bad time for the court. Silent for hours, she sat and stared before her, even as Mary Tudor had done long years before. A terrible tenseness settled upon her. The Council was at court in force. She would see none of them but Cecil and the Archbishop. She listened to the reading of the old Canterbury Tales attentively. Their broad humanity smacked of the way she had walked through life, and eased her introspection, but they were only a phase. She was soon sorrowing again amid her shadows. Nothing in the world was worthy to trouble her and the forced spirit, with which she had kept up the round of habit so long, flashed out utterly. She took no medicine. The doctors found no disease, to which she answered: "I am not sick, I feel no pain, and yet I pine away."

On March 6 she went into the garden in a perverse mood. After that she took no more interest in the nearness of spring. In three days she was nearly dead, lying in a coma. When she was in a stupor her physicians could take charge. On the 11th an abscess in the throat opened and gave her relief. Her ailments were as vacillating as her actions in earlier times. She ate and drank a little, but in a few days, when Sir Robert Carey went in to her, she could only wring his hand and say, "No, Robin, I am not well." Was she wandering? She ended by sighing many times. Was she thinking of Leicester? He, too, had been her "Robin." Alas, there had been so many, and all gone, even to poor languishing Essex. She talked of her symptons with utter clarity to her grandnephew, and he went away mourning her melancholy but with no thought of any madness.

On March 20, she was well enough to order the great chapel made ready for public service the next morning. The court gathered that Sunday in much of a quandary. The morning wore away. Ten changed to eleven. Elizabeth then announced she would hear service in the little chapel, but time dragged on and she got no nearer the chapel than the floor of her Privy Chamber, where, stretched upon three cushions, she heard the service, but would not afterward return to her bed.

The finger of England was on her pulse. Vagrants were pressed *en masse* and shipped to the army in the Netherlands, that they might not riot in London. The fleet was made ready and set to control the Channel. The London authorities set watch. Rurals sought safety for their plate and gold. Cavalry was set to guard the exchequer. Edward Bruce wrote Henry Howard saying, "Cobham and Ralegh are forlorne in our accompts." King James had sent a blue ring to Lady Scrope to await the expected moment. The Queen's own Chaplain, the Bishop of Winchester, composed a public prayer for the Queen's recovery, while the council, in solemn conclave, discussed the propriety of asking her to name her successor before it was too late. The Lord Keeper, followed by Secretary Cecil, put the question to her. "Who should succeed?" "No base person, but a King," she said, putting the belief of a lifetime into a word and that spoken with struggle. Even at the verge of darkness she was still Queen—royalty looking across the gulf set between her and her realm.

On the third day she did not speak. Her eyes were open but staring. One finger was inserted in her mouth. She was put to bed that day, thanks to the courage of Lord Admiral Howard who dared defy her commands. Shrewsbury, Worcester, Cecil, Grey, Knollys were all there. By their orders none were allowed to enter or leave the palace, save the servants preparing the horses and coaches to carry the Councillors to London. The Queen lay with one white hand outside the coverlet, her breathing light. Prayers rose from the inner room, stabbing the impatient silence. She had the luck of a fortunate Queen, not to be deserted then. At last, all left her but her women and Canterbury who prayed aloud as the night grew. She was insistent he continue, but her breathing grew feeble, irregular, then imperceptible. At last Lady Scrope rose from amid the sorrowing attendants and

THE HALTING OF THE TIDE 217

passed from the room. She took off her finger the blue ring James had arranged as a signal he could trust, and, leaning out of the window, threw it to her brother, Robert Carey, who, so soon as he had confirmed the news, made off to Edinburgh to greet James ruler of England, Ireland, and Wales.

There followed a weird procession by night from Richmond to Westminster. Black water lapping grassy banks and a slow journey by the river loops. Under flickering torches the Queen was rowed down Thames, her household following in other barges. It was her final progress full of color and the black melancholy she had envisioned. The river opened to the Surrey meadows and the roar of the overfalls at London bridge rumbled heavily. Wrapped in its cere cloth, soldered in lead, unseen by any after the death at Richmond, her body was watched over by her ladies. For more than a month the funeral was amaking.

3

Sir Walter Ralegh and his Guard standing with lowered points. Bell ringers and knight marshal's men clearing a space in the crowd. Two hundred sixty poor women and sixteen poor men shamble along all in black. Mechanics, servitors, couriers, scullions, hostlers, wood choppers, drawers of the royal household walking to the blast of trumpets. Behind them the menials of the courtiers. Elizabeth the Queen is dead and has no needs more.

The pursuivants at arms striding along. The standard of the Dragon, of the Greyhound, of the Lion, all signifying the burial of a Tudor. The chapel children in cope and surplice, marching, singing in mournful tune. The mayor recorder and aldermen of London passing. The banners of Chester, of Cornwall, of Wales, of Ireland. Lord Keeper Egerton carrying the seals, that for a time mean nothing, in a bag over his shoulder. The French Ambassador parading with a train six yards long. Pembroke and Howard of Effingham bearing the embroidered banner of England guarded by heralds. All these pass Sir Walter Ralegh and his men, waiting. Sir Walter gives the low word of command. The Guard is going too. Elizabeth the Queen is dead and has no needs more.

She rode in waxen effigy upon the royal hearse. She wore her parliament robes, crowned and sceptred, for she was indeed going unto her people. The canopy above was borne by six Earls. The place of Essex, leading the Queen's palfrey, was taken by the Earl of Worcester, walking just behind the hearse. The body, embalmed, sheathed in lead, covered with purple velvet, lay beneath the effigy, resting upon a chariot drawn by four horses trapped in black velvet. The Marchioness of Northampton, the ranking noblewoman of England, her train tended by two countesses, paced on foot the slow, sad measure. Elizabeth the Queen was dead and had no needs more.

A little group followed close upon her. The Lord Admiral, now but a shadow, Buckhurst, the Lord Treasurer, successor to old Burghley, two Earls, a dozen Countesses, the Queen's ladies, the maids of honor, trod to the end their little day of grandeur and power.

Sir Walter Ralegh swung his Guard sharply. Halberd points lowered. Hoods all sable. Suits of sober black. Silence along the short way from Whitehall to the Abbey. Sobs and tears. Words and staid airs. The hollow tread of slow feet upon the stone floor. The lift of the Gothic groining opening into uncertainty, like the sky sweeping palms of Guiana. The procession running on endlessly, a mighty stream like the Orinoco. Ralegh for a time a metaphysician. Somewhere the fugitive spirit of the woman who had jested broadly in rough speech and whose eye had bidden obedience at a glance,—somewhere the threefold soul had gone. Cyril said, "that the souls of women are very womanish; hard and slow to understand hard things." Elizabeth had matched the greatest men in her own will. She had entered her tomb. "In this life the reward of the godly is small." The feet were moving again, more quickly. Ralegh had a Guard now with no purpose. He took them out of the Abbey in order, leaving the candle smoke about the tomb, dim against the dusky screen. An order, whispered, brought his men out into the April air. He had a Guard now without a duty. The unbelievable had come to pass. Elizabeth the Queen was dead and had no needs more.

CHAPTER XVI

LONG LIVE THE KING

ALL the world was weary of religious struggle. When the Councillors arrived at Westminster in the chill dawn and proclaimed their intention "to maintain and uphold King James' person and estate, as our only undoubted Sovereign Lord and King, with the sacrifice of our lives, lands, goods, and friends, and adherents against all force, power, or practice, that shall go about, by word or deed, to interrupt, contradict, or impugn his just claim, or his entry into this Kingdom or into any part thereof, at his good pleasure," the sacred fires burned low. French Huguenots and Catholics had reached an armistice of exhaustion. Lerma and Uzeda dominated weak Philip III, leading Spain away from the defense of the faith and striving for peace with all nations, especially England. The glow of fervor had paled. In the far-off Chinese court, Ricci, the Jesuit, might teach Christianity with all missionary zeal. Europe felt the sloth of fatigue even to Scandinavia and Germany. The war of beliefs was by no means over, but as national propaganda Christ and Anti-Christ appeared a bit worn. The Bible had been translated into German and was soon to be accessible in English. Intolerance was no longer the mode.

In a world so quiet, all bigots cast their eyes upon James. He had said, after his return to Scotland from Denmark, that he blessed God that he was born at such a time of the Gospel and to be King of such a church, the purest church in the world. "And for our neighbor Church of England, what is their service but an ill said mass in English?" When he came to be England's King, he still felt that the "Kirk" of Scotland was superlative. The church of Geneva honored the pagan Yule and the Hebrew Pasch and "What have they from the Word of God for that?" Naturally, the English courtiers turned biblical as they had once been Euphuistic. Wondering, hoping they might meditate upon the nature of the young Scotchman, Catholics, Puritans, and Episcopalians tried to read between the lines, long before James was crowned. Henry Howard, Earl of Northampton, was a Romanist in secret all his life and died an avowed one. He did not fail to plead for toleration. England—so great a kingdom—was worth allowing "a mass in a corner." Cecil had struggled too long with recusants and their plots to favor the Catholics and his youth touched the Puritan vigor that had brought the long wars with Spain. For him, the Church of England, with the King at the head, was the proper medium. "I love not to yield to any toleration." Here was a power he could use to attack Spain or mollify the King; a weapon fitted to his interests. The general reputation of James as a religious man bred doubt, but to Ralegh this outlook could promise nothing. He was too generally reputed an atheist.

When James was travelling south, Sir Walter took his fate in his hands. He thought of Sir Robert Crosse. They had faced the Spanish at Cadiz. Together they would front this monarch from the north. A proclamation was out, prohibiting persons in public office from resorting to the King. Cecil was trying to keep Ralegh in London. Ralegh galloped off with his knightly friend at his back. The proclamation had said resorting to the King injured public business. Sir Walter sought him out to secure the continuance of his legal powers in the Duchy of Cornwall, thus giving the lie to the proclamation. None could deny his devotion to public duty. It was all a Quixotic turning of Machiavell. As Niccolo phrased it, "I conclude then that fortune varying and men remaining fixed in their ways, they are successful so long as these ways conform to each other." Ralegh had felt the wings of fortune brush past. He would not be as Cecil, or Bacon, or Howard, relying upon their snares. He could not match them in dark plans for he had not their resources. What happened in Council he only knew by hearsay. They were at the heart of those things. Well then, how outface them? War? He had never succeeded at anything as well as he had in war. He would fling his powers at the feet of his Prince. For the state, for the prestige of the throne, the prowess of Ralegh offered freely, the reward left unbargained: it was a proud gesture, a bold conception, evading plots and counterplots at a leap. Howard or Cecil would have known better than to do it.

James was a plain man with no grace of person. His eyes were as hard as Elizabeth's with something of the ferret in them. His nose strong, his mouth truculent and testy; he was the soul of suspicion. When Ralegh reached his presence, with his unfaltering gaze and imperious manner, the King felt the force of him and remembered letters from Howard and Cecil. Here was the man. Slyly watching him, James made that awful pun upon his name. Ralegh! Rawly did he think of the great one of Elizabeth. There was a flash of fire in Sir Walter and James passed from pointed pleasantry to a hasty authorization of Ralegh's power in Cornwall. "Let them be delivered speedily, that Ralegh may be gone again," he said to Sir Thomas Lake and when the old favorite had gone with good Sir Robert Crosse still riding henchman at his back, Lord Henry Howard, who even then was attending upon James, knew the triumph of his scheming.

With the royal favor so obviously removed Ralegh's enemies took heart. Said La Rochefoucauld, "Pride is equal in all men; and the only difference is in the means and manner of displaying it." Ralegh's pride had been arrogant, Henry Howard's envious, Cecil's self-congratulatory. Sir Thomas

Lake wrote Cecil to assure him Ralegh had "taken no great root here." . . . Cecil felt it safe to prepare his stroke against Sir Walter.

It is hard to understand the malice of Cecil. Ralegh had been a friend of his father. Ralegh had never put slight upon him. Their wives and children were intimate. Sir Walter almost never wrote a letter to Cecil but it contained a message of kindness from Lady Ralegh. For years they had been partners in privateering ventures, Cecil sharing the profits, Ralegh directing the effort. Ralegh was strong, able, vigorous and Cecil was thwarted, almost misshapen in body. Cecil played with nations: France, Spain, Italy, Denmark, yet was himself a physical cipher. Ralegh was a man of the sword, so Cecil first bound him to do what others directed, and then, when James, who shivered at the drawing of a sword, came to the throne, found his friend no longer serviceable and cast him aside as he would a nation. So far his purpose is discernible. Whatever he had done against Ralegh before James was crowned is clear and logical. The Devonshire man had a way with royalty and Cecil could brook no rivalry, but when James was on the throne Cecil never relented. His malice was deadly, striking at the very life of his friend.

The year was a time of wonders. The Queen died in March. James left Scotland on April 5. On April 25, Ralegh turned back from James at Burghley. Within a week the monopolies of Elizabeth were attacked by James before the Council at Theobald's, the country seat of Cecil, and Ralegh's income from the farming of wines was stopped at once. Two weeks from the interview at Burghley, Sir Walter faced the Council at Whitehall. King James was not present. The plague rendered London unsafe for his royal person, but the Lord President of the Council conveyed his pleasure to Ralegh. The King had appointed Sir Thomas

Erskine, brother of the Earl of Mar, Captain of the Guard. Ralegh bowed and submitted himself. On May 14, the King remitted to him three hundred pounds a year under an altered patent for the Island of Jersey, by way perhaps of mollifying a knight who might prove dangerous. James was always afraid and always inconsiderate. He aimed at popularity in striking at Ralegh. On May 31, the Church took its revenge upon the falling favorite. Durham House had been church property. Bishop Tobias Matthew of Durham had lost the See of Sarum through Ralegh's opposition. Bishop Matthews pleaded the cause of the Church before James at Berwick and squared accounts by securing a royal warrant for Ralegh and Sir Edward Darcy to remove. With very little of Christian charity the Bishop forced them to quit the house by midsummer. It was an indignity at the hands of a man who hardly dared face Sir Walter in earlier days. When a knight began to suffer from the velvet spleen of clerics it was a year of wonders, but the summer was to find greater miracles still.

James was bent upon popularity. He moved out from under the immediate influence of Cecil. Elizabeth had found the royal progress a way to establish contact with her nobles at their own expense. James saw in it the plucking of the English and the assertion of his authority. On Progress he went to Beddington Park as the guest of Carew. It was cleverly arranged. Carew was the uncle of Lady Ralegh.

Sir Walter had written and presented to James the *Discourse Touching a War with Spain, and of the protecting of the Netherlands.* Curiosity had moved the King to give attention to the matter. Sequestered within the beauty of restful Surrey he might never again be so ready to accept Ralegh's services. Sir Walter approached his monarch and undertook to argue the need for attacking Spain and at once. He was making his grand gesture, offering himself as a warrior. He promised to raise two thousand men at his own expense, to lead them, in person, to Spanish territory. For a blow at Spain he would gladly risk his life. He was an older man than the King, gifted in fiery eloquence, with which to support a lifelong conviction, but a little lame and with whitened hair. The destruction of Spain was a theme he had never forgotten through all his fifty-one years. He was vigorous still but he was cautious. To win belief was worth a little time. There must be no coercion. "If any persuade your Majesty to a hasty conclusion for either part, I should suspect him to be more concerned for his own or some other's, than for your Majesty's interest."

James was thirty-seven years old. Never had he felt any desire to go charging into battle at peril of life and limb. That there lived men whose true vocation was war he could not believe. This man was crazed or else deep in something dark and devious. The man was trying to lead him somewhere. Spain yearned for peace. France wanted no English-Spanish alliance. Henry had sent over Sully, who, lost in the multitude of intrigues he found underway, had soon gone home. James suspected such naïve fairness untouched by bargain. His eyelids lowered; the corners of his mouth slackened. He looked down his nose and, surrounded by uncertainty, wondered what was the purpose of this troubled Ralegh. Of course he sought favor, but that was not to be gained in some obscure Spanish town ruddy in flames. The King was suspicious.

Howard and Cecil had warned him. Ralegh had not changed, had not conformed to altered fortune. James pictured England at war, Spanish ships standing up channel, Spanish guns pointed at his palaces. He shuddered at the thought of heading his armies in the field. This man, who stirred such images, was gunpowder. He was all violence and so bold his very manner smacked of disrespect. These favorites of Elizabeth had been a careless, self-willed crew. Essex had dared to raise his hand against his Queen. This man dared do anything if the idea seized him, and his gaze had no touch of becoming diffidence. He feared not God they said, and it was very doubtful that he feared his King. Instead his vehemence frightened James. He would see what Howard and Cecil could make of the man. There was no need for royal attack. It might return upon his own head. He verily believed Ralegh's pride was as great as his own, God's own anointed, appointed by heaven to rule, and his courage—Ralegh's gaze went quite through one. James made no answer.

So the year of miracles wore away. Ralegh received many a buffet, but he followed the court in its movements. Perseverance might bring a change of favor. An emergency might offer him an opportunity. The King reached Windsor in July without Sir Walter having improved his position. James did not dare go to London because of the plague. Something of his prestige demanded he should be seen in the city as England's own, but he loitered, intent upon rural pleasure. To ride out with the King might offer little sport, but Ralegh was playing for the stake of his life. The flat, broad humor, the soiled linen, the garish splendor, the pedantic narrowness: these things had to be borne with in a King. Ralegh waited for his monarch on a clear, cool morning. Summer was at its lush full. From the terrace at Windsor its beauty was at its best. True, Elizabeth's new buildings were a little raw against the soft dull tones of the older castle, but the day was serene and the King would presently ride. While Ralegh waited Cecil came out to him.

Sir Robert announced he came as from the King. His manner was easy without suggested import. He knew Ralegh had the summer in his blood and had no knowledge of all that was making. Sir Walter did not realize the old adventurous spirit, the blend of pride and honor, was a thing of suspicion under James. The morning light was bright. Cecil looked up into his face unblinking and without a false accent told him the King had excused him. He was not to go riding. He was to attend the Lords of Council. They desired to question him. He had often given information. A hundred times his knowledge had served. He never suspected Cecil in the matter. Boldly he strode into the castle, leaving the peace of the summer morning. Sir Robert followed, his shadow long and crooked in the sunlight.

2

James at Windsor seemed a monster to the English. His eyes were large and he rolled them frightfully out of dread, when he spied a stranger. His beard was thin, his tongue too large for his mouth, his body short and thick, his legs weak and poor, his skin soft as taffeta sarcenet and dirty. He despised washing and his body harbored lice while, during his occupancy of Theobolds, the house was infested with fleas. He was a scholar without taste, a moralist who was curious in morality, a philosopher all prejudice and a King all dread.

Queen Elizabeth had been dead less than four months, but the grace and power of her had flown with her passing. She had delegated responsibility and authority. James gave no authority. He was King. Anything beyond his experience was something to be dreaded. The English in bulk frightened him. They were not always well ordered. They were sometimes violent. Even in their religion they were so active. Catholic, Puritan, Church of England, they were likely to rend him limb from limb if they could. Yet he did not mollify them. Instead he sat in his quilted doublet and stuffed breeches, safe from dagger thrusts although reeking in sweat and tried to be the wisdom, the wit, the strength of the nation. All about him milled plot within plot, courtier against courtier, faction against King, throne against throne. The Howards against the Herberts, the Howards against Cobham and Ralegh, the Jesuits against James, Spain and the Spanish Lowlands against England: these were all multiplying an hundredfold. To stem them all, Robert Cecil had to save James in spite of the Stuart egotism. James was his King; he had made him. It was his necessity to guard him, for should the royal Scot fail, Cecil passed with him, and Cecil was at his most dangerous year—he was forty-two.

Plots were everywhere but that had always been true. What court does not carry its tinder carelessly, never heeding the bonfire of the world should the flame strike through? He kept his gaze upon the smouldering discontent. Ralegh was aglow with resentment. The Catholics, such as Sir Griffin Markham and Anthony Copley, were warming to wrath. James had failed them. When Cobham had approached the King about the peace with Spain, which he hoped to arrange through Count d'Arenbergh, James had resented Cobham's activity and had shown it. Cobham had been very open in his dislike of the King ever since, thereby confirming the opinion Howard and Cecil had filed in Edinburgh before Queen Elizabeth's death. Individually, Cecil knew his dangers. It was the threat of combined secrecy that called for his cautious vigilance.

Then, suddenly, he found all the game in his hands. He would put out the fires of retribution at a blow, or rather, without a blow. The government would handle everything through normal channels. There might be surprise to be met. Cecil neither then nor ever knew all the depth and breadth of his discovery.

In 1602, two priests, William Watson and Francis Clarke, sought out James to plead for toleration, or even religious freedom for the Catholics when he should come into his second kingdom. Watson at least gained an audience. James was just then promising, with canny evasion of course, anything to any one, even assuring the Pope that his coming to the throne would be a state of joy to the English Catholics. Watson saw through the honeyed bigotry and, returning to England, became so energetic in his party that he was in prison for a time, but was presently let loose, perhaps with the purpose of allowing him to hasten his destruction. Swiftly he schemed. He and Clarke gained the support of Anthony Copley, scion of a Catholic family, George Brooke, brother of Henry Brooke, Lord Cobham, and a reckless man, and Sir Griffin Markham. Markham was the most interesting of the accomplices. He had served Elizabeth so well she had given him Beskwood in the forest of Nottinghamshire, where he lived like a Robin Hood. A thousand men would have been put to it to take him if he had cared to remain in the forest. All so far enlisted were Catholics. Next, Lord Thomas Grey of Wilton was approached. A Grey of Wilton had fought the Irish and defended the realm against the Armada. It was a truly noble name and one best known in the wars. Lord Grey was a Protestant, more than that, a Puritan within the Church of England who hated "Popery," but who loathed this Scotch King even more. Watson and Clarke were succeeding in building a faction. The final candidate was Sir Edward Parham, a Catholic of good standing. By that time the priests imagined themselves deep as the sea, and as obscure as some of the church fathers.

When Watson enlisted Parham he changed his plans. Originally, the plotters were to surprise the Court at Greenwich on Midsummer Night, arrest the King, and carry him off as a hostage, but without harming him. Meanwhile another wing of the conspirators was to seize the Tower of London, within which the King would be imprisoned until a new government had been formed. Just how quickly the testy, stubborn, but cowardly James might be brought to terms was impossible to predict. It was there that Sir Edward Parham would earn his share in the rewards.

Watson planned that when Lord Grey had successfully surprised the Court at Greenwich, and had the King secure, Parham should attack Grey, rescue the King, and carry him off to the Tower as the only place of safety for his person. The plan so carried out, the King would be very ready to accede to the wishes of his rescuers and be everlastingly grateful to those of the Catholic faith for proven loyalty. Watson never seemed to realize that probably the King would have died in a paroxysm of fear before he had been an hour in custody.

Cecil did not know all the steps of the conspirators; it remained for the jumbled examination to unfold them. He did realize there was just a possibility of the traitors succeeding if foreign aid was given them. Later, he wrote Sir Thomas Parry, Ambassador to France, the reward for which each strove. Lord Grey should be Earl Marshal. Markham would have Cecil's post and be Secretary. George Brooke aimed at being Treasurer. Watson, the priest, longed to be named Lord Chancellor. Cecil knew too that the attempt was postponed because Lord Grey, wise, although only thirty years of age, caught the possibility of Catholic union against him and pleaded his party was not yet ready to move. Three hundred men slept nightly about the Court at Richmond, posted with an eye to proper defense. For the "Bye" or "Surprise" plot Cecil had all in readiness.

The idea that so determined a plot must secure confidence from a promise of foreign support grew upon the crafty Secretary. He knew, through his agents, Lord Cobham met Sir Walter Ralegh frequently. Sir Walter was openly discontented although cautious in his expression. Cobham raged loudly: Cecil was a traitor, the new King had surrounded himself by scoundrels, England was betrayed. He told every one what he felt, even Beaumont, the French Ambassador. He had as many foreign contacts as Ralegh. Together they were the possible influence upon which foreign support of a plot might rely. In June, Charles, Count d'Arenbergh, came to London, in the company of Henry Howard. Cecil saw no perfidy in this affiliation, but when Cobham visited the Count on June 9, and later Cobham and Ralegh conferred at Durham House, which Ralegh had not yet vacated, the Secretary felt assured of treachery. He waited to see what form of Punic faith he had to deal with, waited patiently. Count d'Arenbergh was minister to Archduke Albert who had married the Infanta Isabel. Jointly they ruled the Spanish Low Countries. In his heart Cecil knew Ralegh hated Spain. Was the disaffected knight so broken in mind as to risk his estate of Sherborne upon political dice, a gamble in regime? Was not Ralegh too practical a Machiavellian to so behave? Cecil himself had followed the Florentine maxims to win the favor of his King. Was Ralegh lacking in thoroughness? The vision of the dead Queen, the weakness of dislike, the rebuff of personal affront: these might shake him. So put out, would he not between James and Spain choose to serve his life-long enemy, turn traitor? Cecil watched and listened.

It was Copley who ended the matter for the conspirators. He was a dashing young man, who could not resist the dramatic in the situation. To be an actor one must have an audience. Copley chose his sister. He told her as he went from home that he was engaged upon a great and dangerous undertaking for the good of his country. His manner gave his words ominous weight. His sister repeated his saying to her husband, who could make nothing of it, but thought it important enough to reveal it to old Lord Admiral Howard, while a loyal Catholic wrote to Cecil at the same time enclosing correspondence of the conspiracy. Already the Howards found themselves competing for royal favor with the Herberts. The Lord Admiral hastened to prove his attachment to the King, and caused the immediate arrest of Copley. This was on July 6. Sir Walter Ralegh wrote Cobham of it. Copley was given six days to become thoroughly frightened and then was examined. The "Bye" or "Surprise" plot was tapped at last. They were all in. Markham tried to get from Lord Cobham, through his brother, George Brooke, a passport to clear the country, but Markham did not escape. This was the sole contact of Lord Cobham with the plot, although much of his wild talk was quoted as inspiring the action. The priests, Watson and Clarke, Copley, Brooke, Lord Grey, and Markham were all examined, which resulted in a mystifying mass of testimony, often contradicting itself and involved beyond hope of disentanglement.

Cecil found George Brooke very interesting. The Secretary reasoned since one brother had moved so much in the matter the other might have glanced at it also. George Brooke disclosed his brother's dealings with Count d'Arenbergh through Matthew La Renzi as an emissary. When the examiners touched upon Ralegh, Brooke averred that what was in Cobham's mind was in Ralegh's. Cobham was called to be questioned on July 15, and immediately afterward, Sir Walter Ralegh stepped from the sunlight of the morning at Windsor into the chill austerity of an interview with the Lords of Council. Sir Robert Cecil had bridged the gap between the "Bye" and the "Main" plot by a connecting witness: George Brooke.

The Lords asked Ralegh of the conspiracy to surprise and coerce the King. He denied any knowledge of it. Did he know anything of a plot to replace James by Arabella? He did not. What did he know of the relations of Lord Cobham and d'Arenbergh? Nothing. The Lords let him go, but with orders to confine himself to his house.

LONG LIVE THE KING

There was work to do, work that took the rest of the summer. Prisoner after prisoner was interrogated, questions propounded out of statements. Since George Brooke bridged the gap between the "Bye" and the "Main" the examiners worked upon him unceasingly. Never was greater effort expended. Testimony was cut down to abstract, the interrogators keeping the portions that served their purpose. There is no injustice in saying that the inquiry was one of purpose, not one of exploration. The inquisitors knew what they sought; what they could not find they would create. Those in the "Bye" plot would suffer. Those in the "Main" plot should perish. It was time Cobham and Ralegh went out. On July 17, the strongest statement against Ralegh that George Brooke could give was, "The conspirators, among themselves, thought Sir Walter Ralegh a fit man to be of the action." Six weeks later he had been worked up to deposing that Ralegh, and his brother Cobham, had resolved to destroy the King with "all his cubs." Brooke, Watson, and Copley accused every one suggested to them. They "thought" anything that would relieve their mortal terror, and this "thinking" was entered to be used later as testimony when the trials for life began.

Cobham, linked with Ralegh, was difficult. At first his answers were purely negative. He confessed nothing, made no statement. Then, frightened, he proceeded cautiously to fence. Some of what he wrote was used at Ralegh's trial and lost afterward. He found himself outfaced by men intent upon destruction. On July 20, he admitted he had conferred with d'Arenbergh. More than five hundred thousand crowns were to be put into his hands to be distributed to discontented Englishmen. He agreed with d'Arenbergh to speak first to Sir Walter Ralegh concerning those chosen to share. Oh, it was a hazy affair of hearsay and inference, shadowed by innuendo. When Cobham had served them so well as to connect Ralegh's name with his intentions, the inquirers put before him a note in Ralegh's hand. He read. He checked. Then, angrily, "O traitor! O villain! I will now tell you all the truth," and so burst into a torrent of blame. Ralegh had led him into a false position. Ralegh would never let him be. Ralegh had made him discontented. Ralegh had smirched for him the justice and mercy of their King. Cecil's eyes never shone more brightly than at that. Ralegh was connected with the Main: he had meant to dethrone James and crown Arabella with the aid of the foreign money. Just that might not be proven, perhaps, but something very like it. Cecil would seem more perfect in the eyes of the King he had made when Ralegh and Cobham were gone. They alone had not shared his efforts before Elizabeth's death; they only lay outside the circle of rewards and obligations. Their independence would be the end of them and Cecil would have none to cross him before the King.

So Ralegh was taken from his house and examined by Bishop Bancroft, sitting as a Royal Commissioner at Fulham Palace. The Bishop regarded him dispassionately as a man already disgraced. Ralegh had been forced to resign as Warden of the Stannaries. He saw before him the machinery of a criminal prosecution, which he knew well concerned itself so seldom with equity, so frequently with settling private grudges, or the sacrificing of any victim not adequately defended by influence. Cobham's examination was so fruitful in the eyes of the Commissioners that Ralegh was taken from the presence of the Bishop to the two small rooms in the Bloody Tower, in the very shadow of Traitor's Gate, where philosophy took flight. He could see no way through the mass of folly he knew to be arrayed against him. Cobham accused, retracted, and from August onward struggled to address the Lords as a matter of conscience in Ralegh's behalf. Ralegh admitted Cobham had offered him ten thousand crowns to further peace between Spain and England. Ralegh denied he had made Cobham any answer, for he thought the offer "one of his ordinary idle conceits; and therefore made no account thereof." At the same time he enjoined Cobham to clear him by speaking the truth in an interchange of letters made possible through his jailers' sons: first young Peyton and later George Harvey, together with Edward Cottrell, a Tower servant. To add to the August madness, Sir John Peyton was made Governor of Jersey, the King declaring Ralegh's office forfeit by intended treason. In September, "the Commission of Lieutenancy granted to Sir Walter Ralegh being become void and determined," Ralegh was stripped indeed.

It did not take even many hours in the Tower for Ralegh to scan his position. Ruin had come down upon him. He had no hope of keeping anything but Sherborne, which by his arrangements should go to his son. If he died for treason none could tell what the Scotch James might do. His trial had no connection with his innocence. Death waited just ahead, death and disgrace, with the nodding of heads in approval. All the tribe of lesser men, who had never understood his clear-eyed visions nor dared to front him in fight, would vent their spleen upon those he left. If one died in the Tower—Sherborne was saved for his legal heirs; a monstrous rumor against Cecil and the Commissioners would be sure to stir the air—murder, cruelty, injustice bruited everywhere; and death so won came but a little sooner. Cecil meant murder. To die at his own will was to play his only card with a gallant flirt of the cape, a thoughtful fingering of the pointed beard, a slow roll of the eyes under the brow lifted in surprise. It was to accentuate the trust of the dead Queen in his courage and carry his name clear of a world tumbling about him.

He wrote to Elizabeth Ralegh in great distress, "I am now

made an enemy and traitor by the word of an unworthy man." That for Lord Cobham; and for Lord Henry Howard, "God forgive my Lord Harry, for he was my heavy enemy." Piteously he put his hopeless trust in his oldest friend and most destructive foe. "And for my Lord Cecil I thought he would never forsake me in extremity. I would not have done it to him, God knows. But do not thou know it for he must be master of thy child and may have compassion of him." Ironically, as he knew, Cecil was Master of the Court of Wards, so the boy would be much in the power of the Lord Treasurer. Other sad words he wrote: remembrances to an illegitimate daughter, to his debtors, to Keymis, his faithful captain; a hope that death wipes out memory, hateful jibes, and the taunts of the lawyers as well as their onslaughts upon honor and decency. May death lay him "up in dark forgetfulness." Innocent he was. His son must know he was no traitor and his wife must live to rear his son. Hope and despair live not together. The poor prisoner will destroy himself, trusting in God's mercy. Not a word to be spoken of Sherborne. The less said of the deed he had prepared the better. So ran his curious letter to Elizabeth Ralegh, filled at once with belief and denial of faiths. When he had written he went to dinner with Sir John Peyton, Lieutenant of the Tower.

At table Sir Walter tore open his vest, and being ready drove a knife into his breast. It struck a rib and glanced. There was no weapon handy for a desperate, smashing blow, nor time for another trial. The pain flashed hope. "There! An end!" he said brokenly, and let the knife fall.

CHAPTER XVII

TREASON

JAMES was a pedant, but a stupid scholar. So sure was he his kingship was of God, and so strong were his suspicions of everything strange or foreign, that he scorned the wisdom of Niccolo. His learning was clumsy; his craftiness but natural cunning. "Men who at the beginning of a new government were enemies, if they are of a kind to need support to maintain their position, can be very easily gained by the Prince, and they are the more compelled to serve him faithfully as they know they must by their deeds cancel the bad opinion previously held of them, and the Prince will always derive greater help from them than from those who, serving him with greater security, neglect his interests." Niccolo pointed out sound policy in those words; James ignored them. He had not appreciated the value of Ralegh, nor his willingness to serve. The royal pride stood by the first impression of dislike and shuddered at the warlike spirit of the Devon knight. The bugaboo of violence always put the august brain awry.

Out of his vanity, rather than his ignorance, James scorned to be Machiavellian. He was blazing a path for a will made imperial by God. This relationship with heaven he took very intimately. To himself he was consistent. Howard and Cecil he denied nothing. They had given him secret aid. By them he had newly taken the throne of England. Machiavell advised a prince so placed, "He must consider well the motives that have induced those who have favored him to do so, and if it is not natural affection for him, but only because they were not contented with the state as it was, he will have great trouble and difficulty in maintaining their friendship, because it will be impossible for him to content them." But James felt no need to make content even the faithful who had smoothed his path. Since he had been successful, he believed he was the chosen of God, truly the Lord's anointed. This was not clever, but it saved him any pangs of remorse. It was good to owe only heaven, a debtor that exacted no immediate payment. Yet he frequently departed from his righteous divinity, turned his back upon the Scotch doctrine of eternal reward and punishment, and pondered upon the things of Hermes and Aphrodite. To certain young men, chosen for beauty, "the love the King showed was as amorously conveyed, as if he had mistaken their sex and thought them ladies."[14]

Something of all this Sir Walter Ralegh noted. He recognized his talk of an attack upon Spain had frightened the King. His person offered no passionate temptation to royalty: James was only thirty-seven; Ralegh was fifty-one, a man of presence the King would not have dared approach. In no way could he gain favor. A prisoner in the Tower, his liberty denied him, his friend Cobham chosen as the weapon with which to strike him dead, he saw his fortunes swallowed by his enemies. In despair he had stabbed himself. The knife had not pierced the muscle wall. In ten days the wound was healed, and at once Cecil was notified of his recovery.

The wry little man immediately spread his nets again to end Sir Walter. James was told of the attempted suicide, and with his eyes rolled up to heaven spoke of the soul's salvation almost lost, and sent his prisoner admonition. Ralegh should be probed by a good preacher. To slay the body was bad. To wound the spirit was for the soul's good. James did not come near the prisoner; a man who would use cold steel upon himself might think of murder. Aloof, like a god, he let Cecil work his will. Ralegh lay in the Bloody Tower, his mind clear, seeing all with pitiless clarity. He knew the injustice of the court before which he would appear, the insults and debasement incidental to legal practice. The Lords who would try him had a definite function; they would please Cecil. There was the greatest unkindness of all. The change in Cecil—how puzzling, and too dark to think upon, too murderous of noble instincts and large nature, free of heart, and magnanimous. It was like a dark play. The rabble might hate and welcome. The poor were always armed with envy, but Cecil was not poor, could not be matched by any rival. It was impossible to believe in his deadly hatred, and yet at every turn it was all too apparent.

Meanwhile the populace enjoyed the fall to the full. Ballads were written, appeared in broadside, but lived mostly by word of mouth, sung upon the streets.

> Wily Watt, Wilie Wat,
> Wots thou not and know thou what,
> Looke to thy form and quat,
> In town and citie
>
> Fresh honndes are on thy taile,
> That will pull downe thy saile,
> And make thy hart and quaile
> Lord for the pittie
>
> 'Lordshipp is flagg'd and fled,
> Captainshipp newly sped,
> Dried is the hogshead's hed
> Wilie Wat wilie
>
> Make the best of thy plea,
> Least the rest goe awaie,
> And thou brought for to saie,
> Wily beguilie
>
> For thy skuance and pride
> The bloudy minde beside,
> And thy mouth gaping wide
> Mischievous Machiavell.

> Essex for vengeance cries,
> His bloud upon the lies
> Mountinge above the skies,
>   Damnable fiend of hell
>   Michievous Machiavell."[15]

Miserable verse, heaping all sins upon Sir Walter, but sincere in hatred of the old favorite, and a popular viewpoint looking toward fallen greatness.

The brew was ready at last. It was pale and weak, but the best that could be concocted upon hearsay and disputed confessions. The King's Bench dared not keep the term in London for fear of the plague. Two thousand died of it in a week. The Tower was infected. Sir Walter Ralegh was indicted at Staines on the 21st of September. He was charged with every vestige of treason the arraignment would bear. Then matters lagged. There was no need to hurry the trial. Count d'Arenbergh was the guest of James. His testimony might have undone the prosecution, had he been willing to testify. Of course, no embarrassment was to be his. In October, the Count departed for Flanders laden with royal flattery. After that, any who had hoped for an anti-Spanish policy despaired. On November 10, Ralegh was taken from the Tower in his own coach and carried to the Episcopal Palace of Winchester—Wolvesey Castle. The rest: Brooke, Grey, Cobham, Markham, Parham, Brooksby, Copley, Clark, and Watson rode down in a cavalcade guarded by fifty light cavalry. The state was determined to make a killing.

November 17 saw the King's Bench convened. It was a precious court. The legal lights were Lord Chief Justice Popham and Chief Justice Anderson, Justices Gawdy and Warburton. Popham was a heavy, ugly man, once a highwayman by repute, a bully, a rake, and a gamester. He had advised Queen Elizabeth to pardon Essex. Anderson moved in his shadow which was ample in itself to ruin both Ralegh and justice. Justice Gawdy was ambitious. He was looking forward to the day when he would be Chief Justice of the Common Pleas, which came about at Michaelmas term, 1605. He was not the man to front Popham, nor was Justice Warburton. The King's reign was young and preferment all to win and the rule of a pedant was bound to rest much upon the law. The prosecution was headed by Attorney-General Coke, a bold man, without any human weakness. His second, Sergeant Hele, had represented Ralegh in his suits against Meere, Sir Walter's annoying bailiff. The Sergeant hoped to profit by the fall of Cobham and the conviction of Ralegh was a step.

Sitting as Commissioners of Oyer and Terminer, the royal judges appointed by James were a group as deadly as venom to the defendant.

There sat the Earl of Suffolk, better known as Thomas Howard, who remembered Ralegh's action at Cadiz with envy, and who was also Lord Chamberlain and so bound to reflect the prejudice of James.

There sat the Earl of Devonshire, Charles Blount, who had been an adherent of Essex and had advised Ralegh's court martial on the Islands Voyage in 1597.

There sat in judgment, Sir John Stanhope, Vice-Chamberlain, dependent upon Suffolk's favor for his highest hopes, a man who had smoked Sir Walter's tobacco, but was much under the thumb of Cecil. It was said that Ralegh might have been Vice-Chamberlain himself if Cecil had not aided Stanhope; a doubtful statement.

Lord Wotton presented his commission signed by James, but it had as well been signed by Cecil, for Wotton of Morley was a Cecil man to his toes. By blood he was a sympathizer with Essex and by stature little more than a creature of the Secretary.

Henry Howard, on his way to be Earl of Northampton,

followed upon his long hatred of Ralegh by facing him there in court where judge and enemy promised to be synonyms. James spared no pains to secure a conviction.

There sat Sir William Waad, who despised Sir Walter, who had shared in examining the accused and so hoped to see his findings prove wise. He had been made Sir Walter's keeper in the Tower because of his hatred for the prisoner. Years before he had broken open Queen Mary's cabinet at Chartley Hall. He was fit for any dirty work the trial might involve.

There sat too, unashamed, and without flinching in any degree, Robert Cecil—Baron Cecil by then. Married to Cobham's sister, lifelong friend of Ralegh, he was pushing on past Secretary, past Treasurer, past Baron Cecil, past Viscount, toward the goal of being an Earl. He wanted James in his hands and Ralegh knew his ways, his habit of thought, his long devices. Moreover, where he did not fully understand he was bold to conjecture. Ralegh must be put away from before the face of James. His moment had come. If only some one out of the angry crowds that watched Ralegh leave London had set upon him and finished him, Cecil would have been relieved of a necessary ruthless task. None did. Popular hatred did not rise above flinging stones and mud, and growling in the best fashion of the citizens when stirred by passing circumstance. Cecil had no option but to see the business through.

The jury was as good as another. Sir Thomas Fowler served as foreman. There was no defense counsel, for the practice of the law had no such device at that time. It was Ralegh against the world, against the King, against the battery of intimates upon the bench, all unfriendly, against the professional ambition marshalled at the bar, against the jury, which would receive a charge so obviously mandatory that men of their condition dared not resist, against the traitor's procession with the mockery of the axe edge turned from his neck.

Sir Walter came to the trial carked with anxiety, his body drained of its energy by confinement, his shrewd mind possessed of every item of his danger. He was worn and gray. The exactness of mind necessary to walk amid the pitfalls of the law he had never had. The generous gesture, the large manner, that was all of another time; violent days of turbulence of mind and men far different from James' moment of narrowed eyes, pursed lips, and slowly nodded head. He pleaded not guilty. The jury he put by as with a wave of the hand. "Christian men" and "honest" he called them, advancing his innocency as his strength. Then, before the indictment could be read he went on. "Only this I desire;—sickness hath of late weakened me; and my memory was always bad; —the points in the indictment are many; and, perhaps, in the evidence, more will be urged. I beseech you therefore, my Lords, let me answer the points severally, as they are delivered. For I shall not carry them all in mind to the end."

Was the man mad? Did he know nothing of the close knit mesh of the law, especially when a case was so fragile, so much to be moulded as his? Ah, but he did know. The fellow was clever. Attorney-General Coke rose at once. "The King's evidence," he made the words high sounding, "ought not to be broken or dismembered; whereby it might lose much of its grace and vigor." The Lords acceded to Sir Walter in part. They felt sure that with such help as the bench might legally give the prosecution the verdict they desired was assured.

Sergeant Hele rose to read the indictment.

2

"Men will always be false to you unless they are compelled by necessity to be true." Fifty years of life to learn only that.

Not a man of the court loyal to old favors. No need to look about. A glance at Thomas Howard's big nose and complacent mouth wiped out every hope from Cadiz Bay. The good that men do—buried in the curly, round-cut beard, the low-set ears. Jolly honesty buried in lying craft and envy. Malice in every man on the bench; every man, severally judging in wrath.

Hele was reading; the man's cursed insolence, to prosecute one who had helped the making of him. Sickening familiarity! No matter; the fellow was a clown. Who more fit to introduce a farce? The grimacing fool, his wit was so precious he was in love with it. Arabella! So they were going to conjure with that name. Poor lady! Well, what of her, buffoon?

"She, upon my conscience, hath no more title to the Crown than I have; which before God, I utterly renounce." The numbskull was right. Title, cry that for James too. Out mountebank, what for the claim of your Scotch Sovereign? To smile, one smiled at a farce. One smiled at death. Rabelais dying, "I am going to leap into the dark. Let down the curtain. The farce is over." Smile at death, sadly, yes perhaps, but not at treason. Strange how Arabella spelled destiny. Good Niccolo, "Fortune is a woman. . . . She is a friend to the young." Ah youth!

Hele was speaking in summary. Coke was gathering his papers, ready to begin. A gloomy man; down curving mouth, high eyebrows above pouched lids. He looked along his nose as Hele was finishing with, "You have heard of Ralegh's bloody attempts to kill the King." Hele ended in a flourish without saying anything to the purpose. Coke rose, fixed the Lords with his ferret eyes, and began. Here was a broadside! Stand by to resist boarders.

Flattery at first. The Lords would pardon irreverent things said of the great estate of Kings? Heighten the horror, that was the way of it. Tom Kyd could have done no better. Of course they pardon you, Coke, do they not find themselves in the seats of royalty? Yes, there were two treasons: the "Bye" and the "Main." The "Bye" was that of Lord Grey, Markham, and Brooke, who intended to seize the King while under arms, to make him a subject, to extort pardon, religious toleration, and the removal of his councillors. Aye, Coke, ramble on learnedly. The jury has been long lost, swallowed in pedantry. It was unsafe. The jury might think this had something to do with the trial. Coke concluded. It was time to speak.

Sir Walter Ralegh: "I praye you, Gentlemen of the Jury, to remember that I am not charged with the 'Bye,' which was the treason of the priests."

Attorney-General Coke: "You are not, but their Lordships will see that all these treasons, though they consisted of several points, closed in together; like Samson's foxes, which were joined in the tails, though the heads were severed."

The small eyes snapped. The jury looked doubtful. The check launched Coke upon a tirade. Wow, what a punster. "Perdition" and "Petition"; raw, raw! Even Will Shakespeare would have scorned that, and he loved a pun. The jury had gone for a journey into history. King Edward the Second was murdered. Perkin Warbeck was a traitor to King Henry the Seventh. Edmund de la Pole, Duke of Suffolk, was a felon of the same reign. Coke ranted admirably. Oh, what a thing was treason. Then, suddenly, an attack. It would be argued that Cobham was the state's only witness. That could not save the traitor. Cobham was more than two witnesses. "When a man by his accusation shall, by the same accusation also condemn himself and make himself liable to the same punishment, this is by law more forcible than many witnesses, and is as the inquest of twelve men. For the law presumes that a man will not accuse himself to accuse another." So one confession equalled the testimony of twelve. Then, full throated, the bay of the leader. The horror of treason. The wickedness of traitors. The sweetness of the King's nature: his wisdom, his works of honor. Never a word of the testimony to be presented. Was Coke to go on unchecked?

Sir Walter Ralegh: "I protest I do not understand what a word of this means, except it be to tell me news."

Attorney-General Coke: "I will then come close to you. I will prove you to be the most notorious traitor that ever came to the bar. I charge you with the words."

Sir Walter Ralegh: "Your words cannot condemn me; my innocency is my defense. Prove against me any one thing of the many that you have broken, and I will confess all the indictment."

Coke in a fury. Coke roaring invective. Ah, the hateful ignominy of being a prisoner, of having to face the man of law who had only anger instead of logic. Thou monster! An English face, but a Spanish heart! Arr, for one back-handed slash, from behind a saddle bow, falling fair in fence, upon that law-fattened face, with its beard like a goat's teat. The Count d'Arenbergh entered as a ghost at Coke's will and departed still as a shadow. Cobham stalked in to bleat accusation through chosen passages read sparingly from his statements. Arenbergh's money was to buy peace with Spain. Nonsense! It was to set Lady Arabella upon the throne after deposing James. Coke was clever. Cobham had done these things, Cobham, but why try two men by the acts of one before a King's Bench? Life and limb, and the justice of the land were in jeopardy. Coke must be challenged.

Sir Walter Ralegh: "Let me answer; it concerns my life."

Coke: "Thou shalt not."

Lord Chief Justice Popham: "When the King's Counsel

hath given the whole evidence you shall answer every particular."

Naïve, Popham instructing Coke the accused might speak at last. There was no evidence Coke would ever reach the round of honest proof. How could he? There was none. That was the advantage of innocency. Did these digging dogs expect to unearth a fox in the branchings of his burrow? Coke, bursting with spleen, vituperative, roaring out his stave of rage, bullying as the law allowed, and blaming Cobham's actions upon one. Cobham was not clever enough to concoct the treason of "the Main." To talk alone with Cobham was to be deemed guilty of plotting. So Coke held. Who had talked most with Cobham?—the guilty wretch before the court. "And such was Ralegh's secrecy and machiavellian policy in these courses, that he would never confer with but one at once." Inference! Even the circumstances inferred, but it was necessary to have Cobham very black to make the accused shadow a malignant monster. Cobham's faults as Warden of the Cinque Ports made the Attorney-General foam at the mouth. The man was likely to fall in a fit as he waved his finger, the veins standing large upon his brow.

Coke: "All he did was by thy instigation, thou viper; for I thou thee thou traitor. I will prove thee the rankest traitor in all England."

Too much, far, far too much to stand.

Sir Walter Ralegh: "No, no, Master Attorney, I am no traitor. Whether I live or die, I shall stand as true a subject as ever the King hath. You may call me a 'traitor' at your pleasure; yet it becomes not a man of quality or virture to do so. But I take comfort in it. It is all that you can do; for I do not yet hear that you charge me with any treason."

Was it all he could do? The jury could feel the truth in that answer above all the swagger bludgeoning of Coke. It shamed the savage attacks of the prosecution, and the Master Attorney did not go on, but stood as if dazed, while Popham leaned forward to speak carefully.

Lord Chief Justice Popham: "Sir Walter Ralegh, Master Attorney speaks out of the zeal of his duty for the service of the King; and you for your life; be patient on both sides."

Was it a trial, with the Chief Justice covering Coke? Henry Howard was looking very hard. Cecil sat turned away a little, as if he heard or heeded nothing. The rest gave no sign, but waited indifferently. Perhaps Coke could do more than cry traitor. It was not a trial at all. It was a conspiracy to take life, to pay grudges, to quiet envy bred in other, fairer days. "Whoever conspires cannot act alone," said Niccolo. Coke was up, ready to read his "proofs"; an examination of July 20. Cobham had admitted dealing with d'Arenbergh concerning five or six hundred thousand crowns to be got from the King of Spain. Nothing further was to be done until Cobham had "spoken with Ralegh for distribution of the money" to the discontented in England. Ah, this was close to the mark; the only scratch. No chance to cut and run. Best draw the fire.

Sir Walter Ralegh: "This is absolutely all the evidence that can be brought against me."

Stiffly, like that, was the way to go on telling them. Cobham had been suspected of contact with d'Arenbergh. That was not new. In the dead Queen's time, Lord Burghley that was, and the new Lord Cecil knew of it. When Cecil was written to apprehend the go-between, La Renzi, he did nothing, and later, with the first coming of d'Arenbergh asked the matter remain unmentioned. Robert Cecil was awake now. His eyes were fixed, his attention perfect. To speak out of the pause a denial of affection for Spain could do no hurt.

Sir Walter Ralegh: "I was not so bare of sense but I saw

that, if ever this State was strong, it was now that we have the Kingdom of Scotland united, whence we were wont to fear all our troubles;—Ireland quieted, where our forces were wont to be divided;—Denmark assured, whom before we were always wont to have in jealousy . . . I knew the state of Spain well. . . . Thrice had I served against him myself at sea,—wherein, for my Country's sake, I had expended of my own property forty thousand marks."

So onward, point by point to show the poverty of Spain: lost ships, lost trade secrets, lost valor, lost pride. Spain had no six hundred thousand crowns to tender Cobham. That shown, the only darkening accusation perished. To be charged with love for Spain—have at that.

Sir Walter Ralegh: "And to show I am not 'Spanish'—as you term me—at this time, I had writ a treatise to the King's Majesty of the present state of Spain, and reasons against the Peace."

Let them have that in their very teeth. There was no way left to let them feel one's weight. Nothing mattered if they were conspiring for a man's death, nothing but the little dust and the essence of one's name in aftertime. To some good Englishmen the word Spain was still as a fire devouring them. Union and strength were the King's pride. No tang of offense should be uttered; the last appeal would rest upon the royal will. No harm then to warm English hearts. The court was astir. Faces lightened. Heads nodded. Eyes glowed. Oh, cautious James would hear of it, but would he understand? This heart beat of England was the impulse he had so often feared in Scotland, and now, regnant, hated. It must go to him, this story of a struggle for life, for the court was a conspiracy. Too obvious that to be missed, more certain with each speech.

Coke was bringing in names of men strange to all the charges. The prosecution should have been arrayed in motley. Those on the bench were shifting uneasily. The defense was astray. Life and freedom lay in careless words. Popham, frightened at Coke's wavering, volunteered information to the jury, forgetting he was a judge and not a witness. He told that Cobham had said Ralegh had betrayed him. And that meant only one thing. Ralegh, to betray Cobham, must have been the director, the creator of this nefarious plot of which Cobham knew but part. Every effort related Cobham's treason as being pertinent to the trial. The jury asked for the circumstances of the correspondence between Cobham and the prisoner. Cecil forgot he was on the bench and hastened to testify. "A former dearness" for the prisoner moderated his opinions of the gentleman. Oh, Cecil was exquisite; gentle, considerate, and deadly. Cecil befogging the jury by a wealth of names inscribed upon the actions of Cobham. The jury only heard the correspondence in excerpts. When Cecil ended Coke was up. Much more of Cobham and his contacts. Bah, Cobham could not stand before the court and make the accusations with which he was credited. Try him, by all means try him.

Sir Walter Ralegh: "My Lords, I claim to have my accuser brought here to speak face to face."

They recoiled at that. Good! What said the law? There had been time enough to read the matter in the long days in the Tower. The testimony of two witnesses was necessary to convict of treason. Have at them with that. All might do no good, but one must not perish foolishly. The statute of the first of Edward the Sixth. On foot then and attack. "No man shall be condemned of treason, unless he be accused by two lawful accusers," who in addition, "must be brought in person before the party accused." That was statute the fifth and sixth of Edward the Sixth. There were others of Philip and Mary. There was the warrant of British practice. Biblical canon gave it sanction.

Popham denying the legal references. Justice Warburton protesting such things were unheard of. Both refusing to waive the severity of the law in the name of justice. Equity must proceed from the King. More talk of what Cobham did and said. Cecil urging to speed with the proof. Coke rambling on with little sense but much pomp. Sergeant Philips injecting jeering comment. Justice Gawdy making his sole comment of the occasion in support of the uselessness of the three statutes of Edward the Sixth because they had been replaced by other laws. A crazy time, full of device and treachery. Oh, Cobham, Cobham!

Sir Walter Ralegh: "The King desires nothing but the knowledge of the truth, and would have no advantage taken by the severity of the law. . . . Good my Lords let my accuser come face to face and be deposed."

Popham: "You have no law for it."

Scraps read from the examinations of others; of Brooke, Watson, and again Cobham. The words of those hellish spiders, Clarke and Watson, brought against one. The barbarous threat against "the King and his cubs." Coke, frenzied, crying, "Thou hast a Spanish heart, and thyself art a spider of hell." One's words twisted at every turn. Cobham's "I had from Ralegh a book, written against the title of the King," a silly book, written by a rogue name Snagge and once owned by old Lord Burghley. All foolish wrangling this, that led nowhere.

Only Sir Robert Wrothe of the jury escaped befuddlement. He muttered something. Coke was upon him. "My Lords, I must complain of Sir Robert Wrothe. He said this evidence is not material." Wrothe denied his words and shrank out of sight as Cecil vouched for him. More wrangling about the book and Cobham. Cobham must be had.

Sir Walter Ralegh: "The Lord Cobham hath accused me. . . . Were it not for his accusations, all this were nothing."

Coke: "He is a party, and may not come. The law is against it."

Sir Walter Ralegh: "It is a toy to tell me of law. I defy law. I stand upon the facts."

Evasion, confusion, the casting of much dust, the swearing of one Dyer, a pilot, who heard a Portuguese say King James would never be crowned for Don Ralegh and Don Cobham would cut his throat this time. The inference? That the treason hath wings. A black and hopeless time. The truth sounding strange amid the babel of meaningless words, but the speaking of it needful.

Sir Walter Ralegh: "Consider, you Gentlemen of the Jury, there is no cause so doubtful which the King's counsel cannot make good against the law."

It was true. The charges to the jury—wonderful and weird the fabric, all dependent upon the word of Cobham. And he had changed his word at will. It was time the veracity of Cobham should vanish in a puff. Cobham had not only written statements for the Crown from the Tower, he had written a letter for the Lords. Cecil rising to read, vouching for the hand as being Cobham's. Cecil glancing upon the cowed jury, explaining the letter had been written upon a plea to Cobham to tell the truth at last, and so to the reading.

"Seeing myself so near my end, for the discharge of my own conscience and freeing myself from your blood, which else will cry vengeance against me, I protest upon my salvation I never practised with Spain by your procurement. God so comfort me in this my affliction, as you are a true subject for anything that I know. I will say as Daniel, *Purus sum a sanguine hujus.* So God have mercy upon my soul as I know no treason by you."

When this was read and the marshal of the court had stirred to lead the jury into retirement, there was but a word, the last word which belonged to a man whose life rested upon it.

Sir Walter Ralegh: "Now, my masters, you have heard both. That shewed against me is but a voluntary confession. This is under oath, and the deepest protestations a Christian man can make. Therefore believe which of these have most force."

Fifteen minutes with the court to study in the dying light. The day was almost done. The court sat waiting. In fifteen minutes the jury returned. An age in a moment; life on wing, life at rest. Then the inevitable word for which the beginning of the trial had been planned and which could be balked by no last minute confusion of the jury.

"Guilty."

3

Sir Walter Ralegh desired the King should know the wrong done. Since Cobham was his only accuser and Cobham had retracted his statements Coke had wronged Sir Walter at every turn.

Popham denied the Knight had had any wrong and proceeded to pronounce judgment, which he did with great thoroughness, not omitting to remind Ralegh he had best believe in Heaven and abandon the atheisim of Hariot. Then he spoke that savage, awful sentence which once had broken Essex at every word. Ralegh heard it with composure, unmoved by any ferocity of Popham.

Ralegh prayed that the jury might never have to answer for its verdict. Speaking to Henry and Thomas Howard, to Blount and Cecil he asked that they intercede with the King to grant him honorable death without the disgrace of hanging and quartering. Cecil, having attained his end, wept tears of friendship. If no pardon could be won from the

King Ralegh asked that Cobham die first. He knew that Cobham dared not die without confessing his lie in the early statements. Even so late there was a chance for life, but if it failed, the memory of Ralegh would go down untarnished. He was more than fifty. He had lived much, but he would save his pride, even the other side of death.

CHAPTER XVIII

ROYAL MERCY

JAMES heard of the trial, of Ralegh's good temper, his wisdom, his courage, of Coke's surprise at the success of the prosecution. Shrewsbury was able to relate that Sir Walter "Wrought both admiration for his good parts and pity towards his person." The Earl of Mar had wept for him. Cecil had shed tears to heighten the case against him, an exercise in legal poignancy, giving sincerity to the damaging words. This pushing roisterer might be ungodly, but he had met his fate in full manliness. Well, he was ended. The Court had done its duty and the finding was what Cecil thought good.

In contrast, only the Friday after Sir Walter had heard his stunning sentence, Lord Cobham faced the Lords in the same room, the great "Arthur's Hall" at Winchester. Word of that too came up to James seated at Wilton House. Cobham cringed. Poor of mouth, trembling, without a grain of spirit, he heard the indictment. Ralegh, Arenbergh, any one but himself was to blame for his predicament. His case collapsed in short order. All, they had them all then, Cecil could say: Watson, Clarke, Brooke, Grey, Markham, Cobham, Ralegh. This very grouping was an irony. Neither Grey nor Markham would ever have had a share in any undertaking in which Ralegh had a part; yet the net swept them all toward death.

As the word of what manner of man Ralegh had proved on trial went over England, there was a singular reaction. He had been hated in success but, baited at the bar, his life sought by a Scotchman on an English throne, his conviction aided by Cecil who was himself disliked by the people, the popular imagination swerved through pity to love. A legend of the nation was reversed. Ralegh the hateful had become Ralegh the heroic. From mouth to mouth the account of the trial journeyed, growing weirdly wonderful with much bandying about. To the factions who loved James none too well it was fuel: the anti-Spanish party, slighted West Countrymen, eclipsed survivors of Elizabeth's day, brave spirits who saw no action, no bravery, no loot to be won under the new dynasty, the anti-Scotch party who saw poor Scotchmen flocking into London town. From this minority the cry was taken up by the masses as a truth out of gospel and went everywhere.

James caught wind of it from two gentlemen he had sent to Winchester to bring him a private report. One, Roger Ashton, an Englishman, was infected at a breath, "Never man spoke so well in time past, nor would in time to come." When the other, Scotch as the King himself, came, James hoped for the dour truth, but that gentleman was even more enthusiastic. Whereas, when he saw Sir Walter Ralegh first, "He was led with the common hatred that he would have gone a hundred miles to see him hanged, he would, ere they parted, have gone a thousand miles to save his life." Meanwhile the Queen interceded for Sir Walter. James' own host, the Earl of Pembroke, sued for the prisoner's life. The young man's mother had charged him of all her blessing to employ his own credit and his friends and "though she does little good, yet is she to be commended for doing her best in showing *veteris vestigia flammae.*"[16] Vestiges of old passion, or merely the loyalty of Mary, the sister of the long dead perfect knight Philip Sidney, the effort gave James thought, and thought with him meant delay. Besides, the Spanish ambassador had approached the Councillors about the matter pleading his fear that Ralegh's death would make Spain more than ever unpopular. What could be his object? James paused. Philip had always counted on Elizabeth in his struggles with France. Not directly of course, but more upon the theory he should have one, either France or England, as a foil to use against the other. Elizabeth had never been the Queen in the sense James was King. James was the nation as the Cecils had been earlier. Ralegh was a menace to the Spanish peace if he lived, which, with a little care, might be continued indefinitely, to the profit of both nations. Ralegh dead might establish a popular legend upon which popular feeling would force a war with Spain as a revenge for his death. Was the wave of popular love of him apt to last? A pestilential fellow, as Cecil had promised! James paused.

Ralegh's mood of the trial lived on. His enemies had massed in attack. The end had never been in doubt, but he had displayed the unjust folly of their success; that, a man as clever as Robert Cecil would never forgive him. He had followed High Sheriff Tichborne to the prison with the pride of his early days but little sobered, "Yet in such sort as a condemned man should." He had been condemned upon a possibility that he had known of his friend's desire to control the royal policy by spending Spanish money. There was the baleful truth. In his secret heart he was entertained by the ludicrous clumsiness of his foes. They could have done so much better had they been only a little more fortunate in their knowledge, but they had done enough. The vast bazaar or exchange he had planned to erect upon the site of Durham House, once the old palace was razed, would never be. A Scotch Captain of the Guard strutted before the King. Jersey had a new governor. All was stripped and looted from him. The learning of the King might have made him cry with Virgil excusing the inhumanity of Dido in her rule,

"A fate unkind, and newness in my reign
Compel me thus to guard a wide domain."

Niccolo had quoted that where he spoke of whether it were better to be loved or feared. Robert Cecil had had no such excuse for his disloyalty. Such malice must have grown out of fear, which was flattering, but of no avail against a death sentence. The masses of England were despicable but useful. The King tried not to be hated by his people. He was forever listening, learning. He had ears everywhere. The King, too, dared not incur the hatred of Cecil and the Howards. To plead for life could do no harm. Life was necessary to undo all the other harms which had befallen. Once pardoned, he could begin again the climb toward position in the state and the use of those powers he felt still strong within him. He would even stoop to beg of the Councillors. From them he could hope for no freedom but only deferment. "The law is passed against me.... If I may not beg a pardon or a life, yet let me beg a time. Let me have one year to give to God in a prison and to serve him," he wrote, declaring the power of the law exceeded that of truth. To the King he wrote more classically, "If the law destroy me, your Majesty shall put me out of your power, and I shall then have none to fear, none to reverence, but the King of Kings." He was slaying the bugaboo of atheism, protesting himself a subject of the King, and pleading for his life, standing upon necessity, not upon justice.

James let the parade of death begin. The evidence against Ralegh was slight. The conspirators might, at the moment of death, let the truth fly. One at a time, beginning with the priests, he would send them to the scaffold.

The two priests died on November 29, 1603. Dreadful punishment, to be hung, drawn, and quartered. Watson died first, contrite enough in spirit, regretting he could not pay for all upon whom he had brought ruin. He was alive when cut down from the hanging, which in no way delayed the quartering. Clarke thought himself a martyr, a zealot even at death. After the hanging, he still lived, in accord with the letter of his sentence. He "strove to help himself and spake," but was stretched upon the scaffold despite his struggles and the executioners fell to their bloody work with a will.

George Brooke was executed on December 6, 1603, but the extreme sentence was remitted to beheading. "There is somewhat yet hidden, which will one day appear for my justification," he said, wondering at the mystery of the plot beyond his ken. When the axe fell and the headsman lifted up the severed head with "God save the King," only one voice responded. Sir Benjamin Tichborne, the High Sheriff, alone did his duty. James knew of these things by messenger. The humor of the people was not what he would have liked. The execution was in protection of their King's interest, yet they showed no enthusiasm of loyalty. Later in his days his tetchy vanity, as God's anointed, would not have let him moderate his action, but he was newly come to a throne in a strange country. There had been little reassuring since his arrival. Even his capital was so ridden with the plague that he had not dared to go into London to be regularly crowned. His caution was natural and wise, yet, still seated at Wilton House, he signed the warrants for the execution of Markham, Grey, and Cobham on Friday, December 10, and planned to have Ralegh follow on Monday. Then he worked out a pretty scheme to get at men's dying thoughts.

Ralegh, finding time passing with nothing done, weighed the pro and con of his situation. Lady Ralegh had sued Cecil to save her husband. Every turn had been tried. Ralegh decided life was over and drew aloof to the heights his philosophic mind made possible. On December 9, he wrote his wife farewell. He pleaded that she travel, with a high heart, the road of life. "Your mourning cannot avayle me that am but dust." He was able to speak what had long been in his mind, "I plainly perceive that my death was determined from the first day." The letters he had written the Lords, begging his life, he asked her to try and recover. He warned her against those who, thinking him rich, would pretend affection for her, but spoke not so to dissuade her from marriage, "for that will be best for you—both in respect of God and the world." With a commendation of them both to God, a note on money due and debts owed, a plea she care for their boy, and a final wry farewell, "May God hold you both in his arms," he waited the headsman.

On December 10, at ten in the morning, Sir Griffin Markham walked out to the scaffold in the yard of the prison at Winchester. Ralegh saw him move up, sad and heavy. He prayed. He said good-bye when the High Sheriff stayed the execution. With the air of an actor he said to Markham, "You say you are ill prepared to die, you shall have two hours respite." Then the condemned was led away and locked in Arthur's Hall. Grey was led to the scaffold, also to be led away after he had confessed a faulty heart, and had been prepared for death.

Lord Cobham was very queer upon the scaffold. He strode toward the block, a bold man, contemptuous of the death dealt there. Gone was his cowardice before the Lord Commissioners. Did he know the issue of the scene? His prayers reeled from his tongue with assurance. Had he been pledged to confirm the finding of the Court concerning Ralegh with his reward promised? He spoke of his offense against the King. Sorrow and regret he felt for his folly. For all he had said of Sir Walter he affirmed, "It is true, as I have hope of my soul's resurrection." Ralegh had had his way. Cobham was going to execution before him, yet Cobham said nothing startling, nothing illuminating. He had contradicted himself so often it was difficult to be sure just what he had meant to say of Sir Walter. The King's men were content. They took his statement to mean he still accused Ralegh of treason. So much they had hoped to establish by the little scene, but Cobham, moving upon apparent death with composure, with brazen determination; no wonder that raised a question. Many were sceptical. Did he know the royal intent? Was that the reason so patent a coward dared to pass nonchalantly close to the keen edge? Whence the required courage to trust a mere promise? With what relief or suspicion he must have heard the Sheriff announce he was to be confronted with other prisoners. Grey and Markham were brought out. Sheriff Tichborne asked the trio, standing before the block, three questions of the King's making:

"Are not your offenses heinous?" General admission.

"Have you not been justly tried and lawfully condemned?" That was true.

"Is not each of you subject to due execution, now to be performed?" To Grey and Markham all this must have seemed an unnecessary torture, but to Cobham, who had clung to his testimony, it would have been maddening had not he had implicit faith in and knowledge of Tichborne's next move. The Sheriff spoke quickly,

"Then see the mercy of your Prince, who of himself hath sent hither a countermand, and hath given you your lives." The crowd cheered. Grey pledged himself to deserve life, while Cobham called upon God to witness his repentance was unfeigned. He was always calling upon God to attest his statements, and feigning anything efficiently was beyond him. His statement was characteristic.

James, who could not stand the sight of a dagger, had sent three men through a hell to demonstrate his cleverness. While they suffered his cruelty he had sat at Wilton, comparing the prisoners with all the dry pedantry at his command. Now Grey, now Cobham, now Ralegh, he turned and twisted all upon his philosophical spit, while courtiers applauded, wondering to what the character examination was leading. The lesser men stood in the antechamber, while the names of the condemned were toyed with to give amusement to the Sovereign who would himself likely have gone mad under the torture inflicted at Winchester. When he had tired of his play, and his self-praise cloyed, he brought forward the climax which he rounded off with the utterance he hoped sounded like the words of a Daniel, "And therefore I have saved the lives of them all." Wilton rang with applause of God's anointed in his stuffed doublet and padded breeches.

As for Ralegh, he watched the comedy from his cell at Winchester, he saw Markham leave the scaffold, then Grey, then both return to join Cobham while Tichborne harangued them and the folk in the prison yard cheered. A fool could have caught the gist of the action. Beaumont, the French ambassador, wrote that Sir Walter saw the performance with a smile upon his face, but Beaumont was not in the Winchester cell. Perhaps it was but a fragment of the great legend of Ralegh. When the news of the reprieves reached French Henry he ordered Beaumont to discover if Spanish gold spent by Ralegh had brought them about. Even so close to death Sir Walter's powers appeared weird and wonderful to any who did not know his true plight. If he smiled a little at his own torment, catching a glimpse of its futility, plumbing the King's intent from the chill retirement of his cell, it would only be the functioning of a mind against which the stupid power of a self-infatuated James would bring attack after attack until it faced the truth for the last time. A smile at fifty-one is seldom pure and never simple.

2

It was not in Sir Walter's mind to make light of Kings. To have his life from James was no blow to his pride. It was a grant within the duty of a monarch. He felt the disgrace of having sued for the support of the Lord Commissioners, but mostly because his plea had gone unheeded. From Winchester he wrote James, thanking him for his life; a letter filled with that flattery the Scotchman loved so well.

"Seeing it hath pleased your Majestye to breathe into dead earth a new life, I among others do presume to offer my humblest thanks and acknowledgments, which (God knows) can neither be expressed or presented." He quoted Latin twice, he offered turgid, weighted sentences, with the flash of vainglory, the swashing gesture. A sombre divine could have written no more of involution, of wordy stupidity. The old crowd of the Mermaid would have roared at it. Ralegh was courting the learnedly witless, for James was so enamoured of his own proclivities that he was far on his road to absurdity.

On December 16, 1603, the convicted prisoners were taken to London. Ralegh was assigned the apartments he had left in the Bloody Tower. Midwinter was a gray time in the old pile. He might see a stretch of the Thames when the fog swirled aside. Turning from the waterside he could look down upon the Lieutenant's garden. A passage led from behind his rooms, through a doorway, out on the terrace. There the air might be raw and cold, but the sky was overhead and the dank chill of the moist walls was lost in striding back and forth across the breathing space. For the King's convenience, he was snatched away to Fleet Prison for a time, and again, for unknown reasons, for a shorter time, but by the summer of 1604 he was fixed in the Bloody Tower.

The permanence of his imprisonment Ralegh could not believe. Somewhere, in something, he would find a way to unlock the doors, but that was not enough. He must step back into his King's grace. Life without a hand in the government he could not conceive. He suffered the imperishable illusion of affairs. From time to time, especially in his later weary time, he offered to go to Holland, to accept confinement upon Sherborne Hundred, but he could never have done either of them. He was oblivious of his position. His mind was still an instrument to serve James, his spirit soaring after greatness, which might come suddenly once this check were passed. He might well have been innocent for any thought he gave the crime of which he had been declared guilty. He thought instead of the unjust bonds which held him. Whether in his heart guilty or innocent, he remembered only the injustice of the trial and set his eyes upon the work he could do if free. Tramping the Terrace, forever after known as Ralegh's Walk, he wrestled with his anger and his wrongs by giving rein to his prophetic vision of opportunity. James would find a saying of Niccolo's true—a saying concerning the minister who thought more of himself than his Prince. Cecil was deep. It was necessary to pretend to vast patience, which scorned unbelief, when dealing with the little man, but James would find in the end there was nothing so dear to Cecil as his own way and reward. Old Burghley had not always taken his own, but Robert showed no weakness, **not a single, wavering scruple.**

Poverty was not easy to bear in the Tower and Ralegh was but a wreck of the financial power he had been. On July 30, 1604, the Crown conveyed a sixty year tenure of Sherborne and ten other Dorset and Somerset manors for Lady Ralegh and young Walter. James had enjoyed the vanity of his own cleverness in the reprieves; he reached after the further self-flattery of beneficence. Sherborne brought Ralegh an income of about fifteen thousand dollars in our values, but for the pomp and pageantry of the Court he was no longer fit. His plate, his rich hangings, many of the things he had gathered in Durham House, had gone, and debts of long standing clamored to be met. Yet for **actual** privation and penury, Sir Walter knew nothing of either in the Tower. With him were Lady Ralegh, Walter, and two servants. Within a year after his imprisonment, a second son, Carew, was born. He saw Hariot, his physician Doctor Turner, Doctor John, a surgeon, and Hawthorn, a clergyman, whenever he would. Visitors came and went freely, ranging from nobility to the Indians he had brought back from the Chief Topiawari in Guiana. He entertained as he chose, and if the throngs who once climbed to his study in Durham House were greater in number, the Tower guests were as various in interest and importance.

From the first, the Tower shook Ralegh's health. He was not a well man when convicted. For two years or more he had been taking excursions to Bath to take the waters. A lifetime of activity had consumed his body. He was very shortly writing to Cecil, "I have presumed at this tyme to remember your Lordship of my miserable estate—daily, in danger of death by palsey, nightly, of suffocation, by wasted and obstructed lungs." None heeded. Who better pleased if the Tower should prove too much for Ralegh than his enemies? In 1605, he related again his symptons to Cecil. They were more pronounced but he had hardened to the conditions under which he lived. "I complain not of it. I know it vain for there are none that have compassion thereof." Even if Cecil cared he manifested no interest. He was prone to make light of Ralegh's ailments, but Doctor Turner, on March 26, 1606, recorded the progress of the prisoner's distress. "All his left side is extreme cold, out of sense and motion, or numb; his fingers on the same side begin to be contracted and his tongue, in some part, insomuch that he speaketh weakly, and it is to be feared that he may utterly lose the use of it." A threat of general paralysis, this, and certainly much advanced over the two years. It was enough to engulf a man. Why not sit back, let the darkness of the years creep on, wiping all out, squaring all accounts, clothing one's memory in a pathos of softening pity, and so revenging the wrong of the unjust sentence?

Ralegh wanted no pity, no pathos. His mind was as clear as ever. Every fair day he dragged his body out upon the terrace while the people looked on. His enemies said he was keeping his memory alive among the citizens. There was more in it than that. He was reminding himself there was a world beyond prison walls, a world toward which he was working, and to which he must not become a stranger. It was unthinkable the King would cast away his abilities, his peculiar knowledge. Some day release would come. He would not believe that justice would miscarry forever. Grey and the others complained at the comparative liberty of Ralegh. Ralegh held he should not be imprisoned at all, especially when Papists who had plotted against the King were freed. He worked upon every acquaintance. Cecil had to tell Lady Ralegh in 1604 that it was not the time to move for a pardon. "It could not yet be done." Meanwhile time passed, weeks to months, months to years. Ralegh refused to count them as stolen from his store yet left to him. The Howards could not bend him to humility or abate his energies. Cecil was gaining no greater success in his absence from court than he had won in Ralegh's presence.

Two friends had risen in the Court. James' Queen had, from the first, opposed the Howards, and most of all Henry Howard, whose policy and person she despised. Her likes were strong and her position able to support them. She made George Carew her Vice-Chamberlain, who, finding his kinship with Sir Walter and the favor of his Queen supporting one another, was too cautious a man not to recall Ralegh often to the royal mind. Anne of Denmark was "bold and enterprising," to quote the Frenchman Sully, and the predatory in Ralegh, the freedom of mind, his presence appealed to her so strongly that she took Prince Henry with her to the Tower, that he might catch something of the spirit of the man. Prince Henry promised to be much more of a man than his father. Anne was determined he should grow up no poltroon fit only for a silken throne. She saw her husband's reign did not sit easily upon the nation. Who could better prepare her son to rule wisely than this old fox of Elizabeth's day, steeped in learning, knowing Machiavellian policy so well that he had never been brought to bay until his enemies stuffed every post of power and, working together to crush him, had mewed him up within four walls, where still he seemed a more proper man than any two or three who had crushed him. Nothing of Henry Howard was missing in that attack and the Queen's wit was stirred. She would match him later if she had her way and she saw the light. For Ralegh she was freedom and a blow to his enemies. He would sit in the sun again. For herself she was power, to put her will upon the Councillors through Ralegh would please her. For Prince Henry she was an anxious mother, knowing the cowardice, the vicious virtues of the King, flesh of her flesh and yet not a man to her liking. She saw that Ralegh knew her liking for him. She heard Prince Henry say, "Who but my father would keep such a bird in a cage!" with keen pleasure. She directed the Prince be allowed to enjoy the company of Ralegh as a youthful penitent going unto a confessor who understood the passions of life and who, from the great heart of him, might pour into young ears the secret of his manhood which the Tower could not take from him.

CHAPTER XIX

THE LONG YEARS

WHEN the plague lingered only within the Tower among his prisoners, James dared to enter London. It was an hour of pomp. All ranks and callings sought to do him honor. Men marched in procession, the best of every sort. Among the eight actors chosen were Shakespeare, Burbage, Heming, Cundell, and Lawrence Fletcher. To each of them was granted four and one-half yards of red cloth. It was not every day that brought a new King to town, and the occasion passed swiftly enough. Hardly had Parliament opened before the Commons began to quarrel with him, but for the moment all was pleasant. James was intent upon uniting Scotland and England. The English thought that only meant Scotch lords would be able to hold British land. They would have none of it. James paused in deliberation, trying to see his way to a policy of toleration, until the Gunpowder Plot frightened him nearly out of his senses, after which there was no more delay. He persecuted vigorously. He held no more aloof from his problem of the sects; he assailed the Catholics openly.

In August, 1604, with Ralegh safe in prison, James wrote a congratulatory letter to the Archduke Albert. He was glad the Spanish peace had come at last. He was proud to treat with such "eminent instruments" as Count d'Arenbergh who was so adequately possessed of "sufficiency, prudence, and integrity." In a year the Count had ceased, in the royal mind, to be a traitor to both Albert and England by making offers to discontented Britons ready to open civil war. In a year the sole evidence upon which Ralegh was convicted was no longer believed by James. The Count had integrity, not a suddenly acquired virtue, and the King had Ralegh safe under lock and key, with none to rise and brand the trial of the royal bench a lie, the charges arrayed against the prisoner a malicious device to forward the Spanish peace and pay the grudges of the Howards and Cecil. The Count may have had integrity, but if so, King James had none.

To Ralegh in the Tower, the world moved on with startling haste. Bacon of the heavy jowl and feral eyes uttered his *Advancement of Learning*. Cecil was made Earl of Salisbury. Prince Henry had his own household quite apart from his father, and gave every evidence of having a mind of his own to boot. In the prison, nothing seemed to change—the scale of time was too generous. Sir Walter defended himself as well as he could. Sir William Waad had displaced Sir George Harvey as Lieutenant of the Tower. Waad annoyed his prisoner in every way possible—trivialities that in captivity bulked large: building a brick wall beyond the gate to cut off a view of the outer world, restraining exercise upon the terrace, compelling all his victims to keep to their cells after the afternoon bell, excluding guests without reason. Yet Sir Walter stood him off in many matters. Waad was a spy, able to nose out a plot. He missed in discovering whatever Ralegh may have known of Cobham's conspiracy. In the Tower, every motion of his prisoner was examined. Shortly after Ralegh stood in his Tower room and saw the *Sarah Constant*, the *Goodspeed*, and the *Discovery* sail for Virginia, bearing one of his own faction, Captain John Smith, he was interrogated upon the actions of his first warden, Harvey. There was some glancing aside into his personal affairs. The years did not teach him fear rapidly enough to please his enemies, but the King fortunately turned his face away to glance at other matters.

Through all the prison years, Lady Ralegh sided always with Sir Walter. "True wife," he had called her, writing in expectation of execution, and true wife she proved. She bore him Carew Ralegh within the shadows of the Tower. Her pride matched his. She was as insolent toward his enemies as he. Neither sought compromise, nor looked for quarter. Both set their faces toward a clouded future, and fought zealously for the last poor right left them. So long as she could, she lived in the Tower, although it was unhealthy, often touched by the plague, and girt with rules which straitened her life there.

The one friend she hoped to find was the King. Then she showed no pride; only a piteous will to plead and plead for justice. She went upon her knees at Hampton Court. With young Walter and the babyish Carew she sought the royal presence, always hoping for an altered mind, a kindlier heart. This James seemed to dislike, but there was no avoiding the woman. She was fighting for her own with all she had, and no rebuff held her long quiet. Against her the odds were heavy enough to begin with, and they were not lightened as time went on, revealing a changed King.

There was at court a young man named Robert Carr, who one day rode into the tilt yard, and by ill jousting broke his leg. He lay at the royal feet, so beautiful despite his pain, that James loved him at once, amorously, and out of his misfortune the young man mounted a new steed of royal favor.

James' affection was difficult and singular. He displayed his lust with abandon. The Earl of Holland and some others refused his Majesty's favor under the conditions Carr subscribed to. Holland was even so bold as to turn aside and spit after the King had kissed him wantonly. Carr's person was not rugged. His straight nose was well moulded. His lips were pursed to a Cupid's bow, set off by his combed and pointed beard. His ears were pierced for pendant rings. He was by no means so stupid as to disregard his opportunity. He looked upon Ralegh's Sherborne with desire. It put James to some trouble to secure it for him, but a slight flaw in the conveyance served to help. Ralegh wrote Carr, pleading for the interests of his wife and children. Lady Ralegh appealed directly to the King. James had to have it for Carr: Sherborne was lost for Ralegh. Carr never even acknowledged his letter concerning the matter.

This way led madness. To sit impotent in the Tower, waiting for blow after blow, required the mask of the Gods. Ralegh needed to be impenetrable, armored with indifference and calm to fling back Henry Howard. He succeeded. "We had a bout with Sir Walter Ralegh, in whom we find no change, but the same boldness, pride, and passion that heretofore hath wrought more violently, but never expended itself in stronger passion," wrote Howard. Ralegh kept his pride a thing absolute, apart from his forbearance and quiet hope. He saw a far-off light. He waited, and he did not stoop, for his mind was content in its visions. Sometimes his spirit grew very weary, but his view was clear. "Tacitus says, we ought to submit to what is present and should wish for good princes, but whatsoever they are, endure them, and Machiavel terms this a golden sentence, adding, that whosoever does otherwise, ruins both himself and country." Ralegh had long reasoned thus, but only in the Tower did he come to understand his thought's significance. When Sherborne was finally wrung from him he hoped to never hear of it again. He was trying to express life in other symbols.

Waad allowed him to convert a little hen house in the Tower garden into a still house. An operator was hired and distillation was carried on all day long. Something, too, of an assay furnace Sir Walter contrived for testing ores. He mixed balms and ointments for the ladies. His Simple Cordial had the properties of a general medicine of tonic qualities.

His Great Cordial was a potent remedy, sure to turn back death in every illness except where poison was concerned. He experimented with tobacco curing, striving to bring an English sort to equal the Virginian. Roving friends brought him materials from far away. His science was most shadowy in its conventions, and his inquiries were often fruitless. They produced wonder in him, filling his mind so completely that time grew unimportant and unkindness lost its stinging force. He needed most just such success. One secret he learned: that sea water could be distilled into fresh, a fact he was to carry with him on his last voyage to Guiana, and which was not used afterward for two hundred years.

There was too much of bitterness in him for poetry in those days. It was the mind not the heart he sought to exercise. More than ever, he devoured books by the chest. His Report of the *Truth of the Fight about the Isles of Azores* had appeared in 1589. In 1596, his *Discovery of Guiana* had been addressed to Charles Howard and Robert Cecil. He had published no other prose before entering the Tower. There, the restraint nurtured a consuming energy in him. He had thought himself worn out after his return from Guiana, yet he had had never a buffet, had he but known. His fall swept away so much. His hair grayed, his shoulders stooped a little, his manner still imperious, but veiled. Where once he spoke quickly, in the Tower he turned his words over in the womb of a great silence, choosing those to be born. Those he spoke were sometimes cryptic, sometimes ironic. He repressed his natural utterance, which gave fuel to the fire within him and sent his pen scampering over pages of prose. Hariot and Jonson he took more into his confidence than most. To Sir Robert Cotton he wrote for the loan of rare old books and manuscripts: the works of Sigeberti, Gervasius Tilesberius, Foresti of Bergamo, Nöel Tailleped, Peter de Icham, and Alexander Evesham, dealing with the history of

England, traces of the Druids, monastic legends, and scholarly commentary. From history he caught the color of life, and, warming to his interest, put the great fire of him into a prose that none matched.

He wrote of government and the Court from which he was shut away. He conceived of the King as something more royal and nearer to heaven than James ever dared to be. His distrust of the mob made him urge the King to get rid of his ministers in *The Prerogative of Parliaments*, setting forth that attempts to bind the King by law justified his breach of it, "his charters and other instruments being no other than the surviving witnesses of unconstrained will." Flattery? Perhaps, but Ralegh was always an aristocrat. James' vanity was prodigious, but so was his power and Ralegh must get out of the Tower before he could begin to climb again. Yet he could not put Machiavelli behind him, even though he was in eclipse and the days of heroic gesture gone from him. He wrote *The Cabinet Council* in an improved style of Florentine argument. Looking upon the English state as he knew it he produced *Maxims of State* in the very shadow of the great Niccolo's *The Prince*. The heavens did not fall, nor did the King move. His mind was of a heavy cast and his prejudice stronger than his curiosity. Why heed what a prisoner in the Tower wrote?

For Prince Henry there was the sea and Sir Walter to write of it. The lad was keen for ships, and Sir Walter turned out a *Discourse of the Invention of Ships, Anchors, Compass, etc.* It was done in a godly and learned style, with proper references to biblical example and ancient precept. For a long time the author had been a captain by sea. Frankly, he pointed out the conflict to come between Dutch and British merchants. He wrote specifically of ship building, of design, of armament and personnel. He wrote as the hero of Cadiz. Prince Henry read, came and talked with him, and fell completely under his spell. No wonder the poor prisoner began to dream of fairer days.

There was a rift between Prince Henry and his father wide as the world. Anne, the Queen, inspired something of her own distaste for the King in their son. With Carr and the host of Scotchmen who were storming England for fame and fortune, the King had his heart and hands full. In turn, William Herbert, Earl of Pembroke, was Anne's favorite and much in attendance upon his Queen. In sympathy, Prince Henry was close to his mother, but perforce lived much upon his own. He was grown to be a fine lad. Hauteur sat in his eyes. A fine brow, delicate lips almost womanish, a strong nose, ears large and set low, a good jaw: such was his face, a countenance of cultured youth unspoiled by dross. He was canny, but not niggardly. Often he came to the Tower, for he was in spirit more an Elizabethan than any at the Court, and he caught the ways of Ralegh as youth sometimes can do such things; by instinct rather than understanding. He found Sir Walter's friendship flattering and he fell so far under the elder man's spell as to imitate his swaggering walk.

To James his children were but instruments to fasten upon political advantage, and he had no exaggerated ambition. Always he lived with caution. The idea of marrying Prince Henry to the daughter of Savoy was brought forward. Ralegh took sides with the Prince against it and wrote his reasons powerfully. No compromise crept into his lines. As always, he was logical and without fear in his opinions. A new light was dawning. There had never been a chance with James. It was useless to waste energy upon him. When a match to marry Lady Elizabeth (the daughter of James, whose issue was later to bring George I to the throne) to the Prince of Piedmont was proposed Sir Walter wrote a second time on royal matches. His was a voice from another world than the suppliant Court, and despite anything his friends could do, a voice that dared to speak roundly, and not with too much heed for policy.

Living in the Tower a life of shadow, thoughts of life and death were always stirring. Ralegh was out of his age, which had died. His friends were a broken circle. Men and women long dead rose to him in spite of his multitudinous activity, and out of memory he perceived the inevitable end. Fear of ideas he never had. His facile mind faced the logic of ending life, wrestled with it, and sought no solace in blind faith. The soul, what was it? Belief, on what founded? When he had thought long he wrote *A Treatise of the Soul.* It was a tour into the realm of metaphysics, a groping after truth. Medieval reasoning: the seeking authority at biblical sources and amid the classics, he always enjoyed. There was time in the Tower for even its sustained meditation. In *The Sceptic* he became more purely a logician "neither affirming, nor denying, but doubting," for this paper was the defense of a man's right to doubt, a fit subject for the years beyond fifty.

For a long time he had glanced at the history of England with discerning eyes, reading everything, talking with all whose scholarship made them worthy. An idea had grown upon him. *The Reign of William the First* and *A Discourse of Tenures before the Conquest* were both thumb-nail sketches pointing toward the work he had in mind. Peace, and the sluggish drift of events made it seem that England with her new colony in America, the only attempt at settling Virginia in which Ralegh had had no part, had emerged into power. The story of her rise began in the darkness of early ages, and most of the men who had rounded it out were with the dead Queen. He had known them and their ways. He had read voluminously of other ages. He would write a *History of the World* upon a scale fitted to the grandeur of the subject. The proportions were gigantic; his resources by no means adequate, but he would begin. The four great empires of the world should precede the story of England. Latin was not a closed book to him. Spanish, French, and Dutch he had. For Hebrew and Greek he would have to depend upon his friends. At the beginning there was no need to have the end more than in sight—time would open the way.

One common fault of chroniclers could be dismissed. There was no longer any hope of pardon. Merit, intellectual power availed nothing with King James. Some day, some scheme to bring wealth to the Crown might overcome the malice of Howard and Cecil and succeed in unlocking the gates. Meanwhile, Ralegh would write history as he conceived it. James believed history should be a mere chronicling of events without judgment or evaluation. Since there was no reward to be hoped for Ralegh freed his mind without temptation.

History was to be courted as Elizabeth once had been. It was to become "the grave mistress of a man's life." He intended to acknowledge virtue where he found it, and not make secure the great. Once he completed the earlier portions of his history, he would be at home amid English things. "I have been permitted to draw water as near to the wellhead as another." His insight was as good as his experience. He had been in the camps and on shipboard. Kings and common soldiers, he knew the ways of both. He knew that "discourse of magnanimity, of national virtue, of religion, of liberty" might encourage virtuous men, but the common soldiery knew only spoil. Whatever it might cost, he would write what he thought of these things as he saw them.

He opened his story in Paradise. The same man who delved into the bald insincerities of Machiavel told the biblical story with the aloofness of a god looking upon his handiwork. Curious, that tendency to keep religious and secular thought far apart, so typical of the Renaissance. Even Niccolo paused at the threshold of the things he thought. Ralegh ended his first book with the death of Semiramis, the second at the sacking of Jerusalem by the Chaldeans, the third with the deaths of the rival leaders of Thebes and Sparta, the fourth with the perishing of Pyrrhus at Argos. The fifth book tells the tale of Rome with grandeur and dignity reaching at his latest the year 130 B.C. Ben Jonson and Thomas Hariot saw this *First Part of the History of the World* through the press. Doctor Robert Burrel, as a cleric, learned in sacred literature, lent his Greek and Hebrew scholarship. The book was actually published on March 29, 1614, a massive folio of one thousand, three hundred fifty-four pages and sold at approximately twenty-five shillings.

Through all its pages, Ralegh preserved a lofty clarity of mind, which, when Macedon had fallen before Rome, and the book drew toward a close, led him to burst into that glorious apostrophe to Death, stately as a cathedral chant, tone under tone, rich and rounded:

"It is Death alone that can suddenly make a man to know himself. He tells the proud and insolent that they are but abjects, and humbles them at the instant, makes them cry, complain and repent, yea, even to hate their forepast happiness. He takes the account of the rich, and proves him a beggar, a naked beggar, which hath interest in nothing but the gravel that fills his mouth. He holds a glass before the eyes of the most beautiful, and makes them see therein their deformity and rottenness and they acknowledge it.

"O eloquent, just, and mighty Death! whom none could advise, thou hast persuaded; what none have dared, thou hast done; and whom all the world have flattered, thou only hast cast out of the world and despised; thou hast drawn together all the far-stretched greatness, all the pride, cruelty, and ambition of man, and covered it all over with these two narrow words, Hic Jacet!"

The Ralegh tradition had been growing through the ten

years of his imprisonment. His book sold well and was read everywhere. Princess Elizabeth carried it with her to Prague. Prince Henry was all admiration. Hampden studied it. Oliver Cromwell recognized the puritanism in it to be unsmirched by narrowness. Only King James read it with anger. It was a saucy book. Ralegh had censured Princes, not all of them more than a thousand years dead. Ralegh did not continue his task. The book was never adequately suppressed. Before 1829 it reached eight editions. For Ralegh there were more important matters at hand than longer courting the "grave mistress." After all, the Tower was a prison.

There was hope in Prince Henry. He hated Carr. He hated the Spanish party, willing to buy peace at any price. He hated them for trying to marry him to Spanish princesses in the name of the wealth to be added to England by such union. Ralegh had an antidote for all that. He knew that Spain was not so wealthy as dreamed. His sailor friends told him how for four galleons there had once been, there was but one; harbors that had boasted a forest of masts were empty. From him Prince Henry learned that the Spanish thrust for power was worn out and grown lazy. Ralegh kept his view before the princely eyes. The youngster had the fire of the days of Drake and Hawkins. He was independent in his life at Otelands, keeping a Court of magnificence and quite his own. Princess Elizabeth was with him. They had a retinue of one hundred forty-one; fifty-six above stairs, eighty-five menials, and this number always growing. It was not false to the best Machiavellian doctrine to stretch every energy toward friendship with him. Ralegh had despaired of aid from James. Queen Anne would pass from the picture, although she was favorably disposed, and so an encouraging factor in any case. Ralegh gambled his all upon the only hope left to him.

The best card he had to play was Guiana. Promises of wealth and wonder he made easily. James stopped them all, but that did not deter their being made. They were an excuse to keep Ralegh's plight before Queen Anne, who lived apart at Denmark House, revelled luxuriously, not always with fitting attention to decorum, and watched her son, who loved best of musical instruments the trumpet, grow into maturity. In turn, the youth consulted Ralegh in everything, and heeded his counsel.

That his efforts might not seem all talk, Sir Walter approached the Court with a scheme for sending out his faithful Keymis to Guiana. He played upon the King's cupidity. Gold! There was something to move the Scotch heart. He could, of course, do nothing unless he won the approval of the Council. There he had a hope as he weighed the balance of power in the making. There was a sombre fellow, secretly an enemy of Carr, a manly man, rising rapidly; Sir Ralph Winwood. He was aggressive, and bound to be of weight; a large man with a full, flashing eye, a heavy determined mouth, and a retreating forehead above bulging brows; a man of imagination and yet of much honesty. James appreciated him despite his anti-Spanish leanings and his friendship with Ralegh. From his retirement within the Tower, Sir Walter could weigh matters dispassionately, and his information was not slight. He knew Carr, now raised to Somerset, was involved with the large haunting eyes, the demure lips, the rounded, dimpled chin of Frances, Countess of Essex. It was easy to forecast the favorite's disgrace, for Carr was genuine in passion, given to extremes and so sure to lose fortune. With his eye upon circumstance, Ralegh tried to strike a bargain with the Lords in an agreement he drew in 1611:

"If Keymis, after being guarded to the place, shall fail to bring to England half a ton, or as much more as he shall be able to take up, of that slate gold ore whereof I have given a sample, then all the charge of the journey shall be laid upon me—by me to be satisfied: but should half a ton be brought home, I am to have my liberty; and in the meantime, my pardon under the Great Seal is to be lodged in his Majesty's hands till the end of the journey."[17]

Incidentally, in another clause of the agreement he let the Council know there was a Spanish settlement on the Orinoco, although later, he was accused of hiding that fact from the King. Gold, not pyrites, he was contracting to present. The matter hung fire without response. Ralegh wrote to Queen Anne, "I did lately presume to send unto your Majesty a copy of a letter to my Lord Treasurer touching Guiana. That there is nothing done therein I could but wonder with the world, did not all the malice in the world exceed the wisdom thereof." But all was in vain. Sir Ralph Winwood might come to be Secretary of State in time. Meanwhile, every device that prevented forgetfulness, that showed a prisoner did not lose initiative nor vigor mewed up within gray walls, was of value. Time would tell, if only it passed before age crippled a man entirely and left no margin for activity. What courage lived in the heart of Ralegh!

In May, 1612, Robert Cecil died and Ralegh wasted no sympathy upon the passing of the Earl of Salisbury. He knew it was the removal of an obstacle to his freedom. Cecil had once been a friend, but recently he had been even more deadly than Carr or the Howards. The King knew a use for Ralegh. Spain was aloof and indifferent to a marriage with the English crown. Ralegh, let loose, would have shown the royalty of Madrid that there was still fire in English stock. The Devonshire adventurer might even have been made to pay for his foray from his own funds, but Cecil said no, and James had an exalted opinion of Cecil's wisdom. Had not the Earl of Salisbury arranged the succession without a hitch? He died leaving the kingdom in a whirl of jealousies and private feuds. Henry Howard was old and as devious as ever. Charles Howard was allowing the King's navy to rot at its wharves, its officers and men both strange to their ships. Parliament was out of hand, and James was being assailed even from the pulpit. Ralegh took heart. He worked more than ever upon Prince Henry. He might prove of service to the Crown at last.

Then tragedy lifted its head from weeping. Prince Henry sickened. Ralegh's Great Elixir, supposed to be a positive cure of any malady not brought on by poisoning, was tried and failed. Prince Henry died in November, 1612. At once the rumor that James had poisoned him found credence. The King was by no means firm in the saddle. It was said Ralegh was to have been freed at Christmas; he remained in prison. Sir Ralph Winwood became Secretary of State. Ralegh refused to lose heart. Time was working in mysterious ways, but the loss of Prince Henry was a blow he had not reckoned with, although it made the interest of the Queen even stronger in the prisoner of the Tower. His kindness to the dead boy was remembered by the mother.

Young Walter Ralegh killed a man in a fight. There seemed to be no peace of mind possible anywhere. The theatres were closed. Masques were not being given. Inigo Jones departed to Italy to measure Palladian palaces and Ben Jonson, with his rival away, and no means of livelihood left, was glad to take young Ralegh in hand and carry him off to France. Young Walter was a callow, youthful cynic. Ben took him to Rouen. Walter studied his books, Ben the French wines, but Walter learned to follow Ben to the tavern. There, one day, taking Ben in his cups, he got the big fellow upon a cart and with the aid of the servants strapped him tight, after stripping him of his clothes. Pushing him along the streets the sixteen-year-old youngster cried out, "Mesdames et messieurs, voyez. Voyez de crucifiement." Ben beat the boy and wrote in rage to Sir Walter. Sir Walter was furious, but Lady Ralegh laughed; it was so like the father in his youth. Ben pushed on with his pupil to Paris, but the King sent a special courier for Ben, ordering him to return to Court. After that, Sir Walter was cool toward Ben, but the boy had been saved; the duel had blown over.

And then the *History of the World* appeared and displeased James with its light treatment of Kings. Christopher Neville stood boldly in Parliament and cried the royal favorites were, "spaniels to the King and wolves to the people." James dissolved Parliament in the face of a petition of grievances, and the realm was in chaos. Henry Howard had himself carried forth from the House of Commons by sixty mounted gentlemen, and rumbled along in his coach to his great house at Charing Cross, only to die of a cancerous thigh. Henry Howard, Earl of Northampton, friend of Carr the favorite, was no longer a factor in the equation, and Ralegh smiled cheerily. Time was winning for him. Thomas Howard, Earl of Suffolk, Carr's father-in-law, by his marriage to Frances, Countess of Essex, inherited the house at Charing Cross, but the most dreaded of his line was gone. Arabella Stuart breathed her last, still a prisoner in the Tower. The old order had changed.

In support of Ralegh had risen a new favorite, George Villiers. The Howards had supported Carr, who was disgraced and out of fortune. Villiers, as rising favorite, hated them, and so loved their enemy, Ralegh. The young man had been chosen by James for the usual charm of person natural to the amatory preference the King always considered in his choice of favorites. Thomas Howard was not a success in Cecil's old berth of Lord Treasurer. The Admiral, Charles Howard, had bungled his administration of the navy. Villiers had easy riding and was a power to consider. King Christian of Denmark came to visit his sister, the Queen, and interceded for Ralegh in one of his drunken bouts at Court. Ralegh battered away at Winwood, the new Secretary, with renewed energy. He refused to blame James openly for his long imprisonment, laying that to his enemies in the Council. "For had his Majesty known me, I had not been where I now am, or had I known his Majesty, they had not been so long where they now are. . . . But to die for the King, and not by the King, is all the ambition I have in the world."

On March 16, 1616, the King's warrant ordered the Lieutenant of the Tower to "permit Sir Walter Ralegh to go abroad to make preparation for his voyage." Sir Ralph Winwood wrote of the going to Guiana "as a matter not in the air or speculative, but real." The day after his deliverance Sir Walter thanked Sir George Villiers in a letter which began, "You have, by your mediation, put me again in the world" and within three months he was in correspondence with men in Holland and France concerning the new venture to Guiana.

2

A tall man, a little stooped, with an eye of fire, whitened hair, but a beard still streaked by black. A man walking down old lanes with an unseeing gaze, looking upon a London long vanished. His tread was heavy, and there was a pause in his gait, as if he looked to turn and turn again, but he strode along with a swing. The surprise in him at the freedom of the streets was the stamp of the Tower. He had come back into the life of the old city. Everywhere he heard inconsequential voices. Men passed him, ignorant of the liberty they enjoyed. To go to prison meant to lose so much; to come out was to live in a dream. He had been shut away a hated man—all of England against him. He emerged a great legend, a man of a thousand stories, and he knew it.

It was a mist, this life of the return. Percy still lay in the Tower, Percy who was Northumberland, but his brother George Percy walked beside talking of days in Virginia. He said that men came and went without wonder—Virginia the dream of old days. Dominion and empire over the water! George Percy had seen with his own eyes the new Jamestown, and George Percy was leading the way to the Virginian woman, who had gone to the races on Newmarket Heath in the company of King James, and before whom Queen Anne forgot her gout. Report named her a King's daughter in her own land.

And so, on walked the two to turn down by Savage's Bell Inn and enter. There the daughter of Powhatan received them, Pocahontas, so different from those earlier waifs, Manteo and Wanchese, the first Virginians to reach London. Percy honored her with a little air of mockery, but the tall man greeted her upon his knee, and kissed that brown hand as he had once reverently graced the fair white one of Elizabeth, and hailed her as a princess. The light of pleasure leaped into the too bright eyes of Pocahontas. Happiness shone upon the young face, already wan, for she was never to escape the deadly touch of English winter. This man was the master of Captain John Smith whom she had once loved. She flushed with pride.

And so the great legends met: Ralegh so near the end with all his greatness gathering about him, and Pocahontas closer to death, but all her story yet to be made. And Ralegh the dreamer hailed Pocahontas for his dream, the vision of that Virginia lost and whelmed away, but greeted her too as a symbol of the grandeur yet to be.

That he might hear a little of the land he had given over, he took her to the Tower where she saw the lions, and old

Northumberland roused himself to give her earrings of pearl set in silver, but when that was ended, Ralegh went down alone to see the *Destiny* growing on the stocks, his ship that was to carry him upon the quest on which he gazed with hope, and more—with faith.

CHAPTER XX

ELDORADO!

THE world of James swung dizzily. Carr, who had so often used him badly, only to rise to be Somerset, had passed from the royal calendar. Convicted of murder, disgraced, he was lost, and another lifted in his place. The King transferred his passionate attentions to his new exquisite, George Villiers, whose loveliness was carrying him on toward the greatness of being Buckingham. Royal leisure was squandered while the realm suffered for lack of guidance.

Internally, affairs were precariously balanced. Ministers were as corrupt as James' favorites. Scotchmen fattened upon English offices. A practice of boldly purchasing preferment grew rapidly. James solemnly indicated that his power was absolute, yet never lifted his hand to make it so. The Commons aired their wrongs to the four winds. The English were really at odds with absolutism. They declared the country devoured by the King's favorites, and James did not dare to touch them. He had lost his people as thoroughly as Catholic Mary had once done.

Foreign affairs received more attention from the Stuart. The old choice was his; which, Spain or France for an ally? A Spanish alliance seemed desirable. There was no more truly royal throne than that of Madrid. James had always longed to marry his children into the line bred in the Escorial, yet he had dealt severely with the Catholics in his own realm. This had not escaped the eyes of all of Europe. He could not hope for a Spanish marriage without according his Catholics peace and liberty. He had only Charles left to offer, but Charles carried with him the English crown. Henry had died. Elizabeth had been married for more than three years to Frederick V, Elector Palatine. It would have done the King little good at the moment to have glanced toward France. Henry IV, before his death in 1610, had dubbed James "the wisest fool in Christendom." Yet despite French logic, Charles was destined to marry Henrietta Maria, and Buckingham as proxy was to bring home the Paris bride. Meanwhile, James dallied. And in far-off Bohemia, the rumblings that were to burst into the clamor of the Thirty Years' War could be heard for the first time.

Sir Walter looked upon all this chaos easily. At sixty-four he understood so much. He had gained his life, for a time. He had regained his freedom, but only upon conditions. He looked upon the unfolding of a new England, and knew he stood alone amid forces only too willing to use and ruin him. There was Villiers, who had helped free him. There was Winwood, who was in need of a violent instrument to forward his anti-Spanish bent. There was Bacon willing to confirm his legal rights under the King's commission to proceed to Guiana in return for information he might later use to become Baron of Verulam. Even Machiavelli offered no aid to the old knight in his last venture, for when the little man had written *The Prince* there were no chapters wasted upon the service due royal fools. The ancient authors Ralegh loved served no better. James would not let him come to Court. It had done no good to approve the absolute prerogative of Kings. James already believed his rights ended only at God. Flattery of an intelligent sort was wasted upon his superlative vanity. Not a single instrument, not a single avenue offered to let Sir Walter rehabilitate himself in England. Guiana, gold, Eldorado: he had to believe in the words of his conjuring; and walk, as it were, blindfolded along a way beset by pitfalls.

Don Diego Sarmiento de Acuna was a tall, thin shadow of a man, and a stalwart hater of Ralegh. The Azores, Cadiz

—these were the deeds of the old pirate. Austere, with something of the sullen, brooding martyr in him, Don Diego watched every move Sir Walter made. There had never been a better Spanish Ambassador. By his patient, relentless work he had almost won for himself the title of Count Gondomar. For Philip III, he was a veritable ear, catching every word uttered in England, meeting every turn for a Spanish advantage. For James he was the only visible instrument to a Madrid marriage. The prestige of such a man was immense, his influence everywhere, yet he failed to have Ralegh's effort prohibited. He could only make the adventure so dangerous, so impossible, that no man with a shred more hope than Sir Walter had, or a touch less need would have accepted the hazards.

Don Diego offered, in the name of his master, to secure a safe conduct for Ralegh to Guiana. He should be taken to the mine and allowed to bring home any gold he obtained. It was an offer of fair words, made that James should feel the friendship of Spain and doubt the peaceful motives of Ralegh, for Don Diego made only one demand. Sir Walter should go in only two ships and unarmed. If he refused, surely the inference was clear; he was sailing in force to attack the colonies of his Spanish Majesty and not merely to find a mine. Sir Walter was not fool enough to believe in the good faith of the offer for an instant. He knew how easily mistakes could be made. Guiana was a long way off and so much could be laid to misunderstanding, after the result to Sir Walter had proved tragic.

Sir Ralph Winwood did not see with the eye of James. He felt the old hatred for Spain. France, with Louis XIII in his teens and rounding rapidly into maturity, was for the moment lost in civil confusion, but was making vague gestures of encouragement to the anti-Spanish party in England. The French Ambassador, Comte des Marêts, conferred with Sir Walter at the instance of Winwood. They saw something of each other while Sir Walter was pouring every shilling he had into the building of his *Destiny*. Des Marêts plumbed the bitterness of the Ralegh pride, which would not forgive the injustice of James nor forget any of all it had suffered. "I thought it well," wrote des Marêts, "to give him good words, although I do not anticipate that his voyage will have much fruit." He sent a report of Ralegh's discontent across the channel to Richelieu, who was even then reaching after the control of France through the favor of the Queen Mother. "A grand marinier et mauvais capitaine," said Richelieu of Sir Walter, just before the death of Luynes. A vague plan for French ships to aid at Orinoco mouth was formulated. Meanwhile a well-found force, able to match any troops the Spanish might present, was made ready in England. Winwood urged Ralegh to attack the Mexico plate fleet if he met it. Ralegh had already told Bacon he intended to do so. The legal mind prompted, "You will be pirates!" And Ralegh, looking upon that deadly mind as from the remoteness of sun-cursed Guiana, answered, "Who ever heard of men being pirates for millions?" Eldorado—there was no place at home. The ministry, the great offices were filled by a new, shrewd generation without the careless splendor of the old. Ralegh did not know their ways, had no foothold to climb. He had only left the heroic gesture before the face of smug futility.

James was always demanding details of the expedition's preparation. He promised to keep them secret. There was the hand of Don Diego. Cleverly he wormed them out of James. Madrid knew every step. James laid the matter before his Council. No harm should befall Spain. Ralegh's friends promised so much. James pledged Don Diego that should Ralegh disobey orders, his life would pay for it. Don Diego made his own preparations to match the hated pirate and waited. There was talk of Prince Charles visiting Madrid —this by way of bait, which James snapped up quickly enough.

Ralegh knew something of where he stood. When Winwood led him to treat with the French Captain Faige, for assistance at the Orinoco, he well knew he was plotting with one rival of England against another. James hoped to urge an Anglo-Spanish alliance by the threat of letting loose an old enemy to Spanish peace, but with a complete washing of the seldom cleansed royal hands. What he did would be on Ralegh's head, which was already conveniently unstable upon its shoulders. Meanwhile, James kept himself so unofficially informed that he could disavow connection with any unfortunately official episode. Poor as he was, Ralegh still had henchmen in Spain. From them he knew, "The alarm of his journey had flown into Spain, and sea forces were prepared to lie for him." Not a single power in the English government would be ready to serve him, should he be compelled to use force upon the Spaniards.

He stood alone facing truth. He had always stood alone; it was nothing new to face the ultimate. In the days that were dead he had had lives through which to work, levers to open channels, the favor of a Queen, but even then he had stood a solitary figure, toying with events, hoping to mould all to his desire. Lady Ralegh, his sons: nothing else of trust and love were left to him. He, an old man, was stooping to build empire with worn out tools and a bowed body. A memory of old fire, a reflection of the dream he had once had of Virginia, a reckless daring of odds he knew too well, a stalwart moving upon thousandfold enmity for a dim and far-off vision: with these he set out for Guiana.

Summer in the West Country. Plymouth entertaining Sir Walter Ralegh in farewell. Seven ships of war and three pinnaces slipping down the Sound and out past Penlee Point:

The *Jason*, the *Encounter*, the *Thunder*, the *Southampton*, and leading the way, with the Admiral in command, the *Destiny*, drawing twelve feet and making a brave show. Stragglers coming up at sea, recognized and saluted, until thirteen ships and one thousand men are bound for the south and west.

The orders of the fleet were martial and succinct. An appeal to God, and a promise to pray and sing a psalm nightly "at the setting of the watch."[18] Blasphemy forbidden lest the curse should depart from neither the ship nor the swearer. Every order to be obeyed, implicitly. Special restrictions upon fires. All to be trained as sailors and soldiers, "making no difference of professions." No private marauding upon the part of any ship. Special sailing orders to be followed faithfully. No ship to be hazarded in attack, "because the loss of a ship to us is of more importance than of ten to the enemy." No gambling, no cowardice, no careless eating, no plundering of the Indians. All to be carried on with an eye to honor and valor.

On June 12, the last glimpse of Devon gone, but the sea rising, with a gale of wind, the fleet driven and scattered, and, from June 25 to August 19, gathering again in the beautiful, hill-girt harbor of Cork. The Admiral feasting with Lord Barry and Lord Roche, riding to Lismore to see Lord Boyle, turning from old thoughts to new, taking his farewell of the broad acres which had once been his. He had begun in Ireland; perchance it was an omen. Farewell at last, and to sea again, keeping together as the ships neared Spanish waters.

Sir Walter Ralegh out again. Housed in his sumptuous cabin, well bedded, the bulkheads hung with paintings and stored with books, he was carrying on in the grand old way at the threshold of penury. He bore his studies with him. A little corps of loyal hearts were his: Sir Warham St. Leger, whose father had shared the early Irish campaigns, a nephew, George Ralegh, a cousin, William Herbert, Captain North, Edward Hastings, and dearer than all, young Walter Ralegh. For the rest, the company was the scum of the country whose joining brought thirty thousand pounds to the venture, but who were not of the stuff to serve well. None in favor at Court dared risk service under him for fear James would remember the association. Pirate, freebooter, unpardoned traitor: these they might call him, but Sir Walter was loosed, and the seas were before him.

Off Cape St. Vincent, the *Southampton* came up with four French vessels, and her captain, Bayley, boarded them. They were taken easily. Sir Walter ordered a fishing net, a small pinnace and some oil taken out of them, for which he paid the French masters. They were then let go. In Madrid, this was called piracy. Bayley, whose duty to his employers in England may have been to prove Sir Walter pirate, demurred at the release of the vessels, and when the fleet touched at Lancerota in the Canaries, and three sailors were killed without retaliation by the Admiral, deemed the mere landing as evidence of his chief's marauding intent, and deserted at once to return to London. There he fell into the hands of a Council in which every man present was favorable to Sir Walter: Arundel, Carew, Compton, Hay, and Zouch. He was thrown into prison and discredited. Of this Sir Walter only knew he had lost a ship from the fleet, and a disaffected captain would be heard in London without any check upon his tongue.

It was not new to him to have men turn back. He was imperious and difficult, and quickly wore a timid man into obstinate caution or even into panic and flight. In this voyage all that seemed different. The pardon left behind in the King's purse, the assured malice of Madrid, the burden of broken years and habitual *mal de mer*, the lack of faith in his men, and a sense of the passing away of the good blades of his youth, so fit for his present work, weighed upon him. He was considerate. Gloom settled upon him and foreboding. He found little pleasure in the shimmer and sheen of depths, blue within blue to the dark under void, nor the flash of rosy creatures making off into the folds of the sea streams. Flying fish leaped and glided from before the cut water. The Admiral was sailing in his *Destiny* and there was no solace to the thought under the great sky bowl: too clearly was his end no longer in his own hands.

In the Lesser Canaries he called at Gomera and found a good harbor, and a governor whose wife was half English, of Stafford blood. Here was the last bit of England to be met. A letter to the Governor, a pair of English gloves, a present to his lady began the interchange of compliments. She was touched and countered by sending the Admiral fruit, rusks, and sugar. He sent some of her gift to his sick in the fleet, but held such as could be kept for the torrid days when they were close to the line. Then bounteously, he returned her favor, but waited till he knew her tastes. Meanwhile, not a sailor dared run amuck. The orders promised hanging to the man who stole so much as an orange or a grape. When sailing time came, the Admiral took from his cabin a fine painting of the Magdalen, and sent it together with lace of curious pattern, rose water, and ambergris to the Countess, who returned her thanks and hurried fresh baskets of fruit and live fowls on board the departing ships. It was a pleasant interlude, all this; a gracious memory to carry on the fortnight cruise toward hazard and danger.

In three days the fleet was beset by sickness. The wind was often ahead. There was no fortune upon the ships. Fifty men in the *Destiny* alone were incapable of duty. The illness strengthened. Two captains and a provost marshal died. Next, as if in mockery, the master surgeon was stricken, and lesser officers succumbed. And day by day the heat boiled. The Admiral went through it all with resolute control. Near Bravo, fifteen degrees above the equator, a hurricane lashed the weakened argosy. One of the twelve went down. The crews of the rest were so reduced they could scarce make repairs. They all seemed castaway in strange seas. A darkness enveloped them in a time of full daylight. They lay becalmed in heat and when rain fell in torrents it gushed below through the opened, sun-dried decks, adding to the misery of the sick and dying. Strange colors flashed along the sea rim. The middle depths were slowly passed, but the voyage grew no fairer. Off Trinidad fifteen lurid rainbows were seen in a single day of squalls and thunder. Through it all the Admiral moved with infinite patience and gentleness, a very different man from the hovering hawk, quick to pounce upon trivial faults. It was his heart that guided him. His mind perchance already saw to the landing, and beyond to the return. He had no bent for self pity.

Fowler, who was to have assayed the gold at the mine, died. John Pigott, who was to have led the forces ashore, died. John Talbot, the Admiral's own companion in the Tower, died, a gentleman of parts and one on whom Sir Walter could fully rely. Francis, the Admiral's cook, died. Crab, the Admiral's servant, died. Only the Admiral's son, young Walter, moved untouched through the pestilence. The Admiral, often drenched by rain, chilled, took cold and fell into a fever which consumed him for four weeks, and even then the fortnight cruise had not ended. Sick and shaken, Sir Walter thought upon the Countess in Gomera, saved his life by a judicious use of the last of the fruit she sent, and saved his ships by keeping the command in his hands, and his journal carefully up to date, so that the fever might not addle his memory and the delirium wipe out the value of his seamanship. Still ill, attended only by his pages, he made his landfall off Cape Oyapoco on November 11, and so northward, soon to anchor in the mouth of the Cayenne. For three weeks there was nothing but rest for the crew. The bounty of the Indians provided roasted mullets, plantains and pineapples, peccaries and pistachio nuts. The Admiral was a great legend among the natives. His name "still lived among them. All offer to obey him." This loyalty touched him. It was so different from the spirit of the English court. He was still weak from illness and the strain of the six weeks passage. A Dutch trader chanced upon the coast. Captain Peter Alley had suffered from fever and had been left dizzy and beyond activity. He was no more use to the expedition. Sir Walter sent him home in the Dutchman, and by him a letter to Lady Ralegh.

"Sweetheart," he began, writing out of weakness. Forty-two of his people in the *Destiny* were dead. The losses of the fleet were detailed, yet made not overmuch of. There, under the cruel light of the tropics, Sir Walter kept his face forward, despising the obstacles passed, and promising better news in his next letter. If he wrote no longer with the fire of youth he dispayed the more courtesy and consideration. With Captain Alley gone he took up his work. He carried the fleet to the Triangle Islands to organize his thrust.

He was still so sick as to be carried about in his chair, and time might prove as valuable as strength. Word of his coming had been sent broadcast to Don Diego de Palomeque, ruling Guiana, El Dorado, and Trinidad, to the Bishop of Porto Ricco, to all the Indies where lived Spanish authority. An armada was sure to gather to come against the outrageous freebooter. Only the smaller ships could ascend the Orinoco. Once entered, they might be cut off by a Spanish fleet. Time passed and still Ralegh could not move. He knew the hardships of such work, but he felt the urge to lead. At last he dared wait not a day longer. Most faithful to his cause since the voyage of 1595, Captain Keymis was the man best fitted to ascend and find the mine. Two hundred fifty men in five ships were given him, and the other five remaining took station at Trinidad, waiting for the Spanish to come down in force, but in vain. The terror of Ralegh's name made the Spaniards cautious. They gave themselves to no such folly as an attack in the open. The jungle, the river was more to their liking. Besides, it was better to protect the passage north to the Indies than hunt a phantom British fleet at Orinoco mouth.

The Admiral knew his estate. He had ordered Keymis to reach the mine without an act of war. If attacked, they were to resist and drive the Spanish as far as might be. Keymis was not to count too much on his "scum of men," for to be beaten by the Spaniards was not only a misfortune but a national disgrace. Defeat must be avoided. The Admiral's nephew George Ralegh was second in command, but Keymis was to take sole responsibility; on his judgment Sir Walter relied. With him he risked even young Walter. It was a gamble for the Admiral's freedom. Should the gates of the Tower once again close there would be no re-opening. Never before had Ralegh been so helpless, so much in the hands of others. All too quickly the short run to Trinidad from the Triangle Islands was ended, and the waiting begun. On December 17, 1617, the Admiral took up station off Puncto Gallo, his life dependent upon the finding of a mine, location uncertain, by a battalion of men forbidden to make warfare unless attacked, only one of whom could even guess the whereabouts of the garrisoned town of San Thome, which had been moved directly into the probable path of the seekers. All of this the Admiral knew better than any of his men, yet he patiently waited in the *Destiny* the toss of fortune. He recorded in his journal the passage of the days. He drove off the enemy who attacked from San Giuseppe in a half-hearted effort, and lost only one sailor and a boy in the defense. He spent days ashore hunting herbs, watching the strange tropical life of the island. It was a maddening interval, but he bore it with as much fortitude as he did anything in his life. Then on February 14, 1618, the journal was abruptly broken off and never touched more. A letter had arrived that marked the end of the world. Captain Keymis had sent it off on January 8, and it told of the events of New Year's Day.

Keymis had been attacked from both banks of the river, but he had landed at eleven o'clock above San Thome. By nine in the evening, forty-two regulars of the Spanish army came against him. The English were saved by their officers, rallied, and drove the Spaniards back to San Thome. Diego Palomeque arranged his main force before the town. Young Walter led his pikemen, recklessly brave. The forces met. Grados or Erenetta wounded young Walter. Diego was killed. The Spaniards broke. The town was taken and burned. Young Ralegh and Captain Cosmor died and were buried. There was no need to read how Keymis pushed on toward the mine, how George Ralegh went exploring. The English garrison at the taken San Thome had a bad bit of fighting. Keymis was ambuscaded and fell back, although within perhaps eight miles of the mine. All that could wait. Young Walter was dead. The rest did not matter. For that the Admiral had suffered fever, heat, insect pests, loss of his estate. For the time he had no words. He had a letter to turn over and over. Keymis had failed him. The fiery spell of the country entered at last into his blood, his head. It was March 2, before Keymis reached Puncto Gallo, and Ralegh had weighed the matter until he was almost crazed. Keymis in his cabin talked frankly, perhaps not realizing the torture his Admiral had endured in the sixteen days of waiting, perhaps over anxious to justify his actions. He had not opened the mine because of the death of young Walter, because his force was weak and could not have worked the mine cut off from the food in the ships. It were folly to open it for the Spaniards to enjoy, and, here he was dangerously blunt, since the Admiral was unpardoned, and weak almost to death he had no desire to open it for King James.

The Admiral disregarded the loyalty to himself rather than James. Keymis thought he had been within two hours of the mine. Sir Walter spared nothing. Since his son was lost, what did he care if Keymis lost a hundred more, so he saved his credit, and took home proof of the mine to the King. Keymis had betrayed him. Keymis must look to himself and resolve the matter to the King and the State. There had never been man truer, but the Admiral was beside himself with pain of his loss and failure.

Captain Keymis composed a defense addressed to Lord Arundel of the Council. The Admiral read it, refused to approve it, and Keymis retired with an "I know then, Sir, what course to take." The rile of the heat had entered his head. He was as mad as the Admiral, whom he had never forsaken. In his cabin he shot himself with a pistol, but the ball only broke a rib. Strong in his purpose, "he thrust a long knife under his short ribs up to the handle and died." He had suffered, he had failed, and he could not stand the Admiral's censure.

As for Sir Walter, out of the blackness came a great stillness upon him. He saw life once again as something afar off, an array of incidents without sense or rhythm, but cruel and silly. It escaped the pattern of Machiavelli, the generalities of Aristotle, the chronicle of Herodotus. He saw the attack as a puppet show, young Walter charging vainly in the face of futility, the ridiculous river voyage beset by meaningless hardships, the blunders and misgivings of Keymis. And within he knew he too was of this pageant, moving upon injustices and misunderstanding, but through his deadened mind throbbed the pain of his loss. It was twenty days before he could write Lady Ralegh and Secretary Winwood. The latter had then been dead almost five months.

From St. Christopher's he sent word to "dearest Bess." "I was loathe to write, because I knewe not how to comforte you; and, God knowes, I never knewe what sorrow meant till nowe." So with care and considerate preparation he led her on to the fateful sentence, "The Lord bless and comfort you, that you may bear patiently the death of your valiant son." Then his own fortitude shattered, his "brains broken," he cried out in a postscript. "I protest before the majestie of God that as Sir Francis Drake and Sir John Hawkins died heartbroken when they failed of their enterprise, I could willingly do the like, did I not contend against sorrow for your sake, in hope to provide somewhat for you; and to comfort and relieve you."

To Secretary Winwood he wrote of the miscarriage of his fortunes; and his letter rang with mingled courage and despair. He did not disguise his knowledge of the double dealing. He sent enclosed the letter captured at San Thome, which proved how far the Spanish were let into his plans. It had left Madrid for Guiana before the expedition had cleared the Thames; so clear was the double dealing of James. The Admiral had been commanded to set down, "the country, and every river by which I was to enter it; to set down the number of my men, and burden of my ships; with what ordnance every ship carried." This James had forwarded through the Spanish Ambassador unblushingly. Out of so piteous a plight a younger or more timorous man might have made great dole, and with a little caution begged his life from the King. But Ralegh was sixty-five, and had looked cold bloodedly upon the death of faithful Keymis, himself fifty-five, and only four years older than the scheming James. The chill of age left the Admiral his judgment. He made no apology for not working the mine. There were none to whom he owed one since he had lost his son and his estate in the enterprise. True, he included a feeble "his Majestie excepted,"[19] but the tone of the passage itself was defiant of fate and authority, and blamed James directly for the breach of faith.

At St. Christopher's even the chance for a return to the mine in a last desperate gesture was lost. Captains Whitney and Woollaston had been slow to support Keymis just before his defeat. They were very quick to urge the Admiral to go roving for loot from Spanish ships. At Granada they deserted and hurried home to England. Ralegh felt the irony of their duplicity but little. It was but another bolt of ruin, of no more moment than the malicious ship gossip on the way to Newfoundland. He could not even die when and where he wanted. The crews proposed piracy. They were out of hand. Perhaps it was indeed as he had said, his brains were broken. Command was difficult to him for the first time in his life. He crossed the ocean on a northerly passage, reaching up to the height of Ireland. The westerly winds were heavy and scattered his ships. He touched at Kinsale and landed four convicted criminals, whose return to England would have meant their execution. There was no turning out of the clans to do him honor. His grip of friend and foe was gone. Dropping down toward the Scilly Islands he found the summer wind chill and checking to the blood, and the grayness of the north weighed upon him, until royal wrath or none, he was glad to see his rugged Devon shores again.

He sailed into Plymouth on June 21, 1618. The *Destiny* carried on alone to the end of the forlorn hope. There was no flurry of a hero's return about his arrival. He took up his berth, and presently went ashore to find a hushed town, a welcome from his faithful Captain King and from one other.

Lady Ralegh had hastened down from London at King's word of the Admiral's homecoming. Like lovers they seized those minutes. Both knew they were living perhaps their last interlude of mutual confidence before the world assailed them again. They had an instant to live over the moments of warmer blood, to sorrow for their son, and to plan for the threatening days to come. Sir Walter might sail as an Admiral no more, but however untrue the King should prove, there was still one loyalty he could not strip away.

CHAPTER XXI

DEATH!

THREE days before Sir Walter touched at Kinsale, the Thirty Years' war began, and James' son-in-law found himself Frederick V of Bohemia. Europe was ablaze with grumblings. In Portugal, Sebastian writhed under the Spanish yoke. Gustavus II Adolphus led Sweden heroically against Poland and the Tsar. The Romanov family had been five years on the Russian throne. Spain played warily to keep the Netherlands in subjection. In France, Mary de Medici, the Queen Mother, from her exile at Blois sent Richelieu to mediate with the Duke of Luynes. James still dreamed of marrying his Charles to the line of Spain, and admired the confusion upon the continent, while he allowed proclamation in Scotland that sports on Sunday, after church service, were legal.

On May 13, word of the taking and burning of San Thome reached England. The Spanish Ambassador burst in upon James' privacy with the one word of his charge, "Piratas!" James took nearly a month to decide how to dispose of Sir Walter. For all the man had suffered he cared not a fig. Ralegh should be sacrificed; a friendly offering to Spain. How, when and where; whether in England, or, to better mollify Philip, in Madrid: there were the matters that concerned the crafty James. Ralegh had broken the peace, committed scandalous and enormous outrages. All the blame was his, none rested upon the Spanish; that had been arranged before Sir Walter left England. The Spanish Ambassador set out for Madrid to plead James' suit for a marriage. At Greenwich a letter overtook him, promising restitution and punishment in the Guiana matter. The letter was in the handwriting of the newly made Duke of Buckingham. Even George Villiers had turned against Ralegh. On June 11, a royal proclamation denounced the work of the expedition. On June 12, Sir Lewis Stukeley was ordered by the Lord Admiral to arrest Ralegh and bring him to London.

Queen Anne favored a French alliance for Prince Charles, despite the two million crowns of the Infanta's dowry. She detested her husband, and his policy. She gratefully remembered Sir Walter Ralegh. Anything which would check Spain and England from drawing closer was desirable to France. The Queen saw to it that the legend of Ralegh's fabled influence reached the French Court. Spain was and always had been his enemy. Should he safely reach France, he could work efficiently to prevent the Infanta from becoming an English bride. Of course, the whole scheme was preposterous, but the French heeded. It was inferred he was still a power in England. Even if the Spanish marriage were realized it would be convenient to have the goodwill of Anne. After all she was the Queen.

As for Sir Walter, his plight was clear, but broken as he was, unwanted at home, his only haven foreign service, he schemed to secure another opportunity to go to Guiana. A chaos of factional plotting mocked the Court. Winwood's place was taken by Robert Naunton, no friend to Ralegh. Francis Bacon had just reached the eminence of Lord Chancellor. Petty groups were everywhere bickering, and even Ralegh's few friends could not face the King with any solid front. George Carew entered the royal presence and begged for his friend's life upon his knees, but James let him know the matter was closed; Ralegh should die. None other got even so far. Yet in spite of these sureties of malice

Sir Walter looked far away, refusing to take the King's attitude as positive and unalterable.

Stukely came upon Ralegh, Lady Ralegh, and the honest Captain King riding toward London. Stukely could boast sixteen quarterings upon his coat of arms. He was the nephew of Sir Richard Grenville and so related to Ralegh. He had no royal warrant, but Sir Walter did not dispute his authority. They were close to Ashburton at the meeting, yet all four turned about and rode back twenty miles to Plymouth instead of pushing on to London. For more than a week they lay there, Stukely paying more heed to selling the cargo of the *Destiny* than to the custody of his prisoner. Did James intend Ralegh to escape? Anxious as he might be to please Spain, would he be able to face the wrath of his people, should he give Sir Walter over to the hated crown of the Escorial? The delay was unnecessary. The absence of Stukely and his inattention were marked. The government was seeking a way out. If Sir Walter would flee they would be rid of all embarrassment, and the onus would be his. So argued Captain King when he arranged with two Frenchmen: Le Grand and Flory, to carry Sir Walter to Normandy. It was with Captain King he once rowed off to within a quarter mile of the Rochelle bark ready to carry him over the narrow seas, but he turned back. The wrath of the King could not be so deadly, else he had been given no chance to escape the royal anger. If he stayed he might yet win clear, and possibly gain that other trial at the land of the Orinoco.

Suddenly, the Council summoned him to appear in London. Then he was sorry he had not fled. He had faced the tragic farce of such an ordeal in 1603. The old sentence still hung above his head. A Frenchman, Manourie, brought the warrant. He was a spy, a rogue, but something of a chemist. Ralegh disregarded his suspicions of the man, and prepared to use him. It was urgent he secure time to write the *Apology for the Voyage to Guiana* and have it tendered to the King. Face to face with the Council summons it was necessary also to prepare a defense, to weigh the questions involved as well as reach the King. To win that delay Manourie would serve as well as another. If the plight were so desperate that creatures so poor as Manourie, or even Stukely, spelled destruction, then ruin was at hand and there was nothing to do but submit. Faith in either was not to be had, for there was no power left Ralegh to demand it. "Men will always be false to you unless they are compelled by necessity to be true," Machiavelli had said. Even Keymis had failed when he thought his Admiral's might lost through sickness, even swallowed by death.

Sir Walter was content to play in the best Florentine style for his life. He begged an emetic of Manourie. From Salisbury he sent Lady Ralegh and Captain King on to London. He had gone as far toward London as he intended. The King, on progress, would touch at Salisbury. When the royal party came the *Apology for the Voyage to Guiana* should be ready. He took the emetic of Manourie, was seized with illness, and used an ointment to produce pustules upon his breast and arms. Doctors failed to understand his malady. Four days he lay at Salisbury. He used Manourie as an amanuensis. His real ailments were not neglible, but those he induced were more obvious and lasted until his *Apology* was completed and James came to Salisbury on August 1. The *Apology* was largely an attack upon the Spanish attitude; their disregard of peace, their ambush and unwarranted attack; not at all the utterances to please the King. In reckless mood Sir Walter told Manourie Captain King was preparing a boat at Tilbury to carry him into France. Manourie accepted a bribe to help in the escape. Ralegh's fine carelessness and scorn were never more costly. Of course Manourie turned traitor at once. The Queen's favor and care might do much, but even Queens can fail, and the Council was against him, eager for his death. The stratagem of the *Apology* brought no result. There was nothing to do but go on to London.

Perhaps at the request of Queen Anne, the French resident in London, Le Clerc, and David de Novion waited upon Ralegh at Brentford, offering to carry him to France from London. Sir Robert Naunton knew of it. He gave Sir Lewis Stukely license to go any length, but for the time to proceed slowly. How much was France really interested? Would the affair rebound through Gallic channels upon the head of Queen Anne? Even the Secretary of State would be ruined if his monarch were carelessly involved in a deal with France. Sir Walter was taken on to London and lodged at his house in Broad Street, on August 7. On August 9, Le Clerc and David de Novion called to tell him a French bark was ready to take him to Calais where an escort awaited him. Sir Walter preferred to go in a small English ketch. It was a futile independence and it spelled tragedy.

Captain King had trusted a boatswain of his, Hart, and a one-time fellow prisoner with Ralegh, Cotterell. Both betrayed the plan to Stukely, who wormed his way into confidence, showed Ralegh every deference, borrowed ten pounds from him, gave good reasons for a hatred of England, and arranged to flee to France with his prisoner. All this he dared to do under Naunton's license, which he had in writing to make sure he would not be involved. Lady Ralegh, Captain King, Le Clerc, and de Novion were true to Sir Walter, but not another soul in all England. The government was ready to close the play. Stukely had set Sir William St. John and Mr. William Herbert upon the trail, reserving all the credit for himself.

It was Sunday night when Ralegh, with a false beard, and a hat with a green band, went into a wherry at Tower dock.

He would do what was necessary to rest in France from Spanish spleen. Perhaps in a little time the Queen would have made means for his pardon and recalling. It was all heavy in manner, this action of the last resort. Sir Walter, his page, Stukely and Stukely's son, King and Hart shoved off in the wherry to join the ketch at Tilbury. Herbert and Sir William St. John took another wherry, let the fugitive have a start and then, when the heavily laden boat had clearly indicated her course, followed her down river. The tide served. Stukely was enjoying the plan. He asked King if he had not played the honest man. King assured him he hoped he would continue. Herbert's boat drew near. Sir Walter told his watermen he had had a brawling matter with the Spanish Ambassador, which was true enough in a way. Oh, it was a night of veiled diction and speech in parables. If the other boat hailed in the King's name they must pay no heed. They should have ten gold pieces when they carried him to Tilbury. He was escaping to the Low Countries. Stukely shivered a little. Ten gold pieces! Thirty pieces of silver! Judas! With a curse, Stukely bewailed the lack of faith in him. He swore he would kill the first man who did not pull. It was all a dim dream, so unnatural that Sir Walter sat sunken in a stupor while the boat passed Woolwich, lost the ebb tide, and felt the turn of the flood in Gallions Reach. It was there St. John and Herbert challenged them. Sir Walter announced himself in Stukely's custody. Together the two crews gave up the pull. The tide was young and strong. It swept them upstream from Blackwall. The fugitive landed at Greenwich. St. John and Herbert landed too. Stukely arrested Sir Walter and Captain King in the name of the Crown. Sir Walter fixed his eyes upon Stukely. "Sir Lewis, these actions will not turn out to your credit," which was good prophecy, for Sir Lewis shortly died raving mad in the island of Lundy. Sir Walter advised King to insist he was an accomplice of Stukely. The good Captain would have none of that. In the morning he bade good-bye to Ralegh at the Tower gate, still faithful, but understanding the sequel to come as well as Sir Walter. He left his master in God's hand, and went on to his own prison in tears.

The challenge of the Tower was peremptory. There was no consideration for the prisoner. He was searched and his possessions seized. It was a hard impertinence to bear. A golden whistle set with small diamonds, a jacinth seal with a Neptune cut upon it, a diamond ring of nine sparks, a lodestone in a scarlet purse, sixty-three gold buttons with sparks of diamonds, an old seal in silver of his own arms, a wedge of fine gold at twenty-two carats, a Guiana idol of gold and copper, a diamond ring he had long worn, and which Secretary Naunton claimed was the gift of "the late Queen": all these were sealed into a bag and given to Sir Lewis Stukely. A map of Guiana and Nova Regina, a chart of the Orinoco, and a plan of Panama were found upon him, together with five assays of the American silver mine. Clearly, he had been carrying these to France. He was allowed to keep two things; "item: one ounce of ambergris; left him for his own use; item: a spleen stone; left him for his own use."

One bit of property he managed to exempt; a gold encased picture set with diamonds. Had it been of "the late Queen" Naunton would have given the fact a quirk. It was very probably of the only one left to him from other times, one for whom he had lain in the Tower in the dead days, and who with King alone had hastened down to Plymouth to meet him, still, in his old age eager for every minute of his company. The picture was left with Sir Allen Apsley, Lieutenant of the Tower.

The usual devices were sprung upon the prisoner. He was examined by a committee of the Privy Council. Bacon, Archbishop Abbot, Lord Worcester, Naunton, Cæsar, and

Coke questioned to their heart's desire. De Novion was arrested and interrogated. Le Clerc was faced with him at Hampton Court. The Frenchman refused to acknowledge the authority of the Privy Council. Ordered to remain in his house, he was defended by his government. The French could not deny they had stood ready to help an enemy of the British Crown. On the other hand, it did no good to blame the French, when Ralegh's death was the thing desired and Ralegh had rejected their help, preferring to sail in an English vessel. It was more important to attach blame to Sir Walter. Spain was pleased at the British taking of Sir Walter at the moment of flight. At the proper instant, when it was the canny act with which to bind the bargain of the English-Spanish alliance, James would offer up his sacrifice. It was the duty of the Council to find the excuses.

On September 11, Sir Thomas Wilson was made the prisoner's special keeper. He was of the Spanish party. Under Cecil he had been a spy at Madrid and had met Ralegh's own men there while gathering evidence to break the conspiracy of the priests in 1603. Pensioned for that service, and since then made Keeper of the State Paper Office, he attacked Sir Walter viciously. It was a thankless job at the best, and he could make nothing of Ralegh, which daunted him. He moved Ralegh from his room in the Wardrobe Tower, overlooking the Queen's gardens, to an upper story of the Brick Tower. None could see the prisoner. No servant was allowed to care for him. Confession, there was the need of the State; and Wilson worked day and night to get one, promising the King's mercy, forgiveness, even liberty. Sir Walter knew him for what he was and insisted on writing to James. This was to gain time, just as the leisurely baiting of Wilson postponed the inevitable. What strength lay in delay he was determined to have. Wilson added another arrow to his quiver. Lady Ralegh was arrested and encouraged to exchange letters with Sir Walter. She, too, was given in charge of Wilson. They wrote pathetically about their mutual distress, each heartening the other. The King was wearied; Wilson had failed to produce evidence sufficient to make hanging easy and immediate. Heaven only knows what he had hoped to obtain.

On October 15, 1618, Wilson quit, defeated by a prisoner whose left side was powerless, who was lame, whose fits of ague shook him endlessly, and through whose parts ran a shifting numbness. Secretary Naunton had hoped that they would "not long be troubled by that cripple." Certainly Ralegh's endurance was coming to an end, but not before Wilson had failed utterly.

Chancellor Bacon had once told Ralegh that the King's commission to go into Guiana, with the power of command, even unto death was "as good a pardon for all former offenses as the law of England can afford." He had now to find a legal flaw in that argument. The King was set upon disposing of Ralegh without a public trial. He had not forgotten how, at Winchester Sir Walter had won men to him. Coke, no longer Chief Justice, arranged the procedure. Ralegh should be tried by the Council. Under the old sentence of 1603, he was without legal rights since he was civilly dead. The examiners were now to become his judges. He should be charged with abuse of royal privileges, hostile acts against friendly Spain, marauding for private gain. Then he should be executed upon the old sentence. Even such an arraignment took time, but by October 22, the matter was ripe.

The Queen was very near death herself. Bedridden, she wrote to George Villiers, Marquess of Buckingham:

"My kind Dog:
"If I have any power or credit with you, I pray you let me have a trial of it, at this time, in dealing sincerely and

earnestly with the King that Sir Walter Ralegh's life may not be called in question.

"If you do it so that the success answer my expectation, assure yourself that I will take it extraordinarily kindly at your hands; and rest one that wisheth you well, and desires you to continue still, as you have been, a true servant to your Master."

It was almost the last word of a lonely woman, faithful to old memories, although sunk in gloom and the misery of dropsy, and at times nearly distraught. Buckingham was unsuccessful. The wheel of fate was ready and too well ordered. He may even never have tried.

All the rumor and fact of the matter were presented to Ralegh, but so twisted by legal carping as to render his case hopeless. He fought as usual, a good fight, filled with denial of his guilt in 1603 and 1618 alike. The Spaniards had attacked him. The Commissioners overlooked that point and countered by inquiring into his intents which they deemed piratical. Did he think of taking the plate fleet before or after the loss of the mine? There was much bickering, but nothing that even approached the array of testimony in his first trial.

The prisoner had no half-hearted hope in Cecil, no lingering trust that some of his friends might lead him clear as in 1603. They were strange minds to him; men he knew by name or report only, for his kin were not active in the prosecution. He was definitely old, and of another day. The gulf of the years spent in the Tower and the thrust at Guiana had cut him off from these courtiers. Even Niccolo himself could have done nothing with them. To work upon men one must know their hearts intimately, and these Jacobeans had very little heart of any sort. At Winchester, Ralegh had suffered from a conspiracy working upon the King, but the will of James had grown surprisingly and his Council were become but puppets for his whims. Even Bacon filed his wits to please his King.

James kept away from London. He could not think of an axe without shuddering. He wrote meditations upon the Lord's Prayer and dedicated them to his lust for Villiers. He filled Theobalds, the old seat of the Cecils, with fleas, visited his filthy habits upon Otelands, and hunted as close to London as Hampton Court, but came no nearer the trial. In the midst of the inquiry he sent a privy seal to the Commission ordering execution forthwith. His puppets murmured, conferred, and delayed. Ralegh was sent for to come to Whitehall and asked if he had any objections to offer, a pardon to present, or a denial he was the person of the charges. Sir Walter knew the plight he stood in before they informed him he was to be executed under the old sentence. He asked to be beheaded, not hanged, nor drawn, nor quartered. The Council promised so much upon its own responsibility. It had no desire to see the more objectionable punishments practised upon gentlemen of rank. The wheel was always turning.

Again the privy seal brought orders. Proceed according to law. Was James vacillating? Could he be like Elizabeth now and then? The Judges nodded their heads; it was well they had delayed. But obedience was necessary. Francis Bacon drew up the warrant for Ralegh's death, and sent it to James, then in Hertfordshire. James signed it under the date October 28. Bacon then felt safe and sent for Ralegh to come to Westminster. There the procedure followed the law. Ralegh defended himself in a weak voice between fits of ague. He had left the Tower for the last time, in haste, and was ill. His mind at peace, Bacon watched these struggles. The man was theirs. They could strike when they would. Chief Justice Montagu was more just then Coke, both in heart and mind. He knew a great man faced him. He had read the *History of the World.* All his life Ralegh had been a tradition of past greatness. He rose to pronounce sentence. With kindly manner he spoke of the prisoner's valor, his wisdom, and reminded Sir Walter he would need them both. "Fear not death too much, nor fear death too little; not too much lest you fail in your hope, not too little lest you die presumptuously," and at the end, "Execution is granted."

Sir Walter did not blanch. His ague did not make him ridiculous, but spared him for the moment. He was old. He was sick. He was disgraced. Before God, he had never been disloyal, before God, whom he was so soon to meet that he need fear the face of no King on earth. He knew they would come down upon him quickly. Under guard he walked to the gatehouse of the old monastery of St. Peter. From the barred windows he looked upon the Abbey. The head of Sir Walter Ralegh was to be cut off at or within the palace of Westminster. Would that it might come in the light.

Francis Thynne feared he would die too daringly. "It is my last mirth in this world," countered Sir Walter, but promised to be grave enough at the sad parting. To him the path was clear and not very difficult. "The world itself is but a larger prison, out of which some are daily selected for execution." He was as a gypsy welcoming the end of life for its release. The play was over, but the future, for that Machiavelli might still serve him. One "should seem to be all faith, all integrity, all humanity, and all religion." His mind might be free, but it was best to conform that his memory might thrive, and his deeds grow fairer, as the wrong done him by the King grew more evident to all eyes. So he had carried himself with Chief Justice Montagu, and so he proceeded to treat Doctor Robert Tounson, Dean of Westminster. None knew better the lash of convention, and none scorned more to bow. His mind soared to the stars, free in thought, and untouched by fear, but he carried his courage with humility that envy might not distort the truth.

Elizabeth Ralegh flung herself upon the Council. None stirred for her, she was only granted possession of her husband's body when the execution was over.[20] It was not until she came to the gatehouse that she heard he was to die next morning. She went up. They talked of his fame and how dishonor might be put aside. Would the King let him speak upon the scaffold? The King was away, but he might have sent special orders. There was no fear of his coming nearer. The sight of blood sickened him. The thought of it turned Lady Ralegh faint. It was their parting, this time of broken sentences and low words. Out of the shadow that was the Abbey boomed the midnight stroke. Elizabeth rose. He should rest to be strong for the awful moment. All her visit the promise of the Lords had been in her mind, but she had not been able to fit it to her tongue. She tried to go, but turned back. She told him. When he was dead his body was hers. That clear smile that came to him so often met her. "It is well dear Bess, that thou mayest dispose of that dead, which thou hadst not always the disposing of when alive." Broken as she was she tried to match him, left, and wrote to her brother she would send the body to him to be buried in his church at Beddington. "This night he shall be brought you with two or three of my men." It was even the day of his death as she wrote. The unbelievable had come. His head would be sent her. It would be sent in a mourning coach, in a red velvet bag, and its coming would break her heart, but she would never let it go from her. The dawn turned gray as she waited.

2

Fearless of death! Doctor Tounson, Dean of Westminster, encouraging, comforting. There could be no fear where

DEATH

there had never been any. "The soul of man, using will and reason, is immortal." Galen, Strabo, Maschion, Hilarius, Herophylus knew as much. Niccolo never concerned himself with that; it was obvious that men died. The soul rested not upon princes.

"Cowards fear to die; but courage stout,
Rather than live in snuff, will be put out."

Grimly pleasant to write that in the still of night. These puny hearts could not feel the humor of it, ecod, they had forgotten how to laugh. Sidney or Spenser would have answered it. Francis Drake tasted its bitter wisdom, Hawkins clapped shoulder, and grousing Frobisher bellowed his approval. Silken men these gaolers. Time to end the affairs of the Guiana expedition. Time to deny the lies of Stukely and Manourie, and then in the quiet dark a deeper mood.

"Even such is time, that takes on trust
Our youth, our joys, our all we have,
And pays us but with age and dust;
Who in the dark and silent grave,
When we have wandered all our ways,
Shuts up the story of our days!
But from this earth, this grave, this dust.
The Lord shall raise me up, I trust!"

Gray strengthening to white, and in the early morning, Doctor Tounson and the Holy Eucharist. Blessed symbol of what life might offer! Faith universal, and the form a meaning! Far-off candles upon the altar of her chapel where once knelt Elizabeth the Queen amid the incense and soft music; strong sea breath wafting sailor prayers from the ships bound to Cadiz. The early days had been fairer. Time and a blanched sky creeping upon man! Tounson objecting to a plea of innocence upon the scaffold because it taxed the justice of the realm. Guilty, pah! The course of law executes, but in the fact, innocent, innocent to the high heavens. That lies beyond Tounson's function and his excuse.

A breakfast eaten slowly. A pipe of Virginia tobacco. A cup of sack at setting out, a good drink if a man might but tarry by it. Friday, October 29, the morrow of St. Simon and St. Jude! The King had chosen a day indeed for the dying. The pageant in the City in honor of Lord Mayor's Day would draw away the crowd. Two sheriffs, and the Dean for company, a hard way to go up to the scaffold in the Old Palace Yard, but, thanks to God, the ague was absent. Arundel, Oxford, and Lord Compton who had just risen to be Northampton. Hard to make men hear, especially those at Sir Randall Crue's window. Hats off to the gentlemen— will they listen? Oh, death, to salute thee! Will they listen? Aye, more, they will come down. They must know the ague and sickness leave one weak; not afraid. They must know there has been no traffic with France, no planning of service under a foreign crown. So much to say and so little strength. Manourie to explain, Stukely to accuse of wrongs and double dealings, honesty in the Guiana effort to affirm, a denial of happiness and ill-mannered mirth at the execution of the Earl of Essex. And so to the end of earthly affairs.

To stand silent a moment when done, smiling a little wearily. To stand in a hair-colored doublet, under it a black-wrought waistcoat, and below a pair of black-cut Taffety breeches, ash-colored silk stockings. To realize that this was but an end a little sooner than the body would have made its own. And in a minute to know the law's violent hand.

The executioner kneeling for forgiveness. A hand upon the bowed shoulder of the good fellow, a gentle word of pardon. To all a request for prayer. A sea-faring man, a soldier, a courtier about to die. For a long time the course held had been one of vanity. Brave prayers to ascend in such a cause. All doubt, and mystery and curious activity upon the

DEATH

brink of the abyss. The axe! The headsman tries to hide it. To feel it with the thumb. Refusal. Insistence. Compliance. The end, really the end. Keen edge. A symbol too. A bowing of the whitened head. Old lips kissing the steel. A sharp, fair medicine to cure all diseases. The headsman has his axe again and stands confused, abashed before honest courage. He no longer tries to hide the weapon within his cloak. He doffs the robe and spreads it before the block.

A long glance into the faces and a turning upon the scaffold. The body laid prone along the proffered cloak, the head upon the block. When the hands stretch forth the blow is to fall. They gesture. The headsman pauses. "Strike man, strike," in rich West Country brogue, "What dost thou fear?" A long instant. A deadly rustle and a crushing stroke. Another and the head is off, snatched into the air that all may see. The body does not shrink.

NOTES

1. Domestic Papers Temp. Eliz. Vol. LXXXI, No. 39.
2. British Museum, C 32, B 29.
3. Prantl, Professor Carl, *Geschichte der Logik in Abendlande,* Leipsig, 1927. IV volumes. p. 107.
4. Pole, Cardinal Reginald, *Apologia at Carolum V. Caesarum, super libre de Unitate.* Brixae, 1744. Tom I, p. 152.
5. Smith, Charlotte Fell, *Life of Doctor John Dee,* London, 1909. p. 91.
6. Cheyney, Edward P., *History of England,* Vol. I, p. 51.
7. Hakluyt, Richard, *Voyages,* Vol. III, folio i.
8. Hakluyt, Richard, *Discourse of Western Planting,* Cambridge, 1877, Main Historical Society Collection.
9. Fiske, John, *Old Virginia and Her Neighbors,* Boston, 1897. p. 45.
10. Hakluyt, Richard, *Voyages,* Vol. II, f169.
11. Ralegh, Sir Walter, *Works.* Oxford, 1829. Vol. VIII, p. 704.
12. Cheyney, Edward P., *A History of England.* New York, 1926. Vol. I, p. 223.
13. Harington, Sir John, *Nugae Antiquae.* Edition 1804. Vol. I, p. 325.
14. *The Secret History of King James I.* 1690. Preface, p. 6.
15. Percy Society, *Poetical Miscellany.* Vol. XV, p. 13.
16. Williams, *Court and Times of James the First.* Vol. I, p. 26.
17. British Museum. Harleian MSS. 39, p. 340.
18. Ralegh, Sir Walter, *Works.* Oxford, 1829. Vol. VIII, p. 682.
19. Ralegh, Sir Walter. *Works.* Oxford, 1829. Vol. VIII, p. 635.
20. The body of Sir Walter Ralegh is buried near the altar in the chancel of St. Margaret's within sight of the Palace Yard, Westminster, where he died. Lady Ralegh had the severed head embalmed and kept it by her until her death. None knows what later became of it.

BIBLIOGRAPHY

There have been extensive bibliographies of Sir Walter Ralegh compiled, not to mention the listed sources proffered by most of his seventy odd biographers. The titles which follow have served to differentiate this present life from its many predecessors. In this sense alone may they be considered to comprise a Ralegh bibliography.

ADDLESHAW, PERCY. *Sir Philip Sidney.* New York, 1909.
AIKIN, LUCY. *Memoirs of Court of James I.* London, 1823.
ANTHONY, KATHERINE. *Queen Elizabeth.* New York, 1929.
ARTAUD, A. F. *Machiavelli, son genie et ses erreurs.* Paris, 1833.
AUBREY, JOHN. *Letters by Eminent Persons and Lives of Eminent Men.* 1813.
BACON, FRANCIS. *A Declaration of the Demeanor and Carriage of Sir Walter Ralegh.* 1618.
BENSON, E. F. *Sir Francis Drake.* New York, 1927.
BESANT, WALTER. *London in Times of the Tudors.* London, 1904.
BIRCH, THOMAS. *Memoirs of the Reign of Queen Elizabeth.* 1754.
BREWER AND BULLEN. *Calendar of the Carew Papers.*
BRUCE, REVEREND JOHN. *Correspondence of King James VI of Scotland with Sir R. Cecil and others in England.* Camden Society, 1861.
CAMDEN, WILLIAM. *Annals of the Reign of Elizabeth.* 1625.
CHAMBERLAIN, JOHN. *Private Character of Queen Elizabeth.* London, 1921.
CHEYNEY, EDWARD P. *History of England from the Defeat of the Armada to the Death of Elizabeth.* New York, 1926.
DEVEREUX, WALTER B. *Lives and Letters of the Devereux, Earls of Essex.* London, 1853.
EDWARDS, EDWARD. *Life of Sir Walter Ralegh.* London, 1868.
FISKE, JOHN. *Old Virginia and Her Neighbors.* Boston, 1897.
FROUDE, JAMES ANTHONY. *History of England.* London, 1870.
FULLER, REVEREND THOMAS. *History of the Worthies of England.* 1811.
GIBBS, PHILIP. *King's Favorite.* Philadelphia.
GOODMAN, GODFREY. *Court of King James the First.* London, 1839.
GOSLING, W. G. *Labrador: Its Discovery, Exploration and Development.* London, 1910.
GOSLING, W. G. *Life of Sir Humphrey Gilbert.* London, 1911.
GREVILLE, SIR FULKE. *Life of Sir Philip Sidney.* Oxford, 1907.
HAKLUYT, RICHARD. *Voyages, Navigations, Traffics and Discoveries of the English Nation.* 1810.

BIBLIOGRAPHY

HARINGTON, SIR JOHN. *Nugae Antiquae.* 1804.
HARIOT, THOMAS. *A Brief and True Report of the New Found Land of Virginia.* London, 1588.
HAYWARD, JOHN. *Annals of Elizabeth.* ed. John Bruce, 1840.
HUME, MARTIN A. S. *Philip II of Spain.* 1906.
JEFFERSON, THOMAS. *Notes on Virginia.* Philadelphia, 1794.
JONSON, BEN. *Conversations with William Drummond of Hawthorne.* ed. R. F. Patterson, 1923.
JONSON, BEN. *Works.* 1860.
NAPIER, MACVEY. *Lord Bacon and Sir Walter Ralegh.* Cambridge, 1853.
MCFEE, WILLIAM. *Life of Martin Frobisher.* New York, 1928.
POLE, CARDINAL REGINALD. *Apologia at Carolum V Caesarum, super libre de Unitate.* Brixae, 1744.
RALEGH, SIR WALTER. *Works.* Oxford, 1829.
RALEGH, SIR WALTER. *Today a Man Tomorrow None.* London, 1646.
SCHELLING, FELIX E. *Life and Writings of George Gascoigne.* Pub. Univ. Penna. Vol. II, No. 4.
SEDGWICK, HENRY DWIGHT. *Henry of Navarre.* Indianapolis, 1930.
SLAFTER, REVEREND CHARLES. *Sir Humfrey Gylberte and His Enterprise of Colonization in America.* Boston, 1903.
SMITH, CHARLOTTE FELL. *Life of Doctor John Dee.* London, 1909.
SOMERS, LORD. *Arraignment and Conviction at King's Bench Bar.* 1809.
SOUTHEY, ROBERT. *The British Admirals.* 1837.
SPARROW, SIMPSON W. *St. Paul's Catheral and Old City Life.* London, 1904.
STOW, JOHN. *Historical Memoranda.* 1880.
THEOBALD, MR. *Memoirs of Sir Walter Ralegh.* 1719.
VILLARI, PASQUALE. *Life and Times of Machiavelli.* London, 1892.
WALDMAN, MILTON. *Sir Walter Ralegh.* London, 1928.
WELLDON, SIR ANTHONY. *Secret History of the Court of James I.* 1811 (1690).
WINWOOD, SIR RALPH. *Memorials of Affairs of State.* 1725.

INDEX

Throughout this index E stands for Elizabeth, and R for Ralegh.

Abbey, Westminster, Spenser and Chaucer buried in, 185; Biron taken by R to, 204; E buried in, 218, 219; R looks upon, 313
Abbot, Archbishop, examines R, 308
Acantio, Giacoma, E patroness of, 31
Achaei, Prince of, *see* Philopoemen
Adelphi Terrace, 78
Admiral, stranded at Roanoke, 105
Advancement of Learning, by Bacon, 269
Adventurers, *see* White; Hakluyt; Smith, Thomas
Æsop, 100
Agincourt, 191
Agiri, Sergeant, seizes power and is slain, 154
Albemarle Sound, reached by colonists, 102
Albert, Archduke, married to Infanta Isabel, 231; James writes congratulatory letter to, 268
Alençon, Francis, Duke of, and E, 42; Flanders, 43; entertained, 61; becomes Duke of Brabant, 61; repudiated by Henry III of France, 83; death, 83, 92
Alexander, E as, 149
Alexander VI, 4
Alighieri, Dante, *De Monarchia*, 28
All Souls' College, 70
Allen, Cardinal, Irish Jesuit, 46; and the Armada, 112
Alley, Captain Peter, ill, sent home with letter to Lady Ralegh, 295
Amadas, Captain Philip, sails for America, 78, 98; goes to Virginia, 100, 105
Amadas of Savoy, base son of Duke of Savoy, sails with Armada, 114
Amazon, 154
Amazons, living at Topago, 161
Amboise, Truce of, 18
America, North, 39, 59; plans for colonization, 72; Newfoundland becomes E's, 75; Virginia, 78; American colony, 79; Ireland substituted by R for colonization, 88; Lok's map of, 97, 98; Hakluyt's plans for colonization, 99; R never landed in, 110
America, South, Oreliana arrives second time, 154; R arrives, 156
Amoret, E as, 130
An Ager, flagship, Gilbert's fleet, 38
Andalusia, 170
Anderson, Chief Justice, on King's Bench at R's trial, 240, 241
Angelica, E as, 150
Angra, West Indiamen reach, 182
Anjou, Duke of, *see* Alençon
Anne Boleyn, mother of E, 11
Anne of Denmark, Queen of James VI of Scotland, intercedes for R, 256; despises Henry Howard, 266; takes Prince Henry to Tower to visit R, 267; inspires son with distaste for James, 274; William Herbert, favorite of, 274, 278; lives apart in Denmark House, 279; R writes to, 280; interest in R deepened by Henry's death, 281; Pocahontas, 284; favors French alliance for son Charles, 303; near death, writes Villiers pleading for R, 310, 311
Anthony, John, master of *Red Lion*, 38
Antoll, John, sails with R, 39

Antwerp, investiture of Alençon as Duke of Brabant, 61; English fabric trade, 99; channel to Bruges, 114
Ape and the Fox, by Spenser, 131
Aphrodite, James ponders upon, 238
Apology for the Voyage to Guiana, by R, 304, 305
Apostles, Twelve, Spanish ships, 169, 170; *St. Philip* and *St. Andrew* in Cadiz harbor, 172; *St. Philip* and *St. Thomas* burned by Spanish, 173; *St. Andrew* and *St. Matthew* taken by English, 173; *St. Matthew* and *St. Andrew* used in attack against Spain, 178; *St. Matthew* loses mast, worked into Rochelle; *St. Andrew* lost, 179
Apothegms, by Bacon, 16
Apsleie's band, 59
Apsley, Sir Allen, to keep R's picture of E, 308
Aquascogok, burned by Grenville, 101
Aquinas, St. Thomas, *De Regimine principum*, 27; quote from Prantl, 28; quoted by R, 33
Arabia, 4
Aragon, Elizabeth of, 108
Areopagus, Sidney's, approved *Shepherd's Calendar*, 129
Ariel, R as, 84
Ariosto, *Supposes* tr. by Gascoigne, 22
Aristotle, quoted by R, 33, 91; R thinks of, 128; much named, little read, 129, 298
Ark Ralegh, sails under Lord Howard, 140; bought by E, 143
Ark Royal, Howard's ship, 169, 170
Armada, plans for, 112; sails from Lisbon, 113, 114; loiters at the Groine, 115; sighted off England, 115; first encounter with English, 117; failure, 118; results of, 119–124
Arromaia, King of, R meets, 159; confesses fear of Spanish, 159, 265
Arthur's Hall, Cobham tried in, Markham locked in, 255
Arundel, Lord, tries Bayley, 292; Keymis and, 298, 316
As You Like It, by Shakespeare, 188
Ascham, Roger, tutor of E, 12, 14
Ashburton, R and Stukely meet close to, 304
Ashby-de-la-Zouch, 43
Ashley, Kate, kinswoman of R's and friend of E, 12; E's governess, death, 58; and Seymour, 63, 64
Ashton, Roger, sent to Winchester by James, becomes friend of R, 256
Atlantic, 72; R crosses to Trinidad, 156
Azores, 76; Grenville at, 104; send plants for R's garden, 126; English fleet off, 140, 141, 143; Essex and R at Flores in, 179, 287

Babington, Anthony, dies for conspiracy against E's life, 96
Bacon, Anthony, nephew of Burghley, 35; recommended to E by Cecil, 177
Bacon, Francis, at Oxford, 15; *Apothegms*, 16; and Machiavell, 32; nephew of Burghley, 35, 93; captured by Lettice

323

INDEX

Knollys, 139; at Twickenham, 164; recommended to E by Cecil, 177; at Essex trial, 195; clinging to Cecil, 204; at Mermaid Tavern, 205; *Advancement of Learning*, 269; works to become Baron of Verulam, 287; becomes Lord Chancellor, 303; examines R, 308; draws up death warrant for R, 312
Balliol College, Latimer and Ridley burned, 1
Bally, 49, 50 (*see* Lord Roche)
Bancroft, Bishop, R examined by, 234
Baque island, 106
Barlow, Arthur, sails for America, 78, 98, 105
Barn Elms, Walsingham at, 163, 164
Barry Court, 51, 52, 54
Barry, Lord, sedition, 48
Basing House, *see* Hampshire
Baskerville, Sir Thomas, brings word of death of Hawkins and Drake, 167
Bassanière, Martin, honored R, 88, 89
Bath, R takes waters at, 152, 187, 204, 212; Shakespeare takes waters, 212
Bayley, Captain of *Southampton*, 292
Beake island, 106
Bear Gardens, R takes Biron to, 204
Beaumont, at Mermaid Tavern, 205
Beaumont, Comte de, French Ambassador, Cobham tells feelings to, 331; writes of R, 262
Beddington Park, James in progress to, 224
Bedford, Earl of, 34, 81; invited to Rutlandshire by Harrington, 213
Belphœbe, E as, 130, 133, 147
Bentivoli, Pope Julio attacked, 128
Berwick, Bishop Matthews pleads with James at, 224
Beskwood, in Nottinghamshire, given by E to Sir Griffin Markham, 229
Best, John, performs R's duties of Captain of the Guard, 153
Biddeford, 108
Biron, Duc de, contempt for Essex, 201, received by R, 204
Biscay, 9, 115
Blado, published *The Prince*, 29
Bloody Tower, R taken to the, 234; R in, 238; R in, 263
Blount, Sir Charles, duel with Essex, 93; Ranger of the New Forest, 124, 125; R's keeper, 152; incites Essex to discipline R, 180, 181; Commissioner of Oyer and Terminer at R's trial, 241; asked to intercede with King for honorable death for R, 253
Blount, Sir Christopher, step-father of Essex, considered for command in Ireland, 190; as officer under Essex, 191; admits talk of treason, 192
Boccace, studied, 129
Bodleian Library, founded, 174
Bohemia, first rumbling of Thirty Years War heard in, 287; Frederick V of, 302
Bologna, Bentivoli at, 128
Borgia, Cesare, Machiavelli's prince, 28, 32
Boulogne, Commissioner of, E refuses to make R, 191
Bourbons, 7, 121
Bow Lane, Essex retreats down, 198
Brabant, Duke of, *see* Alençon
Brave, fails to reach Virginia, 108
Brazil, R captures ship from, 182
Bread Street, R walks along, 205
Bremen, levied upon for sailors by Parma, 114
Brentford, La Clerc and de Novion wait on R at, 308
Brick Tower, R and Elizabeth Ralegh in, 148; R in, 309
Bridges, Elizabeth, Essex philanders with, 186

Brill, captured by De la Marck, 20; Gascoigne reaches, 23
Briskett, Lodovick, clerk to Council of Munster, Spenser succeeds, 128
Bristol, 72
Bristol Channel, 115
Britomart, E as, 130
Brittany, 10
Brooke, George, joins conspirators against James, 229; to be Treasurer if successful, 230; examined, 232; testimony about R, 233; taken to Wolvesey Castle, 240, 251, 255; death, 259
Brooke, Henry, *see* Lord Cobham
Brooksby, taken to Wolvesey Castle, 240
Bruce, Edward, ambassador of James of Scotland, arrives in London, 203; pledges confidence to Cecil, 203; writes Henry Howard, 216
Bruges, channels dug by Parma, 114
Buckhurst, Lord, kinsman of E, 35; at trial of Essex and Southampton, 198; sentences Essex and Southampton, 200; at E's funeral, 218
Buckingham, *see* Villiers, 286
Buda, 73
Budleigh Salterton, port of, 7
Buonaccorsi, copied *The Prince*, 29
Burbage, Richard, in procession welcoming James to London, 268
Burgh, Sir John, aids Frobisher off Azores, 143; cruises to Azores, 150
Burghley, Lord, Sir William Cecil, becomes Secretary of State, 14; expresses E's thoughts, 20; and E, 33; at the Temple, 36; at Islington, 37; ill, 40, 41; diplomacy, 42, 43; advises E to refuse Barry Court to R, 52; urges E to return freebooters' gains to Spain, 57; cautious and deliberate, 70, 71; twenty years of plans pushed aside, 83; absents himself from court, 84; holds realm in hand, 90; plans for son, 91; and R, 95; R pleads for protection against Armada, 115; uses Walsingham, 117, 127; and Spenser, 131; ill, 164; R writes to, 166; drafts instructions to council of war, 167; proclamation of purpose of E, 167, 168; pleads with Essex, 177; joyful at return of Essex, 183; death, 185; burial, 186
Burghley (the younger), accused by Essex of treachery, 194
Burgrave, Marques, son of Archduke Ferdinand and Philippa Welsera, sails with Armada, 114
Burrel, Doctor Robert, aids R with *First Part of the History of the World*, 277
Buxton, 43
"Bye" Plot, 230, 232, 245

Cabinet Council, The, by R, 273
Cadiz, Englishmen carried to, 9; harbor full of ships, 170, 171; R and Howard attack, 172; falls, 173, 174; wound received by R at, 173, 204, 287
Calais, Wentworth surrenders, 2; taken by Francis, Duke of Guise, 6, 17, 18; English follow Spanish to, 118
Caleta, Essex attempts landing at, 171, 175
Callao, 4
Cambridge, 15; Gascoigne at, 22; takes exception to R's wine patent, 103
Camden, at Oxford, 16, 18, 33, 77; writes of R, 146
Campion, Jesuit, 42
Canaries, 78, 101; R reaches, 156
Canterbury, 61
Canterbury, Archbishop of, 15; reads *Canterbury Tales* to E, 215; prays aloud as E dies, 216

INDEX 325

Canterbury Tales, E listens to reading of, 215
Cape Fear, 106
Cape Race, 75
Cape Verde, 4
Captain of the Guard, Goodier, Paulett, 67; R, 67, 88; Sir Thomas Erskine, 224
Capuchins, to carry the Inquisition to heretic England, 112
Capuri River, 160
Carew, Sir George, remembered by R, 129; to answer for R in Tower, 148; refused to take R on River, dagger fight, 149; writes to Cecil, 150; appointed to council of war, 167, 172; praises R, 176; on second council of war, 177; works St. Matthew into Rochelle, 179; disliked by Essex, 186; in Munster, 191; accused of treachery by Essex, 194; guided by Cecil, 206; Cecil writes to, 210; Anne of Denmark makes Vice Chamberlain, 266; begs for R's life, 303
Carew, Sir Peter, escapes to France, 9
Carews, cried through land as traitors, 8, 9, 65
Carey, Sir Henry, effect of Mary's death on, 11; invited by Harington to Rutlandshire for Christmas, 213
Carey, Robert, visits E, 215; carries ring to James announcing E's death, 217
Carlile, Christopher, son-in-law of Walsingham, interested in American trade, 72; sailed in Moscovy Company, 72
Caroli, cannibals at, 161
Carr, Robert, becomes royal favorite, 270; secures Sherborne, 271; tries for fame and fortune, 274; hated by Prince Henry, 278; Sir Ralph Winwood enemy of, 279; raised to Somerset, involved with Frances, Countess of Essex, 279; married to Frances Howard, Countess of Essex, 282; passed from favor, 286
Carthagena, 103
Castelnau, 46
Castile, Elizabeth of, 108
Castilio, admired by court, 129
Catharine of Aragon, mother of Mary Tudor, 1
Cathay, 97, 99
Catherine de Medici, fear of Guises, 5, 7; and Charles IX, 21; St. Bartholomew, 21; and Machiavelli, 30; Elizabeth thinks of, 121; death, 124, 140
Cavendish, Master, voyage to Virginia, 101, 110
Caycos, 106
Cayenne, R anchors off, 295
Cecil, Sir Robert, 35; attainments, 71; advice of Burghley to, 90; R writes to, 111; E thinks of, 121; calls R brutish, 147; brings R's name before E frequently, 150; seizes spoil from Madre de Dios, 151; with R and Killigrew apportions shares, 152; receives praise of R, 176; takes R to E, 176; recommends Francis and Anthony Bacon, 177; sends two letters to Essex, 178, 179; sent for two months to Henry IV, 185; has ear of E, 185; watches Essex and E, 186; chosen as R's nearest friend, 189; and R support Essex for Irish command, 190; in power, 192; accused by Essex, reads complaints, 193; watches Essex, 196; refutes Essex's charges, 199; content, 200; accused of treason by Essex in statement, 203; Bacon clings to, 204; guest of R at Sherborne, 205; secretly opposes R while posing as friend, 206; satisfied, 207; and James, 209, 210; writes to George Carew of R and Cobham, 210; writes to James of R, 211; libelled, 213, 214; E receives only Archbishop and Cecil, 215; asks E who shall succeed her, 216; attends E on death bed, 216; religious views, 221; prepares stroke against R, 223; hatred of R, 223; James turns from, 224; demands R attend Council, 226, 227; fears combined secrecy, 228; and the conspiracy against James, 230; watches and plots against R, 231 to 234; R writes Elizabeth Ralegh of, 236; denied nothing by James, 237; notified of R's recovery, makes new plans, 238; at R's trial, 240 to 254; asked to intercede with King for honorable death for R, 253; disliked by people, 255; Elizabeth Ralegh pleads for R's life, 259; made Earl of Salisbury, 269; death, 280
Cecil, Sir William, see Burghley
Cecil, William, son of Robert Cecil, entertained by R at Sherborne, 189
Champernoun, Sir Arthur, fealty to Mary, 8; turns fleet loose, 9; effect of Mary's death, 11
Champernoun, Charles, at Oxford, 16; on R's ship, 39
Champernoun, Gawen, father-in-law of Montgomerie, 17
Champernoun, Henry, R joins force of, 18
Champernoun, Sir Philip, father of Katherine Ralegh, 8
Chancellor of the Duchy of Lancaster, Sir Robert Cecil, 71
Chancellor of Oxford, Leicester, 15
Chaplain, see Hakluyt
Charing Cross, Henry Howard dies in home at, 282
Charles of England, Prince, to marry Henrietta Maria, 287; Anne favors French alliance for, 303
Charles V, of Spain, ban against Luther, 30; sidelights upon, 128
Charles IX, of France, son of Catherine de Medici, eager for war, 21; St. Bartholomew, 21
Charybdis, 43
Chastillion, sends Morgues to Florida, 89
Chaucer, Geoffrey, 185, 215
Cheapside, Little Conduit in, 13; Essex and, 197
Chelsea, Howard of Effingham retires to, 184
Chesapeake, 107, 110
Chesepians, reached by colonists, 102
Child, T., and R, 17
China, 79
Christian, King of Denmark, refuses E ships, 166; comes to visit Anne, intercedes for R, 283
Christina, Queen of Sweden, The Prince, 30
Cicero, 33, 128
Cinque Ports, Cobham as Warden of, 194, 247
Civil War in France, fourth, 21
Clares, 7
Clarke, Francis, pleads with James for toleration, 228; plots against James, 229; examined, 232; taken to Wolvesey Castle for trial, 240, 251, 255; death, 258, 259
Clement, Jacques, murder of Henry III, 30, 140
Cleves, Anne of, 63
Clifford, Sir Conyers, appointed to council of war, 167
Cobham, Lord, and Cecil friends, 177; attacked by Essex, 190; accused by Essex, 194; watches Essex, 196; takes possession of garden of Essex House, 198; satisfied with Essex trial, 200; accused of treason in Essex statement, 203; accused of conspiracy by Henry Howard, 209; married to Frances Howard, 209; goes to Sherborne with R, 213; open in dislike of James, 228;

INDEX

loud in his rage, 230, 231; visits Count, later confers with R, 231; Cecil connects R and Cobham with plot, 232; Cobham examined, 233, 234; testimony of Brooke about R and, 233; questioned, blames R, 233, 234; R writes Elizabeth Ralegh of, 236; taken to Wolvesey Castle, 240; R's trial, 240–254; R asks that Cobham die first, 254; tried, 255; action on scaffold, 260, 261; taken to London, 263

Coke, Attorney General, at Essex trial, 195; heads prosecution against R and conspirators, 241–253; examines R, 309; arranges trial of R, 310; at R's trial, 312

Coldwell, Dr., *see* Bishop of Salisbury

Coligny, Admiral, advises Prince of Condé, 19; and Charles IX, 21; and Sir Philip Sidney, 97

Colin Clout's Come Home Again, by Spenser, 130, 131

Colonists, *see* Virginia

Colonna Egidio, member of the Guelphic School, 27

Come, live with me and be my love, by Marlowe, 134, 135

Commissioners of Oyer and Terminer, R's trial, Earl of Suffolk, Earl of Devonshire, Sir John Stanhope, Lord Wotton, Henry Howard, Sir William Waad, Baron Robert Cecil, 260

Compton, Lord, in attack on Essex House, 198; goes to Sherborne with R and Cobham, 213; tries Bayley, 292, 316

Condé, Prince of, advised by Coligny, 19; to enter Flanders, 43; rumors about, 213

Controller, *see* Sir Thomas Parry

Copley, Anthony, angry with James, 228; joins conspirators against James, 229; ends matters for conspirators, 231; examined, 232, 233; taken to Wolvesey Castle, 240

Cork, 47, 48, 51, 52, 87; cedars set out by R, 126

Cornwall, 8, 10, 81, 107, 118, 152, 187

Corunna, besieged, 123

Corunna, Bay of, Armada leaves for, 113; Armada loiters near, 115

Cosmographicall Mappes and Charts, 24

Cosmor, Captain, death, 297

Cotesa, 101

Cottea, 106

Cotton, Sir Robert, R writes for loan of rare books to, 272

Cottrel, assists R in attempted escape, 306

Council of War, first, *see* R, Vere, Clifford, Thomas Howard, George Carew

Council of War, second, *see* Thomas Howard, R, Vere, Carew, Mountjoy, Gorges

Court of Star Chamber, Burghley, 71; Sir Robert Cecil, 71, 91; R dreams of, 187

Courtenay, treachery of, 8

Courtney, Thomas, capture of ships, 47

Cranmer, executed by Mary, 1

Croatan, 106, 109

Crockern Tor, 81

Crofts, urges return of freebooters' gains to Spain, 57

Cromwell, Lord, at sea, 177

Cromwell, Oliver, admires *History of the World*, 278

Crosse, Sir Robert, and R ride to meet James, 221, 222

Crue, Sir Randall, 316

Cuba, R captures ship from, 182

Cuffe, Henry, 93

Cumberland, Earl of, voyage to South Seas, 87; and *Faerie Queene*, 131; in attack on Essex House, 198

Cundell, in procession welcoming James to London, 268

Curiapan, 160

Cusco, 4

Cynthia, E as, 130, 133; E as, 202

Cynthia, by R, 133

Cynthia's Revels, by Ben Jonson, 202

da Padova, Marsilia, *Defensor Pacis*, 28

d'Arenbergh, Count Charles, Cobham hopes to arrange peace with Spain through, 228; comes to London with Henry Howard, 231; and Cobham, 233; guest of James, 240, 248; blamed by Cobham, 255; James treats with, 268, 269

Danvers, leaves Ireland with Essex, 192

Darcy, Sir Edward, lives in Durham House, 78; removed from Durham House, 224

Dare, Eleanor, in Virginia, 107, 109

Dare, Virginia, born, 107, 109

Darien, Isthmus of, Lok's map, 97

Darrel, 90

Dartmouth, 39; R received with joy at, 152

David, Essex as, 191

Davis, John, landfall, 79, 80

Davison, William, sent to E by Leicester, 84; banished, 84; and Mary Stuart, 90; E angry at, 91

de Acuna, Don Diego Sarmiento, and R, 287, 288, 289

de Berreo, Don Antonio, in Trinidad, 156; sends to Spain for troops, 157; taken by R, 157; closes country against all, 163

de Chartes, Vidame, Havre, 17

de Medici, Mary, to marry Henry IV of France, 204; exiled at Blois, 302

De Monarchia, by Dante Alighieri, 28

de Osua, Pedro, and Guiana by way of Peru, 154

De Regimine principum, by St. Thomas Aquinas, 27

des Marêts, Comte, French Ambassador and R, 288, 289

Dee, Dr. John, 56, 79; dines with R at Durham House, 162

Defensor Pacis, by Marsilia da Padova, 28

Defiance, fights Spanish ships, 116, 117

Dekker, Thomas, at Mermaid Tavern, 205

Delight, 73, 75

Denmark, Christian refuses E request for ships, 166, 249

Denmark House, Anne of Denmark lives apart in, 279

Denny, Captain, in Ireland, 47

Dennys, Sir Thomas, sent after Carews, 8

Derby, Lord, kinsman of Queen, 35; E thinks of, 121

Desmond, to be conciliated, 43

Desmond, Earl of, brothers, James and John, 47; estates confiscated, 47

Desmond, James, brother of Earl of Desmond, 47; hanged, 47

Desmond, John, brother of Earl of Desmond, 47

Demosthenes, 129

Destiny, building, 284, 289; to Guiana, 291, 293; at Plymouth, 300; cargo sold, 304

Devereux, Lady Dorothy, sister to Earl of Essex, married Sir Thomas Perrot, 40, 145; slighted by E, 94

Devereux, Penelope, 35

Devereux, Robert, *see* Earl of Essex

Devon, 8, 9; disloyalty stirring, 10; great men of, 11; men assist Montgomerie, 17, 25, 47, 65, 81; R's Irish estate colonized by people from, 126; R's duties carry him to, 152

Devonshire, Earl of, *see* Sir Charles Blount

INDEX 327

Diana, E as, 6, 44, 149
Diana de Poitiers, mistress to Henry II, 5
Dido, in Virgil, 257
Discourse, by Machiavelli, 28
Discourse of a Discoverie for a New Passage to Cataia, A, written by Sir Homfrey Gilbert Knight, 24
Discourse of Tenures Before the Conquest, A, by R, 275
Discourse of the Invention of Ships, Anchors, Compass, etc., by R, 273
Discovery, sails for Virginia, 269
Discovery of a Gaping Gulf, The, by William Page and John Stubbs, 60
Discovery of Guiana, by R, 162, 271
Dominica, 101; Ferdinando reaches, 106
Dominican Friary at Youghal, R seeks peace, 126
Don Alonzo Perez de Guzman, *see* Guzman
Don Antonio, restoration attempted, 123, 124
Don John of Austria, natural brother to Philip II, 3
Donne, John, *The Storm*, 178; at Mermaid Tavern, 205
Dorothy, Virginia, 101
Douay, 15, 42
Dover, de la Marck leaves, 20; E on progress to, 204
Dover Straits, Spanish and English fleets make for, 117
Drake, Sir Francis, 33; return in *Pelican*, 57, 65; returned from Indies, 95; lands at Roanoke, 103; to serve against Armada, 115; trusted by E, 119; attempts retaliation of Spanish, 123; gives up attempt, 124; death, 167, 278, 299, 315
Drury House, Essex and five friends meet at, 196
Dublin, 48; Essex in action near, 192
Duca Valentina, by Machiavelli, 28
Dudley, Guilford, condemned, 8
Dudley, Robert, *see* Leicester
Due Repulse, Essex ship, 169; council held on, 171
Dulce Bellum, by Gascoigne, 23
Durham House, 78, 79; R at, 153; Dee dines with R at, 162; R asks Ferdinand Gorges to meet him at, 196; comings and goings at, 207; R loses, 224; R and Cobham confer at, 231
Dutch, English aid, 20; appeal to French, 21; agree to furnish E with ships, 166; ships commanded by Van Duvenvoord, 168, 177; soldiers, 180
Dyer, attends E, 61; R trial, 252

Eddystone, fight off, 116, 117
Edinburgh, Harrington looking toward, 204; Robert Carey carries ring announcing E's death to James at, 217
Edward VI, son of Jane Seymour, 63; Statute of, 250, 251
Effingham, Lord Howard, kinsman of E, 35; given command of fleet, 115; receives news of Armada's approach, 116; and R urge against boarding of ship, 116; trusted by E, 119; and *Faerie Queene*, 131; attempts intercession for R, 150; *Voyage for the Discovery of Guiana* dedicated to, 150; lends R *Lion's Whelp*, 156; R pleads for new expedition to Guiana, 166; and Essex commissioned in joint command, 167; in command of squadron, *Ark Royal*, 169; decides Thomas Howard and R to lead attack, 172; on *Nonpareill*, 173; lands in Cadiz, 174; growing old, 175; receives patent as Earl of Nottingham, 183; retires to Chelsea, hates R, 184; interposes between Essex and E, 186; besets Essex House, 198; defies E's commands, 216; bears banner of England at E's burial, 218; receives news of conspiracy and writes to Cecil, 231; neglecting navy, 281
Egerton, Lord Keeper, Essex confined under, 194; sent by E to Essex, locked up by him, 197; carries seals attending E's body, 217, 218
Eldorado, City of Gold, 154; reached by Martines, 154, 287, 295
Elector Palatine, *see* Frederick V
Elizabeth, Virginia, 101
Elizabeth, and her gentlemen, 2; description of, 6; defense before Council, 6; as Diana, 6; ascension, effect of ascension on R, and Humphrey Gilbert, 11; coronation, 13; religious attitude, becomes leader of her people, 14; and the universities, 15; and the Huguenots, 17–19; and the Netherlands, 20, 21; Sir Humphrey Gilbert, visits Leicester, 24; and Gascoigne, 24, 25; and the doctrine of Machiavelli, 31, 32; and Burghley, 33, 34; and Alençon, 42, 43; and Simier, 42; and Ireland, 44–54; refuses Barry Court to R, 52; R's cloak, 55; favoring R, 59–61; entertains Alençon, 61; recalls Thomas Seymour, 62–66; compares R, 64-68; pomp of court, 69; gifts to R, 70, 71; becomes "Queen of Seas," 73; refuses R permission to sail, 73, 74; gives R patent for colonization, 77; effect of Alençon's death, 83; anger at Leicester, 84, 85; favors R, 84-88; depends on Burghley, 90; Essex presented to E, 92; joy in Essex, 93; favors R, 95, 96; receives pleas for Virginia colonization, 97–99; wavers, 100; keeps R from America, 111; Pope deprives E of princely titles and dignities, 112; prepares for Armada, 114; rides to Tilbury to encourage people, 116; and Walsingham, 117; sends Spaniards back to own country, 118; is humble, 119; celebrates victory, 120; thinks, 121; seeks to restore Don Antonio, 123; sweeps country into caprice, 129, 130; and the poets, 131–139; and Essex, 139, 140; again receives R, 139; rewards R with Sherborne, 142; buys *Ark Ralegh*, 143; disregards R, 147; hears of fight in Tower, 150; share of *Madre de Dios* booty, 151, 152; disregards R, 153, 163; grants patent to R to explore and settle Guiana, 154; ponders, 163, 164; dallies with Essex and plans new attempt against Spain, 166, 167; disappointed with booty, 174; restores R to favor, 176, 177; vacillates at thought of new enterprise, 178, 179; forbids Essex attack Lisbon, 178, 179; sends for Cecil, 178; cold toward Essex, makes Effingham Earl of Nottingham, 183; sends for R to solve difficulty with Effingham and Essex, 183; fifty-sixth birthday, 185; boxes Essex's ears, 186; birthday tournament, 189; sends Essex to Ireland, 190; countermands Essex appointment of Southampton, refuses to conciliate, 191; refuses to make R Commissioner of Boulogne, berates him, 191; E writes Essex forbidding his return, 192; prepares for possible armed return of Essex, 192; receives Essex, is gracious, changes, orders confinement at York House, 193, 194; confirms truce with Tyrone, releases Essex after a year, 194; has Essex tried, 195; Essex plots against, 196; R close to, 197; sends message to Essex House, 197; quails before own justice, 200; signs warrant, 200; as *Cynthia*, 202; receives

INDEX

Scotch envoys, 203; forbids any book on succession, 204; never more kind to R, 204; knights Carew Ralegh, 204; appoints R governor of Jersey, 205; remembers Seymour and refuses R as Privy Councillor, 206; ailing, 212, 213; scandal, 213; ill, moves to Richmond, receives Venetian Ambassador, sits silent as did Mary Tudor, 214; recalls Essex and Leicester, 215; all England waits death of, 216; Cecil asks who shall succeed, 216; put to bed against commands, dies, 216; body taken from Richmond to Westminster, 217; funeral, 216–218; monopolies attacked by James, 223; difference between James' rule and E's, 227

Elizabeth of Castile and Aragon, 108

Elizabeth, Princess, daughter of James, to marry Prince of Piedmont, 274; carries *History of the World* to Prague, with Prince Henry at Otelands, 278; married to Frederick V, Elector Palatine, 287

Ely House, 163

Emden, 114

Emeria, port of Guiana, 157

Encounter, to Guiana, 291

Ensenore, friend of colonists, dies, 102

Erskine, Sir Thomas, succeeds Ralegh as Captain of the Guard, 224

Escorial, planned by Philip II, 5; Philip dreams in the, 112, 169, 286

Essex, Countess of, 186; Carr involved with, 279; marries Carr, 282; *see* Lady Frances Howard, Frances Walsingham, Lettice Knollys

Essex, Earl of, Robert Devereaux, presented to E, 92; description, duel with Blount, 93; favorite of E, 94–96; rides to Tilbury with E, 116; leads E palfrey, 120; R considers, 121, 122; runs away, on *Swiftsure*, 123; friction with R, 124; *Faerie Queene*, 131; rooted in E's heart, 139; marries Lettice Knollys, raged at by E, 139; commanded into France, 140; success, 153; enters Compiégne, greeted by Henry IV, 164; E dallies with, 166; commissioned in joint command with Howard, 167; waits at Plymouth, 167; in command of squadron, 168; *Due Repulse*, 169; attempts landing at Caleta, 171; seconds R, 172, 173; in Cadiz, praised, 174; soothes E, wooed by R, 175, 176; joins Cecil in R interest, 176; friends with R, made commander in new Spanish effort, commands squadron, 177; and R ride to court, new attempt against Spain, 178; Cecil friendly with, gives up attempt against Ferrol, sails for Fayal but does not arrive, 179; arrives after attack, 180; threatens to court martial R, turns to Howard, accepts R apology, sails for home, 181–183; demands commission of E, made Earl Marshal, 183; affronts E, leaves court, returns, received, 186; public pity, 188; kept informed of R, 189; sent to Ireland, 190; refuses to conciliate, blames troubles on R, 191; goes into action in Dublin, refused permission to go home by E, leaves for London, 192; received by E, confinement ordered by E, 193; makes broad accusations, ordered confined at York House, released, 194; cheered by people, tried, freed, 194, 195; rages against E, approaches desperation, plots against E, 195–198; taken to Tower, tried with Southampton, 198, 199; sentenced to be hanged, 200; dies in Tower courtyard, 201; leaves statement of imaginary plot of R,

Cecil, Cobham, 203; dead a year, recalled by Harington, 214; place taken by Worcester at funeral of E, 218, 226, 316

Essex House, Essex at, 186; gathering at, 197; Essex beset at, 198

Ethiopia, 4

Euphues, by John Lyly, 134

Euripides, *Jocasta* translated by Gascoigne, 22, 33; R consults, 128

Evesham, Alexander, read by R, 272

Ewaipanoma, headless ones, 161, 162

Exeter, news of Mary's death reaches, 7; Agnes Prest in Exeter prison, 10; merchants refuse trade with Virginia, 79

Faerie Queene, by Spenser, 130, 131

Faige, Captain, R treats with for assistance at Orinoco, 290

Falcon, The, of Gilbert's fleet, 38; commanded by R, 38

Falmouth, 76

Fardinando, *see* Fernando

Faro, English land at, 174

Fayal, Essex and R sail for, 179; R seizes, 179, 180

Ferdinand, Archduke, *see* Burgrave

Ferdinando, Simon, *see* Fernando

Fernando, Simon, R captain, 38; crosses Atlantic, 72; lands in Virginia, 101; new voyage to Virginia, 105; difficulties, 106, 107

Ferrol, Howard's squadron off, 178; Essex to strike Spanish fleet at, 178; English fleet off, attempt abandoned, 179; Spanish fleet not destroyed at, 182

Finisterre, R off, 143; Frobisher haunts, 150

Finland, Duke of, urges R to go again to Guiana, 187

First Part of the History of the World, by R, 276, 277

Firth of Forth, Armada driven north of, 123

Fitton, Mistress, in Tower with Lord Pembroke, 145

Fitz Edmonds, in Ireland, 48, 49

Fitz Maurice, James, 46; killed, 47

Flanders, 20, 42, 43, 83, 117, 180

Fleet Prison, R and Sir Thomas Perrot in, 40; R in, 263

Fleet Street, E rides along, 2; victory procession along, 120

Fleming, Captain, spies enemy fleet, 116; at Essex trial, 195

Flerres, Thomas, of R crew, 39

Fletcher, John, at Mermaid Tavern, 205

Fletcher, Lawrence, welcomes James to London, 268

Florence, Duke of, *see* Medices

Flores, Essex at, 179

Florida, 77; Laudonnière's travels in, 89; Grenville takes frigate off, 101

Flory, Captain King arranges for R escape with, 304

Flushing, Gascoigne goes to, 23, 61; Leicester lands at, 83

Foresti of Bergamo, read by R, 272

Fota, 52

Fotheringhay, Mary Stuart dies at, 90

Fowler, Sir Thomas, foreman of jury at R trial, 242

Francis, bark given colonists by Drake, 103

Francis, Duke of Guise, captures Calais and Guines, 6

Frederick V, married to Princess Elizabeth, 286, 287; becomes Frederick V of Bohemia, 302

French Antarctic, by Andrew Thevet, 161

# INDEX 329

Frobisher, Sir Martin, 33; serves against Armada, 115; overtakes R, commands fleet, 143; haunts Finesterre, 150, 315
Fulham Palace, R examined by Bancroft at, 234
Fuller, 55

Gabriel, Harvey, praises *Shepherd's Calendar*, 129, 134
Galateo, 129
Galen, 315
Galileo, 16
Gallion, of Gilbert's fleet, 38
Galter Hills, *see* Kilcolman
Gamage, Barbara, marriage to Robert Sidney, 85
Gascoigne, George, translates *Jocasta*, 22; *Supposes*, 22; overseas, 23; *Dulce Bellum*, 23; and R, 23, 25, 26; and Gilbert, 23, 24; and Leicester, 24; *The Princelye Pleasures at the Court at Kenelwoorth*, 24; and E, 24, 25; *The Steele Glass*, 25; death, 25; R takes motto, 26, 117; R recalls, 122
Gawdy, Justice, R trial, 240, 241, 251
Geneva, 15; church of, 220, 221
Gentlemen Pensioners, *see* Hunsdon, 71
Gerard, Sir Thomas, effort at colonization, 72
Gervasius, read by R, 272
Ghent, '114
Gideon, Essex as, 191
Gilbert, Adrian, 56
Gilbert, Sir Humphrey, and E, 11, 16; first taste of war, 17, 18; Governor of Munster, 21; off to Low Countries, 21, 22; siege of Tergoes, 23; and Gascoigne, 23–26; *A Discourse of a Discoverie for a New Passage to Cataia*, 24; pleases E, 25; comes into own, 37, 38; President of Munster, 44; recommends R, 45; monopoly of discovery and settlement in America, 71, 72; leaves Plymouth for America, 74; takes possession of Newfoundland in name of E, 75; further voyage, death, 76, 110; R recalls, 122
Gilbert, Sir John, Deputy for Devon, 81; welcomes R to Dartmouth, 152; with R in Trinidad, 156; with R in Cadiz, 173
Gilbert, Otho, first husband of Katherine Ralegh, 8
Gilbert, Ralph, voyages to Virginia, 111
Gloriana, E as, 130
Golden Fleece, Knight of the, *see* Guzman
Golden Hinde, The, Gilbert and, 73, 74, 76
Goldsmith Row, R walks along, 205
Gomera, R calls at, 293
Gondomar, Count, *see* de Acuna
Goodier, Sir Henry, Captain of the Yeomen of the Guard, 67
Goodspeed, sails for Virginia, 269
Goodwin, Hugh, left with Topiawari, 159
Gorges, Sir Arthur, separates R and Carew, 149; joins R, landing party at Horta, 180; aids R in entertainment of Biron, 204
Gorges, Sir Ferdinando, second Council of War, 177; asked by R to Durham House, 196; meets R on river, 197; releases imprisoned councillors, 198
Granada, Woolaston and Whitney desert R, 300
Gravelines, 5; materials gathered by Parma at, 114; R follows Spanish to, 118
Gray's Inn, 22
Greene, Robert, at Mermaid Tavern, 205
Greenland, current, 75
Greenwich, 56, 78; Mary Stuart's death warrant brought to, 90; R lays siege to Elizabeth Throckmorton at, 164; James to be arrested and carried off from court at, 229
Grenville, Captain John, with R in Trinidad, 156
Grenville, Sir Richard, at Durham House, 79; to carry planters to Virginia, 100; leaves Plymouth for Virginia, takes frigate, burns Aquascogok, 101; fails to return, 103; returns with three ships to Virginia, 104; commanded not to leave Cornwall, 107, 110; given R's place under Lord Howard, 140; covers withdrawal of fleet with *Revenge*, surrenders, dies, 141; Stukeley nephew of, 304
Greville, Sir Fulke, at Oxford, 16; and *The Prince*, 32; Sir Philip Sidney, 32; attends E, 61; in attack on Essex House, 198
Grey, Arthur, Baron of Wilton, in Ireland, 45, 47, 48; dissolves commission, 51; Barry land to R, 52; sends R home, 53; and R Irish plans, 57; hatred for R, 59, 60; patron of Spenser, 129–131; at sea, 177, 190; takes possession of garden at Essex House, 198; satisfied with Essex trial, 200; attends E on death bed, 216
Grey, Lady Jane, condemned, 8
Grey, Lord Thomas of Wilton, joins conspiracy against James, 229, 230; examined, 232; taken to Wolvesey Castle, 240, 255; led to scaffold, led away, 260; pledges to deserve life, 261; taken to London, 263; complains of comparative liberty of R, 266
Groine, Medina Sidonia loiters at, 115
Guadarrama, Philip II at, 119
Guayaquil, 4
Guazzo, 129
Guiana, R applies for patent to explore and settle, granted, 155; R sails for, 156; leaves, 160; *Discovery of Guiana*, 162; voyages dispatched by R to, 205; recalled by R, 218, 272; R offers to send Keymis to, 279, 287; second expedition to, 290, 301; schemes for new expedition to, 303; map found on R, 308, 315, 316
Guinea, 89
Guines, 6
Guise, *see* Francis, Duke of
Guises, 5, 7, 17, 18, 42, 43
Gunpowder Plot, effect upon James of, 268
Gustavus II Adolphus, moves against Poland and the Tsar, 302
Guzman, Don Alonzo Perez de, Duke of Medina Sidonia, Lord of St. Lucar, given command of Armada, 112; Philip hastens, 113; loiters at the Groine, 115; forbidden court, 119; hastens to make defense against England, 170; burns all Spanish ships in the harbor of Cadiz, 174
Gybberd's, Nicholas, tincture of gold, 40

Hakluyt, 38, 72, 89; chaplain to English legation at Paris, 97; joins forces with R and Sidney, *Principal Voyages*, 97; writes book for E, 98; plans for colonization, 99; R yields trade rights in Virginia to, 108; urges colonization, 110
Hamburg, levied upon for sailors by Parma, 114
Hampden, studies *History of the World*, 278
Hampshire, E and Biron at, 204
Hampton, R lays siege to Elizabeth Throckmorton at, 146; Elizabeth Ralegh pleads with James for R at, 270; James hunts at, 312
Hanworth, 63

INDEX

Harington, Sir John, 93, 185; writes of Essex, 195; looking toward Edinburgh, 204; writes wife of E's infirmities; invites guests to Rutlandshire for Christmas, writes James and sends gifts, 213; recalls Essex, 214
Hariot, Thomas, at Oxford, 16; at Durham House, 79, 89; goes to Virginia, 100; publishes report, 104, 110, 111, 253, 265, 272; and *History of the World*, 277
Hart, assists R in attempted escape, 306, 307
Harvey, Sir George, succeeded as Lieutenant of the Tower by Waad, 269; R interrogated upon actions of, 269
Harwich, Leicester sails from, 83
Hastings, Edward, with R to Guiana, 292
Hatfield, death of Mary Tudor, 1; retirement to, 2, 3; E thinks of, 6, 8
Hatteras, weather of, 103; ship arrives off, 104; White's expedition reaches, 106, 107; R never saw, 110
Hatton, Sir Christopher, and French marriage of E, 42; advises E, 57, 58, 70; accepts R, 81; and Leicester, 84; royal favors, 85, 86; becomes Lord Chancellor, 86; temporary eclipse, 87, 93; befriends Spenser, 131, 163
Havre, offered to E by Huguenots, 17; lost to England, 18
Hawkins, Sir John, 109; to serve against Armada, 115, 119; letter used by Cecil praising R, 151; death, 167, 278, 299, 315
Hawthorn, clergyman, 265
Hayes, R home at, 7, 8
Hayes, Barton, 80
Helarius, 315
Hele, Sergeant, assistant to Coke, 241; reads indictment against R, 243, 244
Heming, welcomes James to London, 268
Heneage, Sir Thomas, 81; sent with orders to Holland, 84; close to E, 85, 86
Henrietta Maria, to marry Charles of England, 287
Henry II of France, wife Catherine de Medici, mistress Diana de Poitiers, 5
Henry III of France, and *The Prince*, 30; murdered by Jacques Clement, 30, 140; repudiates Alençon, 83; E thinks of, 121
Henry IV of France and *The Prince*, 30; assassinated by Ravaillac, 30; abjures Huguenot faith, crowned King, idol of Essex, 140; greets Essex at Compiègne, 164; Cecil goes to, 185; to marry Mary de Medici, 204; sends Sully to James, 225; and James, 287
Henry V of France, Essex compared to, 191
Henry VII of England, fined R's father, 7, 8
Henry VIII of England, father of Mary Tudor, 1; father of E, 11; remembered, 13, 92; listed Earl Marshal in precedence of an Admiral, 183, 186
Henry, Prince of Wales, taken by mother, Anne of Denmark, to Tower to see R, 267; has separate household, 269; *Discourse of the Invention of Ships, Anchors, Compass*, etc. written by R for, 273; talks with R, 273, 274; rift with James, objects to marriage with Savoy, 274; admires *History of the World*, 278; hates Carr, 278; holds court at Otelands, 278; sickens and dies, 281
Henslowe, Philip, 205
Herbert, William, favorite of Anne of Denmark, 274; with R to Guiana, 292; set on R trail by Stukely, 306, 307
Hereford Cathedral Library, manuscripts, 174
Hermes, James ponders upon, 238

Herodotus, 298
Herophylus, 315
Hertfordshire, E on progress to, 94; R death warrant sent to James in, 312
Hesiod, R consults, 128
Hiero, first King of Sicily, 128
Higford, William, on R ship, 39
Hispaniola, 78, 101, 106
History of the World, by R, 18, 275, 276, 277, 282
Holborne, Thomas, on R ship, 39
Holland, Earl of, and James, 270
Hollinshed, 39
Holy Office, 9
Homer, 33, 128
Hood, Robin, Sir Griffin Markham as, 229
Hooker, John, writes R, 39, *Irish History* by, 89
Hooker, Richard, at Oxford, 15
Hope of Greenway, in Gilbert's fleet, 38
Horta, Spanish flee from, 179; seized by R, 180
House of Commons, R speaks in, 187
House of Lords, Essex in, 183
Howard, Lord Charles, *see* Effingham
Howard, Henry, Earl of Northampton, hatred of R, 207; accuses R, Lady Ralegh, Cobham, Lady Shrewsbury, Northumberland, of conspiracy, 209; praised by Cecil, 210; Edward Bruce writes, 216; Romanist, 221; attends James, 222; comes to London with d'Arenbergh, 231; R writes Elizabeth Ralegh of, 236; denied nothing by James, 237; at R trial, 241, 242; R asks intercession with James for honorable death of, 253; writes of R in Tower, 271; old and devious, 281; dead, 282
Howard, Lady Frances, Countess of Kildare, married to Cobham, friend of E, 209
Howard, Lady Frances, Countess of Essex, married to Carr, 282
Howard, Lord Thomas, R Vice Admiral under, 140; praised by R, 141; appointed to Council of War, at Plymouth, 167; in command of squadron, 168; *Mere Honour*, 169; and R attack Cadiz, 172; on *Nonpareill*, 173; on Second Council of War, commands squadron, leaves Plymouth, 177; waits for fleet off Ferrol, sails for Plymouth, 178; Essex turns to, favors R, 181; and R aboard fleet to resist invasion, 192; at R trial, 241; asked by R for intercession with James for honorable death, 253; inherits house at Charing Cross, 282
Humphreys, Doctor, and E, 15
Hunsdon, Lord, effect of Mary's death on, 11; cousin of Queen, 35; attends E, 61, 71
Hyde Park, Keeper of Game in, 71

Iceland, 10
Icham, Peter de, read by R, 272
If all the world and love were young, R answer to Marlowe, 135
Imokelly, 48
Incas, 158, 159
Inchiquin Ralegh, R retains castle of, 212
India, 4, 79, 97
Indians, Manteo, Wanchese, 78, 79, 101; roused by the burning of Aquascogok, 101
Indies, *see* West Indies
Infanta of Spain, 193, 203, 206, 231
Inglatierra, 162
Inquisition, to be carried to heretic England, 43; E and, 44, 46; R in, 49, 50, 55-59; colonization by R, 88, 95; R goes to, 115;

INDEX 331

news of the Armada reaches, 115; Spanish ships crushed, crews landed, 118; potatoes, 126; Essex sent to, 190-192; James made King of England, Wales and, 217, 249
Irish History, by John Hooker, 89
Islington, R at, 36, 37, 66
Isthmus of Darien, 97

James I of England, as King of Scotland, 43; pleads for Udal, 89, 111; warned by Essex to make sure of succession, 193; thinks of succession, 203; trusts in Cecil, 208; seeks R service through Lennox, 208; and Henry Howard, 209; ambitions, 210; Harington sends letter and gift to, 213; sends ring to Lary Scrope to signal E's death, 216; Carey greets as ruler of England, Ireland and Wales, 217; proclaimed King of England, 220; religious views, 220, 221; description of, 222; royal favor removed from R, 222; goes on progress, 224; R offers service against Spain, 224, 225; suspicious, 225, 226; loiters at Windsor, fear of plague, 226; difference between reign of E and, 227; plots and counterplots, 228; Watson and Clarke plead for toleration, 228; conspired against, 229, 230; scorns Machiavelli, 237; believes himself chosen of God, 238; hears of trial of R, Cobham, 255; ponders on R, 256, 257; R asks pardon of, 258; toys with condemned, 261, 262; R writes to, 263; enters London, 268; writes Archduke Albert, treats with d'Arenbergh, 268, 269; disbelieves evidence against R, 269; Lady Ralegh pleads for R, 270; Robert Carr favorite of, 270; gives Sherborne to Carr, 271; rift with Prince Henry, busy with Carr, wishes to marry Henry and daughter of Savoy, 274; displeased with *History of the World,* 278, 282; accused of poisoning Prince Henry, 281; dissolves Parliament, new favorite, George Villiers, 282; orders release of R to prepare for voyage to Guiana, 283; and Pocahontas, 284; and a chaotic world, 286, 287; and Guiana expedition, 288, 289; double dealing proved of, 299; watches continental confusion, decides to sacrifice R, 302, 303; keeps away from London, receives R death warrant, 312
James VI of Scotland, *see* James I of England
Jamestown, 284
Jason, goes to Guiana, 291
Jersey, R Governor of, 187, 194, 205; R loses Governorship of, 235
Jesuits, turn upon Philip II, 30; Persons and Campion, 42; Allen and Sanders, 46; provided to carry Inquisition to England, 112; R, Cecil, Effingham as marked men to the, 187
Jocasta, Euripides, translated by Gascoigne, 22
John, Doctor, R surgeon, 265
Jones, Inigo, leaves for Italy, 281
Jonson, Ben, 33. 85; *Cynthia's Revels,* 202; at Mermaid Tavern, 205, 272; *History of the World,* 277; carries Walter Ralegh (R's son) off to France, 281; ordered by James to return to Court, 282
Julio, Pope, 128
Justices of the King's Bench, Popham, Anderson, Gawdy, Warburton, Montagu, 240
Juvenal, R reads, 128

Kenilworth, Leicester dies on way to, 124
Keymis, with R in Trinidad, 156; sent out with two ships to Guiana, returns, 163; R writes letter from Tower to, 236; to be sent to Guiana by R, 279; given five ships to ascend Orinoco, 296; sends word of young Walter Ralegh's death, 297; attacked by R, 298; dead, 298
Kilcolman, Edmund Spenser at, 128, 133
Kildare, Countess of, *see* Lady Frances Howard
Killigrew, William, R and Cecil to take stock and apportion shares of *Madre de Dios,* 152
King, Captain, welcomes R on return from Guiana, 300; urges R to flee, 304; and Lady Ralegh leave R at Salisbury, 305; attempts escape of R, 306, 307; bids R good-bye, 308
King's Bench, convened for trial of R and conspirators, 240
Kinsale, R touches at, 300
Knollys, Sir Francis, cousin of E, 35; returns, 39; and the Netherlands, 83
Knollys, Lettice, and Sir Philip Sidney, marries Essex, 139; and Leicester, 145
Knollys, Sir Robert, sent to placate E by Essex, 179
Knollys, Sir William, as Lord Deputy to Ireland, 186; sent by E to Essex, locked up by Essex, 197; at Essex trial, 199; attends E on death bed, 216
Kyd, Thomas, known to R, 188; at Mermaid Tavern, 205

La Renzi, go-between, 248
La Rochefoucauld, quote from, 222
Lake, Sir Thomas, and James, 222; writes Cecil of R, 223
Lamoral, hero of St. Quentins and Gravelines, 5
Lancerota, Bayley deserts at, 292
Lane, Ralph, at Durham House, 79; made Governor of Virginia, 100; explores country, 102; returns to England with Drake, 103; searched for by Grenville, 104, 110
Languedoc, R in, 19
Latimer, Hugh, Bishop of Worcester, burned by Mary Tudor at Oxford, 1
Latimore, Lord, first husband of Katherine Parr, 63
Le Clerc, offers escape to R, 306; arrested and questioned, 309
Le Grand, Captain King arranges for escape of R with, 304
Le Moine, brings maps of Florida, 97
Leicester, Countess of, *see* Frances Walsingham, Lettice Knollys
Leicester, Earl of, Robert Dudley, Master of Horse, 14; Chancellor of Oxford, 15; Gascoigne, Gilbert and R, 24; visited by E, 24; R weighs, 33-35; and E French marriage, 42; rivalry for Burghley, 43; R letter to, 52, 53; return to favor, 57; advises E, 57, 58; attends E, 61, 70; recognizes power of R, 81; attempt to become sovereign of Netherlands, 83, 84; as "Sweet Robin," 85; dimmed by time and distance, 87; Burghley hates, 90; presents step-son, Earl of Essex, 92; commands on land against Armada, 115; rides to Tilbury with E, 116; dead, 124, 127; married to Lettice Knollys, 145, 164
Lennox, Duke of, comes to London, seeks services of R for James, 208; refused by R, 210; Cecil checks relations with R, 211
Lerma, dominates Philip III, 220
Lieutenant of the Tower, Sir John Peyton, 236; Sir George Harvey, Sir William Waad, 269

INDEX

Limehouse, Gilbert's home in, 24, 38
Lincoln, Earl of, in attack on Essex House, 198; surprised at E's refusal of mercy to Essex, 200
Lion, to Virginia, 101
Lion, to Virginia, 105; voyage of, 106; returns to England, 107
Lion's Whelp, loaned to R by Howard, 156
Lisbon, Armada leaves, 113; English expedition sails for, 123; E fears Essex may attack, 178
Lismore, Castle built for R at, 126
Little Conduit, in Cheapside, 13
Livy, 33; studied, 129
Lizard Point, Spanish ship beaten off, 118
Lodge, Thomas, *Rosalynde*, 188
Lok, Dr. Michael, map of America, 97
Longjumeau, Truce of, 18
Lopez, Francisco, tells of riches of Guiana, 157, 158
Lord Chancellor, Hatton, 86; Bacon, 303
Lord Chamberlain, Earl of Oxford, 183
Lord Commissioners, *see* Commissioners of Oyer and Terminer
Lord Robert, *see* Leicester
Lord Steward, Lord Buckhurst, 198
Louis XIII of France, 288
Low Countries, 21, 32, 64, 83; Sidney killed in, 86
Lucian, studied, 129
Ludgate Hill, Victory Procession passes up, 120
Luther, Martin, ban pronounced against, 30
Luynes, Duke of, Richelieu to mediate with, 302
Lyddes, Hatton as, 86
Lyly, John, *Euphues*, 134

Mace, Samuel, sent out by R in last effort for Virginia, 111
Machiavelli, Niccolo, 22; unfolded by Gascoigne to R, 23; *Duca Valentina*, 28; *The Prince*, 28–32; *Discourse*, 28, 32, 33, 66, 91, 94, 117; studied, 129, 185, 186; scorned by James, 237, 273, 276, 287
Machiavellian maxims, 29, 30, 32, 40, 66, 94, 122, 127, 150, 153, 160, 175, 186, 187, 221, 222, 237, 238, 244, 248, 313
Mackworth, Captain, in Ireland, 47, 48
Madre de Dios, captured and brought to England, 151
Madrid, 11
Magnus, Albertus, Quote from Prantl, 28
"Main" Plot, 232, 233, 245
Malabar, *Madre de Dios* homeward bound from, 151
Mandeville, writes wonders of Guiana, 161
Manoa, *see* Eldorado
Manourie, brings warrant to R, 304; used by R, turns traitor, 305; R denies lies of, 315, 316
Manteo, received by R, 100; returns to Roanoke, 101; loyal to colonists, 102; White seeks aid of, 109, 110, 284
Mar, Earl of, ambassador of James, arrives in London, pledges confidence to Cecil, 203; wept for R, 255
Marck, Admiral de la, seeks harbor in England, ordered out, takes Brill, 20; Gascoigne joins, 23
Margate, to be protected against Armada, 114
Markham, Sir Griffin, warming to wrath against James, 228; joins conspirators against James; as Robin Hood, 229; to be Secretary in Cecil's place, if successful, 230; examined, 232; taken to Wolvesey Castle, 240, 255; execution stayed, 260; questioned, 261; taken to London, 263

Marlowe, Christopher, in hey-day, 133–135; has friendship of R and patronage of Earl of Oxford, 188; Mermaid Tavern, 205
Mars, 26, 27
Marshalsea, John Udal dies in, 89
Martial, R reads, 128
Martines, reaches Manoa and returns to tell its glories, 154
Mary Spark, sent out by R against Spanish, 87
Mary Tudor, death; résumé of reign; marriage to Philip II; at Hatfield, 1–3; attempt at death of E, 6, 12; effect of death on West Country, 7, 11; dislike for West Country, 8; plot to revolt against, 8; pledge to Pope, 10; undoing of work by E, 14, 67; E compared with, 214, 215
Mascarenhas, Bishop, manuscripts and volumes taken by English, 174
Maschion, 315
Master of the Court of Wards and Liveries, Burghley, Robert Cecil, 71; Robert Cecil has control of young Ralegh as, 236
Master of Horse, Robert Dudley, Essex
Matthew, Bishop Tobias, secures warrant removing R from Durham House, 224
Maxims of State, by R, 273
Medices, John, bastard son of Duke of Florence, sails with Armada, 114
Meere, John, bailiff at Sherborne, 205; hatred of R, 207
Melito, Prince of, natural son of Philip, Duke of Pastrana, sails with Armada, 114
Mendoza, Bernardino de, 39; and Leicester, 43, 46
Mercilla, E as, 130
Mercury, 26, 27
Mere Honour, Thomas Howard's ship, 169
Mermaid Tavern, R at the, 205, 206; recalled by R, 263
Meuse, Brill at mouth of, 20
Mexico, 9, 99
Meyricke, urges Essex to discipline R, 180, 181
Middle Ages, 27
Middle Temple, R of the, 25, 35, 36, 37
Midsummer Night, James to be surprised, arrested and carried off on, 228
Monardus, writes of armadillo, 159
Moncada, Captain Hugo de, lost, 118
Monson, in the *Rainbow*, 182
Montagu, Chief Justice, more just to R than Coke, 312; pronounced sentence of execution, 313
Montcontour, Louis of Nassau retreats from, 18
Montgomerie, Count, at Rouen, 17
Morequito, King Arromaia at, 159, 162
Morgan, Nyles, commander of *Red Lion*, 38
Morgan, Sir William, in Ireland, 49
Morgues, James, publishes "draughts and descriptions," 89
Moses, Essex as, 191
Mount Ralegh, named, 79
Mountjoy, Lord, *see* Charles Blount; on second Council of War, 177
Moyle, in Ireland, 48
Munster, Gilbert as Governor of, 21; E hears complaints of, 44; E unmoved, 46; Captain John Zouch becomes Governor of, 51; suppression of the rebellion of, 57, 59; potatoes planted in, 126; Carew in, 191
Münster, Sebastian, map of America, 97
Muscovy Company, 72, 78

Nash, Thomas, and Thomas Kyd, 188
Nassau, Lewis of, at Montcontour, 18
Natural History, by Pliny, 161

INDEX 333

Naunton, Sir Robert, and Leicester, 32; succeeds Winwood, unfriendly to R, 303; knows of plans for R escape, 306; examines R, 308, 310

Navarre, Henry of, *see* Henry IV

Nec mortem pet nec finem fugio, "I neither seek death nor flee the end," motto of R ship, 39

Neiuport, firewood prepared to burn heretics at, 114

Neptune, Van Duvenvoord's ship, 169

Netherlands, Margaret of Parma to rule in, 7; seething in revolt, 20; E aids William of Orange in the, 21; Robert Dudley for the cause of, 34; Alençon leaves England to govern, 61; Seymour had tasted war in the, 64; Leicester and the, 83; drifting toward war, 86; fabric trade with England, 99; Duke of Parma prepares for victory, 113, 115; E wonders about loyalty of, 185; vagrants shipped to, 216; Spain plays to keep in subjection the, 302

Neville, Christopher, speaks in Parliament, 282

Newfoundland, fishermen shipwrecked in, 9; crews come home from, 10; taken in name of E, 75; Gilbert satisfied with discoveries, 76, 77; projected trade between Jersey and, 205, 300

Newhaven, harlots reach, 119

Newland, estate given to R, 70

Niedhurst, Gascoigne offers services as burgess of, 22; refused, 23

Nonesuch, Essex carried from, 194

Nonpareill, Thomas Howard and Effingham on, 173

Norden, John, prayer for Essex, 191

Norimbega, *see* Northwest Passage

Normandy, threatened by Spain, 10; harlots reach, 119

Norris, John, attempts retaliation of Spanish, 123; gives up attempt, 124

North, Captain, with R to Guiana, 292

North Hall, E at, 94

Northampton, Earl of, *see* Henry Howard, Compton

Northampton, Marchioness of, at E funeral, 218

Northumberland, Earl of, Henry Percy, and *Faerie Queene*, 131; accused with R of conspiracy, 209; writes James about R, 211; in Tower, 284

Northwest Passage to China, Gilbert's project, 21; *A Discourse of a Discoverie for a new Passage to Cataia*, 24; expedition for finding, 28; expedition unsuccessful, 45; Adrian Gilbert plans for, 56; R becomes one of "the colleagues of the fellowship for the discovery of the," 79; Lok's map, 97

Nottingham, Countess of, dies, 214

Nottingham, Earl of, Effingham made, 183

Nottinghamshire, Markham as Robin Hood in, 229

Nova Regina, map found on R, 308

Novion, David de, offers escape to R, 306; arrested and questioned, 309

Nuevo Reygno, Berreo's son in, 157

Nuñez, Doctor, Burghley pays heed to, 40

Ochino, Bernadino, charge of religious train of E, 31

Ocracoke Inlet, barks reach, 78

Oia, river, found by de Osua, 154

Old Bailey, E rides through, 2

Opinions of Mr. Rawley upon motions made to him for the means of subduing the Rebellion in Munster, The, 62

Orange, William of, de la Marck, admiral of, 20; aided by E, 21; and Gascoigne, 23; and *The Prince*, 30; and Alençon, 42; R meets, 61; murdered, 83

Ordace, Diego, killed on Guiana coast, 154

Ore, Fort del, blessed, 46

Oreliana, tries for gold of Guiana, 154

Orinoco, Whiddon sent to examine, 154, 157; reached by R, 158; trip up and return, 159, 160; E funeral likened to, 218; R tells of Spanish settlement on the, 280; R treats with Faige for assistance at the, 290; Keymis ascends, 296; chart found on R, 308

Orkney, crews home from, 10

Orlando Furioso, R as, 150

Ormond, Earl of, Lieutenant of Munster, 47, 49; returns to England, 49; Leicester enmity for the, 57; and the *Faerie Queene*, 131

Orpheus, E as, 149

Otelands, Prince Henry and Princess Elizabeth keep court at, 278; James at, 312

Othello, Shakespeare, 163

Oxford, Latimer and Ridley burned at, 1; visited by E, 15; R at, 16, 17; R leaves, 18, 70

Oxford, Earl of, married to Elizabeth, daughter of Burghley, 40; Sir Philip Sidney and, 93; and the *Faerie Queene*, 131; Lord Chamberlain, 183; patron of Marlowe, 188; carries animus for R to E, 204, 316

Oyapoco, Cape, R makes landfall off, 295

Padua, Walsingham studies law at, 117

Page, William, *The Discovery of a gaping Gulf*, by, 60

Palomeque, Don Diego de, R coming announced to, 295; defends San Thome, 297; dead, 297

Pamlico Sound, 2 barks reach, 78; reached by colonists, 102

Panama, pearl fisheries of, 4, 99; R urges E to strike at, 143; plan found on R, 308

Parham, Sir Edward, joins conspiracy against James, 229, 230; taken to Wolvesey Castle, 240

Parker, Matthew, Archbishop of Canterbury, 15; and *The Prince*, 32

Parma, Duke of, success, 42; in Netherlands, 96; prepares for victory Armada, 113, 114

Parma, Margaret of, natural sister to Philip II, 3; to go to the Netherlands, 7

Parminius, Stephanus, at Oxford, 16; names E as "Queen of the Seas," 73; death, 75, 76

Parr, Katherine of, wife of Latimer, wife of Henry VIII, wife of Thomas Seymour, 64

Parry, Sir Thomas, knighted and made controller, 14; conspiracy against James, 230

Pasch, Hebrew, honored by Church of Geneva, 220, 221

Pastrana, Duke of, *see* Melito

Paulett, Sir Anthony, Captain of the Yeomen of the Guard, 67

Paunsford, Richard and William, servants of R, 37

Peckham, Sir George, efforts at colonization, 72

Peele, George, writes farewell, 123; and R at Oxford, 188

Peirson, John, *Reasons Why the King of Scots is unacceptable to the People of England*, 89

Pelham, in Ireland, 47

Pelican, Drake's ship returns, 57

Pembroke, Countess of, *see* Mary Sidney

INDEX

Pembroke, Earl of, *see* William Herbert
Pembroke, Lord, married, 35; refused Ranger of the New Forest, 124; scandal with Mistress Fitton, flung into Tower, 145; invited by Harington to Rutlandshire for Christmas, 213; at funeral of E, 218; sues for R life, 256
Pemisapan, son of Ensenore, rouses tribes against colonists, 102; murdered by colonists, 102
Percy, George, talks to R of Virginia, 284
Percy, Henry, *see* Northumberland
Perrot, Lady Dorothy, *see* Dorothy Devereux
Perrot, Sir John, illegitimate half brother of E, 35; sent to Munster, 44
Perrot, Sir Thomas, married to Lady Dorothy Devereux, 40, 145; duel with R, 40
Persia, 4
Persons, Jesuit, 42
Peru, 154
Petrarch, studied, 129
Peyton, Sir John, R attempts suicide while dining with, 236
Philip II of Spain, married to Mary Tudor, 1; Mary's desire for, 2; effect of Mary's death on, review of reign, and Margaret of Parma, 3; early preparations for war, English hatred for, 4; Escorial, 5; disliked by West Country, 9, 10; and the Netherlands, 20; and Jesuits, Machiavelli, 30; rampant, 96; longs for salvation of heretics, 99; feared by E, 100; plans for the Armada, 112, 113; tries to mislead the English, 115; takes failure calmly, sends fleets against Plymouth, 143; England sends expedition against, 166, 167; ill, 170; dead, 185
Philip III of Spain, dominated by Lerma and Uzeda, 220; and de Acuna, 288
Phillips, Miles, brings stories of mistreatment of English sailors by Spain, 9
Philopoemen, Prince of Achaei, R likened to, 116, 117
Phœnicians, brought by tin industry to England, 81
Piedmont, Prince of, to marry Princess Elizabeth, 274
Piers, Captain, in Ireland, 49
Pigott, John, dead, 294
Plague, attacks English, 18; in London, 223, 226, 240
Plato, R quotes, 33; R thinks of, 128
Plautus, R reads, 128
Pliny, R quotes, 33; R consults, 128; *Natural History*, 161
Plutarch, R consults, 128
Plymouth, Gilbert as member of Parliament from, 21; fleet forced back to, 39; Gilbert leaves, 72, 73; ships under White sail for Virginia from, 105; to be protected against the Armada, 114; expedition sails from, 123; Philip II sends 60 ships against, 143; Essex and Howard waiting in, 167; second expedition against Spain sails from, 177; Howard returns to, 178; Essex returns to, 183; R leaves for Guiana, 290, 291; R reaches, 300; R and Stukeley return to, 304
Pocahontas, meets R, 284
Poland, Gustavus II Adolphus leads against, 302
Pole, Cardinal Reginald, Mary confesses to, 10; and *The Prince*, 31; death, 31
Pope, Ghibellines deny he is the sun, 27; forwards rebellion in Ireland, 42; San Josepho bears banner of, 46, 121; *see* Sixtus

Popham, Lord Chief Justice, sent by E to Essex, locked up by him, 197; on King's bench at R trial, 240; R trial, 247, 248, 250, 253
Portland, to be protected against Armada, 114, 115; R at, 116; invading ships appear off, 117, 118
Portland Bill, R goes to sea from, 117
Porto Rico, 2 barks reach, 78
Porto Ricco, Bishop of, R coming announced to, 295
Portsmouth, R sees importance of, 115
Powhatan, father of Pocahontas, 284
Prague, Princess Elizabeth carries *History of the World* to, 278
Praise of Music, The, dedicated to R, 89
Prantl, Professor Carl, quote from, 28
Prerogatives of Parliament, The, by R, 273
Prest, Agnes, visited by R and mother, 10
Preston, Amias, challenges R to duel, is refused, 212
Prince, The, by Machiavelli, 28; copy by Buonaccorsi, 29; published by Blado, 29; excerpts from, 29, 30; R and, 33, 273, 287
Princelye Pleasures at the Court at Kenelwoorth, The, by Gascoigne, 24
Principal Voyages, by Hakluyt, 97
Privy Council, 6, 22, 39, 40, 53, 57, 64, 71, 81, 86, 91, 96, 124, 141, 142, 143, 166, 187, 308
Privy Councillors, Hatton, 68, 86; Burghley, 71; Cecil, 71; Shrewsbury, Worcester, 207
Psalms of David, versified by Henry Howard, 209
Puckingham, Keeper, at Kew, 164
Puna, Incas garden of pleasure near, 158
Puncto Gallo, R takes station off, 296; Keymis reaches, 297
Puntal, fort at, 170, 172
Puritans, excited against Catholics, 42
Pyrenees, 121

Queen Mary, *see* Mary Tudor
Queen of the Seas, E as, 73
Queenhithe, Essex goes to, 198
Queenstown, built later, 52
Quito, river Oia rising east of, 154

Rainbow, Vere on the, 173; Monson on the, 182
Ralegh, R sends the, 73
Ralegh, galleon, offered by Carew Ralegh in attack against Panama, 143
Ralegh, Carew, son of Walter and Katherine Ralegh, 8; at Durham House, 79; offers galleon *Ralegh* to E, 143; knighted by E, 204
Ralegh, Carew, son of R and Elizabeth Ralegh, born in the Tower, 265; taken by Elizabeth Ralegh to plead with James for R, 270
Ralegh, Elizabeth, Elizabeth Throckmorton, description, 144; and R, 144-147; in Tower with R, 148; urges Cecil not to assist R with Guiana expedition, 155; accused of conspiracy by Henry Howard, 209, 224; receives letters from R in Tower, 236; sues Cecil to save life of R, 259; sixty year tenure to Sherborne conveyed to, 264; in Tower, 265; sided always with R, 270; pleads with James at Hampton Court, 270; laughs at young Walter's pranks, 281; receives word of death of Walter, 299; welcomes R home from Guiana, 301; leaves R at Salisbury, 305; arrested, 309; pleads with council, 314; granted R's body, 314
Ralegh, George, with R to Guiana, 292; second in command to Keymis, 296

INDEX 335

Ralegh, Katherine, mother of R, widow of Otto Gilbert, wife of Walter Ralegh, daughter of Sir Philip Champernoun, 8; takes R to visit Agnes Prest, 10

Ralegh, Margaret, daughter of Walter and Katherine Ralegh, 8

Ralegh, Walter, father of R, distrust of rulers, 7, 8; carries Carew to France, 9; fears Queen, 9; effect of Mary's death on, 11

Ralegh, Walter, R, son of Walter and Katherine Ralegh, 8; visits Agnes Prest, 10; effect of E ascension on, 11; and Kate Ashley, 12; at Oxford, 16; joins Henry Champernoun for first taste of war, 18; in action, 19; back from war, 21; off for Low Countries with Humphrey Gilbert, 21; learns discipline, 22; and Gascoigne, 23–26; and Leicester, 24; takes motto, 26; and Machiavelli, 32, 33; and Burghley, 34; struggle for notice, 35; in Middle Temple, 35, 36; at Islington, 36, 37; goes to sea, 38, 39; duel with Sir Thomas Perrot, 40; gains friends, 41; in Ireland, 45, 47, 54; headed for court, 51; receives Barry land, loses Barry Court, 52; letter to Leicester, return to England, 52, 53; and the cloak, 55; solution of Irish problems, 56, 57; first audience, 58, 59; serves E, 60; entertains Duke of Alençon, meets William of Orange, 61; description, 62; need of the court, 70; gifts from the Queen, 70, 71; refused permission to sail, 73, 74; takes up quest of colonization, 77; dreams of an empire, 77, 78; leases Durham House, 78, 79; plans for Northwest Passage, 79; elected to parliament, knighted, 80; Warden of Stannaries, Lieutenant of Cornwall, Vice Admiral of Cornwall, 81; pleads with Leicester for frankness, 84, 85; struggle for privilege, 85; suspected of sympathy with Spain, 86, 87; in E's favor, 84–87; colonization in Ireland, becomes Captain of the Guard, 88; E favorite, 89, 90; effect of death of Mary Stuart, 91; endures nearness of Essex, 93, 94; enjoys release, 95; sends fourth expedition to Virginia, looks for trouble with Philip II. 96; works for Virginia, 97, 98; turns to colonization, 100; difficulties at home, 103; sends ship to Virginia, 104; plans new expedition to Virginia, 105; more difficulties, 107; works secretly, yields trade rights to Adventurers, 108; still hopes for Virginia, 109–111; provides for defense against Armada, 114, 115; goes to Ireland, 115; in West Country, 116; goes to sea, 117, 118; writes of the coming of the invincibles, 118; receives rich ransom, 119; considers Essex, 121, 122; sails under Drake and Norris, 123; receives booty and prizes, friction with Essex, 124; returns to Ireland, seeks peace at Youghal, plants potatoes, trees, etc., 125–127; trusts to time to cure E of Essex, 127, 128; and Spenser, 129–135; poems, 135–138; received again by E, 139, 140; Vice Admiral under Thomas Howard, 140; relieved, ordered by council to warn Howard, praises Howard, 141; E gives lease of Sherborne to, 142; begs E to strike at Panama, leaves Gravesend outward bound, commanded to return, continues, finally turns back, 143; meets, seduces and marries Elizabeth Throckmorton, 144–147; placed in Tower, 148; travels in custody of Blount to Dartmouth, takes stock of *Madre de Dios*, apportions shares, returns to Sherborne,

152; offers services, at Durham House, 153; first thoughts of Guiana, sends Whiddon to examine Orinoco, applies for patent, 154; equips expedition and sails, 155; arrives in Trinidad, 156; burns St. Joseph, captures Berreo, leaves for the mainland, 157; reaches Orinoco, 158; meets Topiawari, 159; gains accurate idea of Guiana, 160, 161; attitude toward E, 162; E ignores, 163; waiting and hoping, 166; appointed by E to Council of War, recruiting, 167; in command of squadron, 168; on *Warspite*, 169; off Cadiz, 171; attacks Cadiz, wounded, 172, 173; results of expedition, 174, 175; woos Essex to reach E, taken to E, restored to favor, 175, 177; friends with Essex, on second Council of War, commands squadron, 177; and Essex ride to Court, new attempt against Spain, 178; and Essex at Fayal, 180; reprimanded by Essex, apologizes, 181; left at St. Michael, sails for England, 182, 183; sent for by E to solve difficulties with Essex and Effingham, solves problem, 183; hated by Effingham, 184; seizes opportunities, 186–188; surrounded by enemies, tries to overcome enmity, 188; chooses Cecil as friend, keeps contact with Essex, 189; is refused commissioner of Boulogne, retreats to Ireland, 191; invited home by E, 191; spends month as Vice Admiral on fleet, 192; accused by Essex, 194; watches Essex, 196; again close to E, 197; takes possession of garden of Essex House, 198; at Essex trial, watches execution, 200, 201; accused of treason by Essex, 203; E kind to, receives Biron and Sully for E, 204; Governor of Jersey, 205; at Mermaid Tavern, 205, 206; opposed by Cecil, 206; refused Privy Councillor, friend of Cecil, 207; James seeks services through Lennox, 208; refused, 209; accused of conspiracy, 209; Cecil's changed attitude toward, 210; watches James, 211; conveys Sherborne to himself for life, refuses challenge of Amias Preston, sells Irish holdings, 212; goes to Sherborne, takes Cobham and Compton with him, 213; attends E's body, 217–219; reputed atheist, 221; rides with Crosse to meet James, 221, 222; stripped of incomes and powers, 223, 224; offers James services against Spain, 224, 225; Cecil tells him to attend Lords of Council, 226; discontent, 228; and Cobham confer at Durham House, watched and plotted against by Cecil, 231; questioned, ordered confined to home, 232; testimony of Brooke about, 233; accused by Cobham, 234; sent to Bloody Tower, 234; letter to Cobham pleading for truth, loses Wardenship of Stannaries, Governorship of Jersey, Commission of Lieutenancy, 235; writes wife and attempts suicide, 236; recovers, ponders on injustice, 238, 239; indicted, taken to Wolvesey Castle, 240; trial, 240–254; found guilty, pleads for honorable death, 253; James hears of trial, popular favor changes in favor of, 255, 256; meditates, 257; asks for pardon, 258; prepares for death, 259, 260; watches Grey, Markham, and Cobham leave scaffold, 262; taken to Bloody Tower, 263, 264; in Tower, 263–267; ill, 265; comparative liberty, 266; befriended by Anne of Denmark, 266, 267; James disbelieves evidence against, annoyed by Waad, watches ships sail for Virginia, 269; loses Sherborne to Carr, 271; experiments, reads and writes prose, 271-275; visited by Prince Henry, 273, 274; no longer hopes for pardon, 275; looks to Prince Henry for aid, 278; offers to send Keymis to Guiana, tries to bargain for liberty, 279, 280; released to prepare for voyage to Guiana, 283; meets Pocahontas, 284; off for Guiana, 290-301; death of Walter, 297; finds command difficult, sails to Plymouth, 300; welcomed by Elizabeth Ralegh, 301; arrest ordered, 303; summoned to appear, 304; works for delay, 305; escape offered, 306; taken to London, 306; attempt to escape, 306, 307; in Tower, 308; defense, 312; sentenced, 313; bids Lady Ralegh farewell, 314; dead, 316

Ralegh, Walter, son of R and Elizabeth Ralegh, Sherborne conveyed to, 212, 264; in Tower, 265; goes with mother to James at Hampton Court, 270; kills man, taken to France by Jonson, 281; goes with R to Guiana, 292; with Keymis, 296; dead, 297

Ralegh's Walk, terrace of the Bloody Tower, 264, 266

Ralegh's Works, *History of the World*, 18, 275; *Sonnet to Spenser*, 132; *Twenty first and last book of the Ocean, to Cynthia*, 133; *If all the world and love were young*, 135; excerpts from, 136, 137, 138, 277; *Report of the Truth of the Fight about the Isles of Azores*, 141; *Discovery of Guiana*, 162, 272; *Discourse touching a War with Spain, and of the protecting of the Netherlands*, 224; *The Prerogatives of Parliaments*, 273; *The Cabinet Council*, 273; *Maxims of State*, 273; *Discourse of the Invention of Ships, Anchors, Compass, etc.*, 273; *A Treatise of the Soul*, 275; *The Sceptic*, 275; *The Reign of William the First*, 275; *First Part of the History of the World*, 277; *Apology for the Voyage to Guiana*, 304, 305

Ravaillac, Henry IV assassinated by, 30
Reasons Why the King of Scots is unacceptable to the People of England, by John Pierson, 89
Red Lion, of Gilbert's fleet, 38
Reign of William the First, The, by R, 275
Revenge, covers withdrawal of fleet, 141
Rheims, 42
Ricci, Jesuit, teaches Christianity in China, 220
Rich, Lord, at sea, 177
Richard I, Cœur de Lion, 7
Richelieu, and *The Prince*, 30; and Marêt, 289; sent to mediate with Duke of Luynes, 302
Richmond, E leaves, 56; Court at, 78; R lays siege to Elizabeth Throckmorton at, 146; Court moved to, 214; E's body carried to Westminster from, 217; Court guarded at, 230
Ridley, burned by Mary Tudor at Oxford, 1
Roanoke, Wokoken Island, two barks reach, 78; colonists land at, 101; home of colonists, 102; fifteen men landed at, 104; John White lands, 109
Robtes, John, on R ship, 39
Roche, Lord, captured by R, 49, 50
Rochelle, *St. Matthew* worked into, 179
Roe, fails to reach Virginia, 108
Roebuck, Grenville's fleet, 101; offered in attempt against Panama, 143
Romanov family, on Russian throne, 302
Rosalynde, by Thomas Lodge, 188
Ross Bay, ships to get salt at, 106
Rostellan Castle, 52

Rota, ships bound to, 171
Rouen, Count Montgomerie at, 17; siege of, 140
Royal Charter, to Gilbert, 38
Russel, Sir William, refused to take command of Irish affairs, 190
Rutland, at sea, 177; sojourns abroad, 195; invited by Harington to Rutlandshire for Christmas, 213
Rutlandshire, Harington invites guests to, 213

Sacharissa, Waller, 85
Salisbury, R pauses at, 305
Salisbury, Bishop of, preaches on victory, 121; Dr. Coldwell as, 142
Salisbury, Earl of, Robert Cecil becomes, 269; William, son of Robert Cecil, later becomes, 189
Sallust, studied, 129
Sand, George, and Mary Stuart, 91
Sanders, English Jesuit, 46
Sandys, Archbishop, and E, 43
San Giuseppe, R attacked from, 296, 297
San Josepho, in Ireland, 46; sent to England, 48
San Sebastian, monastery in, 170
San Thome, town of, 296; Keymis lands above, captures, 297; word of capture reaches England, 302
Santa Cruz, Ferdinando lands at, 106
Santa Cruz, Marques of, dead, 112
Santleger, Sir Warham, *see* St. Leger
Saracens, 112
Sarah Constant, sails for Virginia, 269
Sarum, See of, Bishop Matthew lost, 224
Savage, Sir Arthur, aids R in entertainment of Biron, 204; introduces Lennox to R, 208; intermediary between R and Lennox, 211
Savoy, Duke of, *see* Amadas
Sceptic, The, by R, 275
Scilly Islands, 64, 300
Scotland, 43; Spanish ships around, 118; James leaves, 223
Scrope, Lady, wears black for Essex, 195; James of Scotland sends ring for her to signal E's death, 216; leaves E's death bed to send ring to James by Robert Carey, 216, 217
Scylla, 43
Sea Beggars, *see* de la Marck
Secotan, reached by colonists, 102
Secretary of the Crown, Davison, 90, 91
Secretary of State, *see* Lord Burghley, Robert Cecil, Sir Ralph Winwood, 205
Selden, at Mermaid Tavern,
Semiramis, First part of *History of the World* ends with death of, 277
Seneca, R reads, 128
Serpent, sent out by R against Spain, 87
Seville, West Indiamen bound for, 182
Seymour, Henry, to serve against Armada, 115
Seymour, Jane, mother of Edward VI; third wife of Henry VIII, 63
Seymour Place, 63
Seymour, Thomas, intention to marry E, 6; R likeness to, 62, 63; tried and executed, 64; recalled by E, 206; married to Katherine Parr, 64
Seymour, William, and Arabella Stuart, 206
Shakespeare, *Venus and Adonis*, 144; reads *Discovery of Guiana*, 162; *Othello*, 163; *As You Like It*, 188; compares Essex to Henry V, 191; at Mermaid Tavern, 205; welcomes James to London, 268

INDEX 337

Shepherd's Calendar, by Spenser, 128; becomes the fashion, 129
Shepherd of the Sea, R as, 130
Sherborne, given to R, 142; administered from Tower, 148; R superintends building of new home at, 187; visited by R as often as possible, 204; R, Cobham and Compton at, 213; secured to R's legal heirs, 235; sixty year tenure given to Elizabeth Ralegh, 264; given by James to Carr, 271
Shirley, urges Essex to discipline R, 180, 181
Shrewsbury, Earl of, oyle of staggs blood, 40; made Privy Councillor, 207; with E at death, 216; praises R, 255
Shrewsbury, Lady, accused of conspiracy by Howard, 209
Sidney, Sir Henry, 32, 35; never rewarded, 86, 127
Sidney, Mary, Countess of Pembroke, recalls love for R, 144; mother of Earl Pembroke, 256
Sidney, Sir Philip, at Oxford, 16; Sir Fulke Greville and, 32; and the Earl of Oxford, 40; friend of R, 58; attends E, 61; killed, 86, 93, 103; R joins forces with, 97; plans with Drake for colonization, 103, 256
Sidney, Robert, marriage, 85; considered for Irish command, 190; in attack on Essex House, 198; invited by Harington to Rutlandshire for Christmas, 213
Sidonia, Duke of Medina, *see* Don Alonzo Perez de Guzman
Sierra de los Gazules, Spanish Mountains, 171
Sigeberti, read by R, 272
Simier, and E, 42, 57
Sixtus V, Pope, aids Philip II, 112; E knows thoughts of, 117
Sluys, 114
Smerwick, County Kerry, 46, 47
Smith, Captain John, one of R faction, sails for Virginia, 269
Smith, Thomas, R yields trade rights in Virginia to, 108
Smithfield, E rides through, 2
Smyth, Sheriff, met by Essex, 197
Society of Jesus, accused by followers of Luther, 30
Somerset, Countess of, *see* Frances Howard
Somerset, Earl of, E writes to, 13; brother of Thomas Seymour, 63; Carr raised to be, 279
Somerset House, 78; procession leaves, 120
Somerset Place, E rides to, 2
South Seas, 87
Southampton, Earl of, friend of Essex, 93; patron of Shakespeare, 144; married to Elizabeth Vernon, 145; at sea, 177; troop commander, 191; leaves Ireland with Essex, 192; sojourns abroad, 195; surrenders with Essex and goes to Tower, 198; tried in Westminster Hall, 198, 199; sentenced to be hanged, 200
Southampton, to Guiana, 291; captures four French vessels, 292
Sparrow, Francis, left with Topiawari, 159
Spenser, Edmund, assistant Secretary under Grey, 45; at Kilcolman, 128; and R, 129, 130; *Faerie Queene*, 130; *Colin Clout's Come Home Again*, 130, 131; meets E, 131; sonnet to R, 132; dies, 185; missed by R, 189; Mermaid Tavern, 205, 315
Spicer, Edward, reaches Hatteras, 107
Squirrel, in Gilbert's fleet, 73, 75, 76
St. Andrew, see Apostles
St. Bartholomew Day, 21
St. Domingo, 103
St. George's Channel, 126

St. Ives, R lands at, 183
St. James, 78
St. John, Sir William, set on R trail by Stukely, 306, 307
St. Johns, Newfoundland, 75
St. Johns, Antigua, Ferdinando, 106
St. Joseph, Berreo at, 156; taken and burned by R, 157
St. Lawrence, Day of, 5
St. Leger, Sir Warham, in Ireland, 47, 53; wih R to Guiana, 291
St. Lucar, Lord of, *see* Guzman
St. Mary Port, Medina thinks of, 115
St. Matthew, see Apostles
St. Michael, R left at, 182
St. Pauls, E celebrates victory in, 120
St. Philip, see Apostles
St. Quentins, 5
St. Simon and St. Jude, 316
St. Thomas, see Apostles
Staines, R indicted at, 240
Standen, Sir Anthony, praises R, 176
Stanhope, Sir John, Commissioner of Oyer and Terminer at R trial, 241
Stannaries, Warden of, R becomes, 81; R loses, 234
Stannary Parliament, 81
Steele Glass, The, by Gascoigne, 25
Stolney, 70
Storm, The, John Donne, 178
Strabo, 315
Strand, victory procession passes on the, 120, 197
Strasburg, 15
Strozza, R reads of, 128
Stuart, Arabella, R meets, 95; and William Seymour, 206; and James, 209, 232, 244; dead, 282
Stuart, Mary, brought to Buxton, 43; death warrant, dies at Fotheringhay, 90, 163
Stubbs, John, *The Discovery of a gaping Gulf*, 60
Stukely, Sir Lewis, goes to Virginia, 100; ordered to arrest R, 303; meets R, returns to Plymouth with him, 304; betrays R, 306, 307; dead, 307; given R possessions sealed in bag, 308; R denies lies of, 315, 316
Suetonius, 33; R reads, 128
Suffolk, Earl of, condemned to block, 8
Suffolk, Earl of, *see* Thomas Howard
Sully, received by R, taken to E, 204; sent by Henry IV to James, 225
Supposes, by Ariosto, translated by Gascoigne, 22
"Surprise" Plot, *see* "Bye" Plot
Sussex, 22
Sussex, Earl of, friend of R, enemy of Leicester, 58, 70
Swallow, in Gilbert's fleet, 73, 75
Sweden, led by Gustavus II Adolphus against Poland and the Tsar, 302
Sweet Robin, Leicester as, 85
Swiftsure, Essex on, 123

Tables of Ortelius, Gilbert and the, 24
Tacitus, R quotes from, 33, 66, 271
Tagus, 200 ships burned on the, 124
Tailliped, Nöel, read by R, 272
Talbot, John, dead, 294
Talbot, sixth Earl of Shrewsbury, brings news of death of Mary Stuart, 91
Tam marte quam Mercurio, as much for Mars as for Mercury, motto of Gascoigne, later of R, 26
Terceres, Strozza at, 128
Tergoes, siege of, 23

INDEX

Thames, 78; fires to warn of Armada lighted along the, 117; E body rowed down the, 217; R sees the, 263
Theobalds, gaiety of reception recalled by E, 164; Council at, 223; James at, 227, 312
Thevet, Andrew, *French Antarctic* by, 161
Thirty Years War, first rumblings heard in Bohemia, 287; begun, 302
Thomessin, the pirate, 64
Throckmorton, Arthur, brother of Elizabeth Ralegh, 147; with R in Cadiz, 173, 174
Throckmorton, Elizabeth, *see* Elizabeth Ralegh
Throckmorton, Sir Nicholas, father of Elizabeth Throckmorton, 144
Thucydides, R consults, 128
Thunder, for Guiana, 291
Thynne, Captain, *Ark Ralegh*, 140
Thynne, Francis, fears R would die too daringly, 313
Tibullus, pondered by R, 33, 91
Tichborne, High Sheriff, followed by R to prison, 257, 259; questions Cobham, Grey, and Markham, 261
Tiger, leaves for Virginia, 101
Tilbury, E rides to, 116
Tilesberius, read by R, 272
Tipperary, 87
Tonson, 4
Topago, Amazons living at, 161
Topiawari, King, *see* Arromaia
Tounson, Doctor Robert, and R, 313, 314, 315
Tower, Leicester's armor in the, 92; R prisoner in, 111; Pembroke and Mistress Fitton flung into the, 145; R and Lady Ralegh in the, 148; Essex, Southampton in, 198, 200, 201; to be seized, James to be brought to, 229, 230; R reflects in the, 235, 236; R, Cobham, Grey, and Markham in the, 263; Lady Ralegh and Walter in the, Carew Ralegh born in the, 265; R leaves the, 283; Northumberland in the, 284; R again in the, 308, 316
Traitor's Gate, R in the shadow of, 234
Treatise of the Soul, A, by R, 275
Treaty of Trodesillas, 4
Tredgar, Nyles Morgan of, 38
Triangle Islands, R organizes fleet off, 295
Trinidad, R reaches, 156; marvels of, 160, 161; R expedition off, 294; vessels take station at, 296
Triple Alliance, perishes, 185
Troyes, Peace of, 18
Truth of the Fight about the Isles of Azores, by R, 272
Tsar, Gustavus II Adolphus leads Sweden against, 302
Tudor, Mary, *see* Mary Tudor
Tully, 129
Turks, 64
Turner, Doctor, R physician, 265
Twenty first and last book of the Ocean, to Cynthia, by R, 133
Twickenham, Bacon at, 164
Tyburn, Essex and Southampton to be drawn to, 200
Tyrone, Essex concludes truce with, 192-194; truce confirmed, 194

Udal, John, pleaded for by R, 89
Ulster, 192
Unico Aretino, 129
Uzeda, dominates Philip III, 220

Valdez, Don Pedro de, deserted by countrymen, 118

Van Duvenvoord, Admiral, commands Dutch, 168; in the *Neptune*, 169; knighted, 174; in new attack against Spain, 177
Van Meteran, Emanuel, Latin History of Low Countries, 118
Vegetius, R consults, 128
Venetian Ambassador, received by E at Richmond, 214
Venus, E as, 149
Venus and Adonis, by Shakespeare, 144
Vere, Marshal, appointed to Council of War, 167; on *Rainbow*, 173; receives booty, 175; and R friends, 177; on Second Council of War, 177; E complains about Essex to, 186
Vernon, Elizabeth, marries Earl of Southampton, 145
Verulam, Baron of, Bacon works to become, 287
Vervins, Peace of, France signs the, 185
Vigo, Englishmen carried to, 9; set fire to, 124
Villiers, George, new favorite of James, hates Howards, likes R, 282; thanked by R, 283; to be Buckingham, 286, 287; turns against R, 303; Anne of Denmark pleads for R to, 310, 311
Virgil, Dido in, 257
Virgin of the North, E as, 6, 80
Virginia, receives name, 78; first expedition to, 78, 79; fourth expedition to, 94; R struggles for, 97; expedition of planters, 100; colonists explore, reach Secotan and Chesepians, famine and trouble with the Indians, 102; Drake brings relief, colonists return to England with Drake, 103; R ship arrives, finds no colonists, relief expedition arrives, 104; new expedition under White, 105-107; *Brave* and *Roe* fail, 108; White lands, no trace of colony, 109; R never saw, 110; R thinks of Virginia, 126, 131; compared with Trinidad, 156; voyages despatched by R to, 205; new colony in, 215, 284
Voyage for the Discovery of Guiana, by R, 150

Waad, Sir William, Commissioner of Oyer and Terminer at R trial, 242; displaces Sir George Harvey as Lieutenant of the Tower, annoys R in every possible way, 269, 271
Wales, James I, King of England, Ireland and, 217
Walker, John, mapped part of coast of America, 72
Walsingham, Lady Frances, Countess of Essex, daughter of Sir Francis, marries Leicester, mother of Earl of Essex, works for son, 92
Walsingham, Sir Francis, and E French marriage, 42; letter from R, 51; burial, 52, 140; advises E, 57, 58; letter from R, writes Grey, 59, 70, 72; and Gilbert's monopoly, 72; and Leicester, 83; health failing, 91, 97; proves worth, 117, 127; *Faerie Queene*, 131, 163, 164
Wanchese, received by R, 100; returns to Roanoke, 101; turns against colonists, 102, 110, 284
Warburton, Justice, on King's Bench at R trial, 240, 241, 250
Wardrobe Tower, R moved from, 309
Warspite, R ship, 169, 170; enters Cadiz harbor, 172; fight of the, 172, 173; dinner on the, 181
Warwick, Lady, 94
Waterford, 87

INDEX 339

Watson, William, pleads with James for toleration, 228; plots against James, 229, 230; to be Lord Chancellor, if successful, 230; examined, 232, 233, 251, 255; dies, 258
Welsera, Philippa, see Burgrave
Wentworth, surrenders Calais, 2
West Country, news of Mary's death reaches, 7; dislike of Mary for the, 8; feeling about the marriage of Mary and Philip, 9; dislike for Philip, 10; and the Huguenots, 11, 16, 17, 18, 64, 65, 81; R in the, 116; R pays for victualling of parts of, 187, 290
West Indian Marguerita, 156
West Indies, 99
Westminster, Essex taken to, 194; E's body carried from Richmond, 217; R at, 312
Westminster Hall, prepared for trial of Essex and Southampton, 198
Westphaling, Doctor, and E, 15
Weymouth, R wants protection for, 115; duties carry R to, 152
Whiddon, Captain Jacob, sent out by R to examine the Orinoco, 154; with R in Trinidad, 156
White, John, at Durham House, 79; becomes Governor, 105; voyage of, 106; unwillingly returns to England, encounters difficulties, prepares two ships, 107; R yields trade rights in, 108; contracts for three ships, 108; lands at Roanoke, 109; leaves, 109, 110
White Tower, R watches execution of Essex from the, 201
Whitehall, 61, 69, 78; E to be confined at, 196; E's body carried from, 218; R faces Council at, 223; R brought to, 312
Whitney, Captain, urges R to go roving for loot, deserts, goes to England, 300
Whyte, Rowland, 190
Wight, Isle of, to be protected against Armada, 114, 115
Williams, Sir Roger, and Essex, 123; and R, 124
Wilson, Sir Thomas, made special keeper of R, 309; keeper of Elizabeth Ralegh, 310
Wilton, Baron, Arthur, see Lord Grey,
Wilton House, James at, 255, 259, 261
Winchester, Bishop of, composes public prayer for recovery of E, 216

Winchester, Episcopal Palace of, see Wolvesey Castle
Winchester, Marchioness of, carries train of E in victory procession, 120
Winchester, R at, 262
Windebank, watches as E boxes Essex ear, 186
Windsor, James reaches, 226
Winter, Admiral, in Ireland, 47
Winwood, Sir Ralph, enemy of Carr, 279, 280; becomes Secretary of State, 281, 287; disagrees with James, 288; leads R to treat with Captain Faige, 290; dead, 299
Wokoken Island, Roanoke, 78; colonists land, 101
Wolvesey Castle, R carried to, 240; Brooke, Grey, Cobham, Markham, Parham, Brooksby, Copley, Clark, Watson, carried to, 240
Woodstock, E visits, 25
Woollaston, Captain, urges R to go roving for loot, deserts, goes to England, 300
Worcester, Earl of, coach carried Essex from Nonesuch to Westminster, 194; sent by E to Essex, locked up by him, 197; made Privy Councillor, 207; attends E on death bed, 216; leads palfrey of E at funeral, 218; examines R, 308
Wotton, Lord, Commissioner of Oyer and Terminer at R trial, 241
Wrothe, Sir Robert, on R jury, 251
Wyatt, Sir Thomas, plot to revolt against Mary, 8; condemned to block, 8

Yelverton, at Essex trial, 195
Yeomen of the Guard, end victory procession, 120
York House, Essex confined at, 194, 195
Youghal, 48; R colonizes, 88; R becomes mayor of, 115; R sails to, 126; R rests at, 127, 128
Yule, honored by Church of Geneva, 220, 221

Zouch, Captain John, Governor of Munster, 51; tries Bayley, 292
Zurich, 15
Zutphen, Sidney killed at battle of, 86, 103

SBS.
192 4/8 4º
60922